Career Mobility in a Corporate Hierarchy

Career Mobility in a Corporate Hierarchy

JAMES E. ROSENBAUM

Center for Urban Affairs and Policy Research
and
Department of Sociology
and
School of Education
Northwestern University
Evanston, Illinois

1984

ACADEMIC PRESS, INC.

(Harcourt Brace Jovanovich, Publishers)

Orlando   San Diego   New York   London
Toronto   Montreal   Sydney   Tokyo

ACADEMIC PRESS, INC.
Orlando, Florida 32887

United Kingdom Edition published by
ACADEMIC PRESS, INC. (LONDON) LTD.
24/28 Oval Road, London NW1 7DX

Library of Congress Cataloging in Publication Data

Rosenbaum, James E., Date
  Career mobility in a corporate hierarchy.

  Includes index.
  1. Occupational mobility. 2. Promotions. 3. Occupa-
tional mobility--Longitudinal studies. 4. Promotions--
Longitudinal studies. I. Title.
HD5717.R67   1983   305'.9   83-22406
ISBN 0-12-597080-3 (alk. paper)

PRINTED IN THE UNITED STATES OF AMERICA

84 85 86 87   9 8 7 6 5 4 3 2 1

To Ginny and Janet

Contents

Foreword

The status attainment model, formulated by O. D. Duncan in the early 1960s, is one of the few instances of a conceptual paradigm in the Kuhnian sense, having guided research in a substantive field of sociology. This paradigm has proved to be a rich and fertile structure. For more than a decade it has provided the intellectual core for research in stratification. Prominent researchers have been associated at one time or another with the status attainment model. Considerable funding has been made available to researchers working within this tradition, and several of the most extensive social surveys of the period, such as OCG I, OCG II, and the Wisconsin study of high school seniors, were designed to address issues that arose within this framework.

During the 1960s and 1970s, much basic information about the socioeconomic achievement process was gleaned from this model. With the accumulation of research results that addressed questions raised by the model, the implications of the status attainment approach have been gradually fleshed out. Status attainment nominally is built around the multiple themes of intergenerational mobility, the transmission of advantage across generations, the consequences of early childhood experiences for subsequent achievement, and the determinants of status and earnings at various points along the life course.

The different themes of the model have not proven to be equally tractable to exploration with the status attainment model. The research topics that have been amenable to this formulation are those that focus either on intergenerational linkages or on the influence of factors in early youth, prior to labor market entry. Thus, disentangling the effects of various parental influences has been a much-investigated topic, including distinguishing among genetic contributions, the transmission of material advantage, and the more subtle impact of parents' expectations for their offspring. The methodological apparatus of path analysis is also pertinent. Introduced to sociologists by Duncan and associated with the initial versions of the status attainment model, it has enhanced our ability to analyze "indirect effects" and thereby enlarged our comprehension of the workings of such variables as IQ and educational attainment, which mediate between parental characteristics and the respondent's achievement in the labor force.

The research questions that have not been adequately addressed within the status attainment formulation concern the impact of labor market institutions on individual achievement. Parental characteristics and respondent's education may well be the principal factors responsible for a person's first job, but thereafter, they recede in importance as determinants of earnings and status over his or her work life.

In most organizations, the opportunity for salary advancement and promotion is formally structured, and these institutional specifications differ by industry, by firm, and even by unit within a single corporation. In short, it matters very much where one is employed, what sort of work rules apply, and what the context is with respect to organizational demography. Yet, despite the evident importance of these considerations for an understanding of socioeconomic achievement, little attention is given to institutional variables in the status attainment formulation.

To speak of the neglect of certain variables and aspects of the achievement process is not the same as dismissing the paradigm as wrong or inadequate. The essence of a research paradigm lies in its simplification of reality, which permits the achievement of normal science. The simplification occurs along particular lines, in that certain variables and processes are singled out from the larger domain of potentially relevant factors, while others are downplayed. A successful paradigm is one in which the research questions that are stimulated by its formulation are viewed in the wider discipline as important questions; at the same time, the attendant simplification of reality does not interfere with obtaining useful results. Measured against these criteria, the status attainment model has been a most fecund framework.

As the body of results on issues for which status attainment is an effective formulation has expanded, the limitation of the paradigm with respect to exploring other topics that impinge upon socioeconomic achievement has become increasingly bothersome. We have now learned a considerable amount about the role of individual-level factors whose values are determined prior to labor force entry, while our understanding of the mechanisms of career evolution remains meager. Recognizing this situation, several young sociologists began in the late 1970s to explore themes in the achievement process that are not readily encompassed by the status attainment formulation.

Some of the most interesting work in this new sphere was done by James Rosenbaum. In a 1979 paper in the *American Journal of Sociology*, which provides the body of Chapter 3 of the present volume, Rosenbaum examined promotion rates for different categories of employees within a large bureaucracy. He found that age-specific promotion rates differ substantially by occupational category and that the various rates are, themselves, sensitive to the pattern of corporate growth. In a second 1979 paper, much of which is incorporated into Chapter 2, Rosenbaum began the task of formulating models of career evolution that provide a suitable framework for examining individual work histories within a firm.

This volume elaborates some of the same themes that were addressed in the 1979 papers. The new material, however, contains a more explicit treatment of organizational structure and its implications for career evolution than was present in the articles. The approach in this book is manifestly a multidimensional view of the career process, a view that takes account of diverse issues relevant to career specifications; thus, major sections are devoted to attributes of jobs, the use of job evaluation systems by corporations, and the psychological implications of age-grading in career structures. Rosenbaum also notes recent work by economists, pointing out how human capital theory complements the "tournament" model of mobility, which is a major organizing theme of the book.

If status attainment research has unfolded within a fairly compact paradigm, this is not the case with respect to research into the institutional bases of achievement. Here there is little consensus on matters of study design or methodology; nor is there even agreement on what questions should be asked. In one approach to institutional issues, researchers have continued to use representative samples, often of the national population, to which structural information has been added that usually involves characteristics of industries that were available from a different data set. The advantage of this approach is that it permits the findings to be generalized to a known population.

Rosenbaum and a few others have adopted a different strategy. They have sacrificed the benefit of working with a representative sample, conducting instead what is essentially a case study. As a consequence, we cannot say how typical these results are, whether they apply to many companies or to just a few. The advantage of this research design is that it permits an exploration into the fine details of the achievement process, into how corporations go about structuring opportunity for their employees. My own view is that more studies of this sort will be necessary before we are in a position to characterize career structures in a way that is applicable to the diversity of firms and industries associated with a representative population sample.

Seymour Spilerman
Columbia University

Preface

In setting out on this inquiry, I felt a great sense of adventure. I had obtained the complete personnel records of a large corporation covering a 13-year period. Although they took an unpretentious form—computer tapes gathering dust in a basement archive—and were encoded in arcane ways that required hundreds of hours of programming work just to be read, the tapes held the promise of revealing the hidden structure of the organization's selection system.

The importance of these data becomes evident when we realize how extensively theory and research about careers are based on the assumption that employees can assess their career prospects accurately. If research were to cast doubt upon this assumption, much of what we accept about career selection systems would come into question. Economic and psychological theories contain a strong presumption that employees know all about selection procedures. Researchers make the same assumption when they study careers by analyzing employees' perceptions.

Unfortunately, research suggests that this assumption is often mistaken. Studies that compare employees' perceptions with career realities find that even middle-level managers misperceive their career system (see Chapter 1). On closer scrutiny, the reasons for misperceptions are not hard to find. Organizations do not explicitly state many of their career policies or the career patterns that result; indeed, official descriptions tend to be vague, ambiguous, and sometimes misleading (see Chapter 1). In addition, promotion systems are difficult to perceive, and employees' hopes about opportunity distort their perceptions of the actual promotion system and their chances in it.

The complete personnel records of this large corporation provide a rare opportunity to study actual patterns of career mobility over a long period of time. Since this study is not subject to the distortions of individuals' perceptions, it is able to view organizational careers with more clarity, objectivity, and comprehensiveness than is generally possible. As a result, it gives an entirely new picture of the systematic properties of organizational careers.

For organization planners, policy-makers, and theorists, conceptualizing career systems may be an even greater problem than perceiving them. The tournament model proposed here suggests a new conception of the ways that organizations allocate employees' career incentives. Although job security is often considered an incentive, it is more likely to be a prerequisite to a more powerful incentive: the opportunity to compete for future rewards. Without job security, employees demand full compensation in the present (demands that would increase wages in the early career, according to Lazear's estimates [1981]). With job security, future opportunities can be powerful and inexpensive motivators, since a single promotion can motivate many employees. In providing a new conception of the ways organizations allocate employees' promotion opportunities throughout their careers, the tournament model may help organization planners, policy-makers, and theorists to see the structure of incentives in career systems and to envision alternative ways that career systems may be redesigned to offer career incentives to more employees over longer portions of their careers.

Although this volume addresses familiar issues about inequality and career mobility, studying these issues in a single organization permits them to be investigated in new ways. This volume studies the kinds of mobility issues that preoccupy individuals as they proceed through their careers in an organization, it studies the set of options and incentives available for various kinds of employees, and it suggests a model of the social processes that determine career selections. I hope readers will feel some of the sense of adventure that I experienced as I proceeded to discover the inner workings of this large corporation.

Acknowledgments

Since careers have implications for many disciplines, I have tried to relate this study's findings to many fields, both within sociology (sociology of stratification, organizations, and education) and across disciplines (economics, organization behavior, and social psychology). Many friends and colleagues in various fields have contributed to this endeavor. I particularly thank Chris Argyris, Scott Boorman, Rosabeth Kanter, Melvin Kohn, Lee Rainwater, Albert J. Reiss, Seymour Spilerman, David Stern, and Victor Vroom, who strongly influenced this research from the outset, and Christopher Jencks, Barbara Lawrence, and Myron Roomkin, whose extensive critiques greatly improved many of the later chapters. I am also indebted to Frank P. Romo, who began as my research assistant and became my valued colleague. Many other colleagues offered support and suggestions about various pieces: Donald Black, Paul Burstein, Frank H. Cassell, Dale Dannefer, George Farkas, Fred Goldner, Mark Granovetter, J. Richard Hackman, Eric Hanushek, Robin Leidner, Charles E. Lindblom, John W. Meyer, Bernice Neugarten, W. Russell Neuman, Robert Robinson, Rachel Rosenfeld, Len Rubinowitz, Barry Seltser, Shelby Stewman, and Don Treiman. Their ideas, criticisms, and encouragement greatly improved this work, and credit for whatever merit resides in this book must be shared with them.

In analyzing these data containing 20 million pieces of information, standard statistical packages were totally inadequate. David Bruce came to my rescue, and I am greatly indebted to him for the extraordinary dedication and proficiency he brought to this project. After I moved to Northwestern University, Vernon Keenan and William Stiers continued this work and contributed greatly to the project.

I am also greatly indebted to the employees of ABCO who entrusted these data to me and who openly shared their views and experiences. We commonly speak of the courage involved in science, the courage to submit to examination regardless of what will result. These managers showed this courage in entrusting the records to me, and I hope my product justifies their efforts. To justify their trust, I have made every effort to protect the identity of the corporation and individual employees. (Though frustrating readers' curiosity, these efforts may make more such studies possible.) My greatest regret, in this regard, is that promises of confidentiality prevent me from personally acknowledging the individual employees who contributed so much to this study.

For the production of this book, I am also indebted to many individuals. Miriam Klein, Kathy Polit, Mary Ann Gariti, Mary Bucholtz, and Madelyn Townsley deserve particular recognition for their dedicated and able typing of the many drafts of this manuscript.

I was fortunate in receiving extensive support for this project from various institutions. I am indebted to the Manpower Administration, U.S. Department of Labor, for the two grants that provided most of the funding for this project, and to Dr. Robert Foster and Ms. Bonnie Coe for their support as project officers. I am also grateful to the National Institute of Mental Health and the Russell Sage Foundation for the portions of this work that they supported. Of course, the opinions presented reflect only my own views, not those of supporting institutions. I am also indebted to Yale University and Northwestern University for the supportive environments they provided, and particularly to Charles E. Lindblom, David Wiley, and Margaret Gordon for allowing me the time to devote to this work. During periods of tight budgets, when there are strong pressures to constrain research into narrow, money-making projects, these leaders provided support and encouragement for my efforts to extend the original narrow project reports into a more conceptually based work.

Finally, and above all, to my wife and daughter, Ginny and Janet, I wish to express my deepest gratitude. Ginny provided support and intelligent criticism at all stages of this work, and Janet provided a continual reminder of the strong natural growth-needs in us all, to which social institutions must become more responsive. To them, I dedicate this work.

Career Mobility in a Corporate Hierarchy

CHAPTER 1

The Study of Career Stratification in Organizations

Introduction

Inequality raises a fundamental problem in our society: How can a system with unequal attainments preserve equality of opportunities? In the United States, norms demand that individuals be offered equality of opportunity, but these norms also permit outcomes to be unequal. Since outcomes at any period become inputs at the next, a perplexing dilemma arises: To what extent do early selections to unequal positions curtail subsequent advancement opportunities?

While this dilemma has received considerable attention in studies of socioeconomic mobility across generations, it is also a central issue for intragenerational mobility, that is, the study of mobility through individuals' careers. Career selections take many forms, and they occur at various times. Selections occur when individuals enter the work force, and subsequent selections may periodically occur throughout their work careers. How are individuals' opportunities affected by the selections occuring at various times? This question stresses the importance of timing, and it asks not only *which* factors have effects, but also *when* they have their effects.

On a priori grounds, we have little basis for knowing how the conflict between opportunity and inequality is settled. Societal norms permit inequality of outcomes even as they prescribe equality of opportunity; and they fail to specify how the conflict can be reconciled. Moreover, social science theories do not specify how the conflict can be resolved. Economic theories, such as human capital theory, are built on assumptions of open opportunity which deny structural constraints, while structural theories contend that selections severely limit opportunity.

Although the conflict between opportunity and inequality exists throughout society, this conflict is likely to be particularly acute in a single organization. Careers are likely to be patterned by several aspects of organizational structures: authority and status classifications associated with jobs, hierarchical shapes and vacancy chains (White 1970a), and specific personnel policies about careers. However, the countervailing influence of opportunity norms are also likely to be stronger within organizations; indeed, company "cultures" strongly emphasize opportunity norms. Moreover, since attainments are easier to discern in organizations, individuals can more easily evaluate whether an organization is living up to these norms than would be possible in large labor markets. As a result, structural inequalities and opportunity norms may both be stronger within organizations than they are in larger society, and the conflict between opportunity and structure may be even more acute within organizations than it is in larger society.

By studying how this conflict is handled in a large corporation, this investigation combines two important fields of sociological interest—stratification and organizations—and it permits significant extensions of central issues in contemporary stratification research. Work carried out since 1970 has focused renewed attention on the structural properties of occupational mobility (Sørensen 1977; Vanneman 1977; Breiger 1981, 1982) and on more fine-grained classifications of occupations (Stolzenberg 1975). However, even when occupations are divided into 435 detailed categories, the resulting categories are not very homogeneous: Nearly two-thirds of income variation is still *within* occupational groups (Jencks *et al.* 1972, pp. 226). Moreover, for individuals in many occupations, changes to other occupations are rare, and the main kind of advancement is within an occupational or organizational hierarchy (Lipset and Bendix 1952; Spilerman 1977; Spenner 1981). As a result of such findings, the study of structural effects on attainment has begun to focus on firms (Kanter 1977; Baron and Bielby 1980). By considering specific jobs in organizations, the researcher is able to investigate the compensation processes by which actual jobs and job classifications become related to earnings and the matching processes by which individuals become allocated to jobs (Granovetter 1981). This study extends this new thrust, and, by having information over several historical periods, it seeks to investigate the dynamic features of organizational structures and their effects on economic outcomes.

In addition, rather than studying attainments at a single point in time, this is a study of individuals' attainment over time: the study of careers as coherent entities of sociological interest. Careers have received increased attention since 1970. Some studies have suggested that psychological changes may be affected by organizational structure, but this research has rarely described such career structures in detail (Hall 1976; Van Maanen 1977; Schein 1978; Bailyn 1980). Internal labor market theory also describes distinct segments in organizations that offer different career opportunities, but these segments describe very gross distinctions (Doeringer and Piore 1971). For instance, the primary sector contains many different segments which offer different career lines, some of which even preclude further advancement (Spilerman 1977, p 583). Status attainment research provides some descriptions of intragenerational mobility (Blau and Duncan 1967; Jencks et al. 1972, 1979), but it ignores some important aspects of careers:

> Jobs in that literature are treated implicitly as independent entities rather than as linked components of coherent trajectories, . . . the models are insensitive to the fact that changes in status and earnings . . . are to some extent "scheduled," . . . [and that] education gets converted into status and earnings not in some vague or random manner but in relation to career lines. (Spilerman 1977, pp. 584–585)

To understand the ways that attainments change over time, it is necessary to study the properties of careers as coherent entities: how and when they are affected by background factors like education and how these relationships are affected by changes in historical circumstances.

This study describes attainments in terms of the detailed job classifications in an organization and analyzes the ways that individuals' careers evolve and are affected over time by various background factors and previous attainments. It investigates the dynamics of the social structure: how the process of matching individuals with jobs changes over different periods of a career and over different historical circumstances (Granovetter 1981). Moreover, as Spilerman notes, "career lines constitute an intermediary structure, relating the behaviors and life chances of individuals to 'macro' organizational units, thereby linking two important levels in sociological analysis" (1977, p. 586). Consequently, this book concludes with a consideration of the implications of this structural analysis for individuals' behaviors and lives.

This volume reports the results of a study of employees' patterns of career mobility in a large corporation, which shall be called ABCO (not its real name). ABCO employed between 10,000 and 15,000 employees in the period studied, making it slightly larger than the median corporation among the Fortune 500. It is an old, well-established, autonomous, investor-owned firm, having offices in many cities and towns across a large geographic region.

This chapter begins by considering what studies of organizational career selection systems and organizational job status systems can contribute to the sociological study of mobility and stratification and to the social-psychological study of employee motivation. The discussion then indicates why vacancy approaches to the study of careers, though useful for showing hierarchically imposed limitations, cannot adequately address some aspects of organizational careers. Moreover, personnel policy descriptions and employee perceptions, which should be good ways of obtaining descriptions of organizational career selection practices, are found to yield vague, fragmented, and sometimes contradictory portrayals.

The problem arises from the difficulty in conceptualizing careers and the conflicting forces that shape them. These conflicts are reviewed, and they are related to the dominant theoretical approaches. A new model, the tournament model of career systems, is proposed, which is the conceptual focus for this study. The chapter concludes with a summary of the research questions addressed in the following chapters.

Stratification in Organizations

As mentioned earlier, the study of career opportunities in organizations is useful theoretically because it integrates two important areas of sociological interest—it is the study of stratification in organizations. Although a large proportion of the work force is employed in large organizations and although mobility and stratification have been extensively studied, researchers still have very little information about career mobility in organizations.

While most mobility research has studied changes in occupational attainments, most professionals, managers, and skilled workers tend to stay in the same occupation throughout their work lives (Reynolds 1951, pp. 19–36; Lipset and Bendix 1952; Blau and Duncan 1967). In such occupations, which have many status distinctions and diverse career ladders within them, classic measures of occupational status will be insensitive to career mobility (Blau and Duncan 1967). Occupational status scales such as Duncan's socioeconomic index

(SEI) also have some anomalous characteristics. The lowest professional occupation has a score very similar to that of the highest manual occupation (Blau and Duncan 1967, p. 121). Moreover, when high-status professionals, say chemical engineers (SEI = 90–96), working for a manufacturing firm, are promoted to a position of high-level executive (SEI 75–79), they take a large status drop in occupational status score. It is hard to imagine in what respect this promotion represents *downward* mobility.[1] While these problems do not preclude the usefulness of occupational status scores in some contexts, they do suggest the value of other status distinctions. Given the large segment of the American work force employed by large corporations, the analysis of promotions within large corporations can augment our understanding of intragenerational mobility in society.

The present study investigates changes of status and authority within an organizational hierarchy, and it is able to do so in terms of the actual social classifications made by the organizational hierarchy—classifications which have extensive implications. These status and authority categories define many aspects of employees' work lives: the kind of workspace they receive, how that workspace may be furnished, what kinds of assistance and services they can expect, how much they are paid, and how they are paid (Goldner 1965; Ladinsky 1975; Kanter 1977). They also have great meaning and importance to individuals, defining the discretion, autonomy, and complexity in one's work, factors which have been shown to influence individuals' values outside the workplace (Kohn 1969; Kohn and Schooler 1978).

By studying a single organization, this research can analyze organizational structure at an even more fine-grained level: analyzing the effects of jobs. While sociological research has studied the effects of occupations on economic and status attainments, investigators have noted that the underlying patterns can probably best be seen at the fine-grained level of jobs (Featherman 1973; Kelley 1973a,b). The study of stratification in an organization can focus on actual jobs—their attributes, composition, and effects on earnings and subsequent attainments—in effect, providing a test of whether job effects are fully expressed by job status scales.

In studying attainments in terms of the actual units used by the organization (jobs, statuses, authority levels, earnings), this research provides a description that is likely to resemble the actual processes operating in the organization because it describes relationships in terms of the organization's own labels and categories. Longitudinal

---

[1]One could contend that the engineer gives up some prestige in becoming an executive, but the contention is at best equivocal.

analyses of mobility patterns for different employee groups suggest dynamic mechanisms in terms of actual social classifications in the system.

From a theoretical viewpoint, attainments in an organizational status system are in many ways better indicators of status than the customary occupational status scores. If the Weberian notion of status is viewed as a consensual system of deference, status in an organization is the epitome of this notion, for the small size and institutionalized character of the status system assure an almost total consensus far beyond the interrater reliability of occupational status scores in larger society.

In a sense, it is like studying the status system of a small community: The relatively small group of individuals "residing" in a corporation (fewer than 15,000 employees in ABCO) agree on which jobs each individual holds, what status ranking each job receives, and how status rankings are to be interpreted in terms of rewards, perogatives, autonomy, and deference. Some of their agreements are codified into formal rules and institutionalized into prescribed practices. For instance, the status rankings of jobs are precisely codified by most organizations, and in ABCO, as in many corporations, an extensive job evaluation procedure (described in Chapter 4) is used to make the status assignments standardized and widely accepted. Similarly, formal rules tend to define the implications of the various status rankings. A job's status ranking defines its salary range, its benefit package, its office size, its furniture, and whether the individual who holds it gets an outside office with a window. As an advertisement indicates, "You know you've made it when you have a Bigelow [carpet] on the floor," and in ABCO, employees do not get a carpet of that quality until they reach the top status category in the middle-management level. A job's status ranking also defines how much discretion one has about job tasks, how often one reports to a supervisor, and one's latitude to spend the afternoon at the golf course or (for some low-status jobs) to go to the bathroom without permission.

Moreover, like a small community, organizations develop highly articulated norms for interaction. Although the formal compensation system and job evaluation system explicitly prescribe some of these norms, many implicit norms have also developed to specify numerous subtle aspects of interaction (who can interrupt whom, who steps aside in a crowded hall, who "volunteers" to get coffee). The extensive implications of organizational status systems for deferential behavior and the near-total consensus on these statuses and their implications make organizational statuses, in some ways, a better representation of the concept of status than occupational status scores.

In addition, as in a small community, these statuses can easily be communicated throughout the organization. Formal personnel records make the information very readily available, and the organization's size makes it easy to communicate shared understandings about how to interpret the status nuances connoted by particular jobs and job moves.

Organizational statuses also reflect distinctions which are not indicated by status scales derived from occupations. Authority and promotion relationships within occupations and organizations are not reflected in occupational status scales, as indicated by the previous example of the occupational status decline that occurs when a chemical engineer is promoted to a high-level executive position.

Organizational statuses also provide a better test of the extent that status might be associated with (and determined by) individual attributes. The finding of a modest relationship between individual attributes (e.g., education) and occupational statuses across many employers (Featherman and Hauser 1978), may occur either because different employers have different practices or because most employers have vague and diffuse practices. In contrast, within a single organization, the relationship will clearly indicate whether organizational selection practices are determined by these individual attributes.

Finally, these organizational status classifications provide a better test of the extent to which careers have a structure of their own. The effects of early statuses on later careers are more likely to operate within a small demarcated community in which these statuses have common social meanings and in which they are likely to be widely known and understood.

The consensus about the statuses associated with jobs, their extensive explicit and implicit implications for rewards, deference, and authority, and the small-community characteristics of organizations which make an individual's history of job statuses known and readily interpreted throughout the organization suggest that job statuses are likely to have particularly strong effects on individuals' career opportunities.

Why Study Job Status Attainments?

This study analyzes careers in terms of employees' earnings, status, and authority attainments. Surely there is more to careers than these materialistic and status outcomes. Individuals seek variety, autonomy, challenge, and interpersonal influence from all aspects of their lives, including their work (Argyris 1964; Hall 1976). In limiting its empirical analyses only to status, authority, and earnings attainments, does this study assume that all employees are "status seekers?" Not at all. Even though individuals seek many kinds of rewards from work besides status, authority, and earnings, organizations allocate these nonstatus rewards to jobs in ways that are related to job status. As this study will show, jobs are structured in organizations so that regardless of whether one wishes more variety, autonomy, challenge, or interpersonal influence in one's work, one can only get more of it by advancing in the status hierarchy.

As Chapter 4 notes, organizations sometimes make this explicit. Job evaluation systems actually formalize this relationship by using these nonstatus features of jobs as factors in the determination of job worth and job status. Jobs which offer greater variety, autonomy, challenge, or interpersonal influence are evaluated as having more value and conferring more status. To attain jobs with these nonstatus qualities, an employee must advance up the status hierarchy.

Although this study only measures career attainment in terms of status, earnings, and authority attainments, a wide range of nonstatus rewards are also at stake. This makes it all the more important to understand how status attainments are structured and allocated, for they are the basis by which individuals obtain many psychological rewards, including opportunities for personal growth at work.

Beyond the Pyramid Imperative: The Need for Studying Subgroups and Career Timing

The shape of organizational hierarchies imposes unavoidable constraints on the possibilities of career advancement. Since most organizational hierarchies are shaped like a pyramid, with many more low-level than high-level positions, an organizational pyramid must inevitably present barriers to the advancement of employees. This simple logic dictates that the average employee's advancement must slow down over time. Because this constraint is an unavoidable consequence of the pyramidal shape of hierarchies, it may be described as the pyramid imperative. Most organizational observers, responding to the inevitability of these premises, have stopped their analysis at this point, either resigning themselves to the futility of reform or calling for radical changes in the pyramidal shape of hierarchies.

This perspective has been extended in several important ways over the past decade. Among jobs in a hierarchy, it is only vacant jobs which offer advancement opportunities. Consequently, patterns of filling vacancies will affect career advancement options within organizational hierarchies. White (1970a) showed how jobs are linked in distinctive vacancy chains. A high-level vacancy tends to be filled by individuals from a limited set of lower-level jobs, creating a new vacancy which in turn must be filled from a limited set of jobs at the next lower level, and so on.

White (1970a, p. 282) notes the obvious limitation of this approach in ignoring individual attributes, and Bartholomew (1968) suggests more complex models that combine the vacancy approach with the analysis of individual attributes. Stewman and Konda (1983) have used such procedures to model the ways that promotions from any position are affected by organizational growth or contraction, cohort size, or exit rate. These models focus on the relationship of organizational structure to individual demography, and they provide techniques for projecting the distribution of individuals in the organization in the future, given hypothetical conditions (Stewman 1981). Indeed, Stewman and Konda (1983) suggest that the pyramid imperative may not always apply, and they show how the ratio of vacancies to lower-level individuals can increase at one level in the hierarchy under hypothetical circumstances despite its decreases in all other levels of the hierarchy. Although this model is far more sophisticated than the pyramid imperative and comes to somewhat different conclusions, it has the same elegant simplicity to explain important parameters of career systems from structural properties.

However, like the pyramid imperative, the vacancy approach is more suited for analyzing the way that shape, growth, and exits influence careers than it is for analyzing the influence of individuals' attributes, the jobs they occupy, or their job histories. While in principle the vacancy approach can be extended to include such factors, and Stewman and Konda show procedures for analyzing a few individual attributes, the procedure quickly becomes cumbersome when several attributes are considered.

The fundamental insight of the pyramid imperative and the vacancy approach is that organizational shapes and vacancies impose important restrictions on the average employee. However, it isn't clear that organizations have any "average employees." Even a very steep pyramid (which narrows greatly at each successive level) may offer substantial advancement opportunity to a small elite subgroup of employees through the highest levels of the hierarchy, and the shape of the organizational pyramid and its number of vacancies may have very little impact on their careers. A small elite group could continue receiving the same high promotion rates even when there are few vacancies. In contrast, if a large segment of the work force (the "secondary labor market") was identified by policy or practice as having no advancement opportunity, then the particular shape of the organizational hierarchy or the number of vacancies would not affect the advancement opportunity of this segment. Indeed, the present study even finds that some segments of the primary labor market are not helped by increasing growth. Obviously, these possibilities can only be ascertained by analyzing various subgroups of employees.

The impact of organizational shape also fails to specify when employees will be selected for advancement, and time is a crucial dimension of careers. Description of organizational hierarchies and vacancy chains can either ignore career timing or adopt assumptions about it, but the question of career timing is an empirical matter which is determined by organizational policy and practice. Even if there are only a limited number of vacancies available, organizations have great latitude in determining whether promotions are to be distributed in the beginning, middle, or end of employees' careers and what this timing will imply about individuals' later career options. While some employee groups may not expect to receive their first promotions until after their first 5 years in the organization, individuals in other employee groups who have not received a promotion in their first 5 years may be unlikely ever to receive one. For some employee groups, an early promotion may indicate the first of many future advancements; for others, an early promotion may be as much advancement as one can expect for one's entire career.

While the shapes of organizational structures surely affect career advancement chances, organizations are not run as chance lotteries. Personnel selection systems introduce many other kinds of constraints in determining which employees will be considered for advancements, when employees will be considered for advancements, and what their rate of advancement will be. Although Stewman and Konda's models provide a powerful method for understanding certain kinds of structural constraints on careers in organizations, analyses must also consider important components of selection systems, particularly how they differentiate employee subgroups and define the timing of careers.

Personnel Policy Descriptions

Organizational policies provide the most direct approach to describing the selection procedures determining organizational careers. Organizations formulate personnel policies based on human resources planning in order to assure that they will have candidates qualified to fill upper-level vacancies in the future. Human resources planning has led to new kinds of policies and programs for recruitment, training, and career development (Wellbank et al. 1979).

Some examples of such programs are detailed in a report by the Conference Board, a nonprofit, business research group (Shaeffer 1972). The companies themselves provided the descriptions, so these reports provide a picture of public self-presentations, not necessarily reality. While the four programs described in this report cannot be considered representative, the Conference Board selected them because the corporations they represent are leaders in human resources planning, and these programs were presented as positive models. Consequently, quite apart from their descriptive value, they are meant to have prescriptive value as ideal models.

Some similarities are evident across the programs described. All stress the importance of early identification of talent, the use of education for identifying talent, and the use of special "developmental experiences" to give these employees better training. Macy's department store reports that "college graduates are advanced more quickly than those with less education, and MBA's have been moved ahead even more rapidly than the college graduates . . . and have been given special assignments in the financial, operating, and administrative areas in addition to the experience that all managers get in merchandising" (p. 67).

Uniroyal's early identification program (EIP) is described as "the gateway to the promotional mainstream to top management within the company" (p. 76). It consists of giving special "developmental assignments" to exceptionally able young executives who have been nominated by their supervisors.

The initial management development program at AT&T selects a small number of highly able young employees to receive a series of challenging assignments which are conducive to managerial growth and development. This program was based on some earlier research at AT&T which suggested that young managers who had received more challenging jobs were more productive and attained higher levels (Berlew and Hall 1966; Bray, Campbell, and Grant 1974).

The First National City Bank of New York (Citibank) describes the most elaborate program. It is a program with four different career tracks. Track 1 is for professional and technical appointments (e.g., for filling jobs in computer programming, engineering, and law). Track 2 is the "fast-track" program in which exceptionally able new recruits become bank officers within 2 years, and is similar to the EIPs described in the preceding. Track 3 is primarily for holders of nontechnical undergraduate degrees who are hired and trained as personal banking specialists; the more able individuals in this track can go on to become managers of increasingly larger bank branches. Track 4 is for employees from the ranks of tellers or clerks who may move up to supervisory positions or even to junior officers.

While these early selection programs provide different "developmental training" and different associated advancements, the companies emphasize that their programs do not close off opportunity for others. Uniroyal emphasizes that "it is not essential to have either a college degree or an advanced degree" or to be "in the youngest age group" to be selected, and those selected receive subsequent tests; so the program offers no guarantees. Moreover, "failure to be selected for the EIP program does not mean that an individual . . . will not receive special training or that he may not advance to a high level" (Shaeffer 1972, p. 74). Citibank, the organization with the most elaborate tracking system, also presents the most extensive qualifiers in describing its program.

> This report has to do with general employment patterns—not with individual careers. Variations from the bank's staffing patterns always occur. . . . The bank believes it is possible to describe the general shape and pattern of its staffing efforts without prejudging the career of any employee within the organization. No ceiling has ever been placed on individual attainment within the bank regardless of the level at which the person entered the organization. On the other hand, it would be unrealistic to assume that the great majority of rank-and-file employees either want to be or could become president of the bank. (p. 82)

These qualifiers contradict the general thrust of the rest of the report, but they are vague and evasive. They also seem somewhat disingenuous, an impression that is strengthened by the claim that the only ceiling imposed by their track structure is in preventing the majority of bank tellers from becoming bank presidents.

Regardless of the underlying reality of the system, two facts are evident from these reports. First, these reports suggest an ambivalence in these organizations between efficiency and opportunity. These EIPs are clearly intended to take advantage of the efficiencies of early selections, but the companies also stress that these programs do not curtail the opportunities of other employees. Although it is not clear how much the system actually protects the opportunities of individuals not selected for an EIP, it is evident that these companies wish to convey the impression that they do. They want to be perceived as accomplishing efficiency without sacrificing opportunity, and they avoid identifying a conflict between these goals.

Second, to the extent that these reports to the Conference Board resemble the information that these companies give to their employees, the ambiguity in these reports suggests that employees may have difficulty perceiving career systems correctly. Indeed, employees may even get less information than is in these reports. Uniroyal's report admits that it contains information that the company does not give its own employees (p. 74). These findings not only suggest that company reports may not be an accurate indication of what policies they actually implement, but also raise doubts about whether employees' perceptions can give an accurate picture of career systems, a matter addressed in the next section.

Employee Perceptions and Misperceptions

Employees provide another way of knowing what kinds of opportunities exist within organizational career systems. Employees spend 2000 hours a year within work organizations, they are intensely interested in the promotion system, and they spend a great deal of time discussing promotions. The days following the announcement of a promotion are filled with discussions about why the fortunate person got the promotion and why other contenders did not. Even if the firm does not publicly announce its promotions, the word leaks out very quickly. It is regarded as important information by nearly everyone, even those who are not expecting a promotion soon, for it tells them how the system is working and suggests what their future chances may be. With this kind of interest and discussion, employees would be expected to have a very clear picture of how career systems work.

In the 1940s and 1950s there was a great deal of research which described career systems based on employees' perceptions. These studies suggested that ethnicity, family connections, and various other kinds of sponsoring alliances affect promotion patterns in organizations (Collins 1946; Dalton 1951; Kornhauser 1952; Becker and Strauss 1956; Martin and Strauss 1959). These employee reports clearly suggest some additional constraints beyond those suggested by vacancy analysis or by organizational policy statements.

Since few studies have investigated employees' actual careers based on objective organizational data, we have little basis for assessing the accuracy of employees' perceptions. Nonetheless, there are some indications that employees may not perceive the full extent that their careers are constrained by structural factors.

Vroom reports an incident which reveals this quite dramatically. After completing a study of the promotion system of a large corporation using the official personnel records (Vroom and MacCrimmon 1968), Vroom heard a senior manager in the personnel department give a talk on career opportunities in the firm, a talk replete with Horatio Alger stories and vague assurances that this firm offered opportunities for all lower-level managers. Subsequent informal discussion revealed that most lower-management employees fully believed it.

The next day, Vroom presented the research findings which contradicted the general thrust of the personnel official's talk: Employees in finance and marketing had substantially greater advancement opportunities than employees in manufacturing, and employees in personnel had minimal advancement opportunities. The managers were surprised by these findings, and they were shocked when Vroom took individuals' career histories and plugged them into the model to predict likely advancement outcomes. Vroom and MacCrimmon's models, based on simple calculations of promotion probabilities for employees from different departments, came as a complete surprise to these lower-management employees, most of whom had been in the firm for several years.

In another study, Goldner (1970) asked 149 middle managers in a large manufacturing firm whether they expected to be promoted, and he returned 5 years later to see whether they had been. Although over 75% of the sample expected promotions, he found that only 51.8% of those expecting promotions had actually received a promotion in the intervening period. Goldner reports that 14.9% of those expecting promotions were given laterals, 20.2% were still in the same job, and 13.2% were actually demoted. Through detailed analyses of questionnaire responses, Goldner outlines a number of factors that seem to contribute to the misperceptions of these groups.

As part of the present study, I interviewed 163 employees in lower-management and foreman levels, and I found similar kinds of misperceptions. Many of the employees in this sample who had the lowest potential rating (a rating which indicates that an employee has virtually no chance for a promotion) totally misperceived their promotion chances. When asked what they thought their promotion chances would be over the next 6 years, nearly 40% of the employees with this rating ($n = 68$) said their chance of being promoted was better than 50%. Many of these employees did not know their promotion ratings, and the rest did not know how to infer their promotion chances from these ratings.

Kanter's (1977) study further supports these findings. She observed that managers had a "general lack of clarity" about tracks (p. 132). Even employees who were on the fast track learned about it only gradually in "strange and devious ways" (p. 133). They reported noticing the extra attention they were receiving, they began to infer that they were getting special treatment, and later they realized that they were advancing more quickly than their peers. However, "it was often denied by vice-presidents that officer material was judged so low down the ranks," and employees who learned they were on the fast track generally did not discuss it because they did not want competition (p. 133). Similarly, "awareness of being stuck came . . . indirectly" (p. 133), and those who realized they were stuck did not like to admit it to their peers. The lack of official information was accompanied by a lack of informal communication among peers.

Although workers' misperceptions are a classic and pervasive finding (e.g., Chinoy 1955), these findings result from studies of managers, including the people who run these systems on a daily basis. Their distortions could be interpreted as the result of intentional deception, particularly the public presentation by the high-level personnel official in the company Vroom and MacCrimmon studied. However, Vroom believes that this official genuinely believed what he was saying; for soon after learning these results, he was instrumental in getting the company to change these practices. Managers, even high-level personnel administrators, may not be aware of actual practices.

Of course, individuals' misperceptions about their own career chances are easily dismissed as self-interested distortions. However, these reports are not just matters of high aspirations; they also involve incorrect descriptions of reality. Vroom reports that managers did not perceive that promotion opportunity differed for employees in various departments. In my study, individuals' high expectations were associated with ignorance about promotion ratings and misperceptions about how to interpret them. These reports do not seem to be merely wishful thinking. They suggest that reality is difficult to perceive correctly.

The reasons for this are easy to understand. Just as organizations are reluctant to describe the full extent of their career structure, supervisors are reluctant to convey the full implications of a job move to a low-opportunity department or the full meaning of a low promotion rating. Indeed, my interviews suggested that many employees were not even aware that their supervisors had already evaluated their promotion prospects. Although company policy at ABCO mandated two evaluations every year and required that supervisors discuss their evaluations with their subordinates, many managers found ways to evade this embarassing requirement. Hall and Lawler (1969) report similar misperceptions and ignorance about appraisals in a study of research and development (R&D) managers.

Although employees' perceptions are a relatively easy way to discover some of the structural aspects of career systems, the ambiguities in the descriptions provided by company policies make it difficult for employees to see these matters clearly. Ultimately, empirical analyses of actual career moves may be the only way to discover many aspects of career systems.

Two Conflicting Models of the Opportunity Structure

Efforts to describe the selection procedures determining organizational careers have run into two dead ends. Employees' perceptions are important statements about how they see the career system, but their perceptions depart from reality in some important respects. Organizations' reports of their policies, which are meant to provide clear models to other companies, nonetheless show ambiguity and evasiveness. This ambiguity seems to arise from a strong ambivalence between the perceived efficiencies of early selection programs and the concern that early selections may be seen as curtailing opportunity.

The basis of this conflict is described by Turner (1960) in a classic paper. Turner describes two normative systems which stand as ideal types in our society: the contest and sponsored mobility norms.

Individuals in the United States grow up believing that everyone has the opportunity to advance and that, as "the land of opportunity," the United States has no policies or practices which cut off anyone's possibility for advancement or which protect any elite from downward mobility. Turner calls this the *contest mobility norm*. In a selection system which follows the contest mobility norm, selections are delayed and individuals are allowed complete freedom for mobility through most of their careers. Of course, even in a contest system, selections must sometimes occur; but the contest system delays selections and minimizes their consequences. It instills an "insecurity of elite position. In a sense, there is no final arrival under contest mobility, since each person may be displaced by newcomers throughout his life" (Turner 1960, p. 860). Nor are there any final losses, since everyone is kept in the running and offered another chance to qualify for advancement (p. 861).

A selection system following the contest mobility norm embodies several desirable features for an organization. In permitting late mobility, such a system helps to maintain motivation and morale by continually holding out the possibility that one's efforts may have a payoff. Moreover, such a system is quite consistent with Americans' long-standing mistrust of selection criteria. If selection criteria are mistrusted, then a selection system which makes few selections and delays them as late as possible will be relatively less objectionable. Moreover, it would leave maximum opportunity for "late blooming" or late failing to alter individuals' destinies. Such a system also minimizes the chances of errors.

Of course, this minimizing of errors also has its costs; for the later that selection occurs, the less time individuals have to acquire specialized training. Normative ambivalence emerges here because the loss of adequate specialized training is seen as inefficient and, consequently, as undesirable.

In contrast, the *sponsored mobility norm* stresses efficiency. It prescribes that selections occur as early as possible so that the system can maximally benefit from the efficiencies of specialized training and socialization. In a selection system which follows the sponsored norm, individuals are selected for their ultimate careers very early and departures from these early assigned careers are not permitted. Those who are selected for elite status are maximally separated from others, are given specialized training and socialization, and are guaranteed that they—and only they—will attain elite status.

Although Turner attributed this norm predominantly to Britain, it is clear that there are elements of this norm in the United States as well. Surely the United States is a country that values efficiency. The widespread existence of ability grouping and curriculum grouping in public schools (Findlay and Bryan 1971; Rosenbaum, 1976) and of manpower planning in industry suggest the importance this nation attributes to efficiency in the selection of individuals for specialized training. The early selection systems of Plato's *Republic* and Young's (1908) "meritocracy" have a great deal of utopian appeal to Americans.

Which of these normative models is the best description of the opportunity structure in organizations? In many organizations, strong beliefs in opportunity and in efficiency coexist; yet the two often conflict. Rarely is explicit attention given to this conflict, how it might be resolved or, indeed, how contemporary policies and practices deal with it.

This conflict is clearly manifest in the previously reported descriptions of personnel policies in some leading corporations. These policies ostensibly seek to create a sponsored system in which the organization would capitalize on the efficiencies of early selection and specialized training. Yet these organizations could not let their commitment to the contest norm be questioned, so the program descriptions are qualified by contest mobility protections: There are no guarantees for those who are selected for these programs, and there are no barriers for those who are not selected.

This ambiguity and ambivalence in policy statements may seem strange, but it is not unusual. These policy descriptions are very similar to the way high school administrators describe selection procedures for ability and curriculum grouping. In a previous study, I found that high school administrators were very reluctant to admit that their system of grouping students by ability and curriculum might affect students' opportunities to move up to a higher track, and they spoke at great length about individual students who had moved into higher tracks (Rosenbaum 1976). Yet systematic analysis of the school's records showed that only a negligible portion of the students showed upward track mobility. Administrators' evasiveness about this is apparently widespread, for the Coleman Report study of a national sample of schools found that school administrators' responses often directly contradicted the responses of a majority of the teachers and students in the same schools (Coleman et al. 1966, p. 569; Jencks et al. 1972, p. 97).

Of course, corporations can be much more open about their career practices because they are private institutions and are not as responsible to society's norms. Their primary aim is profit maximization, and career practices which presume to promote efficiency contribute to this aim. However, as the movement for "corporate responsibility" suggests, corporations are not totally exempt from society's norms, and this is all the more true for norms which affect the morale of their employees.

Corporations, like schools, are caught in the conflict between efficiency and opportunity. Although corporations are freer to admit their pursuit of efficiency, they are not exempt from opportunity norms. Indeed, as is discussed in greater detail in Chapter 8, corporations, like other U.S. institutions, make use of opportunity norms to stimulate employees' motivation to perform well for the company. They do not wish to admit that their career practices foreclose opportunity for employees.

As a result, it is extremely difficult to get a clear picture of the opportunity structure of most organizations. Public reports such as those to the Conference Board are vague and sometimes evasive, company statements to employees are little better and may be worse, and employees' perceptions are ill-informed and often mistaken. Moreover, judging from Vroom's observations, even higher-level managers may not know the actual situation.

The fundamental conflict between the contest and sponsored norms—between opportunity and efficiency—prevents organizations from being candid on these issues, makes employees confused and mistaken on these issues, and raises serious questions about whether high-level managers are aware of the career system that emerges. Surely this profound conflict makes it difficult for social scientists to trust previous research which has been based only on official policies or employees' perceptions. If we want to understand the actual career system in large organizations, we must examine the actual careers of individuals in these organizations.

Social Science Theories about Opportunity

While the contest–sponsored typology poses the normative constraints on organizational selection procedures, social science theories provide more detailed models and causal mechanisms. Human capital theory in economics and structural theories in sociology and economics (i.e., internal labor market theory) offer counterparts of the contest and sponsored models, respectively, in their emphasis on opportunity or structure. But these theories also go beyond these norms; they elaborate the underlying processes and provide specific hypotheses for empirical study of the issues. These theories provide the basis for a great deal of current research on labor markets and social mobility generally, and they are the basis for much of the research reported in this study.

Human Capital Theory

Human capital theory in economics proceeds from the same assumptions as the contest mobility norm. It posits that labor markets offer open opportunity and that employees' attainments are largely a function of how hard they work and the ability, education, and training they possess. This theory conceptualizes the latter factors—ability, education, training—as human capital. Like physical capital, human capital is increased by investments, and education and training are the primary investments individuals can make in their human capital (Becker 1964; Mincer 1974; Blaug 1976).

This theory suggests an explanation for the shape of career attainments. Investments in education or training are assumed to be costly. Consequently, individuals will concentrate their investments in the early part of their careers in order to maximize the amount of time they have to receive the benefits (amortize their investments). This explains the rapid increase in earnings which occurs in the early part of careers and the leveling off of earnings later in their careers.

Like other neoclassical economic theories, human capital theory assumes that labor markets are perfect markets; thus employers must pay employees what they are worth (their human capital) or else the employees will go to work for another employer. Economic theories do not consider the influence of job structures; structures merely represent labor market imperfections which, according to the theory, will tend to be eliminated by market processes.

Individuals are the active forces in the model. Individuals determine their productivity, and this is the basis for compensation. Indeed, human capital theory contends that individuals create their own productive capacity by the investments they make in themselves.

But investments in education or training do involve a trade-off. While individuals are attending school or receiving training at work, they generally earn less than those who are not receiving formal education or training. Individuals must choose whether they wish to receive greater earnings immediately or to sacrifice immediate earnings to invest in their training. Employees who choose to sacrifice immediate earnings for the benefits of greater training will generally attain much higher earnings in their later careers than will comparable employees who do not make these early sacrifices. In other words, human capital theory contends that great advancement opportunity exists for those who are willing to make the sacrifice.

In this model, the job world is assumed to act like a perfect market. It is not structured, and it does not impose restrictions on individuals' careers. Individuals alone are the main actors in this model. They choose whether and how much they will invest in themselves: how much effort they will expend and how much immediate earnings they will sacrifice to get better training. No barriers exist for able individuals if they choose to make the sacrifices and efforts to acquire the skills necessary for advancement.

Structural Theories

In contrast, structural theories posit a situation comparable to that described by the sponsored mobility norm. The most common version of structural theory, internal labor market theory, posits that organizations make important investments in individuals and these investments segment the work force into separate opportunity circumstances (Doeringer and Piore 1971; Spilerman 1977). Individuals in the primary labor market receive investments from their employing firms, and, as a result, receive advancement opportunities. Individuals in the secondary labor market do not receive such investments; and, even if they invest in themselves, the firm will not respond to these investments. These individuals have no advancement opportunities. In effect, employees in the primary labor market are sponsored by the firm, and those in secondary labor markets are deprived of sponsorship.

Like Caplow's (1954) description of the bureacratic labor market, internal labor markets are characterized by fixed ports of entry, internal promotions as the main way of filling vacancies, and normatively approved, established procedures for hiring, firing, and promoting. Promotions, the central concern of this study, are primarily determined by on-the-job training. Doeringer and Piore (1971) describe what they call the "promotion unit" in which "each job in the progression line develops skills requisite for the succeeding job and draws upon the skills required in the job below it" (p. 21). On-the-job training is often more economical than formal instruction, for it takes advantage of the physical proximity of workers, the use of free time and idle equipment during a production break, the filling in by subordinates during a temporary absence of superiors, and the virtual absence of excess training since training is tailored to the learning capabilities and needs of each trainee.

Since internal labor market theory makes on-the-job training the primary mechanism determining career advancement, entry jobs have great effects on careers. After individuals are assigned to entry jobs, their subsequent careers are largely determined since entry jobs lead into predetermined progression systems. This view differs radically from human capital theory, for it assumes that individual attributes have no influence beyond determination of entry job assignments. Entry jobs lead to distinctive career lines within which future mobility is constrained (Doeringer and Piore 1971). After an individual enters an organization through a particular entry job, "the key decisions about his career follow. The occupational decisions that he made earlier will be of relatively little significance" (Ginsberg 1971, p. 17).

Compared with status attainment research, the real strength of internal labor market theory is that it describes a fine-grained structure of job mobility which status attainment research must dismiss as "random exogenous effects" (Spilerman 1977, p. 522). "What is sacrificed in such a (status attainment) formulation is a comprehension of the mechanism by which background variables operate, because the mechanisms are well defined only at the disaggregated level of the career line" (p. 586).

However, Spilerman suggests that internal labor market theory may not go far enough: "Despite the dualists' sensitivity to institutional factors, theirs is a bare-bones description, in which the considerable variety of labor market structures is reduced to the distinctions between primary and secondary jobs" (p. 582). Refinements of internal labor market theory to discuss multiple segments have not yet led to an adequate description of these segments. What is most lacking is an analysis of the multiple internal labor markets in the primary sector, that is, the multiple career lines of employees who stay with a single employer. This is a focus of the present research.

One other feature of internal labor market theory and other structural theories must also be noted: their assumption that career history is irrelevant. Markov models (Bartholomew 1968; Mayer 1972), status attainment models (Kelley 1973a), and internal labor market models (Doeringer and Piore 1971) posit ahistorical effects. Internal labor market theory is generally interpreted to suggest that career history is irrelevant because present jobs embody the entire effect of past job history. If jobs have clear prerequisites for the kinds of previous training required to do them, or if previous training is less specialized or less valuable than the training one acquires on one's current job, then earlier training will have no independent effects on future career attainment. This would be particularly the case for very early jobs, which, though important for defining one's area of specialization, are probably not as highly specialized as the jobs that follow them.

This ahistorical feature of careers in internal labor markets is most graphically captured in the concept of job ladders. After an extensive review of the literature on internal labor markets, Althauser and Kalleberg (1981, p. 130) conclude that "the concept of an internal labor market should include any cluster of jobs . . . that have three basic structural features: (a) a job ladder, with (b) entry only at the bottom and (c) movement up this ladder, which is associated with a progressive development of knowledge or skill." Most conceptions of job structures are fundamentally based on the model of a skill-based job ladder which allows entry only at the bottom and which involves increased specialization in successively higher jobs. The implications conveyed by the ladder image are precisely those suggested in most discussions of job structures. Like a physical ladder, a job ladder poses barriers to entry except at the bottom and constrains individuals on any particular ladder to remain on the same ladder; jumping from ladder to ladder is a risky trick on job ladders, just as it is on physical ladders. Consequently, the job ladder model implies that all individuals at a given position have the same career history (on the same ladder) and, as a result, that career history is irrelevant, net of present position, in predicting future attainments.

Beyond Human Capital and Structural Theories

Both theories are likely to be too simple. In its pursuit of parsimony, human capital theory ignores many aspects of reality which have obvious relevance, including the structural factors which affect compensation. Critics have noted that human capital and status attainment research construe the problem of inequality too narrowly, explaining inequality only in terms of individuals' attributes, while ignoring the influence of social structures. The human capital model, if taken literally, implies that wage and status attainments would increase without limit if individuals would merely increase their education, an unbelievable outcome which has been contradicted with declining growth in the 1970s (Thurow 1975; Sørensen 1977, p. 966). Studies carried out since 1970 have incorporated social structural measures into their analyses, and they reveal the influence of occupations, industry, firms, and social class which were ignored in the former research (Stolzenberg 1975; Bibb and Form 1977; Talbert and Bose 1977; Wright and Perrone 1977; Beck, Horan, and Tolbert 1978; Baron and Bielby 1980; Grandjean 1981; Spenner, Otto, and Call 1982).

Even economists who take the notion of human capital seriously have begun to note the possibilities of incorporating structural influences in the model. One theoretical analysis shows that wages can grow with experience, even if productivity does not, because giving "overpayment" to senior workers creates incentives for all employees (Lazear 1981), and this predicted lack of association of experience and productivity is supported by empirical work (Medoff and Abraham 1981). In effect, this analysis provides an economic rationale for wage structures which depart from human capital considerations. Another analysis shows that individuals can be compensated in terms of the rank order of their performance, not in terms of the dollar value of their performance (marginal product), and they may receive salaries that are assigned in advance without regard to the dollar value of their productivity (Lazear and Rosen 1981). These analyses are remarkable because they use economic principles to extend economic theory in the direction of structural theory.

Thurow (1975) uses economic and sociological principles to extend the traditional economic analysis much further toward a structural analysis. He argues that labor supply and demand are brought into balance not by the customary model of wage competition, in which wages are adjusted, but by what he calls *job competition*, in which wages are inflexible but jobs confer training to their new occupants so their human capital changes to match the job demands. Thurow adopts the social structural position that individuals are paid wages according to the jobs they hold, the jobs are assigned wage rates according to normative considerations. Consequently, while economic theory describes a process by which individual characteristics directly affect earnings, Thurow's job competition theory indicates that two separate processes are involved: the process of assigning wage rates to jobs and the process of matching individuals with jobs. Like economic theory, the job competition model provides a dynamic mechanism for matching individuals' attributes and their earnings, but the job competition model recognizes structural processes totally ignored by human capital theory.

While economic theories assume too little rigidity, structural theories may assume too much. Internal labor market theories and vacancy theories indicate that advancements occur along rigidly defined routes. Although this may be true in some circumstances, it is unlikely to be true in many others, and it will not be a good description of career mobility patterns in an entire organization. Rather than promoting employees through narrow career routes into managerial positions, organizations often strongly emphasize breadth of experience as a requirement for promotions, and lateral moves through a diversity of jobs and departments are viewed as providing the required preparation. Moreover, job rotations are also portrayed as a way for employees to show that they can handle new challenges and to keep themselves in contention for advancements. While it seems likely that some jobs are better than others for aiding an individuals' promotion chances, the range of advancement routes to a high-level position is likely to be far broader than a single job ladder.

Indeed, ABCO once made an effort to specify its career ladders so that the personnel department could make better manpower planning projections. Obviously, the fact that they undertook this project indicates that some personnel managers believed that career ladders could be easily described; however, they soon found that the reality was more complex than they had anticipated. Great amounts of time and resources were devoted to the project over the course of a year as they tried to map out the antecedent jobs from which each higher-level job recruited. Although some modal patterns were identified for many jobs, the full range of antecedent jobs was difficult to specify for most jobs, and when feeder patterns were combined to make ladders extending over more than two levels, the maps became hopelessly complex. The project was disbanded after a year, a near-total failure except for the knowledge that linkages of specific jobs were very complex.

Granovetter (1981) proposes a more dynamic structural model in which the matching processes which assign individuals to positions will change when the balance between labor supply and demand changes. These matching processes must also explain the ways that employers obtain information about employees ("signals" as described by Spence [1974] and Stiglitz [1975]) and the ways employers keep track of their employees' capabilities over time and decide their subsequent careers. Moreover, Granovetter's earlier findings indicate that the matching process is even more complex than a mere matching of individuals with vacancies. Over half the job placements of individuals in his study were jobs for which no vacancy existed, and in many of these cases, the jobs had not even existed before (Granovetter 1974, p. 14). If jobs are continually being created and destroyed (as is also indicated in Chapter 4), then the matching process raises complexities which some structural theories have assumed not to exist.

Particularly for describing stratification in organizations, Granovetter's model of matching processes may be a better description than either economic or structural theories, but it is also more complex. It posits that individuals' earnings are explained not only by individual human capital, but also by job attainments. It also posits that structure is not as rigid as structural theories sometimes suggest; the distribution of individuals in organizational hierarchies may be responsive to social and economic changes. Of course, research has rarely investigated how structural rigidities limit the responsiveness of attainments. The conception of matching processes paves the way for a dynamic structural model which incorporates elements of structural and economic theories.

Career Systems and the Tournament Model

As this literature review has indicated, the problem of obtaining a coherent picture of the selection procedures determining organizational careers arises largely from the difficulty of conceptualizing the conflict between opportunity and efficiency. The dominant theoretical perspectives tend to be one-sided, stressing one aspect of the conflict without addressing the other. Neoclassical economic theories, represented here by human capital theory, assume free markets and open opportunity, but they are poor models of the structure of demand and of the rigidities imposed by structural constraints. Structural theories describe rigid career ladders that embody the efficiencies of the sponsorship model, but they are not responsive to changing circumstances. What is needed is a model of a dynamic process which regulates structural attainments, similar to Granovetter's model of matching processes.

A model of matching processes determining career outcomes must also specify how matches respond to individuals' career histories. Career history information is particularly important in organizations. In an organization, information about an employee's career history is likely to be readily available; it is contained in company records. Moreover, in an organization, career history information is likely to be meaningful to promotion committee members, who can interpret employees' previous jobs and who know what it takes to get into these jobs and to perform the duties associated with them. In addition, because organizations are small communities with strong norms and policies about many aspects of organizational life, particular kinds of careers are likely to be more valued and, consequently, to affect future career attainments.

This study hypothesizes that a matching process exists which is affected by individuals' career histories. This process, called here a career selection system, or, more simply, a career system, is a system for matching employees with jobs based (at least in part) on employees' career histories. Unlike the human capital model, which posits that individuals' earnings attainments are determined by their human capital attributes, the career system model posits that careers are also affected by earlier career attainments. Unlike some structural models, which stress the influence of vacancies or rigid career ladders, the career system model posits that a dynamic selection mechanism determines which employees will be considered for advancements, when employees will be considered for advancements, and what their rate of achievement will be.

The career system model suggests that selection mechanisms respond not only to individuals' human capital but also to their career histories: the jobs they have held, the timing of their past advancements, and their rates of advancement. Note that these are not attributes of individuals per se, but attributes of individuals in relation to organizational positions. These career history attributes are generalizable roles that some individuals in any cohort could fill, regardless of the individuals' personal attributes and particular performances. By making individuals' chances of future career advancement be a function of their career histories in the organization, the career system can guarantee the availability of candidates for upcoming vacancies and the orderliness and predictability of career transitions. The career system conception is an alternative to the individually based model which underlies so much of the economic and psychological literature.

The particular model of career systems proposed here, the tournament model, describes a career selection system as a series of implicit competitions which progressively differentiate a cohort of employees throughout their careers, each time further defining their opportunities for future attainments. Thus the tournament model provides a resolution of the conflict between opportunity and efficiency by offering initial opportunity to all employees while fostering efficiency by repeated selections to remove employees from the tournament for top positions.

The tournament has a number of implications which are explored in the following chapters. It suggests that selections among the members of a cohort occur continually as their careers unfold, that employees' careers differ in their timetables for advancement and in their rates of advancement (trajectories), and that these timetables and trajectories will be related to employees' ultimate career attainment. Moreover, just as sports tournaments are used to identify the most able contestants, career tournaments may be used to create social signals of ability, which explain restrictions on opportunity and which legitimate investments in the winners of each stage. Finally, the tournament model is a dynamic mechanism which may operate over changing historical circumstances, and social and economic forces may have different effects on careers at different stages and for different employee groups. Some hypotheses about the mechanisms of change are suggested in Chapter 7.

Various aspects of the tournament conception are elaborated in the following chapters, and the subsequent empirical analyses inform, test, and develop the conception. The end result is a model of a general mechanism underlying many diverse career selection practices which organizational policies only vaguely describe. Moreover, this general model provides an overview of the career incentives which career systems hold out to employees through various phases of their careers. While the social psychology of employee behavior tends to stress only current situational influences, it is commonly accepted that individuals are also affected by their past experiences and their future expectations. To the extent that these are patterned by an organizational career system, such as the one described by the tournament model, this model can identify some of the structural sources of individual behavior in organizations.

Generalizability

As an ideal type, this organization can be conceived as a microcosm of stratification and mobility in larger society. This microcosm manifests strata in a formal status hierarchy which are more explicit and more clearly delineated than are statuses in the larger society. Studies of mobility among these strata are also likely to show clearer patterns of mobility than are likely to occur in averaging over diverse practices in the entire society.

Moreover, large organizations like this one employ a large portion of the entire labor force. Roughly 30% of the nonfarm labor force is employed by business enterprises with more than 500 employees (U.S. Bureau of the Census, 1972), and another 20% works for local, state, or federal governments (U.S. Bureau of Labor Statistics, 1976). In addition, major corporations like ABCO influence the rest of the labor market by their visibility as models of personnel practices and by the magnitude of their economic influence on the external labor market.

But there are some important conceptual and empirical distinctions between mobility within a large corporation and other kinds of mobility. Within a single organization, information about an employee's career history is more available, more interpretable, and more trustworthy than is such information when it is transferred across employing institutions. These conditions make many kinds of social labeling processes possible which would be weaker or inoperative across institutions.

Moreover, large organizations treat employees differently than do smaller ones. For instance, larger organizations pay higher wages (Lester 1967; Phelps Brown 1977), and they pay more for education (Stolzenberg 1978). Although the reasons for the effects of organizational size are subject to various interpretations (Kimberly 1976; Hall 1982), this study of a large corporation is likely to obtain findings which differ from those of studies of smaller firms. Consequently, while careers in the microcosm of a single large organization may represent some features of mobility in larger society and may affect mobility patterns more generally, careers in a corporation are likely to differ from mobility among organizations and from mobility within small organizations.

Unfortunately, other attributes of the organization which might aid generalizability inferences cannot be specified here, because I had to promise not to reveal information that would identify this corporation when I was given access to these personnel records.[2] This leads to an unfortunate vagueness in the description of ABCO.

However, it is not clear what further information would be useful for inferring generalizability. Even researchers who identify many features of the firms they study offer few speculations about generalizability implications (Wise 1975, Halaby 1978). Moreover, some of the general dimensions which are commonly used to specify the generalizability of organizational labor markets might not be very useful for that purpose. For instance, one of the main dimensions discussed in the theoretical literature, the distinction between "core" and "peripheral" industrial sectors, suggests predictions about personnel practices which are not supported by empirical research (Cohen and Pfeffer 1983; Jacobs 1983). Reviewing this literature, Baron (1984) concludes that many of the dimensions which have been used to describe organizational environments have been too coarse to explain differences in personnel practices. He proposes that research must focus on more specific dimensions. Ongoing work by Baron and Bielby, Bridges and Villemez, and Althauser and Kalleberg are designed to identify some pertinent dimensions which affect career systems, and may in the future be helpful in assessing the generalizability of these findings. But, at present, the dimensions on which generalizability depends have not yet been identified.

Certainly some of the general findings of this study match findings of other studies: the age-graded career patterns (Martin and Strauss 1959; Kanter 1977; Lawrence 1983, 1984), the job status effects on earnings (Malkiel and Malkiel 1973; Halaby 1978), and the effects of historical context on the careers of different cohorts (Grandjean 1981). These and other such comparisons are elaborated in subsequent chapters. Of course, for many of the specific findings, comparisons cannot be made because appropriate data have not previously been available.

From everything that I know about ABCO, I think that it is reasonable to consider it typical of many other large, well-established corporations. Although the present findings seem unlikely to generalize to small firms, high technology firms (Kanter 1983), or other firms undergoing radical changes in their products or markets, these findings seem likely to generalize to many other well-established corporations. Surely

---

[2]Readers sometimes try to uncover the true identities of anonymous objects of study. Kanter has commented that many people have tried to identify Indsco, and I have heard several different companies identified as the corporation I studied. These rumors serve no useful purpose. If false, they mislead. If true, they only prove that researchers cannot promise anonymity, thus shutting off research possibilities for other researchers. If there is some kind of information about this firm that is needed for particular comparisons, I will try to provide it. In a few years, these data will become old enough to make it possible for me to identify the corporation.

this corporation was not alone in responding to economic growth, contraction, and affirmative action over the period studied, and, judging from reports about career policies, the dominant concerns motivating the career system in this corporation were also salient in other major corporations: Citibank, Uniroyal, AT&T, Macy's (Schaeffer 1972), General Electric (Miller 1979), and Sears (Wellbank et al. 1978).

How does mobility in organizations compare with mobility in larger society? The extensive research on societal mobility since 1960 raises the question of generalizability with special force. That research describes mobility in a larger context, and it would be desirable to place organizational mobility within this context. But the difficulty of making this comparison is that different kinds of social mobility are studied in the two domains. The status mobility studied in most societal surveys (changes in occupations) is not the most important or most common kind of status mobility within organizations. On the other hand, the main kinds of status mobility within organizations (job status and authority changes) are difficult to study in societal surveys. Although some work has begun to analyze changes in authority attainments (Robinson and Kelley 1979), it is difficult to get valid and comparable indicators of detailed authority and status categories across employing organizations. While this makes the findings of organization studies difficult to compare with survey findings, it also indicates a kind of mobility which survey research has largely ignored and which can best be described by studies like this one.

The two kinds of research are comparable in studying earnings, but, as Chapters 5 and 6 suggest, earnings is a lagged outcome which only becomes differentiated well after job status distinctions have been made. If this finding is generalizable, then the detailed study of the timing of career differentiations requires job status distinctions not easily available to survey researchers. Of course, this means that tests of the generalizability of these findings requires more longitudinal studies within organizations.

Survey research does address one aspect of generalizability raised in this study. The longitudinal analyses used in several chapters introduce an additional concern about generalizability: that the sample in the longitudinal analyses is unrepresentative in being more stably employed than most members of the labor force. Of course, this limitation is unavoidable. Careers in an organization can only be studied for employees who remain in the organization.

However, recent work suggests that this is not such a serious constraint on generalizability as one might have thought. Analyzing data from the *Current Population Survey*, Hall (1982) concludes that over a quarter of all workers in the U.S. labor force hold continuous employment with the same employer which will last 20 years or more. Specifically, since the median entry age for male employees in this corporation was 25 years, what portion of the male labor force at this age would remain with the same employer for 13 years? Hall calculates that 27.0% of men in the 25–29 age range can expect 20 years of continuous employment with the same employer. Moreover, this percentage would be larger for a 13-year period and for employees of large corporations like the one studied here. Hall's analyses suggest that these longitudinal analyses, though restricting generalizability, still represent a substantial segment of the labor force.

Questions for this Study

This study describes the career system of a large corporation. Its aim is to investigate how the organizational career system responds to the conflict between opportunity and structural inequalities, particularly to the specific issues raised by the conflict between human capital and structural theories. Since the data obtained contain indicators of actual jobs over historical periods of increasing and decreasing economic demand, dynamic structural issues (similar to those raised by Thurow and Granovetter) may be tested. In addition, analyzing these data longitudinally permits the study of the dynamics of careers and, in particular, of how individuals' early job attainments may affect their subsequent careers.

The study of a single corporation permits more fine-grained analyses of more detailed data than have generally been available. The present data, the complete personnel records of a large corporation over a 13-year period, provide an unusually rich and complete set of information about the earnings, status, and job attainments of all the employees in an organization over substantial portions of their careers. By having longitudinal data, this study can analyze the shape of individuals' career lines over long periods of time, the career timing of promotions, and the timing of effects of various factors. Moreover, comparisons over the historical period covered (1962–1975) permit analyses of how increasing and decreasing organizational growth affect career lines. The main questions under study in the following chapters are summarized next.

Chapter 2: *Do early attainments affect later career outcomes?* This question raises a perennial issue in the study of careers: What is the relationship of individuals' first jobs to their later career outcomes? Studies using employees' preceptions have tried to address this question, but the results have been ambiguous. Although orderly features of an individual's career can often be noted, the basis of orderliness in one career may be quite different than the basis of orderliness in another; and in some careers, orderliness cannot be discerned by any stretch of the imagination (Wilensky 1961). Blau and Duncan (1967) find regularities within broad and abstract categories, but studies of earnings find very little relationship between starting salaries and later earnings. March and March (1977), examining the careers of a single occupational group in great detail, characterize the pattern they find as "almost random careers."

Structural theories, particularly internal labor market theory, contend that early jobs are strong determinants of later career attainments. Human capital theory stresses that careers are determined by individuals' investments through their first decade, and it implies more flexibility than structural theories portray. Chapter 2 examines this question by describing how early jobs and early job moves are related to the ways that careers subsequently unfold over time.

Chapter 3: *Does age affect career advancement?* Human capital theory ignores age; it interprets time in terms of experience. However, economists do customarily use age to compute a variable they call "previous experience," which is posited to have a positive effect on earnings (net of tenure).

In contrast, sociologists have long considered age as a status characteristic. Research suggests that age is a socially significant status in society (Neugarten 1973; Riley 1976; Dannefer 1982), and, as such, it may have consequences for employees' careers in organizations. Observers of organizations have noted that informal norms seem to exist about age and, in particular, that a relatively young age (30–40 years) tends to be considered the cutoff point for an employee to be considered for career advancement in some organizations (Chinoy 1955; Martin and Strauss 1959; Lawrence 1983, 1984). If age is an important influence on organizational careers, then economic analyses of employees' earnings within firms (Weisbrod and Karpoff 1968; Wise 1975a; Halaby 1978; Medoff and Abraham 1980) may have misconceptualized the meaning of their age-derived experience variables. Only a few studies have analyzed age effects per se (Klevmarken and Quigley 1976; Bartlett and Jencks 1978), and they find that it has important negative effects.

While much of the earlier research on the relationship of age and promotions was based on employees' perceptions, the present study examines these questions with personnel records of individuals' actual career moves. Moreover, by examining the issue across time periods of increasing and decreasing organizational growth, we can test the durability of the observed patterns and the extent and ways that they change. Subsequent chapters introduce age into multivariate analyses of longitudinal data, which permit an examination of the changing effects of age on a cohort's career advancements. Finally, by studying these issues in a single organization, this research discovers patterns which suggest the normative rules that might have generated them, and it can compare these outcomes with the ways that key managers describe the promotion system.

Chapter 4: *Does job composition influence the compensation jobs offer?* While human capital theory posits that employees' human capital determines their earnings, structural theory emphasizes the structural influences of jobs on earnings. In actual practice, large organizations often use compensation systems which set pay not only by individuals' contributions, but also by the contributions jobs require from individuals in terms of qualifications, tasks, and working conditions. Chapter 4 describes the job evaluation procedures used in this company and examines to what extent the compensation differences among jobs are explained by human capital factors, other kinds of individual attributes, or structural considerations in the organization. The outcomes of job evaluation procedures, besides being of descriptive interest in themselves, are also of theoretical interest because, in principle, job evaluation seeks to apply human capital considerations for determining job compensation. The present analyses provide a way of testing to what extent these theories explain the salaries associated with jobs.

Of course, even prior to answering these questions, it is necessary to discover some elementary properties of jobs in an organization, properties which heretofore have not been examined. Is an organization composed of a constant set of jobs? Are jobs stably valued or does the value of jobs vary over changing social and economic circumstances? Are jobs filled by the same kinds of individuals over time? Even these elementary questions have not been empirically analyzed for a large corporation. Taking the hundreds of jobs in this corporation as the units of analysis, Chapter 4 seeks to answer these questions.

Chapter 5: *What are the effects of human capital and structural factors on the career attainments of a cohort over time?* Unlike the previous questions, most of which can be answered by simple descriptive analyses, the test of these two theories requires analysis of the relative effects of various factors, and multivariate analysis is required for such an examination. While human capital theory contends that human capital attributes have gradually emerging influences on earnings, structural theories contend that age and other status factors also have effects, that their effects occur primarily at the outset, and that their effects are most apparent on job attainments. Consequently, the theories differ in three respects: which attributes have influence, when they have their influences, and what kind of attainment is affected.

Chapters 5 and 6 use multivariate analyses to consider the timing of effects of various factors on earnings, authority, and status attainments in the corporate hierarchy. The analyses incorporate the standard human capital factors (education, experience, and a proxy for ability) and factors suggested by structural theories (particularly age and college status). The analyses in Chapter 5 indicate that selections in the authority structure operate as a real system, which is distinct from the earnings system, and that the authority structure has an important influence in mediating the effect of individual characteristics on earnings. Specifically, many of the factors which influence earnings only after employees have been with the organization for a few years have already had an influence on their authority level attainments at the very outset. Moreover, the level system in the authority hierarchy seems to operate as an amplifying system for increasing college effects on earnings, assuring that graduates of preferred colleges continually receive ever-greater earnings, although these colleges have no further direct effects on earnings (net of level). The findings are interpreted as providing little support for human capital theory, but they provide strong support for structural effects independent of individual attributes.

Chapter 6: *Do early jobs and earnings have continuing effects on career attainments?* Chapter 6 extends the previous analysis in several ways. First, it studies a more fine-grained indicator of structural attainment than Chapter 5, an indicator which includes the status distinctions within authority levels. Second, it investigates whether early jobs have continuing effects on attainment after controlling for intervening attainments, permitting a test of whether structural effects are historical or ahistorical. Third, it also permits a test of a hypothesis suggested by human capital theory, that is, that employees face a trade-off between receiving higher early earnings and receiving greater future career advancements. Two sets of analyses are conducted, one controlling for job status and the other controlling for individual jobs (as dummy variables). Besides permitting a more rigorous test of the hypotheses, these analyses permit job status effects to be compared with the effects of jobs.

Chapter 7: *How do these patterns change over periods of increasing and decreasing growth?* Ultimately, the test of the durability of structure requires analyses over historical periods. Chapter 7 analyzes changes in career patterns over periods of increasing and decreasing growth. A dynamic structural model is proposed which explains the selection process in terms of the relative balance of supply and demand. Though resembling economic theory, this theory differs from economic theory in positing structural limitations on the responsiveness of career patterns. Two sets of hypotheses are proposed to describe these structural constraints.

One set of hypotheses—called the developmental hypotheses—contend that individuals' careers become increasingly enmeshed in the career structure over time, so that they become increasingly less responsive to external forces as they unfold. The other set of hypotheses—the selectivity hypotheses—contend that the balance of supply and demand for particular kinds of individuals, rather than affecting their earnings directly, affects which individuals are selected into available positions, which, in turn, affects individuals' earnings. Consequently, although economic theory may lead to correct predictions of changes in earnings outcomes in many cases, the mediating role of structure introduces constraints on the responsiveness of earnings for certain kinds of employees in ways not predictable by economic theory alone. The developmental and selectivity hypotheses provide a dynamic structural model that more closely describes the actual institutional practice and accounts for a fuller range of circumstances.

These hypotheses are tested on random samples of corporation employees over the four periods between 1965 and 1975. Comparisons of multivariate analyses over these periods reveal considerable stability of certain general patterns, and the changes which occur tend to support the hypotheses.

Chapter 8: *What are the implications of this career system for the socialization of employees?* Sociological research has mostly addressed life-cycle questions using survey methods and, consequently, has been unable to obtain many good indicators of social context effects. Even studies in specific social contexts have often relied on individuals' perceptions of social contexts, without obtaining objective indicators. Chapter 8 develops a conception of aging as a stratification phenomenon which is affected by the career opportunity structure in institutions. Chapter 8 shows how this study's findings about career patterns might create distinct career stages for different kinds of employees. These findings suggest the possibility that the organizational career structure may contribute to aging, particularly to stratification aspects of aging. In addition, further hypotheses are proposed about the ways that an organizational career structure may differentially socialize different employee groups. The chapter concludes by considering policy implications of this analysis.

Chapter 9: What are this study's implications for conceptualizing organizational career systems? Organizations are complex phenomena; they are difficult to see and difficult to conceptualize, so it is not surprising that managers and employees are confused, conflicted, and vague in the ways they portray them. The pattern of careers is hard to discern, even at a descriptive level, because of the large numbers of individuals involved and the many factors that any analysis must include. The task is made additionally difficult by the fact that personnel policies are confusing on these issues, reflecting the fundamental conflict in social norms. This study is distinctive in that it describes and models organizational careers in an entire corporation over long periods of time, using an unusually detailed and accurate dataset.

Our analysis of human capital and structural theories is really an effort to understand how much and what kinds of structuring the organization incorporates into the career system. The tournament model provides a particularly good way of reconciling some of the conflicts between the human capital and structural theories, for, like a sports tournament, career tournaments make structural attainments into signals of ability. Chapter 9 explores some of the implications of this model, most notably as they affect the conception of ability in organizations and as they may create differential options for ability to emerge at different points in the career system.

Chapter 10: What are this study's implications for organization personnel policies? The final chapter considers the policy implications of this study. The tournament model may be used both to reconceptualize and to redesign career systems in organizations. It can help employees understand their career options, and it can help organizations' planners redesign career systems to make a better resolution of the conflicting ideals. Some specific policy implications are proposed.

While the particular findings of this study contribute new kinds of empirical evidence to the sociological literature, the more general contribution of this study is to show the ways in which this ultimately irresolvable normative conflict becomes manifest in policies and practices which fit neither ideal exactly. It is hoped that an awareness of this conflict and the ways in which it becomes manifest in practice for organizational career systems may aid in our understanding of what forms organizational career systems may take and why they do so. This, after all, is the first step toward addressing the dilemma between opportunity and efficiency, which is a core issue for society.

CHAPTER 2

Tournament Mobility:
A Longitudinal Analysis
of the Pattern of Career Moves

Introduction

Promotions and demotions—changes in status within an organization or occupation—are important events in most people's work lives.
They may be the most common form of mobility for some segments of
the labor force, and they are important functions in organizations and
occupational groups. Yet while there have been many systematic studies of mobility among occupations since Blau and Duncan's (1967)
pioneering work, there have been few longitudinal analyses of promotions and demotions within occupations or organizational hierarchies.
  This chapter presents an empirical analysis of the flow of individuals
along sequences of jobs—what I shall call career mobility.[1] The analysis

[1]This follows the definition of *career* by Thompson, Avery, and Carlson (1968, p. 7), as
"any unfolding sequence of jobs," which is also accepted by Spilerman (1977) but differs
from Wilensky's (1961) use of the term "career" to refer only to orderly careers.

follows the career mobility of a single cohort through a large corporation over a 13-year period, using the official personnel records. Because of the extensive checking procedures used to verify these records, these data provide an unusually accurate source of time-series information on career mobility.

The conceptual focus of this chapter is the issue of whether early career positions and changes in status affect later careers, apart from the intervening positions held. This issue has been discussed in the status attainment, Markov, and organization-career literatures. One version of a historical model—the tournament model—is described, and a number of hypotheses derived from it are tested. The empirical analysis supports the historical-effects position, finding that very early job moves are related to subsequent mobility even a decade later after employees have moved on to second and third jobs. Indeed, mobility in the earliest stage of one's career bears an unequivocal relationship with one's later career, predicting many of the most important parameters of later moves: career ceiling, career floor, as well as probabilities of promotion and demotion in each successive period.

Theoretical Background

Historical Antecedents of Mobility

The central issue of the present inquiry is whether individuals' career histories are associated with their future careers independent of their current positions. This issue is being argued on several fronts. In some status attainment research, a historical model is proposed that shows income and occupation at a given period as being directly influenced by income and occupation at all previous periods; Featherman's (1971) analyses provide some support for this model. Kelley (1973a, p. 492) offered empirical analyses challenging the historical model and concluded that "as a man's career progresses, past failures are forgiven and past successes forgotten." Subsequent exchanges between Featherman (1973) and Kelley (1973b) elaborate on the issue, but the question of historical effects remains unresolved. Both, however, agreed that investigation of sequences of jobs and job characteristics would be useful in resolving the question.

Markov models provide another way to analyze historical effects by using simple transition matrices that show the probabilities of moving from each time 1 position to each time 2 position. In Markov analyses, inferences are made about the consequences of transition matrices based on simple assumptions. As Mayer (1972, pp. 312–313) states:

> The basic principle which distinguishes Markov models asserts that the status category a person will occupy in the future depends only on the status category he occupies at present and not at all on the categories he has previously occupied. This is sometimes referred to as the principle of path independence. . . . [If two people] have different status histories, but their status levels at the time recorded are identical, . . . a Markov model would make identical predictions about their future [mobility].[2]

Tests of path independence are rare because of the paucity of mobility data at three points in time. Consequently, some major work in this area admits that this may be an unrealistic assumption, but then stresses models based on this assumption because the mathematics is more tractable (Bartholomew 1968, p. 9). Hodge investigated the path-independence assumption using several sets of data on intergenerational and intragenerational occupational change. Each analysis showed slight departures from path independence, particularly for intragenerational occupational changes; but for the most part his findings, like Kelley's (1973a), supported the path-independence assumption. March and March (1977), analyzing careers of school superintendents, also found support for Markov models.[3]

One troubling finding has been a tendency for Markov models to underpredict the number of nonmobile individuals (Blumen, Kogan, and McCarthy 1955; Hodge 1966). Although this finding has not been used to question the path-independence assumption (which is sometimes called "the Markov property"), it has led to adaptations of the Markov model that modify its other two assumptions. One class of semi-Markov models, questioning the *stationarity assumption* (i.e.,

---

[2]Markov models, as usually applied, make two other assumptions. The stationarity assumption asserts that the probability of mobility over a fixed time internal is independent of when it occurs in that interval, and it depends only on the length of the time interval (McGinnis 1968; Ginsberg 1971; Mayer 1972; Sørensen 1975). The homogeneity assumption asserts that all persons have identical transition probabilities (Blumen, Kogan, and McCarthy 1955; Goodman 1961; Bartholomew 1967; McFarland 1970; Spilerman 1972).

[3]Tuma's (1976) study of job leaving is not directly pertinent to the analysis of upward mobility; however, it might be noted that she found conflicting evidence regarding path independence, with number of previous jobs and duration of preceding job being historical variables that violated the path-independence assumption. Stewman (1975, p. 313) discussed some characteristics of simple transition matrices that gave vague support to the path-independence assumptions, but he did not break down the transition matrices to investigate whether the same job had different effects depending on previous job histories. His description (p. 305) seemed to indicate that the way his data were recorded did not permit the antecedents of promotions to be traced.

that a given length of time has the same effects regardless of when it occurs), posits a decline in mobility with increasing age (Mayer 1968) or duration of stay (McGinnis 1968). Another class of semi-Markov models, questioning the *homogeneity assumption* (i.e., that all individuals have equal mobility chances), posits that a cohort can be distinguished as either movers or stayers (Blumen, Kogan, and McCarthy 1955; White 1970b). Along these lines, Mayer (1972) proposed that all persons are originally movers, but that some become stayers over time.

It is not clear why semi-Markov models have ignored career histories. Although history is incorporated in a limited sense in the age-decline and duration-decline models, none of the semi-Markov models questions the path-independence assumption. A path-dependence semi-Markov model would posit that an individual's early mobility history influences later mobility and so might be called, for simplicty, a historical model (although nonstationarity models are also historical in a more limited sense). Of course, historical effects are difficult to study, but detailed analyses of historical effects may contribute to more realistic assumptions and to more appropriate applications of models.

Much research on organizational careers has dealt with the question of historical effects, and its conclusions contradict the path-independence assumption in the status attainment and Markov literatures. Since the 1950s, many researchers have studied job mobility, and they have emphasized the crucial importance of career paths. Organizations quickly "size up" new employees and allocate them to different training and socialization experiences (Becker and Strauss 1956; Berlew and Hall 1966; Peres 1966; Campbell 1968; Van Maanen 1977; Schein 1978). Furthermore, this selection and allocation is repeated, with later assessments being based not only on age and duration (nonstationarity) (Roth 1963; Jennings 1971; Bray, Campbell, and Grant 1974; Kanter 1977), but also on one's particular career history (Dalton 1951; Glaser 1964; Jennings 1971; Faulkner 1974) and one's advancement on the "correct" path (Kanter 1977).

Unfortunately, although these studies have described selection and socialization processes in extensive detail, they have been far less thorough in examining actual long-term career patterns. Patterns of career moves are rarely described in detail, and many studies (e.g., Martin and Strauss 1959) have relied on respondent reports so that they seem to be descriptions of ideal careers rather than actual job moves (which might be less simple to report). The difficulty of obtaining appropriate longitudinal data is understandable and may explain why these microlevel studies of organizational careers have never been integrated with macrolevel studies in the status attainment and Markov literatures. Systematic longitudinal studies of actual career paths would permit a more direct test of the path-dependence issue in organizations.

Contest, Sponsored, and Tournament Mobility

Ahistorical effects have been described somewhat differently by Turner (1960), who presented two ideal types of mobility—contest and sponsored mobility. Contest mobility systems delay selection and allow individuals complete freedom for mobility and thus are totally ahistorical. Sponsored mobility systems select individuals for their ultimate careers very early and allow no freedom for departures from these early assigned careers. They are ahistorical in the sense that a later position is predicted by the immediately preceding position, and earlier positions do not improve the prediction.[4]

Reformulating Turner's ideal types, I have proposed a tournament mobility model which is a historical model (Rosenbaum 1976). In the *tournament mobility model*, careers are conceptualized as a sequence of competitions, each of which has implications for an individual's mobility chances in all subsequent selections. Although tournaments can be constructed with numerous variants in the rules, the central principle involves an important distinction between winners and losers at each selection point. Winners have the opportunity to compete for high levels, but they have no assurance of attaining them; losers are permitted to compete only for low levels or are denied the opportunity to compete any further at all. As in a contest model, winners must continue competing in order to attain high levels, for there is no assurance of continual advancement; but, as in a sponsored model, early selections have irreversible consequences for losers. The tournament results in a progressively greater winnowing down of the winner's cohort at each successive stage. In contrast, the losers are relegated to "minor tournaments" for lesser positions. Unlike sports tournaments which eliminate losers, the career tournament retains losers but lowers and narrows their options.

The tournament model grew out of research on mobility patterns in a school track system and in students' postgraduate careers. The research

---

[4]Turner proposed his models as ideal types to describe normative systems, not actual mobility patterns. However, one kind of research suggested by his ideas "is an exploration of different channels of mobility . . . to discover the extent to which mobility corresponds to each of these types" (Turner 1960, p. 865). The present chapter is an attempt to pursue this suggestion.

revealed a tournament pattern in which students who were moved out of the college track at any time between grades 7 and 12 had no chance of getting back in that track and very little chance of getting into college, regardless of how hard they strived (Rosenbaum 1976). In contrast, students who remained in the college track at the end of each year had the possibility of remaining in that track, but they could still be dropped in the next year.

In some ways, the tournament model is an abstract formulation of some of the observations in the organizational careers literature. It posits that assessments in an employee's first few years have profound and enduring effects on later career outcomes (see Berlew and Hall 1966). It also posits that assessments occur repeatedly, and an employee must continue to pass these hurdles in order to advance. However, the tournament model goes beyond most of the career literature in hypothesizing some further patterns: for example, the relationship of early promotions to specific career outcomes such as future promotion chances, level attainments, and career ceilings and floors. Although these hypotheses are consistent with findings in the career literature (Kanter 1977), the actual patterns of career mobility over long periods of time have rarely been described.

Hypotheses of this sort have rarely been tested because time-series data over a sufficiently long interval are difficult to obtain, and that, in fact, was a limitation in the tracking study. The data available in the present study are unusual in permitting analysis of career mobility over a 13-year period, thereby providing the first opportunity for testing these hypotheses in an organizational context.

Level Mobility in an Organizational Hierarchy

In the 1970s and 1980s, research on mobility in the United States has largely focused on occupational status changes. This is a particularly valuable approach to mobility between generations, but when applied to intragenerational (career) mobility, it overlooks the patterns of mobility within occupations or organizations that may be the most common form of mobility for some segments of the labor force.

In many occupations, change of levels (or status) in an organizational or professional hierarchy is the main kind of advancement. Most professionals, managers, and skilled workers tend to stay in the same occupation throughout their work lives (Reynolds 1951, pp. 19–36; Lipset and Bendix 1952; Blau and Duncan 1967). In such occupations, which have many status distinctions and diverse career ladders within them, the classic type of occupational status score will be quite insensitive to career mobility. In addition, as previously noted, occupational status scores have certain anomalous characteristics, and the hierarchical authority levels may provide a more consistent hierarchical indicator of attainment in the sense that level increases are accompanied by increases in earnings, job challenge, etc. The problems with occupational status scores do not necessarily preclude their usefulness in some contexts, but they do suggest the need for considering other status distinctions.

Sociologists have increasingly used income as a measure of attainment, but income is also ambiguous as a measure of position within a stratification system. Organizations often have elaborate schemes that give higher-level employees increasing proportions of their compensation in a form other than salary, such as deferred compensation, stock options, insurance, pension, prerequisites, and other fringe benefits (McLaughlin 1975). Moreover, these other forms of compensation are becoming increasingly common for nonmanagement employees (e.g., in Scanlon Plan types of profit sharing). A single indicator of income is therefore likely to be incomplete or misleading.

By contrast, the level categories in organizations often have extremely concrete referents. "A title on the door means a Bigelow on the floor," so the advertisement goes; and the guidelines defining the meaning of each level in an organization hierarchy are often just that explicit. Whether one is in the nonmanagement, foreman, or lower-management level indicates the kind of workspace one receives, how that workspace may be furnished, what kinds of assistance and services one can expect, how much autonomy one has in executing one's job, how much latitude one has in one's hours, how much one is paid, and how one is paid (Goldner 1965; Ladinsky 1975; Kanter 1977). If status is conceived as the prestige accorded to people on the basis of their occupational position, then level categories provide a fine-grained delineation of the most important status distinctions within organizations (Evans 1975; Matras 1975, p. 300).[5]

---

[5]A few researchers have studied similar kinds of internal status distinctions. Chains of job vacancies have been analyzed (White 1970; Stewman 1975), and models for analyzing individuals' career patterns have been proposed (Rosenbaum 1976, 1977; Althauser and Kalleberg 1977; Kanter 1977; Spilerman 1977). In effect, many of these studies have adopted the economists' notion of "internal labor markets," which posits structural constraints in institutions, and have attempted to explain these constraints more clearly (Caplow 1954; Slocum 1968; Doeringer and Piori 1971; Stolzenberg 1975; Cain 1976; Talbert and Bose 1977).

Method and Analysis

Setting, Data, and Sample

The data for the analyses are taken from the computerized file of the complete personnel records of ABCO between 1962 and 1975. The only information selected for the present analyses was the level category. There are eight levels in the corporation: (1) nonmanagement, (2) foreman, (3) lower management, (4) middle management, (5) upper middle management, (6) lower top management, (7) vice president, and (8) president; however, only the first five levels are used in these analyses. Each of these levels has a very clear meaning within the organization, and although space prevents much description, the labels just listed convey the general location in the hierarchy. For descriptive purposes, perhaps the simplest numerical description of each level would be the mean and standard deviation of the annual salaries at that level (see Appendix 2.A).

The sample studied is composed of the employees who entered the corporation between 1960 and 1962 and who remained with it through at least 1975. This permits the analysis of 13 years of career mobility for the newcomer cohort of 671 employees who began in the same starting level.[6] Personnel records were available only for the years 1962, 1965, 1969, 1972, and 1975, permitting analyses of 3-year intervals for all but one period. (Values were multiplied by 0.75 to make the percentages comparable for the 1965–1969 period.) The 3–4-year spans are fortuitous. Observations of other corporations suggest that employees expect that high-potential managers will advance every 2 or 3 years (Kellogg 1972; Kanter 1977).

Analytic Strategy

The aim of the study is to describe the patterns of moves of an employee cohort, testing particular relationships suggested by the tour-

[6]The company's policy was for all employees to enter the company at the bottom level. However, 16 of the 687 employees entering between 1960 and 1962 had already attained a higher level by December 31, 1962. In a sense, these few individuals may be considered to be on the fastest tracks, which have their own career trees. These individuals are considered with the other 671 for the tests of Hypothesis 2 (path dependence). Because of the small number of people involved, these individuals are not considered in the analyses of the subsequent hypotheses, although their career tree is presented in Appendix 2.B. (It should be noted that all dates represent the level as of December 31 of the year given.)

nament model. The aim is descriptive analysis, not causal inference. These analyses do not seek to assert that early career paths cause later career mobility. Rather they seek to ascertain whether early career paths are related to later career mobility. Regardless of whether such a relationship indicates a unique causal influence or a mediating influence for other causal factors (e.g., sex, ethnicity, supervisors' ratings), the existence or nonexistence of such a relationship would have important implications.

In the first place, if such a relationship were discovered, it would identify highly visible social signaling cues about individuals' career futures (Spence 1974). Because of the diversity of selection criteria and irregularity of their application (Kanter 1977) and the invisibility and lack of clarity of selections (Goldner 1965), employees often have difficulty inferring their likely career futures. This unclarity is even more true in judging other employees—supervisors, peers, and subordinates—for whom the relevant attributes (education, supervisors' evaluation) are often unknown to observers (Berg 1971, p. 78). Regardless of whether previous career paths have a causal influence on later careers, if they are related to later careers, then they are clearly visible signals which may influence the way employees are regarded and treated by others. Even as a phenotypic phenomenon, this would illuminate an important stratification process in organizations which may have ramifications for social interaction.

Furthermore, the state of knowledge about organizational careers is such that the very basic descriptive knowledge is lacking. Are there patterns of career paths in organizations? Are early career paths related to employees' likely career futures? If so, what aspects of early career paths are related and how early does this phenomenon appear? Does such a relationship continue to hold, even after controlling for present position (i.e., does the path-independence assumption apply to careers in organizations)? These basic descriptive questions are fundamental to an understanding of organizational careers and, in particular, for understanding whether Markov or semi-Markov models, which require the path-independence assumption, can be applied to organizational careers.

Given the aim of this chapter, nonparametric statistical techniques are quite appropriate for the analyses. Although multivariate tests are commonly used, they are not necessary for these hypotheses, and they have the disadvantage of requiring assumptions about the shape of promotion probabilities (e.g., as linear, logarithmic, or logistic). At this stage of analysis, the choice was made not to constrain the relationship with such assumptions because neither theory nor empirical work suggested a particular functional form. Of course, the costs of these assumptions are also accompanied by certain advantages of multivariate analyses, particularly if one desired to model the complete status attainment process in an organization. However, the hypotheses to be tested here are straightforward, descriptive ones intended to test specific relationships in organizational career paths, and they can be tested very suitably by nonparametric tests (Goodman 1962). Multivariate analyses of these issues are presented in subsequent chapters, particularly Chapter 6.

Hypotheses

Implicit in the tournament model are several hypotheses, some of which make it distinct from the contest model, the sponsored model, or an ahistorical (path-independence) model. Refutation of some of the hypotheses would amount to support for one or more of the other models.

Hypothesis 2.1. The existence of career patterns: In a corporation, career mobility does not resemble a random, open-opportunity model; employees have a limited number of career paths open to them.

Hypothesis 2.2. Path dependence: Employees occupying the same position have different promotion chances that are related to the path by which they come to this position.

Hypothesis 2.3. Early promotion paths: Employees receiving early promotions have very different promotion chances than employees not receiving early promotions.

2.3.1. Employees promoted in the earliest period have a *much better chance of being further promoted* than employees not promoted in the earliest period.

2.3.2. Employees promoted in the earliest period have a *much better chance of attaining management levels* (levels above foreman) than employees promoted in later periods.

2.3.3. Employees promoted in the earliest period have a *higher career ceiling* (maximum possible position) in their first 13 years and they have a *better chance of reaching this ceiling* than employees promoted in later periods.

2.3.4. Employees promoted in the earliest period have a *higher career floor* (lowest possible position) in their first 13 years than employees promoted in later periods.

Hypothesis 2.4. No assurances of later promotions: Early promotions do not offer assurances of continued mobility; employees promoted in the earliest periods are not assured of later promotions.

Hypothesis 2.5. Later promotion paths: Because the tournament specifies that you have to continue winning to stay in the competition, employees promoted in the earliest period must also be promoted in the second period to have a good chance of attaining middle management (level 4) in their first 13 years.

Existence of Career Patterns

The first hypothesis is actually a general proposition which is elaborated and tested in all of the analyses. Each subsequent hypothesis further describes another way in which careers are defined and patterned in ways that close off opportunities for large numbers of individuals in the organization. The net result of all of these hypotheses, if confirmed, would be to reject the applicability of a contest model to these patterns. Of course, this would not necessarily conflict with Turner's contention since he was describing people's normative beliefs. It might, however, conflict with the expectations some employees may initially hold if Chinoy's (1955) findings apply, and it might also conflict with messages some companies convey to employees; however, these are merely conjectures. The first hypothesis is stated only as a conceptual hypothesis, stating a conceptually important point of which everything else is a refinement.

Path Dependence

The issue of Hypothesis 2.2 is whether the path that an employee takes to get to his or her current position is related to the later career. The paths may be modeled by a set of two-dimensional coordinates, with time the horizontal dimension and level the vertical one. The path-dependence hypothesis asserts that people in position C (Figure 2.1) have different career opportunities which are related to whether their careers proceeded by a path of early promotion and subsequent plateau (through position A in Figure 2.1) or by a path of early plateau and subsequent promotion (through position B in Figure 2.1).

Since path dependence asserts that time 3 positions are related to time 1 positions after controlling for time 2 positions, path dependence can be tested for each time 2 position by simple statistical tests (Goodman 1962) which test the path-independence hypothesis as a null hypothesis. The strategy for testing this hypothesis will be to test the

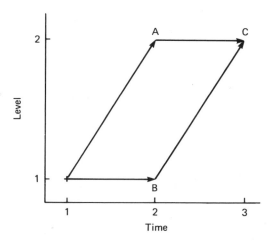

FIGURE 2.1. Parallelogram illustrating historical effects in mobility.

relationship of 1969 to 1962 positions, controlling for 1965 positions; then to test the relationship of 1972 to 1965 positions, controlling for 1969 positions; and finally to test the relationship of 1975 to 1969 positions, controlling for 1972 positions. In this way, separate tests of path independence, at three different periods, can be made.

Table 2.1 presents the results of testing the relationship of 1969 level

Table 2.1

Relationship of 1969 Level to 1962 Level for Employees Who Were Foremen and Lower Management in 1965

1965 level: foreman[a] 1962 level	1969 level			
	Foreman	Lower management	Middle management	Total
Nonmanagement	11	31	8	50
Foreman	6	3	1	10
	17	34	9	60
1965 level: lower management[b] 1962 level		Lower management	Middle management	Total
Nonmanagement		9	8	17
Foreman		2	2	4
Lower management		0	2	2
		11	12	23

[a] $\tau_c = -.203$; $p = .02$.
[b] $\tau_c = .181$; $p = .17$.

to 1962 level for employees who were foremen and lower management in 1965.[7] The results indicate that 1965 foremen who came from non-management levels after 1962 had a significantly better chance of promotion in the subsequent interval than those who were already at foreman level in 1962. However, although the path-independent null hypothesis can be rejected for 1965 foremen ($p = .02$), it cannot be rejected for 1965 lower management.[8] Apparently all new employees who had made it as high as lower management by 1965 had virtually the same promotion opportunities independent of their earlier level.

Table 2.2 presents the results of testing the relationship of 1972 level to 1965 level for employees who were foremen and lower management in 1969. The data for 1969 foremen suggests that a relationship may exist, although it falls short of the .05 level of significance ($p = .09$). However, if the two demotions (in the first column of the table) are ignored, the remaining table, which portrays no-move and promotion paths, is significant at the .05 level. The data for 1969 lower-management indicates that the path-independence hypothesis cannot be rejected. Both tables indicate a tendency for employees who were promoted between 1965 and 1969 to have a better chance of subsequent promotion; in fact, no one who remained at the same level between 1965 and 1969 was promoted in the following interval.

Table 2.3 presents the results of testing the relationship of 1975 level to 1969 level for employees who were foremen and lower management in 1972. The data for foremen indicate a modest, significant association ($p = .03$). The data for lower-management indicate virtually no associa-

---

[7]The tables for nonmanagement and middle management (level 4) are omitted because they tend to be one-dimensional and do not permit comparisons relevant to the path-dependence hypothesis.

The appropriateness of statistical tests with samples of an entire universe is debatable. The rationale for their use is the assumption that there is a random element to these results. If, hypothetically, the events described here were run repeatedly (under the same conditions with equivalent cohorts), some variation in outcomes is likely to occur. A statistical test may be considered to test whether the observed findings differ from the pattern produced solely by chance (Hanushek and Jackson 1977, Chap. 1). The interpretation is controversial, and some do not agree with the use of such tests in these cases (Berk 1977). The controversy is not resolved. I report the statistical tests for readers who are interested. Those who are not may, of course, disregard them.

[8]The chi square test is not used in these analyses because it can reject the null hypothesis in tables larger than 2-by-2 tables when nonlinear relationships exist (e.g., when a U-shaped relationship exists). Since the path-dependence hypothesis posits linear relationships, tau b and tau c permit more appropriate tests. They also indicate the degree of association. Tau b is the appropriate test for square tables and tau c is the appropriate test for rectangular tables. The customary standard of significance, $p < .05$, is applied through these analyses.

Table 2.2

Relationship of 1972 to 1965 Levels for Employees Who Were Foremen and Lower
Management in 1969

1969 level: foreman[a] 1965 level	1972 level			
	Nonmanagement	Foreman	Lower management	Total
Nonmanagement	2	89	15	106
Foreman	0	16	0	16
	2	105	15	122
1969 level: lower management[b] 1965 level	Lower management		Middle management	Total
Nonmanagement	21		0	21
Foreman	29		4	33
Lower management	11		0	11
	61		4	65

[a] $\tau_b = -.054$; $p = .09$.
[b] $\tau_c = -.010$; $p = .43$.

Table 2.3

Relationship of 1975 to 1969 Levels for Employees Who Were Foremen and Lower
Management in 1972

1972 level: foreman[a] 1969 level	1975 level			
	Nonmanagement	Foreman	Lower management	Total
Nonmanagement	1	60	1	62
Foreman	1	93	8	102
	2	153	9	164
1972 level: lower management[b] 1969 level	Foreman	Lower management	Middle management	Total
Foreman	0	15	0	15
Lower management	1	59	2	62
	1	74	2	77

[a] $\tau_c = .051$; $p = .03$.
[b] $\tau_c = .021$; $p = .31$.

tion. Actually, the most noteworthy trend in these tables is the drastically reduced mobility for all levels (possibly indicative of a recessionary economy), which makes the hypothesis difficult to test in this time interval.

Although some tendency is noted toward path dependence in some of the lower-management analyses, little can be inferred with certainty because the total number of promotions from this level is small. However, in the first three periods, these tests provide strong evidence for rejecting the path-independence null hypothesis for the foreman level. During employees' first decade in the company (1960–1969), foremen who have experienced recent promotions are significantly more likely to receive further promotions than those who have stayed at the same level.

Early Promotion Paths

This section presents analyses of the early selection hypotheses. Although careers could be analyzed by using four consecutive transition matrices, four transition matrices are difficult to read simultaneously. A clearer way of presenting the same information is a career tree, which portrays the career paths followed by all individuals during their employment in the organization. The career tree illustrated in Figure 2.2 shows the careers of all newly entering employees in 1962 (i.e., 0–2 years tenure) who remained in the company through 1975, the five levels being shown vertically and the five points of time being shown horizontally.

Since the previous analysis rejected the path-independence assumption for some levels, a career tree must distinguish between employees at the same level who arrived there via different paths. There will be several lines at each level, a separate line for each person with a different previous career. Consequently, even in a career tree such as this one, in which all employees begin at the same position, the number of logically possible career lines is enormous. For example, each level position in 1975 could be filled from any one of five levels in 1972, each of these could be filled from any one of five levels in 1969, and each of these could be filled from any one of five levels in 1965. If all of these possible paths had even a slight amount of randomness so that even a small proportion of the possible paths were occupied by at least one individual, the resulting career tree would be dense maze of parallel and crossing lines, extremely difficult to draw and to decipher.

However, the analyses of pairs of transition matrices have shown a large number of empty cells, indicating that the vast majority of possi-

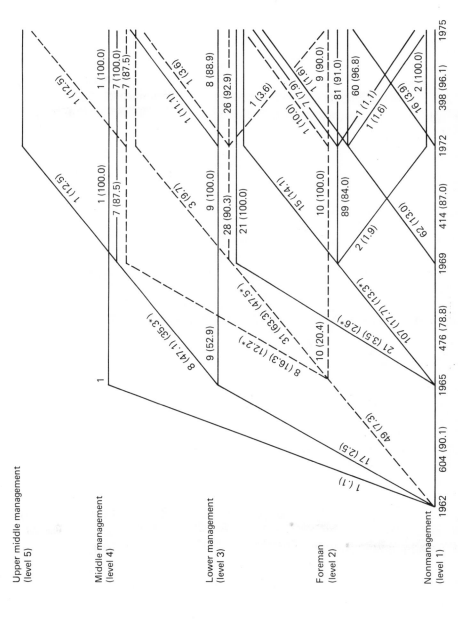

FIGURE 2.2. Career tree for 1960–1962 entering cohort: level placements in 1962, 1965, 1969, 1972, and 1975. Numbers in parentheses are percentages. Asterisk indicates percentages adjusted for the longer time period in 1965–1969 (multiplied by 0.75).

ble moves have not been taken by any employees. The mobility process is clearly a highly ordered one, one that may lend itself to a fairly clear career tree.

As was suspected, even with all five time periods portrayed together, the career tree depicted in Figure 2.2 is fairly clear, with no position having more than four paths feeding into it and with only three positions having more than four paths emanating from them. The simplicity and clearness of these career paths may be taken as evidence of the existence of ordered career patterns, therein supporting Hypothesis 2.1. Career mobility does not at all resemble the random, open-opportunity situation suggested by the contest model. Compared with the hundreds of possible paths, the careers in this company follow a limited number of paths.

Of course this is not to say that job paths would be this clear. Indeed as noted in Chapter 1, the organization's own efforts indicate that job paths are not very clear. But in terms of authority-level categorizations of attainments, the patterns are quite clear.

A key feature in this career-path diagram is that it does resemble a tree structure, with paths branching out from a common starting position and from each successive position. Groups of employees proceeding along each career path tend to be differentiated during each time interval. However, this does not always happen, and whether it happens and the degree to which it happens is highly related to historical features at the beginning of an individual's career. The early promotion path hypotheses posit four kinds of career outcomes that may be associated with early promotions.

In the tournament model, although no explicit competition event is ever held, as is the case in Landau's (1965) model, and although the decisions about losers are never publicly declared (Goldner 1965); processes approximating tournament competitions occur. Because the competitions are not public events and do not come at well-defined periods, some assumptions must be made about when each competition ends and about which contestants have "lost." Quite arbitrarily, for the sake of this analysis, it was assumed that "competitions" occur roughly every 3–4 years[9] and that an individual has "lost" the "competition" if he was not promoted during the 3–4-year period.[10] This too

[9]Interviews with informants in this organization give some support to the 3–4-year period, although it is only anecdotal evidence. Ideally it would be desirable to look at other time intervals, but the present data do not permit this. Observations of other corporations also supports the use of this interval (Kellogg 1972).

[10]Since this analysis does not take account of kinds of status attainment other than promotions, it clearly oversimplifies, as do many analyses of mobility. For some indi-

is possibly an arbitrary labeling, for corporations may have other ways of rewarding employees besides promotions, and sometimes lateral moves (job changes at the same level) are required to prepare the employee for a subsequent promotion (Rosenbaum 1977). To the extent that an ordered pattern exists in which promotions occur more or less frequently than 3–4 years and to the extent that "winners" are rewarded and advanced in the tournament without being given a promotion, the analysis will discern *less* structural order than actually exists. However, as we shall see, the analysis finds a great deal of order even under these crude assumptions.

The tournament model emphasizes how crucial each loss in a competition is, for a loss removes the individual from the main tournament. Although there may be subsequent competitions in minor tournaments, the rewards and chances of winning are greatly *diminished* in minor tournaments. The hypotheses analyzed here emphasize the earliest period because that is the time when the largest number of people are eliminated from the main tournament. The same process occurs in later periods (Hypotheses 2.4 and 2.5), although it does so for smaller numbers of employees. The following hypotheses indicate some of the most important career outcomes that may be associated with wins or losses in the earliest periods of one's career in this corporation.

FURTHER PROMOTIONS   Two versions of Hypothesis 2.3.1 will be tested. Both compare the promotion chances of the winners and losers of the first "competition" (that is, those promoted and those not promoted in the first 3-year period), one taking second-period promotions as the dependent variable and one taking promotions in any of the three following periods as the dependent variable. Table 2.4 shows that the chances of being promoted in the second period are higher for employees promoted in the first period ($p < .001$).[11] This hypothesis resembles the previously tested path-dependence hypothesis, but stipulates the direction of change: It compares level changes rather than levels, and it compares careers of people from a shared origin (time 1 position) rather than comparing those with a shared time 2 position.

---

viduals, upward mobility may not be desired. A professor or a researcher may refuse a promotion to an administrative position, and some manual workers may reject a promotion to foreman or management. An employee may gain informal respect, status, and even authority, without a promotion (however, see Goldner and Ritti 1967). These complexities deserve further attention, but they cannot be addressed here.

[11]Chi-square is used throughout these analyses as the simplest test for relationship in a 2-by-2 table. The stringent standard of significance, $p < .01$, is applied throughout these analyses as the criterion, although the actual significance level obtained is usually reported.

Table 2.4

Comparisons of Promotions

	Promoted first period	Promoted second period					Promoted first period	Promoted 1965–1975		
		Yes	No	Total		(b)		Yes	No	Total
(a)										
	Yes	47	20	67			Yes	49	18	67
	No	128	476	604			No	206	398	604
		175	496	671				255	416	671

$\chi^2 = 69.4$; $p < .001$　　　　　　　　　　$\chi^2 = 38.9$; $p < .001$

	Period promoted	Attained level 3 by 1975				Period promoted	Attained level 3 in 6 yrs.		
		Yes	No	Total			Yes	No	Total
(c)					(d)				
	First	56	11	67	First	40	9	49
	Later	42	86	128	Later	42	84	126
		98	97	195		82	93	175

$\chi^2 = 45.3$; $p < .001$　　　　　　　　　　$\chi^2 = 32.9$; $p < .001$

	Period promoted	Attained levels 4 or 5 by 1975				Period promoted	Demoted		
		Yes	No	Total			Yes	No	Total
(e)					(f)				
	First	22	45	67	First	0	49	49
	Later	0	128	128	Later	4	124	128
		22	173	195		4	173	177

$\chi^2 = 46.9$; $p < .001$　　　　　　　　　　$\chi^2 = 1.4$; n.s.

	Period(s) promoted	Attained levels 4 or 5 by 1975		
		Yes	No	Total
(g)				
	First and second	19	28	47
	First but not second	1	18	19
		20	46	66

$\chi^2 = 7.9$; $p < .005$

These results offer further support and elaboration of the path-depen-dence hypothesis. It should be noted that a negative association be-tween promotions in the first and second periods might have been a conceivable hypothesis, but the present results clearly indicate that this is not occurring.

The hypothesis of a positive relationship between a promotion in the first period and promotions in any of the next three periods (1965–1975) is also strongly supported.[12]

ATTAINING MANAGEMENT LEVELS   Hypothesis 2.3.2, and the following variants of it, compare the promotion chances of the employees pro-moted in the initial "competition" with those first promoted in the second "competition." Unlike the previous hypotheses, which com-pared the initial winners with all initial losers, these hypotheses com-pare the initial winners with the subset of initial losers who subse-quently win. In effect, these hypotheses are comparing individuals whose career paths differ in the time spent at the nonmanagement level.

Table 2.4 shows that employees' chances of attaining a management level by 1975, in their first 13 years, are significantly improved by an early promotion. Although this result seems to support the tournament model, it may only indicate the effect of having more time at the fore-man level for attaining management level. Consequently, a variant hy-pothesis is tested, that employees promoted to foreman in the earliest period have a much better chance of being promoted to lower manage-ment in their first 7 years at the foreman level than employees pro-moted to foreman in the second period.

Comparing employees arriving at foreman level at the end of the first and second periods, the hypothesis predicts a greater promotion rate for the former than for the latter after 7 years. Table 2.4, which com-pares the chances of "early foremen" (i.e., those promoted in the first period) reaching lower management in 7 years (by 1972) and the chances of "later foremen" (those promoted in the next period) doing so in the following 6 years (by 1975), shows a large and highly signifi-cant association.

Because of the longer 1965–1969 interval, the "early foremen" group

---

[12]It should be noted that in this analysis and the preceding one, promotions from different levels are being compared: for the early promotion employees, their promotion rates from foreman level; and for the employees not promoted early, their promotion rates from nonmanagement level. However, the average yearly promotion rate over the 1965–1975 decade is virtually identical for these two levels (2.8% for both), so that cannot explain the large difference between employees promoted early and those not promoted early.

has 7 years to attain lower management level (1965–1972) while the "later foremen" group has only 6 years (1969–1975). However, even if it were assumed that every additional year contributed an equal number of promotions (an assumption which actually overestimates later promotions), and the "later foremen" group's chances were increased by one-sixth; this would not alter the findings very much. Employees who are promoted to foreman in the initial period have a very clear advantage in reaching lower management (81 versus 33%), an advantage that is not merely a function of having 1 more year to get there.

CAREER CEILING   The career-tree diagram clearly indicates that employees promoted in the earliest period are the only ones to attain levels four or five, the middle management levels, thus supporting Hypothesis 2.3.3. Just over one-third of this group attained middle management, while none of the 128 employees who attained foreman after the first interval attained middle management in their first 13 years. As Table 2.4 indicates, this association is highly significant; here is social structure in action. Although this analysis considers the career ceiling only in the first 13 years of employees' careers, other analyses of these data suggest that the probability of promotions declined exponentially over time, which would suggest no reversals of the pattern observed here if the time were extended further (see Chapter 3).

CAREER FLOOR   The career-tree diagram clearly indicates that employees promoted to foreman in the earliest period were never demoted back to nonmanagement during the period considered here, while four of the employees promoted to foreman in the later periods were demoted back to nonmanagement. However, Table 2.4 indicates that this relationship is not statistically significant. Although Hypothesis 2.3.4 is descriptively accurate, it describes a weak relationship; and the null hypothesis cannot be rejected with any certainty.

The small number of demotions is an interesting finding in itself, but since this analysis only includes a relatively young cohort, it is likely to underrepresent the actual incidence of demotions. However, downward level mobility may not be very common in industrial management. As Goldner (1965) noted, demotions are often clouded over by ambiguities that make it unclear whether a demotion has occurred. Although Goldner presents no counts of the actual number of demotions, many of the examples he cites are not literally demotions in the sense of moves to lower levels, but are, rather, moves to jobs at the same level but with less responsibility.

The early selection hypotheses were all confirmed, with the exception of the "career-floor" hypothesis. They show the various disadvantages of not being promoted in the first period. These disadvantages are so extensive that it seems reasonable to conclude that employees not promoted in the first period are no longer competing in the same system with employees who were promoted in the first period.

No Assurances of Later Promotions

In the tournament model, although employees promoted in the earliest period have much better career chances, employees' career chances may be drastically reduced in subsequent competitions. This contrasts with Turner's sponsorship model in which employees promoted in the earliest period are assured of attaining a high level.

The career-tree diagram clearly indicates that employees promoted in the earliest period are not assured of attaining any level above foreman. Nor are employees who receive two-level promotions in one period or those who receive two promotions in successive periods assured of another promotion in the next interval. Although this career tree indicates better career chances for early promoted employees, there is no juncture which indicates a 100% chance of promotion.

Later Promotion Paths

The tournament model suggests that every selection period is important, not just the first one. This section considers the career paths arising from second-period selections for the employees who had been promoted in the first period. Second-period paths are harder to test because data were available only for two later periods (covering only 6 more years) and thus it is not possible to be confident that periods after those studied would not alter the observations here. Furthermore, since second-period paths pertain to promotions to levels above foreman, and since promotion probabilities are diminished at these levels; differential advantages of various paths may be difficult to identify. Even with these limitations, however, the findings are surprisingly clear.

The career-tree diagram (Figure 2.2) clearly indicates that although employees promoted in the first period have many advantages, these advantages are largely dependent on their also being promoted in the second period. The employees promoted to foreman in the first period had a very good chance of being promoted again, but *only if* they were promoted in the second period. Of the 10 foremen not promoted in the second period, only 1 was promoted in the next two periods. The same pattern was found for employees promoted to lower management in the first period. This marked decline is probably not peculiar to the third period, for the nonmanagement promotion rate in this period showed very little decline. These findings suggest that this very marked falloff after the second period is the result of a distinctive process shaping these paths. Table 3.4 presents the comparisons to test Hypothesis 2.5, and the statistics indicate large and significant associations.

Higher Levels and Later Career Periods

It is difficult to extend the analysis above the fourth level because of the small number of promotions at higher levels, and it is difficult to extend the analysis to later periods because analysis of third-period effects allows only a single period for examination. Of course, by selecting another cohort with slightly greater tenure in 1962, the analysis could consider employees with more than 13 years' tenure in 1975; but those analyses could not be related to the crucial early years of employees' careers.

However, although these analyses have only followed this cohort to the fourth level and have virtually ignored the four highest levels, they have followed employees to an important level in the corporation. The shape of the organizational hierarchy reveals this quite simply: Only 1.4% of the employees are in the fourth level, and only 0.6% of the employees are in the four levels above level 4. The average salary for employees at level 4 in 1975 was over $28,000, which is considerably above the $22,000 average salary of level 3 and the $18,000 average for level 2. Level 4 also offers opportunity for promotions to top-level positions. Analyses of a later cohort (tenure of 7 to 9 years in 1962) showed that two of the 14 employees in level 4 in 1962 attained a vice-presidential position (level 7) by 1975, while none of those in the third level or below had.

Although the time span studied was only a fraction of employees' work lives, it was apparently the stage in which most of the rapid advancements occurred. Among all of the nonmanagement employees who remained in the organization between 1962 and 1975 (3995 employees) only 29 employees attained level 4 or above (0.7%). In comparison, although the 0–2-year cohort analyzed in this chapter constituted only a small number of the total group, it included 22 of these 29 employees.

It is unlikely that extending the analyses to later career periods would alter the findings substantially. Numerous researchers (McGinnis 1968; Mayer 1972; Sørensen 1975) have noted a tendency for career mobility to show an exponentially declining probability, and, indeed, cross-sectional analyses of the corporation's data revealed such a pattern (see Chapter 3). Consequently, when very low promotion rates are found for some paths during the last two periods, it seems likely that subsequent periods will not show dramatic increases. The inference that employees not promoted in the last two periods have been virtually eliminated from the competition for higher positions is a speculation, but it would seem to be a very plausible inference.

Discussion and Summary

Implications of the Tournament Model

Beyond its specific findings, this analysis has provided some support to what is described here as the tournament model. This model makes several kinds of contributions. One is the hypotheses it suggests. Although the empirical tests of the hypotheses do not make the tournament model itself necessarily correct, its usefulness stems from its heuristic value for suggesting a comprehensible mechanism underlying the empirical relationships.

Moreover, the fact that the pattern of career mobility in this corporation so closely resembles a model derived from a study of track mobility in a high school is particularly provocative. Although no contention of genotypic similarity is asserted, the phenotypic similarity raises intriguing speculations about the correspondence between the social relations of production and the social relations of schooling (Bowles and Gintis 1976).

The tournament model also suggests some interesting speculations about the "functions" of an organizational selection system. Ideologically, tournament mobility seems to represent a form of Social Darwinism in which repeated competitions select the "fittest" managers. This may be viewed as particularly appropriate for selecting managers, because the survivors of a tournament gain the image of "winners," a social label that might enhance a leader's authority over subordinates. It therefore combines the efficiency of sponsored mobility (early selection) with the flexibility of contest mobility; and by doing this in successive iterations, it responds to the limitations of managerial decision making (March and Simon 1958).

However, the tournament model also suggests some "dysfunctional" consequences. As I have noted in another context, a tournament model is likely to create self-fulfilling prophecies (Rosenthal and Jacobson 1968) in which early winners are seen as "high-potential people" who can do no wrong and who are given additional opportunities and challenges, while those who do not win in the early competition are given little or no chance to prove themselves again (Rosenbaum 1976). The early winners will receive a challenging socialization process which will help them to develop themselves further, while the others will receive a custodial socialization process which will homogenize them to fit undemanding, alienating roles (Rosenbaum 1975). Furthermore, since the tournament poses the continual threat that any loss (any momentary lapse that prevents a promotion in any period) will have permanent detrimental effects on one's entire career, even people who have won all previous competitions will perceive the costs of risk taking to be too great. The "instant-death" character of a loss in the tournament will tend to discourage innovation and to encourage conformist, "safe" strategies (Whyte 1956; Argyris 1964; Rosenbaum 1976).

Perhaps the main contribution of the tournament model is that it describes the organization career system in a way that suggests an underlying logic, and, consequently, it provides a framework for relating organizational structure at the "macrolevel" with employee perceptions, attitudes, and behaviors at the "microlevel." It seems quite likely that employees in the corporation will have a cognitive representation of the stratification processes in their organizational hierarchy, and this cognitive representation may approximate the tournament model. Employees may not have pictures of such explicit career trees, and they may not have worked out the numerical relationships between first-period selections and subsequent promotion opportunities; however, they may have intuitions approximating these relationships.

Of course, the implications of these cognitive representations will go beyond dispassionate cognition: They will be major influences on the way employees view themselves, their work, and their life chances. The changes in career behavior as employees go from the "advancement" stage to the "maintenance" stage in their careers have been noted (Hall and Nougiam 1968; Levinson 1978), but the relationship of these stage changes to the organizational structure is not clear. The tournament model suggests an organizational opportunity structure which might elicit exactly these phases of career behavior. Further studies are required to investigate the links between organizational opportunity structures and employee career behaviors.[13]

---

[13]The tournament model is proposed to explain individual career mobility in certain kinds of institutional contexts. It is most likely to occur in organizations which are *pyramid shaped* (i.e., organizations in which the number of individuals declines at each successively higher level). However, it is not clear that this is either a necessary or sufficient structural condition for tournament mobility. It is not necessary, for, even if every level had the same number of individuals, higher-level positions could be partially

Summary

The objective of this analysis has been to suggest certain ways in which analyses of mobility across levels might contribute to organization and stratification research and to describe patterns of level mobility in one organization. Since no analyses such as these have been made, even a descriptive noncausal analysis may have potentially great payoffs for yielding insight about organizational careers. These analyses have presented an initial effort in this direction; they suggest several specific implications for future inquiry.

First, the analyses have described mobility in different terms from those previously discussed in the literature. They have pointed to the fine structure of mobility within an institution. Obviously, by using more refined status categories, much greater amounts of vertical mobility have been found than would have been if only occupational changes had been considered. More importantly, patterns in the sequencing and timing of mobility that have not been previously noted by empirical research have been discovered here.

Second, the analyses suggest that the path-independence assumption needs to be questioned in applications of semi-Markov models to organizational careers. Although nonstationarity and mover–stayer models are adequate for some aspects of these data (e.g., the declining promotion rates within each level over time), these models have little to say about the historical antecedents that seem to be associated with subsequent mobility. Although there are ways that nonstationarity and mover–stayer models can be construed to model these findings, these

---

filled from outside, thereby maintaining competition at lower levels. It may not be sufficient, for pyramid structures can conceivably operate by sponsored or contest models of mobility. Employees could be sponsored from the very outset for certain ultimate levels, and this may tend to happen in family- or group-dominated firms (Dalton 1951). Conceivably a contest could operate where "second chances" were encouraged by training programs and job-rotation systems; however, a contest system may be difficult to achieve given the social-labeling effects of initial losses. Pyramid structure and tournament mobility are likely to be related, but they need not necessarily be related.

The tournament model, being a historical model, is probably contingent on situations in which information about a person's history is carried along with the person. If a single organization did not keep career-history information or did not value it, then a tournament might be less likely. However, such a lack of concern about career history does seem inconsistent with available evidence on organizational selections (Caplow 1954; Goldner 1965; Slocum 1968). If a person moves to another organization and his/her career history is not known (or is not important) to the new employers, then the tournament model might be less likely to extend to interorganizational careers. The extent to which these premises are true requires examination in subsequent research.

findings offer support for the potential value of models which question the path-independence assumption. In addition to nonstationarity and mover–stayer modifications of Markov models, the tournament mobility model provides a rationale for a third, path-dependent class of models.

Furthermore, these analyses offer some support for Featherman's historical model in the Kelley–Featherman interchange. Since both Kelley (1973b) and Featherman (1973) had suggested that a more fine-grained analysis of actual job moves was the central question in their dispute, the present analyses may be a useful contribution, indicating one instance where job mobility is clearly related to previous career histories.

It must be stressed, however, that this study tests path independence in a particular situation: studying individual mobility within a single organization. These findings may not have relevance for other kinds of mobility to which Markov and semi-Markov models have been applied: job moves across different organizations or occupations (Hodge 1966; Kelley 1973a; Tuma 1976; March and March 1977) or chains of job vacancies (Vroom and MacCrimmon 1968; White 1970a; Stewman 1975).

Third, these anslyses have pointed to the initial period in an employee's career in this corporation as an important selection period.[14] The stratification literature has recognized that mobility may become less frequent by middle age (Blau and Duncan 1967, pp. 178–188), and the organizational careers literature has noted the importance of early job experience and performance on later careers (Berlew and Hall 1966; Hall 1976, chap. 4); however, little research has been done on the timing of mobility events. The present analysis shows that by at least the third year of employment, an employee's eventual career chances have been fundamentally affected. These findings suggest that an employee's career is not a series of equal contests. Early competitions are more strongly associated with career outcomes than later competitions, and they are associated with many aspects of career outcomes: career ceilings, career floors, and the probabilities of promotion and demotion in successive periods.

---

[14]One cannot infer that the first period necessarily "caused" this selection. The cause of the selection might have occurred much earlier, acting via an employee's initial job placement, education or school performance, or other categorical "signals" (Spence 1974). Promotion rates may also be influenced by vacancy chains, by period effects caused by company growth or contraction, or by differences in the quality of new cohorts due to tight or loose labor markets. None of these possibilities has been examined here, and they cannot be rejected as contributing causes of mobility. Regardless of causality, however, the patterns described here do indicate the relationship among mobility events.

Appendix 2.A: Mean and Standard Deviation of 1975 Wages by Status Level

Level	Number of cases	Mean wage ($)	Standard deviation wage ($)
Total cases	12,860	14,326	5,265
Nonmanagement	9,365	12,525	2,808
Foreman	2,434	18,205	2,659
Lower management	796	22,096	1,341
Middle management	187	28,392	1,911
Upper middle management	56	38,463	2,977
Lower top management	9	46,103	3,461
Vice-president	13	63,144	10,121

Appendix 2.B: Career Tree for 1960–1962 Entering Cohort for Employees Attaining Foreman or Lower-Management Levels by December 1962 ($n = 16$)

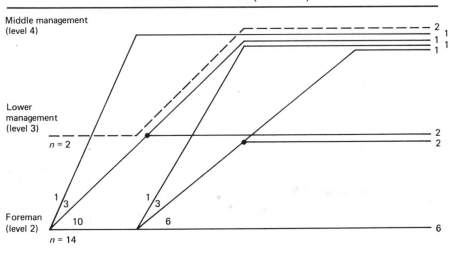

CHAPTER 3

*Changing Patterns of Promotion
Chances during Periods of Growth
and Contraction*

Introduction

This chapter analyzes the age distribution of upward mobility in the corporation and considers the ways in which the age–promotion relationship is altered for different kinds of employees at different levels in the organizational hierarchy and across time periods of increasing and decreasing organizational growth.[1] Consequently, these analyses can examine the stability of promotion timetables and the ways in which promotion timetables are altered in periods with greater or fewer job vacancies.

Careers in organizations and social mobility in society have been extensively studied in sociology; however, there has been remarkably

[1]Downward mobility is rare in most organizations, as numerous researchers have noted (Dalton 1951; Martin and Strauss 1959; Kanter 1977). The present study also finds extremely low demotion rates, too low to be considered here.

little analysis of career mobility in organizations. Stratification research using Markov models devotes considerable attention to mobility, but it tends to ignore individual attributes.[2] Early research on organizational carers provides qualitative descriptions of employees' perceptions, but the lack of extensive quantitative analyses gives a vague, and sometimes contradictory, picture of organizational career structures. Since 1980, important quantitative work has begun, as reviewed in Chapter 1.[3]

The present analysis is able to address some of the same issues as the older qualitative analyses of organizational careers, not merely to restate previous findings, using numerical data, but also to reveal qualitatively different processes which have gone undetected in that research. Promotions in this corporation are analyzed over a 10-year span, using the official personnel records. Moreover, these analyses are distinctive in that they investigate changes in age–promotion patterns over different historical periods in which the organization experienced pronounced growth and subsequent declines in growth.

Examining Promotions: Reasons and Models

Why Study Promotions?

Although it has not been a common part of stratification or organization research, the study of organizational promotions can have important implications for both fields. First, the analysis of promotions provides a different perspective on social mobility from that generally considered in current stratification research. Given the large segment of the U.S. labor force working in large corporations, the analysis of promotions within large corporations can augment understanding of intragenerational mobility in society.[4]

[2]White's (1970a) study of mobility among Episcopal clergy considers seniority effects on vacancy replacements rather than on individual mobility. Stewman's (1975) study of mobility among state police is a noteworthy extension of vacancy analysis, and Stewman and Konda's (1983) work incorporates a few individual attributes.

[3]Studies by Baron and Bielby (1980), Althauser and Kalleberg (1981), Grandjean (1981), Veiga (1981), Stewman and Konda (1983), and Lawrence (1983) are examples.

[4]A number of studies by economists and sociologists have used salary as the dependent variable (Weisbrod and Karpoff 1968; Duncan, Featherman, and Duncan 1972; Stolzenberg 1975; Wise 1975a; Spilerman 1977); however, as I note in the next section, salaries are not always a good indicator of status, and they may not even be a good indicator of income in some cases.

Second, promotions are an important control mechanism in organizations. An enduring problem for organizations is how to stimulate the motivation of employees. Organizations can apply three means of controlling employees: coercive, utilitarian, and normative (Etzioni 1964, p. 59). Most control procedures fall into one of these categories: Punishments are coercive, pay incentives are utilitarian, and symbolic statuses are normative. However, promotions combine two of them, utilitarian and normative control, offering both material rewards and symbolic statuses. Moreover, promotions can be held out as possibilities for a far larger number of people than can possibly receive them. Consequently, the possibility of receiving a promotion is likely to be an extremely effective control mechanism over a fairly broad group of employees.

Third, the distribution of a whole constellation of employee attitudes and behaviors may follow the contour of an organization's promotion curves. One's chance of receiving a promotion is likely to have far-reaching effects on one's aspirations (Chinoy 1955), job interest (Pennings 1970), and leadership style (Hetzler 1955; Levenson 1961). Indeed, promotion chances may be a fundamental determinant of a wide variety of other attitudes and behaviors and are perhaps more important than an individual's personal traits or level in the organization (Rosenbaum 1976, 1977; Kanter 1977).

Models of Career Mobility

Social mobility is a general concept in sociology which includes many kinds of phenomena: geographical movement, occupational changes, changes between institutions or firms, and changes of status within institutions. Social mobility can entail two different kinds of comparisons: those between generations (intergenerational mobility) and those within a single career (intragenerational or career mobility). Promotions represent a specific kind of career mobility: intragenerational status advancements within a single institution.

There are conflicting lines of thought about the relationship between mobility and age. The first prediction comes from the Markov literature and its stationarity assumption, which posits that mobility rates are independent of time. Although this assumption has been contradicted in some applications and, as a consequence, generally abandoned in the Markov literature (Blumen, Kogan, and McCarthy 1955; Bartholomew 1968; McGinnis 1968; Mayer 1972), I shall subsequently note some support for it in the organizational careers literature (Dalton 1951).

A second prediction, which departs from the stationarity assumption, expresses mobility rate as an exponentially declining function of time, that is, $P(t) = (R)^t P$, where $P(t)$ is the later promotion rate at time t, P is the initial promotion rate, and R is the constant proportion at which promotion rates decline.[5] In contrast to the assumption of a constant mobility rate, this function posits a rate which declines by a constant fraction in each successive period. For example, if the rate of decline were 50%, then in each successive age interval, promotion chances would be half of what they were before. This kind of function creates a nonlinear curve on which the initial declines are largest and successive ones progressively smaller.

This formulation has been examined by Mayer (1972) and Sørensen (1975). Using synthetic cohorts constructed from the Blau and Duncan (1967) occupational changes in a generation (OCG) data, Mayer (1972) found that the exponential-decline model explains the patterns of occupational mobility for different age groups quite well. Similarly, analyzing retrospective career histories of a national sample of men, Sørensen (1975) finds comparable declines in mobility, both in terms of occupational prestige and in terms of job moves, over the sample's first 15 years in the labor force.

A third prediction is suggested by the human capital model in economics. The human capital model posits that people acquire education and experience as "investments" in their "human capital," and that these investments have positive payoffs in the labor market. This model predicts large salary increases over time, particularly in the initial decade of work when most on-the-job training occurs (Mincer 1974). After the first decade, Mincer (1974) suggests steadily declining investments in human capital. Although economists generally use this model to explain changes in earnings, it would seem reasonable to use it to explain promotions. If the initial decade of on-the-job training has a positive impact on human capital and if increases in human capital lead to more promotions, then increases in promotion rates in the initial decade of employment and subsequent decreases as investments in human capital decline would be predicted.[6]

It is not clear which, if any, of these models pertains to promotion chances in an organization. The stationarity assumption has usually been examined for job moves in open labor markets, which differ from

[5]R is sometimes expressed as e^{-c} for computational ease.

[6]Human capital theorists also tend to cite differences in individual rates of return on investment, which makes clear predictions difficult. This is one of the less desirable features of human capital theory and will not be considered in the present analysis. For the purposes of the present analysis, the human capital model is distinctive and makes its primary contribution in explaining the rising rates in the early years.

organizational promotions in being more affected by employees' choices (Tuma 1976, p. 349) and less affected by structural constraints (Doeringer and Piori 1971). This assumption may be more suited to describing centralized and structured organizational promotions.

On the other hand, the human capital model has been applied to open labor markets (Mincer 1974) and to single organizations (Wise 1975a, 1975b), but mostly for explaining salary increases. However, salaries are not always a good indicator of status since employees can obtain higher salaries without necessarily acquiring higher status; for example, by productivity bonuses, changes in individual credentials (e.g., education), longer hours, department or job-specific pay changes, or cost-of-living adjustments. Furthermore, salary is not even necessarily a good indicator of income since compensation schemes often give employees increasing proportions of their salary in nonsalary forms when they are promoted (e.g., deferred compensation, stock options, insurance, pensions, perquisites, and other fringe benefits) (see McLaughlin 1975). These practices, currently common for managers, are increasingly common for nonmanagement employees. Consequently, in some respects, promotions may be better than salary increases as indicators of status and income changes, and analyses of the distribution of promotions may complement economic research and reach somewhat different findings.

There are only a few empirical studies of promotions in organizations; however, these too arrive at conflicting results. Dalton's study of promotion in a manufacturing plant found that ages of promotion varied enormously—nearly as much as the ages in the entire work force. Although the mean ages reported seem to me somewhat low and suggest some preference for youth, Dalton concludes that his data suggest "the absence of a pattern based on age criteria" (1951, p. 408). Dalton's view of his findings comes close to the Markov stationarity assumption.

In contrast, two other studies suggest very clear age limits for promotions. Chinoy (1955) suggests from his study of automobile workers that promotions to foreman level are not made after the age of 35. Martin and Strauss (1959) also note sharp age limits for promotions. They report that "identifiable timetables of progression exist. Individuals must have moved through the foreman ranks and be ready for middle management at latest by the time they are around 35 years of age. Otherwise they tend to remain in lower-management positions" (p. 206).

Like Mayer's and Sørensen's findings, Chinoy's and Martin and Strauss's observations predict a decline in mobility over time; however, the latter studies suggest that employers may make certain ages final cutoff points beyond which no promotions take place. Their career timetable description predicts a more precipitous mobility decline than the exponential-decline model.[7] This view seems to have been accepted in most of the current literature on careers (Slocum 1968).

The conflicting conclusions of these studies are difficult to interpret, for the authors do not present extensive empirical analyses. Martin and Strauss do not report data on promotions by age, and their findings seem to have come from employee descriptions of promotion practices, not from analyses of actual promotions. Although employee perceptions are important in their own right, they may not be a good description of reality on the issue.[8] Dalton analyzes actual promotion data; however, he reports only the mean and range of promotion ages, without any consideration of the distribution of promotions within the age range.

Although models and research findings suggest several plausible predictions, none offers much insight into the operation of organizations. The Markov, semi-Markov, and human capital models were not developed to reflect any specific processes or constraints which occur in organizations; and, as Sørensen (1977, p. 976) notes, "most of the proposals for improving the Markov model are *ad hoc* proposals that are not based on an explicit theory of the mobility process." On the other hand, the Dalton and Martin–Strauss findings do come from studies of organizations, but neither provides a theoretical rationale for its findings. Consequently, even if one or more of these predictions were supported, the reasons would not be clear. Before testing the predictions, I shall present an alternative model of career mobility which takes account of some processes in organizations.

[7]Actually, the shape of the curve predicted by the exponential-decline model may vary a great deal, depending on the rate of decline. If each successive promotion rate declines by 50%, and the initial level of promotions is 70%; then promotion chances become less than 1% after 6 years. In contrast, if successive promotion rates decline by only 20% starting from the same initial level, it takes 20 years for promotion chances to become less than 1%. However, in neither case would a clear cutoff point be evident as in the Martin–Strauss career-timetable model, which posits a precipitous decline to no promotions at a certain age.

[8]First, such reports may be distorted, either because they reflect organizational norms which may conflict with actual practices, because the sampled employees have distorted perceptions owing to their vantage point, or because the sampled employees distort their reports in systematic (motivated) ways. Second, even if basically accurate, such reports may be overstated or excessively general, and actual practice may be somewhat different. Quantitative analyses of actual promotions may reveal less sharp age cutoff points than respondents report to researchers, and quantitative analyses are more suited for describing variations in the implementation of a policy for different groups of employees.

An Efficiency–Motivation Model of Career
Mobility in Organizations

   This model of career mobility in organizations begins from the recognition that promotions serve two different, and possibly contradictory, functions in organizations. On the one hand, they serve an organization's need to recruit employees to higher levels. As such, promotions will be decided on efficiency criteria and awarded to employees who are judged most likely to contribute to the organization. Even after noting the difficulty of measuring potential contribution and the possibility of systematic biases and unsystematic errors in these decisions, some researchers have taken this model to be an approximation of the ways organizations actually decide promotions (Wise 1975b). Indeed, Williamson (1975, p. 77) suggests that promotions are better selection devices than hiring because they "permit firms to protect themselves against low productivity types, who might otherwise successfully represent themselves to be high productivity applicants, by bringing employees in at low level positions and then upgrading them as experience warrants."

   On the other hand, promotions are also one of the most important rewards in an organization, and, as such, they must be allocated in a way that gives hope and motivation to the maximum number of employees (Dreyfuss 1938; Stinchcombe 1965; Edwards 1979). There are two reasons for this. First, as just noted, promotion chances are likely to be an effective way of controlling employees, offering the possibility of material rewards and symbolic status to a far larger number of people than can possibly receive the actual promotions. Therefore, organizations are likely to benefit in terms of employee compliance and commitment to the extent that promotion chances are extended over as large a group as possible.

   Second, U.S. norms about opportunity tend to encourage employees to believe that they retain the chance to improve their status throughout their careers. Turner (1960, p. 860), calling this the "contest mobility norm" writes that it encourages delaying "the final award as long as practicable [in order] to permit a fair race." Although Turner's discussion is primarily applied to schooling, studies suggest that workers and managers often retain expectations of promotions at later ages (Chinoy 1955; Sofer 1970; Kanter 1977). By extending the possibility of promotions to the largest number of employees, an organization avoids the appearance of unfair exclusion of some groups from continuing opportunity.

   The efficiency and motivating functions may be contradictory if an organization clearly identifies one group of employees as potentially able to contribute much more than others. For instance, it is a common belief in organizations that young employees can contribute more because of the greater amount of years they may spend in the work force. If such organizations decided promotions solely on efficiency considerations, young employees would be the only ones receiving promotions, in much the way Martin and Strauss describe. However, this would totally neglect the reward aspect of promotions, and it would encourage widespread disengagement by middle-aged and older employees. Consequently, organizations may attempt to reconcile these two conflicting considerations in order to attain a reasonable balance of efficient promotions along with some distribution of promotions by age.

Although the specific arrangement may vary from organization to organization, some general features of a plausible distribution of promotions may be inferred. First, the common belief in the greater potential contribution of youth suggests that organizations will show a marked preference for promotion of youth. Second, motivational and fairness considerations will encourage organizations to allocate some promotions to older age groups, although only a small number may be considered necessary to stimulate motivation and feelings of opportunity. Third, motivational and fairness considerations also encourage organizations to avoid sharp discontinuities in promotion chances between adjacent age groups so that no age group suddenly perceives itself disproportionately deprived relative to its immediately younger cohort (Runciman 1966; Pettigrew 1967; Rainwater 1974). These features may be restated as hypotheses: (1) youth-preference hypothesis—young employees will be given preference over older ones for available promotions; (2) contest mobility hypothesis—older employees will retain some chance of promotion, albeit small; and (3) gradual-decline hypothesis—promotion rates will tend to decline gradually, with no sharp cutoff points beyond which promotions decline precipitously.

Interestingly, one specific form these three hypotheses could take is described by an exponential-decline function. Consistent with these hypotheses, an *exponential-decline function* portrays a curve on which the highest promotion chances occur at the outset, declines are always a fixed proportion of one's current chances, and promotion chances become increasingly rare without becoming impossible (i.e., the curve is asymptotic to the X axis). Of course, proportional declines are only one form of gradual decline, and the exponential-decline function is only one specific form that these hypotheses could take. However, proportional declines may be a particularly appropriate form of gradual decline, for research suggests that deprivations are perceived in proportional, rather than absolute, terms (Rainwater 1974).[9]

However, the efficiency–motivation model is unclear about a number of points. First, it contradicts the stationarity assumption, which posits that mobility rates are independent of time, and it partially contradicts the human capital model, which may be interpreted to predict a modest increase in promotions in early career when individuals make initial investments in their on-the-job training, defer immediate rewards, and subsequently receive increased rewards. Second, it is not clear how employee attributes or organizational levels affect this model. Does this model operate in the same way for college-educated and less-educated employees? Does it operate in the same way at different levels in the organizational hierarchy? Third, it is not clear how this model is affected by changes in organizational growth. During increasing growth, are youth given even more preference, do all groups benefit equally, or are all qualified young employees already promoted so that the additional promotions "spill over" to older employees? During declining growth, are the promotions of older employees preserved or are they sacrificed to maintain the promotions of young employees? These questions are addressed in the following analyses.

Age versus Tenure

After Mincer's (1974) impressive demonstration that years of experience is the more important determinant of earnings than age, some comment is required on the use of age in this analysis. Although Mincer's evidence is compelling, two features of his analysis distinguish it from the present one. He studied earnings, not promotions; and he studied large samples in external labor markets, not internal labor markets. In particular, within the primary segment of the internal labor market, employees tend to remain with firms, and firms' investments in employees will tend to be based on this assumption. Even taking a human capital perspective, employers will be more likely to

---

[9]This model contradicts some of the models summarized previously. It contradicts Dalton's (1951) conclusion of a constant promotion rate, and it contradicts the clear cutoff point and precipitous decline predicted by Martin and Strauss's career timetable. However, like Dalton's findings, it suggests that older employees receive some promotions, although at a much lower rate than Dalton suggests; and, like Martin and Strauss's (1959) findings, it suggests that young employees get preference and that substantial promotion declines occur with age, but not to the extent suggested by the career-timetable description. Although it contradicts each model in some respects, this model predicts some of the central elements of each study, suggests the relationship between them, and even provides a theoretical rationale for the Dalton and Martin–Strauss findings.

invest training and promotions in employees who have more years to stay in the firm, which is calculated by the number of years until age 65 (discounted by an adjustment for exit rates). Consequently, even human capital theory predicts that age will be an important determinant of promotions in the primary segment of the internal labor market.

The more important theoretical consideration for the present analysis is the sociological analysis of age statuses. Sociologists have amassed a large literature on the status properties of age which tend to affect individuals' social conditions at different times in their lives (Foner 1974, 1980; Neugarten 1973; Riley 1977; Kalleberg and Loscocco 1983). This viewpoint can be extended by contending that age stratification affects organizations' promotion decisions. This view is elaborated in Chapter 8, and it permits these findings to be related to life-cycle issues.

In any case, empirically it matters little whether age or tenure was chosen as primary, since the two are very highly correlated and, indeed, they are inseparable for college-educated employees in these data. This chapter does study age effects, controlling for tenure, for noncollege employees, and subsequent chapters separate the effects of age and tenure by using an entry-age variable. Although economic theory does have a great deal invested in whether age or tenure is chosen, it is not clear that sociologists do since tenure could possess status properties. Nonetheless, as subsequent chapters show, both age and tenure have independent effects on earnings, status, and promotions.

Analysis

Setting, Data, and Analysis

This study investigates employees' job-level changes in ABCO in three time periods over the decade 1962–1972. The data for these analyses are taken from the computerized file of the complete personnel records of the corporation for the years 1962, 1965, 1969, and 1972. These years were chosen because they demarcate fairly homogeneous periods in terms of organizational growth: 1962–1965 were years of modest growth, 1965–1969 were years of rapid growth, and 1969–1972 were years of virtually no growth.[10] (These periods are discussed more fully in a subsequent section.)

[10] I considered adding the final period in these data, 1972–1975, to these analyses. Unfortunately, the graphic method limits the number of distinct curves one can portray. In the present case, the 1972–1975 curves show considerable overlap and crossing of the 1969–1972 and 1962–1965 curves. Moreover, since this period of contraction ex-

   The goal of this section is to ascertain the applicability of the various models for describing employees' promotion chances over their careers. This chapter analyzes promotion rates of white males as a function of their ages, for each of the just-mentioned periods. The use of simple promotion rates—the proportion of white males in a given age group promoted during the period (expressed as a percentage)—makes these analyses straightforward.[11] The focus on a single type of employee, white males, in effect controls for sex and race without requiring statistics which necessitate many assumptions (e.g., regression). The present analyses are limited to white males because they constitute the largest and most promoted group in this corporation (and most others) during the period studied. Consequently, the analyses may be considered to represent the best career chances that were offered at the time and to represent most of the career mobility during these periods. The analyses will be comparable with those of Dalton (1951), Chinoy (1955), and Martin and Strauss (1959), which also focused on white males. The limited number of minorities and females in various age categories make these groups difficult to study in this type of analysis, but the career patterns of minorities and females are analyzed using other procedures in subsequent chapters.

   These analyses present promotion rates from the three lowest levels in the corporation. *Nonmanagement level,* the lowest and largest level in the organization hierarchy, comprises workers in craft, service, clerical, and maintenance functions. *Foreman level,* the second level, includes both the supervisors of nonmanagement personnel and the highly trained technical staff (programmers, engineers, etc.) who have equivalent pay, privileges, and promotion chances. *Lower-management level,* the third level, may be considered the lowest managerial level because most employees at this level tend to be more involved with managerial functions than with day-to-day production. As the

---

emplified the same changes as the period of declining growth, little new was suggested. Chapter 7 permits similar comparisons for 1972 and 1975 attainments in a multivariate model, and, by using regression lines, which smooth out random variation, more curves can be portrayed without overlap.

   [11]The dependent variable, promotion rate, is calculated as the proportion of employees present through the entire 3- to 4-year period who were promoted during the period. If employees who left the company during the period were disproportionately less promotable, my calculations would overestimate promotion rates by not including these exits in the denominator. However, some exits may be due to "raiding" of desirable and highly promotable employees, and other exits may be unrelated to promotability; so it is not clear a priori whether or to what extent the exclusion of exits biases the findings. In fact, when exits are included in the denominator, the curves are not shifted markedly and no substantive conclusions presented here are altered.

common pyramid metaphor suggests, each successive level is considerably smaller than the one below it, and these three levels include 97% of corporation employees. Although there are two middle-management levels and three top-management levels above these, all five of those levels have fewer employees than the lower-management level.

The following analyses report promotion rates for 3-year periods. A promotion is defined as a move from one of these three levels into one above and does not include moves within these levels. The 1962–1965 and 1969–1972 curves report the actual promotion rates for the given periods; and, for comparability, the curves for the 4-year 1965–1969 period are appropriately adjusted (multiplied by 0.75) to represent promotion rates over 3 years. To minimize misleading percentages, promotion rates based on fewer than six cases are not presented. The age distribution of the sample of all white males in this corporation is presented in Table 3.1, broken down by level and education.

The concern of these analyses is the structure of promotion chances at different points in employees' careers. The age distribution of promotion chances can be examined longitudinally by following a single cohort of employees through their entire careers or cross-sectionally by analyzing the age distribution of promotions during a single time interval. A longitudinal analysis has the advantage of studying the same individuals, in effect controlling all personal attributes. However, given the difficulties of obtaining longitudinal data for an entire career, of controlling for cohort effects (some entering cohorts may be better than others), and of controlling for period effects (some periods offer more opportunity than others), longitudinal analysis was judged too unwieldy for this initial effort. Instead, cross-sectional analyses of the age distribution of promotion rates were performed for each time period. Obviously, the usual difficulties of inference from cross-sectional analyses apply (Farkas 1977). In particular, there is the risk of misattributing a cohort effect to age. However, by replicating these analyses in different periods, it can be discerned whether age categories exhibit similar effects when different cohorts occupy them.

Furthermore, one reason for analyzing promotion curves is to understand the promotion structure that employees perceive, and cross-sectional analyses may be the most appropriate type of analysis for this purpose. I would assume that individual employees are not likely to make complex adjustments for cohort effects in inferring their promotion chances. Rather, individuals probably view the age distribution of recent promotions cross-sectionally to infer the way the system operates and their place in it. If this assumption is correct, the present analysis, devoid of complex adjustments, may be the most appropriate

Table 3.1

Number of White Males in Each Level in 1962 by Age and Education

Level	Age									Total
	16–24	25–29	30–34	35–39	40–44	45–49	50–54	55–59	60–65	
B.A.										
Nonmanagement	50	113	44	7	6	2	1	3	1	227
Foreman	2	30	32	11	11	7	6	6	1	106
Lower management	0	22	61	40	12	7	6	8	3	159
Non-B.A.										
Nonmanagement	188	494	756	472	354	152	122	115	29	2682
Foreman	0	6	30	103	116	63	70	67	9	464
Lower management	0	1	11	48	46	19	56	35	7	223

model for an employee's cognitive map of the organizational promotion structure.

Promotion Chances as a Function of Age

The first set of analyses considers employees' promotion chances as a function of age for employees at each of three levels. It will be recalled that Chinoy (1955) suggested that promotions of nonmanagement employees to foreman level were always at a low rate and that promotions are not made after the age of 35. Martin and Straus (1959) also suggest that foremen are promoted to lower management only until the age of 35 and that lower-management employees are promoted to middle management only until "40 or, at a maximum, 45."

The present analyses tend to confirm these general descriptions in many respects. As Figure 3.1 indicates, young, nonmanagement employees have a rather low promotion rate, and their promotion chances decline after the age of 35. Young foreman and lower-management employees have high promotion chances; but foremen's promotion chances decline sharply after age 29 and lower management's promotion chances decline sharply in the 5-year period after age 29. The decline for these two levels occurs 5 years earlier than Martin and Strauss indicate, but this is a minor difference. In many respects, Chinoy's and Martin and Strauss's qualitative descriptions are quite good portrayals of these quantitative results.

However, there are some aspects of the quantitative findings which previous qualitative reports did not suggest. The qualitative descriptions suggested a clear cutoff point beyond which promotion chances decline precipitously and end. No such point is evident here for any level. No sharp declines occur for nonmanagement; their promotion chances decline gradually over the 25 years after age 35. Although sharp declines occur for foremen and lower management before age 35, employees at this age still have real possibilities for promotions (about 15 and 7%, respectively). After age 35, foremen's promotion chances decline only gradually; and lower qualitative reports of negligible promotion chances are evident in these data, but only very late in one's career (age 50 or 55).

Obviously, given the fact that the examination here is of promotions occurring in a different organization a decade after Chinoy's and Martin and Strauss's studies, it is not certain that such findings apply to their settings. However, one of the risks of respondent reports and qualitative data is that they may tend to suggest more clear-cut patterns

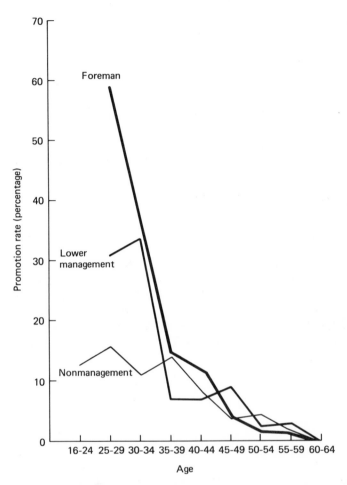

FIGURE 3.1.   Promotion rate for 1962–1965 by age for each level. Percentages based on fewer than six cases are not portrayed.

than actually exist and may be particularly inaccurate about transition states. The findings reported here suggest this may have happened. Chinoy's and Martin and Strauss's findings are well replicated here for early and late careers; however, their findings are not supported for the middle part of employees' careers.

In contrast, the exponential decline provides a very good description of the entire career of foremen. Solving $P(t) = (R)^t P$ gives $R = $ anti-$\log(t+1 \log [P(t)/P])$. By inserting the foreman promotion rates for successive ages from Figure 3.1, R's between .86 and .91, with a mean of .88 and a standard deviation of .02 are obtained. Thus, the promotion chances for foremen decline at an average rate of 12% per year (with an actual range between 9 and 14%). As is visibly evident, the exponential-decline model does not provide a good description of the promotion chances in the other two levels; however, the declining portions of these curves do reveal some tendency toward having initial large declines followed by smaller declines.

Education

The following analyses consider the possibility that the age–promotion relation may be different for employees with different levels of education. Many studies have found that better-educated employees have greater opportunities (Berg 1971; Wise 1975a). The commonly used regression models implicitly assume that the effect is additive, in other words that education has the same incremental effect for all employees regardless of their age and other characteristics. The present analyses permit the shape of the relationship to be examined directly.

Figure 3.2 presents the age–promotion curves for employees who have completed 4 years of college (B.A.'s) and for those who have not (non-B.A.'s). The most striking difference between the employees with a B.A. and those without a B.A. is the magnitude of promotion rates; those with a B.A. tend to have greater promotion chances than those without a B.A., at least until age 35 or 40.

However, this is clearly not an additive difference, for the corresponding B.A. and non-B.A. curves for each level do not have the same shapes. Comparisons of B.A. and non-B.A. curves for each level reveal that a college education has its primary benefit for young employees. Although college education gives an enormous advantage to employees under age 35, it gives employees over this age no advantage over less-educated peers.[12]

These quantitative findings suggest that qualitatively different processes may be at work for B.A.'s and those who lack a B.A. The B.A. curves show a sharp decline and early termination of promotion chances. Age 40 is the end of promotion chances for foremen, and age 45 is the end of promotion chances for lower-management. This pattern

---

[12]Note that this analysis is not limited to direct education effects. The benefits of a B.A. shown here may be mediated by job positions. Job position effects, though not analyzed in this chapter, are analyzed in Chapters 5, 6, and 7. Note that B.A./non-B.A. comparisons for nonmangement are not possible for older groups because there are too few B.A.'s in those groups.

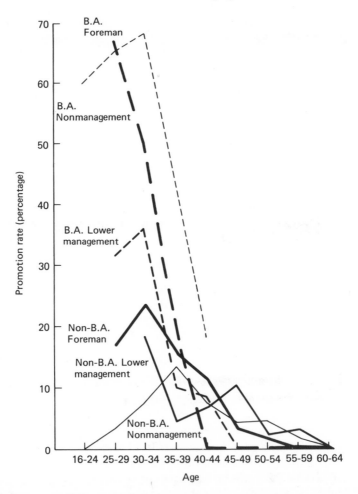

FIGURE 3.2. Promotion rate for 1962–1965 by age and education for each level. Percentages based on fewer than six cases are not portrayed.

of sharp linear decline and termination of promotion chances resembles the Martin–Strauss model described earlier. Although this model did not work very well in describing the promotion chances of all employees in this company, it does much better at describing the promotion chances of college-educated employees.

In contrast, the non-B.A. curves do not show a sharp decline in promotion chances. The declines for the non-B.A. curves are more gradual, particularly at older ages. For nonmangement and foremen, the declining portions of the curves resemble an exponential decline.

For nonmanagement over age 40, promotion chances decline at an average rate of 10% per year (with a range of 8 to 13% and $SD = 2.3\%$). At foreman level, promotion chances decline at an average rate of 11% per year after age 35 (with a range of 7 to 13% and $SD = 25\%$).[13] The lower-management curve does not show an exponential decline, but its decline is not rapid. The exponential-decline model tends to apply to the non-B.A. curves; the precipitous-decline model does not apply to any of them.

Again, it is difficult to interpret this result. The present findings may differ from Martin and Strauss's because this organization operates differently from the organization they studied. However, given their reliance on qualitative data from a few respondents, and given the omission of the college–noncollege distinction in their discussion, it is possible that similar relationships existed but were overlooked in their study. Of course, this is only speculation.

Effects of Increasing and Decreasing
Organizational Growth

The preceding analyses considered promotion patterns by age and education in a single historical period; however, one may wonder how promotion patterns are affected by increases or decreases in organizational growth. The analyses in this section consider the promotion patterns for two subsequent periods, one of increasing growth and one of declining growth, as well as for the initial period. Repeating the previous analyses for subsequent periods permits testing of the persistence of the 1962–1965 patterns in the context of changing growth and it permits examination of the specific kinds of changes in promotion curves which can occur with increasing and decreasing growth.

In the 1962–1965 period, this corporation, like the entire nation, was experiencing neither recession nor extremely rapid growth, and the period might be considered to represent a modest growth rate. The number of employees increased about 2.5% per year during this period. The following 4-year period, 1965–1969, was one of extremely rapid growth, and the number of employees increased about 5.8% per year over this period. The next 3 years, 1969–1972, were a period of virtually no growth, and the number of employees increased by only 0.2% per year.

Not surprisingly, the aggregate promotion rates for each level tend to

[13]The equation in the last paragraph of the preceding subsection is used to obtain these results.

Table 3.2

Percentage of Employees Promoted from Each Level in Each Period

Level of origin	1962–1965	1965–1969[a]	1969–1972
Nonmanagement	11	15	11
Foreman	14	22	12
Lower management	12	12	6

[a]Entries adjusted for longer period (multiplied by 0.75).

correspond to the growth patterns for the company as a whole, albeit not perfectly. Between 1962–1965 and 1965–1969, when the company experienced increasing growth, promotion rates increased for the two lower levels but not for lower management (see Table 3.2). In 1969–1972, the period of decreasing growth, the nonmanagement promotion rate returned to its original rate, the foreman rate fell below its 1962–1965 rate to 12%, and the lower-management rate dropped to 6%, half its former rate. These promotion rates correspond quite well to company growth patterns (with the partial exception of lower management). It should be noted that the periods considered here do not represent conditions of contraction; consequently, inferences are limited to the effects of increasing and decreasing growth.

Figure 3.3 present the promotion rates from nonmangement level for each of the three periods. The curves all have a parabolic shape, with an increase in promotion chances in the initial age intervals and a subsequent decline.[14] As noted in the 1962–1965 curves, the B.A. curves for all years are much higher than the non-B.A. curves; and, after reaching their peak, they show a more rapid decline than the latter. The non-B.A. curves show a gradual decline, remaining above 0 until the age of 55 or 60. The general features observed in 1962–1965 are replicated in subsequent periods.

Certain patterns can also be discerned in the changes over these periods. Between the first two periods there was a large increase in the nonmanagement promotion rate (from 11 to 15%); however, not all age and education groups benefited equally. This can be seen in Figure 3.3 by comparing the distance between comparable curves. For B.A.'s, most of the benefits of organization growth have gone to the 35–44 age group. Among non-college-educated workers most of the additional promotions have gone to younger employees (particularly ages 25–34).

[14]Only the 1965 curve for B.A.'s shows no increase, which is in part because the youngest age interval contains too few individuals to be included.

It is noteworthy that the age groups with the highest promotion chances in 1962 (ages 25–34 for B.A.'s and ages 35–39 for those who lacked a B.A.) showed minimal increases in promotion chances, as if there were a ceiling on their promotion rates.

The change in the next interval (between 1965–1969 and 1969–1972) shows a similar pattern. Between these periods, expansion declined, and promotion rates returned to 1962 levels (11%). However, once again, not all age and education groups were equally affected. Middle-aged B.A.'s, who benefited most in the previous expansion (those aged 35–44) were severely hurt by the contraction, as were those under 30.

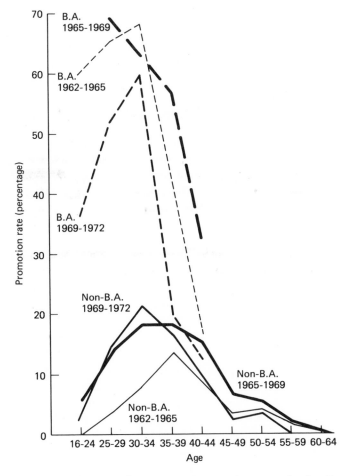

FIGURE 3.3. Promotion rate from nonmangement by age and education for each period. Percentages based on fewer than six cases are not portrayed.

For non-college-educated employees the largest decreases hit older employees, while younger employees largely retained stable promotion chances.[15]

Turning to the promotions from foreman level (Figure 3.4), it can again be noted that all three periods have similar curves. The B.A. curves are much higher than the non-B.A. curves, but the former show precipitous declines with age, while the latter show gradual declines with nonzero promotion chances through age 60. Again, the general features observed in 1962–1965 are replicated in subsequent periods.

Across these periods, promotion chances increased for foremen between 1962–1965 and 1965–1969 (from 14 to 22%) and then decreased in 1969–1972 (to 12%). During the increase between the first two periods, young B.A.'s (aged 25–34) experienced large increases. Non-college-educated employees also experienced increases, particularly younger employees. During the decrease between the second and third periods, the promotion curves for both employees with a B.A. and those without a B.A. returned to almost exactly the 1962–1965 pattern.

Finally, turning to lower-management promotions (Figure 3.5), the two later periods show some patterns similar to those observed in the first period curves, although the resemblance is less for this level than for the other two. For B.A.'s, all curves show a marked decline between ages 30 and 40, and no promotions after age 45 or 50. For non-college-educated employees all curves show a marked decline before age 40 and small promotion rates after that age. These curves are much less smooth than those for lower levels, in part because of the smaller cell sizes.[16]

In sum, promotion chances in two additional periods largely replicate the first-period findings. The general shape and magnitude of the age–promotion curves for each education group and level are extremely similar over the three periods. In addition, some inferences

[15]It might be noted that this cycle through a period of expansion and subsequent leveling off did not return nonmanagement employees in 1969–1972 to the same circumstances that group had in 1962–1965. The gross promotion rate was about the same in the first and third periods (11%), but it was distributed differently. First, the promotion chances of non-college-educated employees increased from 1962–1965 to 1969–1972 (from 7 to 11%), while the promotion chances of B.A.'s decreased (from 61 to 43%). Second, there was a pronounced shift to promoting younger employees, Particularly those without a B.A. aged 25–34. While the non-B.A. 1969–1972 promotion curve almost follows exactly the 1962–1965 curve in the age groups over age 35, younger employees in the later period had much greater promotion chances than those in the earlier period.

[16]For instance, the large increase at age 45 in 1965 for college-educated employees and the large increase at age 45 in 1962 for non-college-educated employees each represent the promotion of only two individuals.

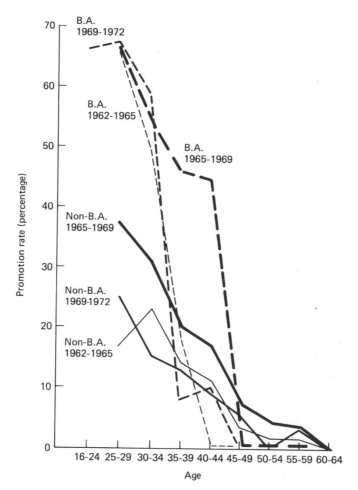

FIGURE 3.4. Promotion rate from foreman by age and education for each period. Percentages based on fewer than six cases are not portrayed.

about the effects of increasing and decreasing growth on the age–promotion relationship are suggested for nonmanagement and foremen.[17] First, the findings suggest that the most favored group, B.A.'s aged 30–40, neither benefit from increasing growth nor are hurt by declining growth. Second, the data indicate that other groups benefit from increasing growth and are hurt by declining growth, with middle-aged

[17]The simple generalizations seem to apply less well to changes in lower-management promotions.

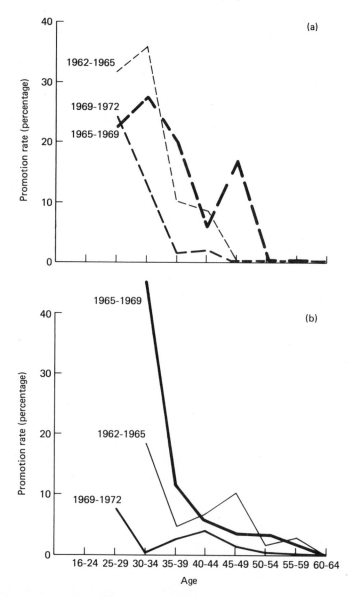

FIGURE 3.5.   (a) Promotion rate of B.A.'s from lower management by age for each period and (b) promotion chances of non-B.A.'s from lower management by age for each period. Percentages based on fewer than six cases are not portrayed.

B.A.'s (aged 35–44) and young non-college-educated employees experiencing more change than other employees.[18]

These findings add a dynamic component to the previous hypotheses. Those hypotheses indicated that most promotions are allocated to youth and only a few promotions to older employees and that a gradual decline occurs in the intervening years. These findings suggest that a ceiling effect operates in this preference pattern, so that an increase in promotions does not benefit the most favored group, but rather it spills over to other groups. This "spillover effect" benefits primarily somewhat older B.A.'s (ages 35–44) and young non-college-educated employees. However, the spillover effect is just that; and when promotion rates return to their earlier levels, it is the groups which have received the spillover, and not the most favored group, which receive fewer promotions.

Age Effects on Promotions, Controlling for Tenure

The primary aims of this analysis have been to describe and model age–promotion patterns and to compare the results with previous models of career mobility. This has been a descriptive analysis, specifying and extending the organizational careers literature and some of the descriptive modeling literature. However, the analysis has not considered whether age is actually responsible for these patterns or whether the patterns are due to duration effects. To what extent do these findings indicate company unwillingness to promote older employees, and to what extent do they indicate company unwillingness to promote employees who have had sufficient time in the company to show their capabilities and who have presumably shown themselves unable or unwilling to be promoted?

Although different from the central issue of this chapter, this question leads to a useful extension of the foregoing analysis. In effect, it asks whether age would have comparable effects after controlling for years of experience in the company (hereafter called tenure). This question has rarely been addressed because few studies have had separate indicators of age and tenure. The present data include both.

The strategy for studying age effects independent of tenure will be to analyze dummy variables for the various age intervals in a regression of promotions.[19] Dichotomous promotion variables (1 if promoted be-

---

[18]The youngest B.A.'s experience changing promotion rates as nonmanagement but not as foremen.

[19]Alternative formulations might control for years on the job or an indicator of ability or job performance, but these were not available in the present data.

tween 1962 and 1965, 0 if not promoted) were regressed on a linear tenure variable and the age dummy variables. (Separate analyses, including a tenure-squared term, produced very similar results, so they are not discussed here.) Regressions were run separately for college-educated and non-college-educated employees. The coefficients for each age dummy variable can be interpreted as the extent to which belonging to a specific age category contributes to promotion chances independent of tenure effects.

Unfortunately, the extremely high correlation between age and tenure for B.A.'s ($r = .96$) created problems of multicollinearity, and the resulting coefficients could not be interpreted. Besides making these cases impossible to analyze, this high correlation suggests that the question of independent effects of age and tenure may not be a meaningful one to ask in this situation. Their effects occur simultaneously for B.A.'s.

However, age and tenure were somewhat less highly correlated for non-college-educated employees ($r = .91$), and the regressions produced interpretable coefficients and no indication that multicollinearity was disturbing the results. These coefficients are reported in Table 3.3 and plotted in Figure 3.6.

The results are strikingly similar to the curves obtained previously (Figure 3.2). The nonmanagement curve corresponds almost exactly to the raw promotion curve except for the negative constant (representing the "coefficient" for the last age interval, 55–65 years), which only offsets the positive tenure effect to produce zero promotion chances. The most noteworthy difference is a more precipitous drop after age 39 in the age-effect figure. This suggests that the age effect on promotions, after controlling for tenure, decreases more sharply after age 39 than is suggested in the actual promotion patterns. The effect of tenure in this regression is small and positive (.003), and if the average 40-year-old employee had 20 years of tenure, this coefficient would raise his promotion chances 6%, to roughly the level indicated on the actual promotion curve.

Other departures also can be noted. The age effect on 35–39-year-old foremen drops slightly less than the actual promotion curve does, and the age effect on 55–65-year-old foremen remains slightly higher than the actual promotion curve. However, the latter positive age effect is something of an artifact, for it only offsets a negative tenure effect in the foreman regression to lead to zero promotion chances.

The central conclusion to be drawn from these analyses is that the age effects almost exactly parallel the pattern indicated in the actual promotion curves. Of course, this can be further indicated by the very

Table 3.3

Age Effects on Non-B.A. Promotions from Each Level, Controlling for Tenure

Level	Unstandardized regression coefficients on age dummy variables and tenure								
	16–24	25–29	30–34	35–39	40–44	45–49	50–54	55–65 (constant)	Tenure
Nonmanagement	.132	.145	.195	.300	.162	.184	.181	−.140	.0030
Foreman	—	.090	.154	.136	.100	.020	.008	.044	−.0013
Lower management	—	—	.140	.038	.068	.134	−.002	−.002	.0002

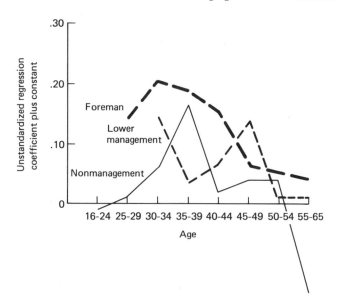

FIGURE 3.6. Age effects on non-B.A. promotions from each level, controlling for tenure. (From regression analysis using age dummy variables.)

small tenure coefficients which range between .003 and −.0016. Even after 35 years of tenure, these coefficients would only add 10.5% to the promotion curves or subtract 5.6% from them. It can be concluded that for B.A.'s the effects of age and tenure act simultaneously and for all practical purposes must be considered inseparable. However, for non-college-educated individuals, age clearly has a significant influence independent of tenure.

Conclusions

Instead of one pattern of promotions over time, these analyses have found two main patterns. The non-B.A. pattern is generally described by the efficiency–motivation model, which hypothesizes that the age–promotion curves will have three attributes: youth preference, gradual declines, and some promotion chances for older employees. The aggregate and non-B.A. analyses support these hypotheses for all three periods.

These three hypotheses may be supplemented and made more specific by the human capital prediction of increases in the initial years. It may also be made more specific by the exponential-decline model, which tends to apply after the initial years. The exponential-decline model describes foremen's promotion chances in the aggregate and non-B.A. analyses. Although it does not describe the entire promotion curves of the other two levels, the declining portions of their aggregate and non-B.A. curves do tend to exhibit large declines followed by smaller declines. Given the number of factors influencing the composition of each cohort and the specific needs of promotion openings, I take these findings as encouraging, though qualified, support for the exponential-decline model. Evidently, this specification is modeling some important features, albeit imperfectly.

In contrast to the non-B.A. pattern, the B.A. pattern for foreman and lower-management levels tends to emphasize efficiency exclusively and to resemble the Martin-Strauss timetable model, showing a precipitous linear decline and no further chance for promotion after age 40 or 45. However, it should be noted that the decline occurs over a rather lengthy period, between ages 25 and 45, so the career timetable is not as rigid as Martin and Strauss (1959) suggest.

In fitting the Martin-Strauss model as well as it does, the B.A. pattern suggests that the efficiency of early selections may be a primary consideration for B.A. promotions. This inference is also supported in the ceiling effect discerned for B.A.'s, which suggests that the company tends to promote nearly all potentially qualified B.A.'s (including, possibly, even those about whom there are some doubts), so that there are no additional qualified employees to be found when there are more positions.[20] This may be done because of a belief in the efficiency of selecting youth and with little regard to preserving the motivation of older B.A.'s. This practice may indeed be efficient; regardless of the ability of young employees, early selections permit more time for training and socializing employees, as Turner (1960) notes.

Analysis of these patterns over time also shows the dynamic properties of the early selection process. The spillover pattern quite clearly benefits young and middle-aged non-college-educated employees, and middle-aged college-educated employees, but not the oldest (over 45) college-educated or non-college-educated employees. These spillover groups are treated as reserve sources of promotable employees, while other employees are not even treated as promotable reserves. Appar-

---

[20]Of course, it is possible that the company places a quota on young B.A. promotions; however, none of my informants was aware of such a practice.

ently, the concern with efficient early selections even extends to spillover promotions.[21]

However, there can be some dysfunctional consequences of early selections, and non-B.A. and aggregate patterns resemble an alternative model in which efficiency is tempered by a concern for preserving the motivation of most employees. In the following, some speculations are presented about the implications of these patterns for employee perceptions and behaviors.

Implications for Employees and the Organization: Some Speculations

These findings indicate that promotions operate differently for young, college-educated employees: Their promotion rate is much higher than that of the other groups, and it is sustained at a much higher rate[22] but does not rise further. These patterns suggest certain hypotheses about employee perceptions and behaviors, assuming that employees perceive these promotion patterns fairly accurately; and they suggest a hypothesis about structural requirements of this promotion structure.

First, and most simply, it can be hypothesized that young, college-educated employees will see their promotion chances as much higher than those of other employees, as fairly unrelated to increasing or decreasing organizational growth, and as declining quite rapidly with age.

Second, it can be hypothesized that these employees will perceive an urgency to receiving promotions quickly. Some researchers have observed that young employees in comparable organizations exhibit a high degree of ambition and achievement motivation, which these researchers have attributed to the individual's personality or character traits (Maccoby 1977). Other researchers have remarked on the anxiety, insecure conformity, and pressured feelings of young employees in such organizations, which these researchers have attributed to the pressures of their work tasks (Whyte 1956). Without disputing either interpretation, the present analysis suggests another explanation: Promotion patterns require that young, college-educated employees attain

---

[21]This suggests also that the older employees who do get promotions may be unusual: Either they are unusually talented, and there are no other older employees qualified to receive spillover promotions; or they are tokens to maintain the motivation of older employees, and no others are needed for this purpose.

[22]This is true except for the youngest B.A.'s in nonmanagement in 1969–1972 whose decline seems to be due to a company-wide shift to promoting women from this level.

promotions in a very short period of time or else they will not be promoted. Employees may exhibit ambition and anxiety not merely out of personal ambition to get to the top, but also because an early promotion is the only way to get any promotion at all.

The problem is compounded by the fact that the promotion curves for all levels begin their sharp declines at about the same time. The young, college-educated employee who gets promoted from non-management after age 30 is not only facing a sharply declining promotion curve at the foremen level, but also the promotion curve for lower management is also declining so rapidly that the gate may be practically closed by the time the employee attains that level. For the college-educated employee leaving nonmanagement at age 30, the end is already in sight; the chances of getting to lower management are very small, and the chances of getting to middle management are negligible.

Third, it may be hypothesized that non-college-educated employees will perceive their promotion chances as lower than those of college-educated employees; however, the non-B.A. promotion patterns have some features which might dissipate feelings of deprivation. First, although non-college-educated employees' promotion chances are much lower than those of B.A.'s in the initial years, their chances rise while those of B.A.'s decline sharply. Second, when their chances decline, they decline gradually. Third, their chances end only toward the very end of their careers (age 55–60). Relative to college-educated employees, non-college-educated employees' promotion chances are not good; but relative to their own chances in previous intervals, their chances increase more and decline less, a pattern which is likely to minimize feelings of deprivation (Runciman 1966; Pettigrew 1967; Rainwater 1974). Non-college-educated employees are likely to maintain some expectation of promotion throughout their careers, but their expectations are never likely to rise or to fall so rapidly as to bring on painful disappointments. In some ways, the gradual decline of their promotion curves might be considered an ideal "cooling-out" mechanism, diminishing the chances of promotion at such a slow rate that those who fail have plenty of time to prepare for the fact before they have to admit that it has happened (Goffman 1952; Clark 1960).[23]

Fourth, it may be hypothesized that this organization's promotion

[23]Implicit throughout this analysis has been the question of how organizations manage the problem of ambition. Ambition is a complex issue because employers want promising employees to be highly ambitious but ambition creates frustration and low morale when promotion chances are low. Goldner (1965) has shown some of the informal procedures organizations use to manage ambition, and the promotion curves presented here suggest another structural aspect of the cooling-out process.

structure not only identifies highly talented people, but also may require a certain number of such people to be so labeled, regardless of the
actual talents of a cohort. Numerous observers have noted that organizations treat some employees as particularly talented, giving them the
most visible and challenging jobs and rewarding them with the earliest
and most frequent promotions. The usual interpretation is that this
indicates organizational responsiveness to highly capable employees
(Bray, Campbell, and Grant 1974), and colloquial descriptions reinforce
this interpretation: "water walkers," "high-potential people," "boy
wonders," or "superstars" (Kanter 1977, p. 133). However, an alternative interpretation is that water walker is a role in the organization,
filled regardless of the capabilities of the individuals selected to fill it.
The findings presented here suggest some support for this interpretation. All B.A. employees enter this company at nonmanagement level
with the median entry age of 25, and 10 years later (age 35) the promotion rate from lower management begins its sharp decline. If a water
walker is operationally defined as an employee who receives three
promotions in 10 years, the company must have water walkers in order
to fill openings in middle management with a substantial number of
college-educated employees (who in fact make up 66% of that level).
Under the present situation, the age–promotion curves require that
some employees be labeled as particularly talented, regardless of the
actual talents of a cohort. Of course, this has a latent function of conferring the mystique of water walker on the people who are to be candidates for top management.

Obviously, these are only speculations. I have not presented any data
on employee perceptions or the labelling process. However, these speculations suggest some of the ways in which organizational structure
may influence employee perceptions and feelings, and labels, and they
suggest the value of integrating such structural analyses with traditional analyses of employees' perceptions.

CHAPTER 4

The Attributes of Jobs and Their Changing Effects on Earnings and Promotions

Introduction

Economic theories generally conceptualize earnings in terms of market forces. However, for the many individuals who are employed by large organizations, earnings are not defined so much by market forces as by organization compensation systems which define the value of various jobs. Economists and sociologists have devoted considerable effort to testing their theories in terms of inputs and outcomes; but, as a practical matter, compensation systems are often the actual mechanism by which inputs are related to earnings outcomes. Consequently, the study of compensation systems can reveal the underlying processes by which earnings are determined for a large segment of the work force.

Compensation systems also have important theoretical implications. While economic theory proposes that compensation follows from economically rational behavior, sociological theory proposes that compensation must also be a social system which responds to social forces in the organization. For instance, employees share beliefs about which jobs are equivalent and which are not and about how much difference should exist among jobs. Consequently, compensation systems embody a fundamental conflict: How can organization compensation systems respond both to social considerations and to economic forces? This question underlies the conflict between economic and sociological theories, and it is also a very practical one for compensation systems since economic and social forces are very real considerations in organizations. Organizations must find ways to make their compensation systems respond to these conflicting forces.

The study of an organization's compensation system can help in identifying the way that these theoretical issues are manifested in practice. Furthermore, a reform effort to construct a more rational compensation system was implemented in the corporation studied, and this reform can illustrate another, possibly superior, reconciliation of the conflict and also indicate what aspects of the conflict are so enduring that they are not easily disposed of by reform efforts.

Strangely, economists and sociologists have ignored the compensation literature. In part, this may be because this literature is mostly devoted to claims about the virtues of the various systems and the procedural details of how to implement them. Theoretical implications are not discussed. Thus, social scientists assume that this literature is of little theoretical interest.

However, this reaction is seriously mistaken. The compensation literature explicitly reveals how organizations address the difficult task of determining the value of jobs. Economic and sociological theories offer diverse interpretations of the influence of jobs on compensation, but these various interpretations are speculations, and they are rarely compared with actual procedures. For instance, human capital theory considers the value of a job to be derived from the employee qualifications required to do the job's tasks. Sociological theory considers the value of jobs to be derived from social normative processes. The detailed analysis of job compensation systems can help settle the conflicts by showing exactly what kinds of considerations go into job compensation.

The organization under study provides a particularly interesting case for studying the social processes affecting job compensation because, during the period studied, it shifts from a traditional status system to a rational job evaluation system. This affords an opportunity to study the operation of each of these systems and the transition between them.

Moreover, job evaluation is a particularly interesting compensation procedure to consider because it is an explicit attempt to move compensation practices from traditional status considerations to economic rationality. Job evaluation is also of theoretical interest, for it concretely illustrates the conflict and tension between economic and social forces which operate in compensation systems.

Research Questions

The study of a job compensation system must consider how jobs affect earnings. Few studies have been able to do this because the survey data generally available to researchers rarely have good indicators of jobs. This is a particularly glaring omission for sociological research, which stresses the importance of job structures. Sociologists have studied the ways that occupational status categories affect earnings, but it is generally recognized that jobs are the units that determine earnings, and sociologists would study jobs if it were possible to identify jobs in their data (Featherman 1973; Kelley 1973a; Baron and Bielby 1980). The data available here offer an unusual opportunity to study the properties of jobs and to analyze their influence on earnings.

However, before analyzing how jobs affect individuals' earnings, which will be a focus of the following three chapters, the present chapter explores some of the properties of jobs. Although jobs are considered the basic units of attainment, here is really very little known about them. A typical model of organizations assumes that organizations are constructed of a fairly fixed set of jobs and that these jobs have relatively consistent ranking and value, but these assumptions are rarely tested. Consequently, the analyses that follow address very simple, basic questions. Is an organization composed of a constant set of jobs? To what extent do new jobs appear and old jobs disappear? Are jobs stably valued? To what extent does the value of jobs vary over changing social and economic circumstances?

Second, since jobs are defined by a fairly fixed set of tasks, the common expectation is that they will tend to require the same kinds of individual education, skills, and experience over long periods of time. To what extent are jobs filled by the same kinds of individuals over time?

Third, little empirical analysis has been done to investigate the determinants of job salaries. By ignoring social structural features of employment, human capital theory implies that salary differences among jobs can largely be explained by the qualifications of the individuals in the jobs, that is, the human capital in jobs. In contrast, structural theory contends that a job's structural position has large effects on the job's value independent of its human capital composition (Thurow 1975). In addition, as shall be elaborated subsequently, the two theories also posit different relationships between individual attributes and job salaries, and they posit differential responsiveness to economic forces. The present analyses test these conflicting contentions.

Finally, the job evaluation system studied here, implemented as part of a large affirmative action effort, had the aim of assessing job worth in a way which is more rational and less sex biased than traditional rankings. While Chapter 7 shows that individual women received great gains from the affirmative action program, structural change in the compensation of jobs is more difficult to accomplish. Analyses are done to determine to what extent job salaries are affected by the gender composition of the job holders, independent of the jobs' human capital composition, and how this changes over time. These analyses also investigate the extent to which the job evaluation system improves the compensation of predominantly female jobs. The results have implications for assessing the potential benefits and pitfalls of job evaluation systems for reducing the structural sources of sex bias (Treiman and Hartmann 1981).

Economic and Sociological Theories of Compensation

Human capital and structural theories suggest different explanations of the ways job compensation is determined. Human capital theory contends that employees are paid for the productive capacity they bring to their work, that is, the human capital they possess. Although this denies any importance to jobs as aggregate entities, it implies that pay differences among jobs arise because more demanding jobs require more capable employees—those with more human capital. Accordingly, the salaries associated with jobs are determined by the human capital of the individuals who hold those positions.

In contrast, social structural theory contends that pay inequalities are determined by the position of jobs in the status structure of the organizational hierarchy. Since jobs are assigned status based at least in part on the same factors that economic theory sees as determiners of compensation, sociological theory, like economic theory, suggests a relationship between human capital and job salaries. But, while economic theory suggests a direct relationship between the two, sociological theory suggests an indirect one that is mediated by job status. Rewards are distributed according to social norms in order to direct motivation in socially valued directions (Davis and Moore 1945). Inequalities are ways to buttress the normative basis of a social system (Dahrendorf 1968), and these processes operate by social, not economic, principles.

Thurow (1975) develops the economic implications of the sociological approach to income inequalities. He notes that individuals develop their expectations about equity based on past history:

> Distributions of the past are considered fair until proven unfair. This explains why inequalities in the distribution of economic rewards that are much larger than inequalities in the distribution of personal characteristics seem to cause little dissatisfaction, and why people tend to ask for rather modest amounts when asked how much additional income they would like to be making. (p. 110)

Moreover, individuals' expectations are relative to their reference groups: "The happiest people seem to be those who do relatively well within their own reference group rather than those who do relatively well across the entire economy" (p. 110). For example, in his study of several countries, Esterlin (1973) finds that "happiness is almost completely dependent upon one's relative income position within one's own country and almost not at all dependent upon whether one is located in a high-income country or a low-income country" (Thurow 1975, p. 105). In other words, individuals are not so much motivated to attain a particular amount of income as to attain a level of income relative to their reference group.

This approach leads to a very different model for compensation systems. Since it is happiness, not dollars per se, which employers seek to maximize in compensating individuals for their productivity, and since individuals' happiness is derived from their income relative to their peers, compensation systems will seek to make the earnings relationships among jobs correspond to normative values, which are formally expressed by the job status system. Although productivity and productive capacity (human capital) may be components of the norms which define a job's value and, consequently, command more pay, the amount of payment may not be the dollar value of their productive capacity, but only an amount proportional to the job's relative standing on the job status scale (also see Lazear and Rosen 1981).

This sociological model suggests that human capital and job salaries will correspond in terms of rank order, not absolute magnitudes. The ordinal ranking of a job's human capital determines its ordinal position on the job status scale, which, in turn, determines the ordinal ranking of the job's salary. By the sociological explanation, the absolute magnitude of a job's human capital has little impact on job status assignments unless it changes the job's rank order relative to other jobs. Similarly, job status has no intrinsic relationship to the absolute magnitude of a job's salary, only its ordinal ranking. The absolute magnitudes of job salary differences are determined by other considerations (market considerations and equity perceptions, cf. Rainwater 1974). Unlike economic theory, which suggests that human capital and job salaries correspond in dollar value, sociological theory suggests that the *distributions* of the two correspond. Rather than the amount of human capital resources defining the dollar value of jobs, sociological theory suggests that it is the variation in human capital resources among jobs which is related to the variation in job salaries.

Although both views predict that job composition affects job salaries, they predict a different relationship. First, human capital theory predicts that the relationship will best be described by *unstandardized* regression coefficients: Organizations will pay for the dollar value of human capital. In contrast, social structural theory predicts that the relationship will best be described by standardized coefficients: Organizations will pay for the rank order of human capital. For example, while human capital theory contends that each additional percentage concentration of college graduates adds a certain dollar increase in the value of the job, social structural theory contends that jobs that are one standard deviation above the mean in their college graduate percentage will be paid a salary a certain percentage of a standard deviation above the average salary at that level.

Second, the two theories differ in the stability they attribute to job composition. Human capital theory predicts that the value of human capital will vary with the supply and demand for it: A tight external labor market (1965–1969) increases the value of a college education and decreases the value of tenure (as starting salaries increase to recruit new employees), while the reverse is true in loose labor markets (particularly given an oversupply of college graduates, such as after 1972) (Freeman 1976). In contrast, social structural theory contends that organizations tend to preserve the same relationship between human capital composition and job salaries over time as long as the organization maintains the same status structure. As internal labor market theory contends, the organization's status structure defines the pay relationships in the firm, relatively insulated from external labor market processes (Doeringer and Piore 1971).

Third, the two theories also differ in their predictions about the strength of the influence. Human capital theory suggests a strong relationship between the amount of human capital in a job and job salaries. In contrast, the social structural theory suggests that the individual "human capital" in jobs is largely *incidental* to the process and, at best, explains a relatively small part of the value of jobs. Job salaries are determined by historically determined social normative evaluations which are only to a small degree determined by individual "human capital" attributes. The historically determined value of jobs depends on a diversity of other factors that cannot easily fit under the rubric of human capital. Perhaps the foremost among these are social discriminations based on sex and race, which are explicitly examined.

Finally, social structural theory suggests that the relationship between the human capital composition of jobs and job salaries is mediated by job status. This means that a change in the human capital composition of a job will not alter the salary a job offers unless it also alters the status of the job. In contrast, human capital theory suggests that job status systems are largely derived from and responsive to economic forces and do not contribute much uniquely to earnings if one controls for the human capital associated with (and presumably determining) the job's status. According to an economic perspective, instead of being rigid hierarchies into which individuals are allocated, status systems are constantly in flux, responding to changing economic circumstances.

The present study affords an ideal opportunity to test the competing predictions of human capital and social structural theories. Although Thurow finds evidence for normative influences in analyses of the entire economy, normative influences are even more salient and powerful in the context of a single organization. In a single organization, individuals are much more likely to have a common culture, with common perceptions, values, and norms about various kinds of work. Moreover, a single organization is more likely to implement a coherent compensation system than would be manifest in the general economy.

Furthermore, in focusing on jobs as the unit of analysis, normative influence is more likely to be discerned. Although normative influences operate at both individual and aggregate levels, normative influences at the individual level are affected by individual characteristics which are difficult to measure. By analyzing the aggregate level of job compensation, difficult-to-measure idiosyncratic influences are avoided, and the regularities in the normative system's effects may be detected.[1]

---

[1]It should be noted that the normative theory does not explain the origin of norms. Norms are taken as given, passed on through the history of past practice and past beliefs. Different theorists would have different explanations of their origins. Marxists would attribute them to the capitalist social relations of production, while idealists would attribute them to general ideological beliefs in the culture. This is an issue for sociology of knowledge, which is beyond the scope of the present study.

Job Evaluation

All compensation systems seek to compensate employees commensurate with their value to the organization. In recent decades, organizations have devoted greater attention and energy to creating more rational and systematic compensation systems (Akalin 1970; Sargent 1972; Treiman 1979). Until 1972, ABCO ranked jobs on a status scale which was derived from traditional practice. Jobs traditionally considered more important had higher formal status than those traditionally considered less important. This ranking was not very systematic; nor were the principles underlying the ranking particularly evident. The organization made little or no effort to articulate the underlying principles; and, for a long time, this hardly seemed necessary, for the actual rankings were the familiar ones that were ubiquitous in other traditionally organized status systems (e.g., craft positions were more valued than manual, and manual more valued than clerical).

During the late 1960s and early 1970s, these rankings came under increased criticism, and the traditional status system provided neither a basis for justifying its practices nor a procedure for adjusting its rankings to accommodate to the criticism. The traditional status system was criticized for the low status it assigned to jobs predominantly occupied by females. It was also criticized for its unresponsiveness to economic changes. Finally, employees in certain jobs were critical of the rankings of their jobs, and, though specific criticisms in themselves might easily have been ignored in other circumstances, coming during a period of general social restiveness, they were taken as cause for concern.

The corporation decided to shift to a job evaluation system for ranking and compensating jobs, and Hay Associates, a leading consulting firm, was hired to design and implement a job evaluation system. The Hay system is probably the most commonly used form of job evaluation.

Although the issues posed for this chapter are pertinent to a traditional compensation system, they have special pertinence for a job evaluation system. Job evaluation explicitly aims to compensate jobs according to their economic value. As such, it seeks to compensate job holders based on exactly those factors emphasized by economic theories, and, as a result, it may be predicted that it will make job status and compensation even more related to human capital factors and less related to discriminatory factors. A description of job evaluation and a detailed analysis of its relationship to these theories is presented in Appendix 4.A.

Analysis

Mobility and Mortality of Jobs: Defining the Sample

Even before considering these central issues, it is necessary to begin with a simpler, and more fundamental, question about the nature of a job hierarchy. Just in defining the sample of jobs, one must consider to what extent a stable job hierarchy exists in ABCO. There is a tendency to think of large organizations as unchanging, almost physical structures—much like the concrete and steel structures which house them. Organizational charts of jobs in a corporation are drawn as if these diagrams were believed to represent something enduring about the corporation.

White (1970a) formalizes these common assumptions in his model of vacancy chains which assumes a fixed set of jobs that remain in the same positions over time. This assumption is central to White's analysis. His entire analysis is based on the assumption that when someone leaves a job, a vacancy is created. However, to the extent that jobs are destroyed or moved in the organization, no assumption about vacancies can be made, so the pertinence of this assumption to various organizations requires empirical testing.

Organizations sometimes change their organizational structures: Jobs are upgraded, downgraded, created, and destroyed. Technological and economic changes occur, requiring new kinds of jobs while making others obsolete. Political battles over authority and task responsibilities change jobs so that they may be upgraded or downgraded in authority or shifted to entirely different departments and transformed into becoming entirely different jobs. Individual job occupants might become proficient and take on so many additional tasks that they change the nature and position of a particular job. These dynamic processes seem entirely plausible, but the frequency with which they occur is difficult, if not impossible, to predict. To the extent that they do occur, they pose a serious challenge to the notion of a fixed organizational structure; they suggest that old job duties or old ways of organizing duties into jobs will disappear and new duties or new ways of organizing duties will appear in the form of new jobs.

These analyses study the set of job titles which are listed in the personnel records for the years 1962, 1965, 1969, 1972, and 1975. Titles for the three lowest levels in the organization—nonmangement, foreman, and lower management—are considered here. The job title identifications for higher levels were removed from the data to protect the anonymity of employees, since these jobs tend to have few occupants. Of course, the small number of occupants also makes them unsuitable for these analyses.

The main concern of the first analysis is the number of jobs which appear or disappear, that is, those that go from having no occupants to having some occupants and vice versa. However, inferences are more ambiguous for jobs with few occupants, since these jobs could mistakenly appear to have been eliminated when they temporarily have several vacancies. Consequently, the analysis distinguishes between *small jobs* (having 1–4 employees) and *large jobs* (having 5 or more employees). It can be inferred with confidence that jobs with five or more occupants have been eliminated when these jobs subsequently have no occupants.

Table 4.1 shows the pattern of changes in job occupancy. The entries in the table are the number of jobs of various sizes in the years portrayed, for the three different levels considered here. For instance, in nonmanagement, 2 small jobs (1–4 occupants) in 1962 had become empty 3 years later, but no large jobs (5 or more occupants) in 1962 had become empty 3 years later. However, between 1962 and 1969, 26 of the small jobs and 4 of the large jobs had become empty. On the other hand, these data also indicate that even more new jobs were created over these time intervals. Between 1962 and 1965, 31 small nonmanagement jobs and 19 large nonmanagement jobs were created.

The patterns for the other levels show even greater amounts of job disappearance and job creation. While 76% of the nonmanagement jobs existing in either 1962 or 1965 were existing in both years, only 73% of the foreman level jobs and only 56% of the lower-management jobs were similarly enduring. For the 13-year interval between 1962 and 1975, the comparable figures are much lower for all levels, and the difference among levels is even greater: 53% for nonmanagement level, 46% for foreman level, and 22% for lower-management level. For all three levels, most jobs existing in these years were abolished or newly created over the period; persistence is more the exception then the rule.

In considering the possible generalizability of these findings, what is most striking is that this company has not undergone enormous outwardly visible changes. In 1975, it continued to produce the same products and to conduct the same services that it did in 1962; nor have there been any mergers with other companies or divestitures of subsidiaries. It is to all outward appearances the same organization, housed in most of the same buildings and doing largely the same activities it was doing over the entire decade; nor has it had any new leadership changes or organizational "shake-ups" which would explain these

Table 4.1

Number of Jobs Changing Job Size between 1962 and 1965, 1969, 1972, and 1975, by Level[a]

NUMBER OF JOBS IN 1965 BY JOB SIZE

Job size in 1962	Nonmanagement				Foreman				Lower management			
	Vacant	Small	Large	Total	Vacant	Small	Large	Total	Vacant	Small	Large	Total
Vacant	0	31	19	50	0	26	10	36	0	43	5	48
Small	2	82	11	95	14	89	8	111	10	59	4	73
Large	0	5	71	76	1	2	41	44	1	0	12	13
	2	118	101	221	15	117	59	191	11	102	21	134

NUMBER OF JOBS IN 1969 BY JOB SIZE

Job size in 1962	Nonmanagement				Foreman				Lower management			
	Vacant	Small	Large	Total	Vacant	Small	Large	Total	Vacant	Small	Large	Total
Vacant	0	26	14	40	0	20	12	32	0	28	9	37
Small	26	60	9	95	49	55	7	111	34	35	4	73
Large	4	10	62	76	5	5	34	44	1	2	10	13
	30	96	85	211	54	80	53	187	35	65	23	123

(continued)

Table 4.1 (Continued)

Job size in 1962	Nonmanagement				Foreman				Lower management			
	Vacant	Small	Large	Total	Vacant	Small	Large	Total	Vacant	Small	Large	Total
NUMBER OF JOBS IN 1972 BY JOB SIZE												
Vacant	0	20	17	37	0	18	13	31	0	21	4	25
Small	42	42	11	95	63	38	10	111	49	20	4	73
Large	11	12	53	76	12	5	27	44	5	2	6	13
	53	74	81	208	75	61	50	186	54	43	14	111
NUMBER OF JOBS IN 1975 BY JOB SIZE												
Vacant	0	16	16	32	0	9	16	25	0	15	5	20
Small	46	36	13	95	61	41	9	111	58	11	4	73
Large	17	10	49	76	12	5	27	44	5	0	8	13
	63	62	78	203	73	55	52	180	63	26	17	106

[a]Job sizes are divided into three categories: vacant (0), small (1–4 occupants), and large (5+ occupants).

changes. As large corporations go, it is probably more stable and less changed than most over the period considered. The disappearance and creation of jobs indicated in these data are indicative of small changes which gradually evolved over this period from a multitude of particular decisions in various parts of the organization.

The fact that the set of jobs in the organization was so thoroughly altered while showing few major changes in product or in organizational structure suggests that this may be a widespread phenomenon. However, few studies currently exist on the topic. One relevant finding is Granovetter's report that 35% of the job placements of individuals in his study were jobs that had not existed before (1974, p. 14). The Markov research literature has sometimes had data suitable for a test of this issue, but the assumptions of these models have prevented the issue from being studied.

This analysis clearly indicates that customary images of a fixed organizational hierarchy are seriously misleading. Jobs appear and disappear at a surprisingly high rate. White's (1970a) procedure for analyzing mobility in terms of vacancy chains would clearly not apply here, even over the short period 1962–1965. Although the assumptions of vacancy analysis seemed to apply rather well to the Episcopal Church hierarchy White studied, in the corporation studied here, any vacancy that occurred could go unfilled forever while new jobs were being created and filled which had never before been occupied.

Do Jobs Offer Stable Compensation?

The responsiveness of job salaries to historical changes can be analyzed most simply by looking at the gross changes in salaries which occur over time. To what extent do jobs change in the relative compensation they offer over periods of changing economic circumstances and organizational priorities?

The structural model of organizations portrays them as rigid hierarchies. It suggests that jobs retain the same value over time, so compensation would not be very responsive to changes in economic circumstances. However, these expectations are put to a severe test in studying the periods included in these data, for they were times of economic and social change: economic stagnation (1962–1965), followed by booming growth (1965–1969), subsequently returning to stagnation (1969–1972), and contraction (1972–1975). Such changes would be expected to be accompanied by changes in priorities among types of jobs. Furthermore, the shift from the traditional job status system to the job evaluation system took place during this period (in 1972). In addition, an affirmative action program began in 1969 and was extended in 1972, which would be expected to change the relative standing of jobs containing large proportions of women and minorities. In the face of these great changes, to what extent were jobs changing in the compensation they offered?

The compensation offered by a job shall be indicated by the average earnings of all individuals who occupy the job at a particular time, and will be called *job salary* or simply *salary*. There is a large range of job salaries in this organization, even within a single level of the organizational hierarchy.[2] To what extent are these job salaries stable properties of jobs over these periods of great economic changes?

In order to characterize jobs (and not individual employees), the following analyses are limited only to jobs with five or more employees. Since the lower-management level contains few jobs this size, the remaining analyses in this chapter only consider nonmanagement and foreman levels.

The analysis finds only minimal change (Table 4.2). Job salaries in nonmanagement levels remain extremely stable between 1962 and 1975. All correlations are large, with correlations of 1962 job salaries with those in later years showing negligible decline (.98, .97, .96, .96). The comparable correlations in foreman level start at the same magnitude, but the correlations of 1962 job salaries with job salaries in later years show a more pronounced decline (.96, .94, .88, and .84). Despite considerable changes in economic circumstances and organizational practices over these periods, job salaries remained extremely stable for nonmanagement and foreman levels.

Demographic Attributes of Jobs

Before analyzing the effects of the human capital composition of jobs on job salaries, it is necessary to consider a more basic issue: whether jobs can be characterized by different amounts of human capital. At issue here is whether the demographic composition of jobs is a stable property of jobs. If, as human capital theory assumes, jobs differ in their human capital requirements; then jobs should have fairly stable demo-

---

[2]In the year 1962, the job salaries of nonmanagement jobs ranged from $3354 to $8684, with a mean of $5462 and a standard deviation of $1336 for the 171 jobs at that level. Foreman jobs offered job salaries in the range of $4810 to $10,061, with a mean of $8031 and a standard deviation of $1511 for the 155 jobs at that level, and lower-management job salaries were between $9222 and $12,203, with a mean of $11,422 and a standard deviation of $729 for the 86 jobs at that level.

Table 4.2

Stability of Job Attributes by Level: Pearson Correlations

Job attribute	Nonmanagement				Foreman			
	1962	1965	1969	1972	1962	1965	1969	1972
Job salary								
1965	.977				.965			
1969	.968	.980			.944	.952		
1972	.958	.966	.968		.876	.881	.920	
1975	.958	.954	.948	.954	.842	.868	.869	.898
B.A. percentage								
1965	.663				.689			
1969	.944	.726			.702	.638		
1972	.923	.817	.973		.708	.634	.773	
1975	.453	.497	.446	.497	.412	.407	.457	.662
Tenure								
1965	.219				.754			
1969	.179	.505			.501	.649		
1972	.724	.179	.129		.458	.276	.308	
1975	.569	.195	.173	.790	.304	.226	.161	.625

graphic composition. For example, if some jobs require more education than others, then it would be expected that a higher percentage of these jobs are held by college graduates and this should be an enduring characteristic of these jobs. Do jobs indeed have stable demographic attributes?

College degrees are one individual attribute on which jobs might be expected to differ in their requirements. For some jobs all employees might be required to have B.A. degrees, while for others mostly employees without degrees would be recruited. If each job is characterized in terms of the percentage of employees with college degrees, considerable variation is found among jobs. For instance, the B.A. percentage in 1965 ranges from 0 to 100% in the various jobs in foreman level, with a mean of .20 and a standard deviation of .36.

Correlations of B.A. percentage in the various years indicates moderately high stability (Table 4.2). For nonmanagement jobs with five or more employees, the correlation between the B.A. percentages in 1962 and 1965 is .66, and, with the exception of 1975, the correlations among all other pairs of years are above .72. The comparable correlations for foreman level tend to be somewhat lower, but all (except the 1975 correlations) are above .63.

Years of experience in the corporation is another individual characteristic on which jobs might be expected to differ. The tendency might be to select only very experienced employees for some jobs, while only inexperienced employees would be selected for others. The average tenure of job occupants is taken as the index of tenure for each job, and considerable variation is found on this index. When correlations of this index are analyzed over time, for jobs with five or more employees, considerable stability is found (Table 4.2).[3] In foreman level the correlations among the 1960s variables are all above .50, the correlation between 1972 and 1975 is .63, and the correlations between the 1960s and 1970s are more modest. This is the pattern that would be expected if job evaluation or affirmative action altered job tenure requirements in the 1970s.

With one exception, nonmanagement jobs show the same pattern: high correlations between 1965 and 1969 and between 1972 and 1975, and more modest correlations across these periods. The 1962 correlations are the exception, showing greater continuity over the 13-year span than over the shorter spans.

These results clearly indicate the stability of average employee tenure in jobs. This stability is most consistent within the 1960s and within the 1970s, but there is remarkable stability over the entire 13-year span. Given the large influx of new (low-tenure) employees into the organization during the 1960s and the lowering of tenure obstacles to women and minorities when the affirmative action effort took effect (see Chapter 7), this stability is strong testimony to the stability of human capital within jobs.

It should be stressed that the stability of individual attributes in jobs is not because the same individuals stay in jobs. Of individuals in the nonmanagement level in 1962, 32% are in a different job in the firm 3 years later. For foreman level, 38% have changed jobs. If employees leaving the firm during this 3-year period are also considered, the job change rates increase even further. Clearly it is not the same individuals whose attributes are being calculated in these findings.

These analyses may be taken as support for the premise that jobs are

---

[3]The correlations reported here are of tenure variables recoded in 5-year spans during a 20-year period, with years 20 and above merged in the same category. This permits testing of the stability of jobs within broad categories. In particular, it removes distinctions between jobs with average tenures of 20 and 35 years because tenure differences in this part of the tenure range are unlikely to be important statements about job requirements. Indeed, preliminary table analyses of the unrecoded tenure variables indicate many jobs with great instability of average tenure over time in this part of the tenure range. In effect, this recode creates larger correlations than would be evident without the recode, and the correlations presented are probably a better reflection of job attributes.

characterized by different amounts of human capital in relatively stable ways. Having shown that jobs have fairly stable human capital attributes, the effect of these attributes on job salaries may be analyzed.

Determinants of Salaries

Having shown that jobs can be taken as units of analysis and that they have distinct and highly stable composition and salaries, the analysis turns to the determinants of job salaries. Of course, the aim here is not to analyze how jobs affect individuals' earnings; subsequent chapters will address that goal. Rather the aim here is to analyze the properties of jobs.

This section tests two sets of predictions for which human capital and structural theories differ. First, as discussed previously, the two theories predict that the individual attributes in jobs have different kinds of effects on job salaries. Human capital theory suggests that the relationship between the dollar value of jobs and the human capital in a job is best explained in terms of *unstandardized* coefficients, and these will vary with the changing supply–demand situation of the different time periods. In contrast, structural theory suggests that the relationship is best described by *standardized* coefficients, and these are predicted to remain stable over time. The two theories also differ in their predictions about the strength of the influence: Human capital theory predicts a strong relationship and structural theory predicts a weak relationship.

The initial regressions investigate the influence of two job composition variables on job salaries. The results of these regressions are reported in Table 4.3. The regressions in nonmanagement level indicate that the B.A. percentage consistently has a strong, significant positive influence on job salaries in all five periods. While the magnitude of its effects on the dollar amount of job salaries (as indicated by the unstandardized coefficient for job salaries adjusted for constant 1967 dollars) is not stable, increasing 23% between 1965 and 1972, the standardized coefficients remain remarkably constant over most of this period: They stay very close to .300 between 1965 and 1972. Similarly, while the dollar value of tenure varies enormously over this period, the standardized coefficients remain remarkably constant for three of the periods.

These changes in the dollar value of human capital are consistent with the predictions hypothesized from the supply and demand for human capital in the various periods. The dollar value of college graduates increased and the value of tenure decreased during the 1965–1969

Table 4.3

Human Capital Effects on Job Salaries over Five Periods, by Level[a]

Variable	1962	1965	1969	1972	1975
Nonmanagement					
B.A. percentage	16.178*	15.458*	17.508*	18.991*	12.617*
	(2.745)	(3.054)	(4.176)	(4.449)	(4.451)
Tenure	.596*	−.086	−.194*	.759*	.782*
	(.102)	(.068)	(.057)	(.129)	(.151)
Constant	50.358*	63.665*	67.204*	61.566*	65.403*
	(1.840)	(1.661)	(1.809)	(1.965)	(2.448)
R^2 (%)	26.2	10.8	12.1	24.4	18.9
Standardized coefficients					
B.A. percentage	.398	.307	.300	.302	.220
Tenure	.393	−.080	−.242	.414	.400
n	76	101	85	81	78
Foreman					
B.A. percentage	10.799*	9.368*	17.048*	15.075*	12.010*
	(2.939)	(2.310)	(4.453)	(4.801)	(3.962)
Tenure	.209	.171	.058	.531*	.580*
	(.143)	(.124)	(.154)	(.230)	(.221)
Constant	82.038	88.697*	93.118*	93.427*	94.535*
	(3.761)	(2.941)	(3.463)	(5.217)	(5.139)
R^2 (%)	9.0	9.1	10.9	9.5	10.0
Standardized coefficients					
B.A. percentage	.316	.296	.323	.309	.308
Tenure	.126	.100	.032	.227	.267
n	44	59	53	50	52

[a] Job salaries are given in hundreds of dollars. Asterisk indicates coefficients significant at the .05 level. Standard errors for coefficients are indicated in parentheses.

period of increased demand, and these trends reversed in 1972–1975, a period of declining demand.

The regressions in foreman level reveal very similar findings. Again, B.A. percentage has a consistently strong, significant, and positive influence on job salaries in all five periods, and the magnitude of the unstandardized coefficients follows the same patterns as those previously noted in nonmanagement. However, the standardized coefficients remain stable, ranging from .30 to .32 for all years, and their magnitude is remarkably similar to that for nonmanagement. Similarly, although the tenure coefficients are smaller in this level than in nonmanagement, similar patterns are evident.

In sum, the results are inconclusive as a test of the two theories, for they offer support to both theories. The changes in dollar value of human capital (as indicated in the unstandardized coefficients) are those predicted from the changing supply and demand for human capital. The stability in the relationship between the distribution of human capital and the distribution of job salaries (as indicated by the standardized coefficients) is as predicted from sociological theory.[4]

When total explanatory power of the regressions is considered, however, the results indicate considerably less ambiguity. The human capital attributes have only small explanatory power over job salaries; R^2 never gets as high as 27% in nonmanagement level, and it is considerably smaller in foreman level. This limited explanatory power of the two most important human capital variables suggests limits to the relevance of human capital theory in explaining job salaries. Although this is not definitive evidence against the theory (since unmeasured human capital attributes may have influence), the fact that the two most important human capital variables have such limited explanatory power is noteworthy.

Also, contrary to expectation, job evaluation does not increase the explanatory power of human capital attributes. In nonmanagement and foreman levels, the influence (standardized coefficient) of tenure increases with the onset of job evaluation in 1972, but the influence of B.A. percentage remains little different from what it was in the early 1960s. The lack of influence of job evaluation is considered subsequently.

Discrimination and Affirmative Action

Of course, two social processes which depart from human capital predictions are discrimination and affirmative action. Previous research has extensively documented a strong negative relationship between female percentage and earnings in occupational groups (Sanborn 1964; Fuchs 1971; Oaxaca 1973; Sommers 1974; Treiman and Terrell

[4]The negative coefficients for tenure are somewhat perplexing. In addition, the next analysis shows even more strongly negative tenure coefficients when sex and race composition are controlled. Inspection of the actual distribution of job salaries by average tenure in jobs reveals that nonmanagement jobs predominantly occupied by high-tenure employees (i.e., over 20 years) actually have lower earnings than jobs with lower average tenure in 1965 and 1969. Since curves for individuals show an asymptote at high tenure but not a decline, this negative effect of tenure on job salaries seems to be a distinctively aggregate process, by which nonmanagement jobs having a high concentration of high-tenure employees are disvalued. It is as if these jobs are dumping grounds for high-seniority employees. This phenomenon is not evident in the job salary distributions of other years or in foreman level.

1975a; Featherman and Hauser 1976; Hartmann, Roos, and Treiman 1980; Roos 1981), but it has not been possible to study this issue for jobs. The present section examines this question.

In this company, as in most companies, women were traditionally channeled into certain kinds of jobs. Of jobs with five or more employees in 1962, fewer than 5% of jobs in nonmanagement and foreman levels were sex integrated, and no jobs in lower management were held by women (Table 4.4). However, the company's affirmative action program began having a strong impact in 1969; and by 1975, the proportion of sex-integrated jobs (i.e., jobs with at least one individual of each sex) had increased to 33% in nonmanagement, 27% in foreman level, and 47% in lower management. In terms of race, few jobs were exclusively occupied by minorities, but many jobs were exclusively occupied by whites. In 1965, 80% of the nonmanagement jobs and 98% of the foreman and lower-management jobs were held exclusively by whites. By 1975, the situation had clearly improved, particularly in nonmanagement where only 35% of the jobs were held exclusively by whites (and many of these were small jobs with fewer than five employees). The affirmative action program seems to have had great success in increasing the number of integrated jobs.

However, despite these gains, many jobs were unaffected. Even by

Table 4.4

Number of Jobs by Level and Percentage of Females: 1962–1975
(for Jobs Containing Five or More Employees)

Percentage of females	Number of jobs				
	1962	1965	1969	1972	1975
Nonmanagement					
0	47	55	42	34	19
1–99	3	6	7	13	25
100	23	37	34	31	31
	73	98	83	78	75
Foreman					
0	18	25	20	17	17
1–99	2	7	7	13	14
100	24	27	25	18	20
	44	59	52	48	51
Lower management					
0	13	21	18	9	8
1–99	0	0	5	4	8
100	0	0	0	1	1
	13	21	23	14	17

Table 4.5

Stability of Female and Minority Percentages in Jobs by Level: Pearson Correlations

Demographic composition	Nonmanagement				Foreman			
	1962	1965	1969	1972	1962	1965	1969	1972
Female percentage								
1965	.998				.723			
1969	.997	.997			.598	.848		
1972	.991	.993	.995		.464	.656	.621	
1975	.990	.991	.994	.998	.448	.606	.611	.915
Minority percentage[a]								
1965	—				—			
1969	—	.985			—	.013		
1972	—	.959	.974		—	−.039	.074	
1975	—	.948	.968	.981	—	−.043	.029	.458

[a]Race composition was not available in the 1962 data.

1975, the vast majority of jobs were still segregated by sex and over a third were still segregated by race.

Moreover, even the pronounced increase in the number of integrated jobs in nonmanagement between 1969 and 1975 did not have as much effect as it appears, for jobs maintain virtually the same rank order in terms of their female concentration. The correlation between female percentage in 1969 and 1975 is .994 in nonmanagement level (Table 4.5). The foreman correlations are more modest, but even over the period of greatest change (1969–1975) the correlations indicate substantial stability (.61). Similarly, with respect to minority proportions, nonmanagement jobs are nearly perfectly stable among jobs with five or more employees (correlations above .94).[5] No such stability is evident in foreman level, but this could be due to the small number of minority individuals. Despite great improvements in desegregating jobs by sex and race, considerable stability is still evident, particularly with regard to sex. Although the absolute magnitude of these percentages changed, their rank order tended to remain stable. Many jobs can be consistently characterized by their sex composition over this entire period.

In addition, the sex-segregated jobs offered considerably different salaries. The average salary paid for all-female jobs was about 75% of the salary paid for all-male jobs, and this ratio applies both to nonmanagement and foreman levels in most years (Table 4.6). There is a

[5]The records lack an indicator for race in 1962.

Table 4.6

Average Salary in Dollars for Jobs Containing Five or More Employees, by Percentage
Female: 1962–1975

Female percentage	1962	1965	1969	1972	1975
Nonmanagement					
0	6,268	6,988	7,894	10,009	14,679
100	4,530	4,854	5,850	7,590	10,632
Foreman					
0	8,863	10,050	12,345	15,297	19,713
100	6,849	7,440	9,104	11,569	15,722
Lower management					
0	11,160	12,440	14,617	19,368	22,600
100	—	—	—	18,333	21,985

general trend toward slightly greater equality over these years, but the trend is modest (and it shows an unexplainable reversal in nonmanagement level in 1975). Certainly all-female jobs show much less gain than individual females experienced over this period (see Chapter 7).

Of course, the simple association between female percentage and average salary may be highly misleading since jobs may differ in other respects and the apparent effects of female percentage may actually be due to other factors. For instance, jobs may differ in terms of the education and training they require, and economists might suggest that the human capital composition of jobs account for the apparent effects of female percentage.

Regressions were run to study the effects of female and minority percentage on job salaries, controlling for the percentage of college graduates and the average tenure in the job (Table 4.7; 1962 analyses are omitted because 1962 data lack an indicator for race). As economists would predict, the two human capital factors affect job salaries, but the percentage of females and minorities also have significant independent effects (although the latter is rarely significant due to the small numbers of minorities).

The clearest effect of adding these variables to the regression is in explaining additional variance. These variables add 14–30% to the explained variance in nonmanagement salaries and 22–38% in foreman level salaries. The sex and race composition of jobs is clearly an important influence on job salaries.

Female percentage has a strong significant negative relationship with job salaries in all years, even after controlling for human capital composition. In nonmanagement level in 1965, job salaries were $21 less

Table 4.7

Human Capital, Sex, and Race Effects on Job Salaries over Five Periods, by Level[a]

Variable	1965	1969	1972	1975
Nonmanagement				
B.A. percentage	27.841*	22.313*	25.821*	26.522*
	(5.175)	(5.173)	(6.012)	(6.842)
Tenure	−.319*	−.387*	.898*	.586*
	(.099)	(.097)	(.227)	(.259)
Minority percentage	−38.045*	−22.667*	−14.207	−24.159*
	(14.112)	(7.453)	(7.898)	(8.749)
Female percentage	−20.759*	−19.868*	−14.946*	−12.310*
	(4.383)	(5.192)	(5.170)	(5.031)
Constant	75.423*	81.330*	66.212*	75.710*
	(2.874)	(3.290)	(3.640)	(4.473)
R^2 (%)	43.1	39.3	40.3	37.3
Standardized coefficients				
B.A. percentage	.416	.401	.390	.370
Tenure	−.248	−.376	.382	.231
Minority percentage	−.209	−.276	−.172	−.278
Female percentage	−.369	−.339	−.258	−.231
n	101	85	81	78
Foreman				
B.A. percentage	7.116*	10.718*	12.783*	11.022*
	(1.906)	(3.550)	(3.907)	(3.495)
Tenure	.256*	.046	.512*	.460*
	(.103)	(.120)	(.192)	(.195)
Minority percentage	−2.623	−84.099*	−9.941	−1.147
	(13.479)	(22.241)	(6.320)	(5.737)
Female percentage	−10.259*	−8.108*	−10.200*	−8.192*
	(1.122)	(1.011)	(1.417)	(1.460)
Constant	95.278*	103.558*	103.885*	104.559*
	(2.519)	(2.966)	(4.538)	(4.841)
R^2 (%)	40.0	46.7	41.5	32.4
Standardized coefficients				
B.A. percentage	.224	.203	.262	.283
Tenure	.150	.025	.219	.212
Minority percentage	−.011	−.246	−.121	−.017
Female percentage	−.560	−.534	−.541	−.472
n	59	53	50	52

[a]Job salaries are given in hundreds of dollars. Asterisk indicates coefficients significant at the .05 level. Standard errors for coefficients are indicated in parentheses.

for each additional percentage of females, so that the regression estimates that salaries for 100%-female jobs were $2100 less than salaries
for all-male jobs, a figure very close to the real difference between job
salaries of all-male and all-female jobs. Although this difference declines over the periods of increasingly strong affirmative action, even in
1975 it retains a strong significant negative effect. In foreman level, the
decline is less, and it is more erratic (perhaps because of the large
influx of women promoted into foreman-level all-female jobs in 1972).
But even in 1975, female percentage still has a strong negative association with job salaries. Although human capital composition accounts
for some of the earnings differences among jobs (particularly at the
foreman level); even after controlling for this, the salaries for jobs employing a higher percentage of females are lower.[6]

These findings indicate the complexity of making affirmative action
operate in all ways at the same time. Despite the gains over the 1969–
1972 period in improving individual women's earnings and for desegregating jobs, foreman-level female jobs experienced declining value,
which was reversed in the following period. These analyses suggest
that the jobs which had not yet been desegregated were the ones which
remained undervalued.

These analyses clearly indicate the complexity of the effects of the
affirmative action program. Financial penalties that were traditionally
associated with jobs held predominantly by females and minorities in
the earlier period were reduced with the implementation of the affirmative action program; but progress was erratic, and the penalties still
remained to a substantial degree. Despite great changes, these analyses
indicate that traditional patterns are difficult to change completely and
all at once.

Job Status Effects on Job Salaries

As previously noted, the job status classifications in this organization
actually derive from two different systems: a traditional status system
which operated until 1971 and a job evaluation system which operated
thereafter. However, although job statuses were determined by two
different procedures over these periods, the actual status rankings are
strikingly similar (Table 4.8). While the status classifications of jobs are
highly stable within the two systems (i.e., between 1962 and 1969 and

---

[6]The large unexplained changes in the influence of minority percentage may be due to
the small numbers of minorities in most jobs.

Table 4.8

Stability of Job Status for Foreman Level: Pearson Correlations

	1962	1965	1969	1972
1965	.997			
1969	.990	.994		
1972	.849	.848	.867	
1975	.814	.817	.838	.954

between 1972 and 1975, job status correlations are over .95), they are also moderately stable across the two systems (i.e., between 1962 and 1975, job status correlations are over .81 in the foreman level; job status data were not available for nonmanagement).

The stability of job statuses between the 1960s and 1970s casts some doubt on the extensiveness of change introduced by job evaluation. Although described in the job evaluation literature and in organization policy as a thorough reevaluation based on more rational criteria, the resulting rankings are only minimally reordered by this system. One must infer that either the traditional system was a great deal more rational than it had been portrayed, or, more likely, traditional values from the previous system have somehow been inadvertently reintroduced into the job evaluation system. This will be discussed at greater length in the conclusion of this chapter. In any case, the stability of the job status categories does suggest that they can be analyzed as if they were the same phenomenon in all years although the organization constructed them by different procedures.

When job status is introduced into the analyses for the foreman level (recall that data are unavailable for analysis of job status categories in nonmanagement), job status is indeed found to have a very great influence on job salaries (Table 4.9). Of course, its large influence is not surprising since it is the result of traditional status and job evaluation systems which are supposed to determine job compensation. However, while the basis of job status changed from tradition to job evaluation, job status continues to have the same amount of influence in 1969 and 1972 (see standardized coefficients and unique variance in Tables 4.9 and 4.10). Moreover, the total effect of female percentage in foreman-level jobs remains constant from 1969 to 1975 (Table 4.7) and job status mediates an increasing proportion of this influence (21% [1.681 ÷ 8.108] of its influence is not mediated by job status in 1969 and only 3% [0.250 ÷ 8.192] of its influence is not mediated by job status in 1975).

Table 4.9

Human Capital, Sex, Race, and Status Effects on Job Salaries over Five Periods
(for Foreman Level)[a]

Variable	1965	1969	1972	1975
B.A. percentage	−2.559*	−2.781	.509	−1.689
	(.571)	(1.529)	(2.236)	(1.381)
Tenure	.111*	−.079	.437*	.175*
	(.029)	(.049)	(.103)	(.073)
Minority percentage	−7.646*	−26.520*	−2.172	.053
	(3.749)	(9.269)	(3.435)	(2.115)
Female percentage	−.778*	−1.681*	−2.870*	−.250
	(.376)	(.480)	(.887)	(.621)
Job status	3.169*	2.989*	9.164*	9.502*
	(.070)	(.117)	(.567)	(.373)
Constant	61.949*	72.561*	69.731*	73.949*
	(1.017)	(1.704)	(3.230)	(2.151)
R^2 (%)	95.4	91.4	83.2	90.9
Standardized coefficients				
B.A. percentage	−.081	−.053	.010	−.043
Tenure	.065	.043	.186	.081
Minority percentage	−.035	−.078	−.026	.001
Female percentage	−.042	−.111	−.152	−.014
Job status	.973	.894	.812	.949
n	59	53	50	52

[a]Job salaries are given in hundreds of dollars. Asterisk indicates coefficients significant at the .05 level. Standard errors for coefficients are indicated in parentheses.

Contrary to the aim of job evaluation to rationalize compensation and reduce bias; the penalty against female jobs is not reduced, and it is increasingly mediated by the job evaluation system.

Indeed, since nearly all of the influence of female percentage is mediated by job status in 1975, job evaluation may be preserving and legitimating the influence of this factor; and it may be making it less subject to criticism. Job evaluation creates a status hierarchy which continues to mediate much of the effect of female percentage on earnings, in the same way that the traditional status system did. Job evaluation, even in the context of a strong affirmative action program, maintains and possibly reinforces much of the earnings differences among male and female jobs.[7]

[7]Sociological uses of path analysis have a customary practice of treating factors which mediate effects of other factors as not truly causal. Thus in the present analyses the fact that the effects of college degrees on earnings is mediated by job status may be viewed as incidental. However, this is really a theoretical issue dependent on theoretical assump-

Table 4.10

Partitioning of Variance from Tables 4.7 and 4.9 (for Foreman Level)[a]

Variables	1965		1969		1972		1975	
	Unique	Total	Unique	Total	Unique	Total	Unique	Total
Demographic	1.5	40.0	2.1	46.7	5.2	41.5	1.2	32.4
Job status	55.4	93.9	44.7	89.3	41.7	78.0	58.5	89.7
Shared	38.5		44.6		36.3		31.2	
	95.4		91.4		83.2		90.9	

[a]Variance is expressed as a percentage.

Job Effects on Promotion Opportunities

Promotions, even more than earnings, are usually considered to be attainments of individuals. The individualistic achievement norms of our nation encourage this perception. However, although individuals themselves may be responsible for their attainments, various social factors outside the individual may influence whether individual achievements are recognized, valued, or rewarded with promotions. In particular, a person's job may have an important impact on whether that person's achievements are recognized, valued, or rewarded with promotions. For instance, individuals in clerical jobs may have difficulty getting promotions because they are not given the chance to demonstrate the managerial skills that are thought to be nec-

---

tions. According to human capital theory, the effects of job status are indeed incidental. Organizations would have to pay for the value of college degrees regardless of whether the job status system existed. In contrast, according to structural theory, the job evaluation system specifies how much this organization is willing to pay for a college degree. While social structuralists concede that external labor markets constrain organizations to pay a premium for college degrees, they would contend that market imperfections permit organizations wide latitude in the amount and form of this premium and that other organizational features determine how much it will be. Indeed, the practice of job evaluation is implemented with the explicit purpose of making job (and indirectly individual attribute) compensation more rational and equitable in relation to one another. Presumably, organizations only go to the bother and great expense of implementing these programs because they seek to realign pay relationships within the firm. It is noteworthy that job evaluation has little way to take account of external market pay relationships. Organizations evidently believe that they can realign these pay relationships without being totally at the mercy of markets and that job status systems are an instrument for doing this. Like most other sociologists, I concur with this assumption in the inferences I draw from these findings.

essary for promotions. While individuals' achievements may have important effects on their career attainments, their achievements will be differentially rewarded depending on whether the kinds of achievements they can show in their jobs are highly visible, highly valued, and regarded as demonstrating skills and personal qualities thought to be suitable for higher levels.

The management literature explains this in terms of the "visibility" of jobs, and Kanter (1977) describes some of the social psychological processes associated with high visibility of jobs. Signaling theory suggests an alternative view: that certain highly valued jobs serve as a signal to indicate that their occupants are capable and worthy of promotion. An analysis of vacancy chains (White 1970a) suggests another view: that jobs which feed into higher-level jobs will offer greater promotions. Of course these various explanations may be describing different aspects of the same same phenomenon since high-visibility jobs may also be social signals and may obtain some of their visibility and signaling value because they are part of a dynamic promotion chain (e.g., a growing or highly valued department).

Economists describe the differential career opportunities associated with different jobs as "dual labor markets"—one containing jobs which offer no career mobility and one containing jobs which offer high promotion chances (Doeringer and Piore 1971). Of course this dichotomy may even be too simple; it may be only one part of a more extensive job tracking system which selects and channels employees' careers in organizations. Observations and surveys of employees in organizations suggests some support for this hypothesis (Martin and Strauss 1959; Goldner 1965; Kanter 1977); however, systematic analyses of the actual promotion chances associated with jobs have not been done.

The following sections analyze three questions about the promotion chances associated with jobs. First, do all jobs at a given level confer the same promotion chances? If there are differences; do they indicate a simple dichotomy (as the dual labor market suggests), a multilevel stratification system of "discrete wafers," or a continuum where jobs at the same level have various degrees of proximity to the next higher level?

Second, if jobs differ, are these differences in promotion chances stable attributes of jobs, or are they transitory phenomena which change over time?

Third, what determines the promotion chances offered by jobs? To what extent are the promotion chances jobs offer determined by their human capital, race, or sex composition?

Do Jobs Offer Different Promotion Chances?

American norms encourage the belief that all individuals have the opportunity to improve their position in life, and organizations generally reinforce this perception among their employees. According to this norm, it is up to individuals to improve their attainments and anyone can do it, regardless of their present job. Indeed, stories of individuals who began as mail clerks and rose to high executive positions are frequently topics of newspaper reports and company gossip.

Unfortunately, the literature provides little good information on the actual distribution of promotion by jobs. The research on dual labor markets suggests a dichotomy among jobs offering good advancement opportunity; however, the available descriptions tend to be vague (Doeringer and Piore 1971). Chinoy (1955) presented data on the promotion chances of automobile workers advancing to foreman positions, but his data did not attempt to differentiate by job. Do jobs at the same level in the authority hierarchy differ in the promotion chances they offer?

An analysis of the proportion of job occupants who are at a higher level in the authority hierarchy after 7 years indicates clear differences among jobs. In order to make these percentages more meaningful, analysis is limited to jobs with five or more employees, and for simplicity, the analysis distinguishes between jobs offering no promotions over the next 7 years and jobs promoting over 50% of their employees in that period. The analysis finds that in 48% of nonmanagement jobs, no employees were promoted between 1962 and 1969, while in 21%, a majority were promoted. In 66% of foreman-level jobs, no employees were promoted, while in 18%, a majority were promoted, and the distributions were similar for lower-management level jobs (67% and 22%).

Described in this way, one can visualize a dual labor market in each level, with jobs offering no promotions being seen as the secondary labor market and those offering more than a 50% promotion rate clearly being seen as the primary labor market. However, these distributions differ from the dual labor market model in two respects. First, the dual labor market model considers the secondary labor market to exist only in the nonmanagement level of organizations, while it considers management jobs always to be in the primary labor market. These data suggest that many management jobs, which clearly have primary labor market attributes in other respects (job security, wage levels, job conditions), offer no promotion chances over a rather long period of time (7 years can be considered a long time, given the findings of Chapter 3, especially in a period of company growth). Clearly the dual labor market model ignores significant heterogeneity within the primary labor market.

Second, the allocation of promotions is more like a continuum than like the dichotomy suggested by the dual labor market model. Considering promotion rates between 10 and 49% as moderate, this moderate level of promotions is offered by 26% of nonmanagement jobs, 10% of foreman jobs, and 11% of lower-management jobs between 1962 and 1969. Moreover, inspection of frequency distributions indicates no clear gaps in the distribution of promotion chances in this moderate range. The dualistic conception of promotion chances would seem to be an oversimplification of the actual situation, and the actual distribution comes much closer to a continuum.

Are Promotion Chances a Stable Attribute of Jobs?

Of course, the preceding only describes a single time span. By itself, that analysis does not establish that these promotion rates are properties of jobs. A high promotion rate from a job may merely be a chance phenomenon due to unusually competent employees in the job in that period or an unusually high demand for employees in that specialty in that period.

However, analysis of promotions across time periods indicates considerable stability. For this analysis, the percentage of employees who were promoted in each 3–4-year interval was considered, again limiting analysis to jobs with five or more employees. The correlations indicate moderately strong stability for the two lower levels (Table 4.11). In nonmanagement, the correlations range between .51 and .84, with a mean of .68; in foreman level they range from .59 to .81, with a mean of .70.

The correlations clearly indicate that individuals tend to get promoted from the same set of jobs over these very different periods. Economic recessions, changing organization priorities, and affirmative action led to many kinds of changes in this organization over this 13-year period; however, to a great extent, the highest promotion rates are consistently associated with the same set of jobs.

What Determines the Promotion Chances Offered by Jobs?

Having found that the promotion chances associated with jobs are stable properties of jobs, one may wonder what it is about jobs that

Table 4.11

Stability of Promotion Rates from Jobs by Level: Pearson Correlations

	Nonmanagement			Foreman		
	1962–1965	1965–1969	1969–1972	1962–1965	1965–1969	1969–1972
1965–1969	.747			.739		
1969–1972	.565	.844		.697	.682	
1972–1975	.735	.661	.509	.807	.670	.587

leads some jobs to offer greater promotion chances than others? By repeating the analyses previously carried out for job salaries on promotion chances, demographic composition is often found to explain promotions as well or better than it explains job salaries, judged in terms of total explained variance (Table 4.12). The percentage of college graduates in a job has the largest influence, while tenure has a negligible influence throughout. Minority and female percentages are never significant in nonmanagement level. Female percentage in foreman level jobs shifts from an almost significant negative impact to a significant positive impact over these periods. Apparently, the affirmative action program, which did not markedly increase the compensation of foreman level female jobs, did increase the promotion opportunities out of these jobs.

Conclusions

This chapter has tested the premise that jobs are basic units for allocating rewards in an organization. It has investigated whether jobs have stable properties, the extent to which job composition contributes to the allocation of rewards, the nature and extent of the job status effect on job salaries, and how job compensation was affected by the job evaluation and affirmative action programs.

Although the findings of these analyses indicate that jobs are created and terminated more often than is commonly assumed, the jobs which do persist over time tend to have stable attributes—stable job salaries, stable demographic composition, and stable promotion chances—even across periods of changing growth and during which affirmative action programs were instituted. Since many individuals have either changed jobs or left the firm over the period from 1962 to 1965, it may be concluded that this stability is not merely due to the same individuals remaining in jobs but rather that jobs per se have stable attributes.

The notion that jobs have attributes contradicts an implicit assumption of individualistic research. When research on individuals' attainments shows an association between individuals' attributes (e.g., education) and their earnings, the relationship is thought to indicate a direct causal link. However, if jobs define the individuals' attributes required for entry and if they define the rewards they confer, then jobs and the job structure may be important determinants of the patterns of compensation and career attainment. While this interpretation does not

Table 4.12

Human Capital, Sex, and Race Effects on Promotion Chances Associated with Jobs, by Level[a]

Variable	1965–1969	1969–1972	1972–1975
Nonmanagement			
B.A. percentage	1.167*	.584*	.697*
	(.223)	(.171)	(.091)
Tenure	−.002	−.004	−.001
	(.004)	(.003)	(.003)
Minority percentage	.823	.172	−.096
	(.606)	(.247)	(.122)
Female percentage	−.321	−.140	−.114
	(.218)	(.184)	(.084)
Constant	.380*	.351*	.114*
	(.123)	(.109)	(.056)
R^2 (%)	24.7	12.9	45.3
Standardized coefficients			
B.A. percentage	.466	.382	.665
Tenure	−.050	−.132	−.036
Minority percentage	.121	.075	−.073
Female percentage	−.131	−.081	−.117
n	101	85	81
Foreman			
B.A. percentage	.491*	.369*	.473*
	(.079)	(.104)	(.034)
Tenure	.001	.000	−.004
	(.004)	(.003)	(.003)
Minority percentage	−1.368	−.419	−.432*
	(1.401)	(.314)	(.185)
Female percentage	−.136	.010	.069*
	(.082)	(.065)	(.032)
Constant	.129	.065	.084
	(.096)	(.067)	(.056)
R^2 (%)	50.6	35.6	86.1
Standardized coefficients			
B.A. percentage	.650	.556	.888
Tenure	.015	.010	−.095
Minority percentage	−.095	−.158	−.143
Female percentage	−.165	.019	.120
n	59	53	50

[a]Asterisk indicates coefficients significant at the .05 level. Standard errors for coefficients are indicated in parentheses.

reduce the value of analyzing individuals' attainments, it does suggest that such analyses must consider to what extent structural factors are contributing to individuals' attainments.

Consequently, changes in individuals' attainments may not only be the result of individuals' performance; they may also be affected by the ways individuals' personal attributes define the kinds of jobs to which individuals can be assigned, issues which are analyzed in Chapters 5 and 6. Moreover, the organization's responsiveness to changes in social and economic conditions may not entirely be a direct relationship; it may also be partially mediated and limited by the job structure, a contention which is examined in Chapter 7.

On the central theoretical issue of this chapter, whether human capital alone is sufficient to explain job salaries, the results are necessarily ambiguous. The concept of human capital includes a diversity of individual attributes, many of which are difficult, if not impossible, to measure. This makes the theory virtually impossible to refute. However, the limited explanatory power of the two human capital variables considered here is important, for these are the two most emphasized variables in the human capital theory and the variables which have the strongest explanatory power in empirical analyses of earnings. Consequently, although the findings here about human capital effects on job value cannot be definitive, they strongly suggest that human capital composition has a minor impact in determining job value.

The structural contention about the job status effect on job salaries is unambiguously answered by these analyses. The impact of job status is complete and leaves very little room for other factors to have separate influences on job salaries. The compensation for jobs is nearly totally determined by the status to which the jobs are allocated, and other factors have minimal additional impact. The analyses suggest that the weak effect of human capital and the strong effects of sex and race composition are largely mediated by the job status system, and this is true when job status is determined by traditional status conception and after it was presumably rationalized by the job evaluation system.

Job status explains nearly all the variance in job salaries; it mediates nearly all of the influence of demographic variables and has a large unique influence besides. This strong mediating influence casts considerable doubt on the human capital model; for it suggests that the human capital composition of jobs is not compensated directly, but only insofar as it is reflected in the status of jobs. The salary for a job occupied predominantly by individuals with valuable human capital is determined only by the status value of the job, not by its occupants.

By clearly identifying the social value of jobs, the job status system creates an explicit hierarchy into which employees may be allocated on the basis of their presumed value. It may also be a mechanism for defining the distribution of job salaries, for maintaining this at the same relative magnitude over long periods of time, and for maintaining its correspondence to the distribution of individual attributes. The aggregate properties of jobs may be structurally maintained by the operation of the job status system. Consequently, although the relationship between individual attributes and dollar outcomes appears to be an economic relationship, it is actually mediated by the social structure of the job status system.

Policy Implications: The Reexamination of Job Status

These empirical findings clearly indicate the need for more careful analysis of the job status system. Efforts directed at revising job status systems are aimed at the right target: the system which is central to the determination of salaries, which perpetuates the negative value of women's jobs, and which has been largely immune from examination. It is a system created by particularistic political influences and based on traditional values which may not reflect current equity norms and may not even be responsive to current economic conditions. Job evaluation, being an effort to reexamine traditional job status and create a more rational system, would seem to be a hopeful reform for creating equal pay for "equivalent" work.

Job evaluation's most impressive accomplishment is the creation of a process of determining job value which bridges the gaps among competing advocates and which removes the process from particularistic political considerations. It does this by getting competing interest groups to express their views in terms of numbers, by considering abstract factors instead of concrete jobs, and by using "experts" to reconcile conflicts (Sargent 1972, p. 2-34). However, these procedures also make the factor weights less susceptible to criticism and make their biases difficult to discover.

This risk is not just hypothetical; it may be built into the job evaluation procedure. As Treiman (1979, p. 7) notes, "some job evaluation analysts argue that the principal criterion for the validity of a job evaluation plan should be how closely the job worth hierarchy produced by the plan matches the existing wage hierarchy (Fitzpatrick 1949; Fox

1962)." For instance, according to the director of corporate compensation at Eastman Kodak,

> Perceptions of equity, or standards of work value, are so variable and changing among people, among professions, and among various organizations that a single organization must develop its own set of value standards and sustain those standards over a period of time if they are to have meaning and are to influence perceptions of equity. Thus, the organization should use caution in attacking or changing a long-established set of job relationships, regardless of the source of the equity perceptions which originally generated the relationships. (Wing 1972, p. 2-21)

Experimental studies find that, while compensation specialists are not influenced by the percentage of females holding a job, they are substantially influenced by the current salary reported (Schwab 1983). Consequently, the present findings of remarkable stability of job status and job salaries over the 13 years spanning traditional and job evaluation systems indicate a serious defect in job evaluation as a way of remedying past discrimination. Rather than being a means for reforming traditional practices; job evaluation may be preserving and legitimating these traditions and making them less subject to criticism.

The present findings have several implications for assessing the potential value of job evaluation for advancing affirmative action goals. First, they indicate the crucial importance of formulating a coherent and fair job evaluation system if reform efforts are to endure. If the present findings about the enormous numbers of new jobs which appear over time are generalizable, then one-shot efforts at reevaluating jobs will have only short-term benefits as old jobs disappear and others are created.[8] An enduring system for fairly evaluating jobs is necessary if reforms are to have persisting effects.

Second, reform efforts to implement job evaluation, even in the context of a strong affirmative action program, may not overcome the salary disadvantage of female jobs. The conclusion to the interim report of the Committee on Occupational Classification warned that job evaluation procedures use several procedures which raise questions about whether they can be effective in fairly assessing sex-segregated jobs (Treiman 1979, p. 48). In particular, their reliance on market wage rates and

[8]It should be noted that these findings indicate the emptying and filling of particular job titles as defined by the corporation. Organizational policy in this corporation states that when a job acquires or loses one or more significant tasks, a new job title is assigned. How small a change can constitute a "significant task"? Official policy is not explicit. One of the managers in charge of making such decisions stressed that his office looks at requests for job redefinitions critically in order to guard against arbitrary changes being made solely to increase salaries. However, it is just this kind of subjective judgmental processes which have contributed to past discrimination.

subjective judgments raise serious risks that job evaluation will recreate the same biases as traditional status systems. Unfortunately, the present findings provide empirical support for this warning and they suggest that job evaluation may be especially pernicious in providing legitimization for traditional values under the mask of scientific procedure.

Third, to the extent that affirmative action programs help individual women without improving the status of female jobs, they are likely to maintain structural disadvantages for the individuals in female jobs. This not only prevents the individuals who are not promoted out of these jobs from receiving the full benefit of the affirmative action program; but it also remains a structural component of the organization so that when the impetus of the affirmative action program ends, the structure may again tend to recreate the old patterns.

Unfortunately, though directed at the right target, job evaluation has had only modest effects in changing job status or in improving the salaries of female jobs in this corporation (while other affirmative action efforts have created great gains for individual women). Although its procedures are well suited to reducing discrimination from particularistic political influences, job evaluation's reliance on traditional values and traditional wage rates prevents it from addressing the most important sources of the low valuation of female jobs.

Presumably, the subjective job assessments and market-based factor weightings had important influences on these findings, and these may be the best targets for policy change. Currently, there is not sufficient evidence on how these procedures operate (MacArthur 1983; Schwab 1983). However, the present findings suggest that these mechanisms underlying job evaluation need to be scrutinized to discover whether these inequalities are inequitable; and, if so, how job evaluations could be done in other ways to lead to more equitable results.

Appendix 4.A: Job Evaluation—Building a Normative System around Economic Goals

Although there are several different types of job evaluation in use, the point method stands out as the method which is most objective, most easily implemented, and, in fact, most widely implemented (Akalin 1970). Since the point method is also the type of job evaluation used in the company studied here, this discussion is limited to this type of job evaluation.

The *point method* is so named because it evaluates jobs quantitatively in terms of abstract numbers (*points*). Its objective is to measure the content of each job; but rather than trying to evaluate the content of a job as a whole, it measures each job along a number of predetermined dimensions (*factors*) which are considered to define all the components worthy of compensation. There are four main steps in creating a job evaluation system using the point method. First, the factors on which jobs are to be evaluated are identified. Second, a scale is constructed for each factor to demarcate the various levels of worth on each factor, worth being measured in terms of points. Third, the scores on the many separate factors are combined into a composite score with weights for each factor which reflect the importance of that factor. Finally, the composite job evaluation is translated into earnings, in effect converting from points to dollars.

The procedure seeks to ignore the characteristics of particular job occupants and seeks to measure the characteristics of jobs themselves.

> The measurements are based on the job's requirements, responsibilities and conditions when occupied by a fully qualified incumbent performing at the normal rate, i.e., a rate which is neither abnormally high nor abnormally low, but acceptable. It follows that pay relationships determined by evaluation are base-rate relationships and do not reflect pay for any length of service, premium for superior performance, etc. Evaluations, once established, remain unchanged as long as the jobs remain the same. (Sargent 1972, p. 2-11)

This necessarily makes job evaluations highly abstract and somewhat hypothetical, but it is crucial if the evaluations are to be interpreted as describing jobs.

Although the factors for rating jobs can be based on any set of values an employer might have, many job evaluation systems tend to construct factors reflecting three main components: job requirements, job responsibility, and working conditions. These would then be further operationalized. For instance, the system of job evaluation used by the consulting firm Hay Associates would specify each factor as follows:

1. Requirements: education, experience, mechanical ability, job complexity, physical skill, and complexity

2. Responsibility: responsibilities for materials and equipment, effect of one's efforts on subsequent operations, need for alertness and attention to orders, teamwork, and safety of others

3. Working conditions: repetitiveness and monotony, physical requirements, surroundings, and exposure to hazard. (Sargent 1972, p. 2-33)

For instance, of the 18 job evaluation systems reviewed by Treiman (1979, table 2), 9 explicitly mentioned education and experience as the two factors with the greatest number of maximum points. Treiman cautions that his sample is nonrandom and that total points may indicate the most important influences in actual fact (for that depends on the variance in actual ratings given to all factors); however, lacking better samples and information on actual ratings, these data are the best information available for comparison. Treiman's compilation for these 9 systems suggests considerable agreement across systems, with education and experience containing between 30 and 38% of the total possible points in 7 of the systems (the 2 other systems mentioning education and experience allocate more points to these factors, 41 and 52%). Furthermore, 5 of the other systems Treiman reviewed, including the Hay system and the federal civil service system, attributed a comparable amount of importance to the knowledge required by the job (4 of these 5 systems giving this factor 30–41% of total points). In the Hay system, knowledge is often operationalized as education and experience. Similarly, half of the systems listed a "responsibility" factor as having major importance, with 6 of these systems allocating between 24 and 38% of total points to this factor. Despite the limitations of this compilation, it does suggest considerable agreement on the importance of job requirements and some agreement on the importance of job responsibility.

What is most striking to a social scientist is how much the job evaluation factors resemble the factors stressed by economic theory. The specific operationalizations of the requirements factor—education, experience, and ability—are precisely the variables which human capital economists take as the indicators of human capital. Similarly, job evaluation seeks to operationalize productivity in the responsibility factor. Finally, the working conditions factor reflects the same considerations that economists have noted in discussions of personal sacrifice and undesirable working conditions.

These similarities suggest that job evaluation has been explicitly modeled on economic theories, and they convey an image of a compensation system which resolves the fundamental conflict of compensation systems, creating a social status system which is responsive to economic forces. Obviously, any reconciliation which makes the status relationships in an organization hierarchy more responsive to economic forces is likely to reduce some of the criticisms of the existing compensation system and to confer greater legitimacy.

It also creates a system to which economic theories may be particularly applicable. Especially in light of the strong weighting that job evaluation systems give to the human capital "requirement" factors of education and experience (Treiman 1979, table 2), one would expect that the impact of human capital attributes on job salaries would be particularly strong after the implementation of job evaluation. While economic theory may be correct in positing that human capital determines economic value of individuals and jobs in traditional circumstances, job evaluation explicitly dictates that job value be derived from job requirements and responsibilities. Assuming that organizations tend to fill more demanding jobs (jobs with greater requirements and responsibilities) with individuals with greater human capital, one would expect that job evaluation creates a situation in which the correspondence between individual human capital in a job and job compensation would be particularly great.

In theory, job evaluation does differ from the economic theories in its emphasis on evaluating jobs rather than individuals. However, this difference may be more apparent in theory than in actual practice. As a practical matter, job evaluation systems evaluate jobs' requirements by looking at the way they function with particular individuals in them, and the rankings that result are doubtlessly colored by the qualifications of the present occupants. The same may be true for the responsibility factor; the responsibility demanded by a job is surely affected by the responsibilities that a particular job occupant has chosen to assume or not to assume (or that a supervisor has chosen to assign or not to assign to a particular job occupant). In view of these practical considerations, human capital composition is likely to color the evaluations jobs receive, strengthening the human capital hypothesis even further.

By its design, job evaluation appears to be the embodiment of the mechanisms posited by economic theories. As such, it offers a particularly interesting compensation system for social research, a compensation system explicitly designed to reflect the models usually tested. If it actually operates as it is intended to, then one would expect the previous predictions to be even more strongly supported in 1972 and 1975, after the onset of job evaluation, than in previous years under the less systematic and less rationally determined traditional practices.

CHAPTER 5

The Structural Differentiation of Employees and Its Amplifying Effects on Earnings*

Introduction

In explaining earnings differences, economists have focused on the way individuals' attributes influence their earnings. Human capital theory provides a theoretical justification of such analyses. It posits that individuals possess personal assets that contribute to their productive capacity, and these assets are called *human capital*. Attributes such as education, training, experience, and ability contribute to individuals' human capital and, as a result, to their economic value; and it is individual differences in the economic value of individuals' human capital which determine inequalities of earnings.

Human capital theory, particularly as it is formulated by Mincer (1974) posits that individuals play a very active part in defining their

*This chapter was written with the collaboration of Frank P. Romo.

137

own earnings. The differentiation of employees' earnings is due to their differential decisions to invest in themselves (the training they choose to acquire). According to this formulation, higher ability individuals often sacrifice the possibility of receiving higher initial earnings in order to acquire more training. These investments in training lead to even greater subsequent advantages in the human capital they possess and thus to greater subsequent earnings. In other words, individuals' decisions about self-investments are the primary cause of the increased variation in earnings over time.

This theory is elegant in its abstraction and simplicity, and it is powerful in the range of its explanatory power. However, observers of firms have argued that such a theory is too simple, for it ignores the complexities of organizations (Lester 1946; Doeringer and Piore 1971). Moreover, empirical evidence on career attainment processes over time, which would be useful for testing this or competing theories, have generally been lacking.

The social structural theory presented here suggests another view. It posits that the organizational selection system assigns new employees to different entry jobs and that early job assignments have a strong impact on subsequent attainments. Social structural theories vary in the way they interpret these forces. Some versions indicate that status attainments have effects because of their symbolic meanings and their effects on interpersonal interaction (Meyer and Rowan 1977; Collins 1979); other versions suggest that their effects are due to administrative rules or practices regulating career attainment (Doeringer and Piore 1971; Spilerman 1977). Thurow (1975) comes closest to using the human capital conception to explain structural effects in positing that jobs determine human capital because they confer training, but, as a result, they also determine employees' later careers. Regardless of interpretation, social structural theories concur in contending that early social attainments have strong effects on individuals' later career trajectories.

Thus, instead of explaining differentiation in terms of assumed individual self-investments, the social structural theory contends that there is never a possibility of differentiation not occuring, regardless of what actions individuals take. Even if no individuals chose to make additional self-investments, individuals will still be put in different jobs from the outset; and these jobs offer different career trajectories regardless of individuals' investments (within reasonable limits).[1] While

[1]Of course, not every individual in the better jobs may follow the highest subsequent career trajectory, and the better jobs might not lead to higher trajectories for anyone if no one in the better jobs satisfies minimum job requirements. However, social structural

human capital theory posits that individuals' decisions about self-investments determine their attainment, the social structural theory posits that jobs have the primary influence on individuals' attainments.

Social structural theory also differs from human capital theory in suggesting that the most important selections occur at the outset. Human capital theory posits that employees' initial earnings show little variation and most of the variation in earnings only gradually appears over the first decade of employees' careers. Mincer attributes this "fanning-out" process to individuals' differential decisions to invest in themselves, and he stresses that the process is gradual. "Investments are spread out over time because the marginal cost curve of producing them is upward sloping within each period" (1974, p. 14). Consequently, the fanning out of earnings is a process which evolves over time rather than being predetermined from the outset.

In contrast, according to social structural theory, the important selections among individuals are made at the outset of their careers, these rankings remain stable over the rest of their careers, and any subsequent fanning out is only a magnification of the initial selections. In effect, the two theories suggest different timetables for the selections of individuals' ultimate career attainments. While social structural theory suggests that individuals' ultimate attainments are largely determined by initial attainments, human capital theory attributes more openness and less predictability to the process.

Finally, the two theories also differ in the kind of attainment they are trying to explain. Human capital theory focuses only on earnings attainment, and it has virtually nothing to say about jobs or job statuses. Social structural theory focuses on social status or authority levels, although it also contends that these social attainments are primary determinants of earnings. It is commonly assumed that these different kinds of attainment are so highly correlated that the two theories essentially explain the same outcomes, regardless of their emphasis. As shall become clear, although earnings and authority level are highly correlated in the data gathered in this study ($r = .82$), there are some very important differences in their determinants.

As might be expected, the two theories do not differ in their predictions about the effects of the most salient individual attributes. Education and work experience are key variables in all analyses of both theories, and the theories show consensus in their prediction about these; nor is this surprising, for these are salient in U.S. culture, and

---

theory assumes that, on average, early jobs will have an effect on later careers regardless of individuals' actions.

they are often explicit considerations in compensation policies. While one theory explains their effects in terms of human capital and the other in terms of status, as a practical matter, the most immediate reason for their influence is that rules and policies in labor contracts and bureaucratic procedures stipulate that education and experience are explicit bases of compensation. Obviously, education and experience effects alone will not provide a means of testing these theories.

In contrast, factors which are not explicit components of compensation policy are more interesting for empirical tests of the theories. Since the nature of their influence is not explicitly stated, their impact is more problematic, and the theories often have different interpretations of the reason for their impact and the kind of impact they will have. The present chapter analyzes two such factors which are not ordinarily matters of explicit compensation policy: age and college selectivity.

Age Effects

The influence of age as a status has long been recognized in sociology; however, until now, sociologists have not tried to incorporate the age status conception into models of economic attainment, but instead have tended to adopt an economic perspective which regards age solely as an indicator of experience. Economic theories (both marginal productivity and human capital theories) posit that employers offer greater salaries to employees with more experience because they are more productive, and they ignore the status properties of age.

However, earlier sociological work does suggest that age is a socially significant status in society and that it may have consequences for employees' careers in organizations. Observers of organizations have noted that informal norms seem to exist about age and, in particular, that a relatively young age (30–40 years) tends to be considered the cutoff point for an employee to be considered for career advancement in some organizations (Chinoy 1955; Martin and Strauss 1959). If age is an important influence on organizational careers, then traditional economic analyses of employees' earnings within firms (Weisbrod and Karpoff 1968; Wise 1975a; Halaby 1978) may have partially misconceptualized the meaning of age-derived experience variables or may have misspecified estimations of experience effects by ignoring age (see Klevmarken and Quigley 1976; Bartlett and Jencks 1978).

Chapter 3 has already shown that age influences promotions. However, that analysis is only a simple cross-sectional analysis, so it cannot separate age from cohort effects; nor can it completely separate age effects from the effects of experience (because of multicollinearity). The analysis presented in this chapter can separate these influences, and does so after controlling for a number of other influences.

It should be noted that the age variable used in these analyses, age of entry into the firm, is very similar to the variable that economists customarily use to reflect previous experience (that gained before joining the current employer). The calculation of the two variables is highly similar (*entry age* is age minus tenure; previous experience is age minus tenure minus years of education minus 5), and the two are likely to be highly—though not perfectly—correlated in most cases. The main difference here is a matter of context. This variable means something different in a single organizational hierarchy than it does in the open labor markets studied by survey data. As we shall see, the present findings clearly indicate a different pattern of results.

College Selectivity Effects

College effects have attracted the interest of social researchers, but they have been regarded in very different ways. According to human capital theory, graduates of "better" colleges attain greater socioeconomic success because these colleges are more selective and provide a better education. According to sociologists, "better" colleges have more successful graduates because these colleges confer greater status to their graduates and these status properties increase their graduates' chances of success (Kamens 1977; Mayer 1977; Collins 1979). Mayer (1977) contends that colleges actually have implicit "social charters" which sometimes give highly specific social statuses and career niches to their graduates.

Operationally, economists have measured college quality in terms of rankings of the selectivity of colleges, using Astin's (1965) scale, which is based on the average Scholastic Aptitude Test (SAT) score of enrolled undergraduates.[2] Economists interpret this ranking as a rough indicator of individuals' ability, assuming that individuals who attend more selective colleges are generally more able (see Weisbrod and Karpoff 1968; Wise 1975a). However, since more selective colleges are also

---

[2]It should be noted that the Astin scale was formulated in the early 1960s, while most of my sample graduated from college in the 1950s. It is possible that some colleges changed in student body composition after some of my sample members graduated. Although I have no systematic way to adjust for this possibility, my subjective impression is that the colleges which are most heavily represented in the sample would have ranked similarly over the previous decade.

likely to confer more status, sociologists can interpret this as a status scale (Karabel and McClelland, 1983). Of course, it is not an easy matter to decide between these interpretations.

However, empirical analyses can discern whether colleges affect job statuses and earnings, and, if the analyses are longitudinal, they can reveal the timing of these effects. As previously suggested, human capital theory suggests that ability affects earnings gradually over the first decade, so it would predict a gradually emerging effect of college selectivity. Social structural theory suggests that individual status attributes (like college status) affect attainments from the outset. To the extent that longitudinal analyses support one or the other prediction, they shall offer support to that theory and its interpretation of college selectivity.

College Status Effects versus College Selectivity Effects

Of course, although the previously described analyses test the two theories, they only help interpret college effects indirectly. A more direct test is only possible for cases in which colleges confer statuses that differ from their selectivity. The present sample includes two colleges which confer statuses that clearly depart from their selectivity. Including these colleges in these analyses as separate variables permits the analyses to investigate whether college status has different effects than college selectivity.

Sociological research suggests that organizations tend to develop shared cultures which give symbolic status meanings to many aspects of the organizational environment, including employee characteristics (Martin and Strauss 1959; Kanter 1977). If an organizational culture conferred additional status value to a few colleges, and if these socially important colleges had disproportionately greater effects than their selectivity would suggest, then this would raise doubts about whether college effects were entirely due to the ability of their alumni and would support the possibility that college effects were also due to the social status they confer.

The focus of the present analysis is on the ways that socially proximal colleges have impacts which differ from those predicted by the Astin scale. This study compares effects of two socially proximal colleges with the effects of other colleges of comparable selectivity (Astin ratings) to show the distinct effects of their socially proximal status.

Two colleges seem to have special status relationships in the corporation under study here. The two colleges are located geographically and socially close to the organization. The concept of social proximity has been developed elsewhere (Rosenbaum and Romo 1979). In the cases of these two colleges, they are both distinguished by the salience of their activities to the local community, the information exchange programs and consulting relationships that they offer the organization, the organization's additional recruiting efforts at these colleges, and the degree to which their graduates are represented in the management of the organization. On each of these dimensions, these two colleges have far stronger proximity to this organization than any other college from which employees come.

Obviously, there is no denying that this is an analysis of anomalous cases. Of course, that is always the situation when multivariate analysis separates the effects of highly correlated factors. The problem is exacerbated by considering only two anomalous cases. An alternative strategy would be to devise a scale for rating the social proximity of all colleges; however, the timing of effects is more difficult to discern with a scale than with single cases. Moreover, as a practical matter, it is not easy to rank all colleges on several dimensions of social proximity. Romo and Rosenbaum (1984) have found that a scale of geographical proximity has significant effects on attainments independent of college selectivity, but geographical proximity is not an exact counterpart of social proximity for a large corporation like this one. For these reasons and since the two colleges have far stronger social proximity than any others, only these two colleges are used here to reflect the theoretical construct of social proximity in these analyses.

The empirical question for this analysis is whether these colleges affect the earnings of an entering cohort to a greater extent than would be predicted by their Astin ratings. Such a finding would suggest that these colleges have particular status properties in addition to their educational quality properties. The two colleges are here called Prestige U, which is ranked at the top of the Astin scale (Astin 7), and State U, which is ranked in the middle of the Astin scale (Astin 4). The degree to which each has particular status effects which differ from their educational quality effects will be determined by comparisons of their graduates with those of other colleges with comparable Astin ratings.

Plan for this Chapter

The primary aims of this chapter and the ones following are to identify when attainments are differentiated, which individual attributes affect attainments, and how structural mechanisms independent of individual attributes affect career attainments over time. Although previous chapters are a source of hypotheses for these analyses, these multivariate analyses study the effects of structure independent of individual attributes and the ways that structure mediates the effects of individual attributes on later career attainments. These analyses examine the timing of effects on earnings and structural attainments, and the longitudinal analyses also investigate whether structural attainments have continuing influences on later attainments over time. Most central to an examination of economic theory, these analyses examine whether human capital theory misspecifies the earnings determination process by ignoring indicators of social structure. The present study uses data that are distinctive in the kinds of social structural indicators they possess and in that they are longitudinal over a long period, so that they permit analyses which previously have not been done.

These issues are not merely of theoretical interest; they have important practical implications. For instance, if occupational social structures are directly responsible for a large amount of the earnings variance, then the earnings distribution may be relatively unresponsive to changes in market factors or to changes in individuals' educational attainments unless the social structure is also altered. The issue of whether social structure precedes, and in some sense influences, earnings differences has crucial policy implications.

In order to compare the human capital and social structural theories, the present study compares the determinants of earnings and hierarchical level attainments for an entry cohort. Since the theories differ in their primary dependent variable, separate analyses with each dependent variable are done. Because the theories differ in their predictions about the timing of the impact of factors, these analyses are conducted longitudinally over a 13-year period so that changes in the impact of factors can be investigated.

Analysis

Setting, Sample, and Data

This study investigates employees' earnings and level attainments in the authority hierarchy of ABCO over a 13-year period from 1962 to 1975. The sample studied in this chapter is composed of the white male employees who entered ABCO during the decade between 1953 and

1962 and who remained with it through at least 1975.[3] This permits a longitudinal analysis of 13 years of career mobility for the cohort of 1612 employees who entered ABCO at roughly the same time. The present study only had use of personnel records for the years 1962, 1965, 1969, 1972, and 1975, permitting analyses of 3-year intervals for all but one period.

The focus on a single type of employee, white males, in effect controls for sex and race, and it permits analysis of the career patterns for the employee group which had the most career opportunity during the period under analysis. The earnings variation for females and minorities was much less, particularly in the earlier periods; consequently, including them in the analyses would have attenuated some of the effects of the factors considered here. Analyses of the earnings patterns of these groups will be presented in subsequent chapters.

The data for these analyses are taken from the computerized file of the complete personnel records of the corporation. The availability of actual personnel records makes the present research distinctive from most economic and sociological research and offers two important advantages. First, these personnel records offer valid and precise information on employees' salaries, level attainments in the organizational hierarchy, education, college attended, age, and years of experience in the corporation (tenure). Most research has been based on people's self-reports, and the possibilities of distortions or poor recollection are generally a cause of concern. In contrast, personnel records are systematically kept by the corporation's personnel department for the organization's own use, and consequently, extensive data-checking procedures are implemented to assure the accuracy of the information, since mistakes would have important implications for company personnel practices.

Second, these personnel records represent the complete universe of employees in the corporation. Most studies of organizations have had to rely on employees' cooperation, and less-than-perfect cooperation leads to incomplete information or possibly biased samples. For instance, Grusky's (1966) 75% responses rate (in the data Halaby [1978] used) is rather good as questionnaire response rates go; however, it does raise questions about the representativeness of the sample which cannot be completely settled. These data cover all employees in the

[3]This 10-year span for the cohort was necessary to have adequate numbers of employees from the different groups of colleges. In this tenure cohort, the age range was from 17 to 53, but 95% were in the age range 17–35. There is no reason to suspect that this cohort is unrepresentative, with the possible exception of their stability with the firm which will be discussed later. A 3-year cohort is analyzed in Chapter 6.

cohort studied here, and there is no missing information for any individual.

Of course, the use of personnel records does have its own limitations, primarily in omitting some information which a researcher might like to consider. In particular, the present records do not include information on starting salary, marital status, or actual years of education, which previous research has suggested to be worthy of consideration.

Nonetheless, these personnel records do offer a number of the most important indicators which have been used in previous research, and these are listed in the following.

Variables

EARNINGS   Employees' earnings in the company are indicated in the exact amount. There are several indicators in the file. The present research uses actual earnings, not merely base pay. This corporation has a system which pays employees *merit pay*—increased earnings above customary salary which is contingent on a supervisor's judgment about the employee's performance. This system is a particularly pertinent one for this analysis, because it explicitly attempts to implement the "pay-for-productivity" system which economists assume to exist. All analyses of earnings use the natural logarithm of earnings as the variable analyzed, with earnings being standardized to 1967 dollars, following the conventions in economic research. Unless otherwise noted, any mention of earnings as a variable will refer to these transformations throughout this and the following chapters.

TENURE   The corporation kept careful records of years of company experience (here called tenure). Any leaves of absence or other periods when the employee was not employed (except short illnesses) are subtracted from the indicator so that it accurately reflects how long the person has been employed with the firm. This indicator had important implications for retirement benefits, so it was carefully recorded and monitored.

ENTRY AGE   The age that employees entered the company can be easily computed as age minus tenure. This variable can be taken as an indication of an employee's age relative to that of others in his cohort. Since this study hypothesizes that age confers a social status to employees which has effects on their attainments independent of their tenure, entry age provides a convenient indicator of age which, unlike current age, is not highly correlated with tenure ($r = .14$) and consequently does not create problems of multicollinearity. As subsequently noted, this variable closely resembles, both in definition and in empirical correlation, a variable economists commonly use to represent work experience prior to joining the present employer. The reasons for choosing entry age rather than previous experience are noted in the introduction and in the discussion of results.

NON-B.A.   If an employee has a B.A. or B.S. from an accredited college, this variable has a value of 0; otherwise its value is 1. Anyone with more than a college degree is also coded as 0. All employees with less than a college degree are coded as 1. Although this could be a highly heterogeneous group, informants in the personnel department suggested that most employees probably have at least a high school diploma because company hiring practices encouraged, but did not require, a diploma. The "backwards" coding of this variable is done to permit the college variables (described later) to be added.

M.B.A.   The records indicate the highest degree held by employees. If an employee has a master's or higher degree (M.A., M.B.A., Ph.D., M.D., LL.B.) from an accredited university, this variable is coded to have a value of 1; otherwise its value is 0. Since over 80% of individuals with this level of degree held M.B.A.'s, it is designated "M.B.A."

COLLEGE STATUS   College status is represented by seven dummy variables in these analyses (except Appendix 5.A., where some analyses group categories further). All colleges attended by employees in this corporation are coded in terms of Astin's (1965) scale of college quality (discussed earlier). Each of the top four Astin categories are made into a separate dummy variable, and the lower three Astin categories are made into a single dummy variable because of the limited number of employees from those colleges. The two socially proximal colleges were left out of this coding and were made into separate dummy variables: Prestige U, a high-Astin college (Astin rating 7), and State U, a middle-Astin college (Astin rating 4). The analyses presented here omit the middle Astin category (rating 4) from the regressions so that the coefficients for all education dummy variables indicate the effects of that factor relative to the effects of the middle-ranked colleges on the Astin scale.

Analytic Strategy

Before beginning, some features of this sample should be noted. As already noted, this is the study of the earnings of a single cohort of employees who remain in a corporation at least 13 years. Because this study analyzes the earnings of a single cohort over time, many longitudinal comparisons are possible which have not been possible in most other comparable studies. However, a longitudinal analysis of employees in an organization necessarily limits analyses to employees who remain in the firm across the period studied. This makes the sample a somewhat more stable group of people than it would be if it were merely defined as employees present at a single point in time (as is the case with a simple cross-sectional study).

Determinants of Earnings in 1962

The regression of earnings on tenure, entry age, education, and college for 1962 is reported in Table 5.1. In contrast with studies using survey data which rarely explain as much as 40% of earnings variance, the present analysis explains nearly 73% of the variance. The present finding is quite comparable with findings of other studies of single firms which also explain large portions of the variance of earnings (Malkiel and Malkiel 1973; Wise 1975a; Halaby 1978; Rosenbaum 1980), and together these findings suggest this basic model is even more powerful when variations among different firms are removed.

Turning to the specific coefficients, analysis indicates that a college degree is an important component of earnings. Employees without a college degree have about 42% lower earnings than those with a college degree. The particular college an employee attends does not seem to make much difference on earnings, but an M.B.A. does add an additional 6.2% to earnings.[4]

Within this cohort, tenure has a significant influence on earnings, contributing an additional 6.2% per year to earnings. On average, this suggests a 62% difference in earnings between employees with the most and least tenure in this sample (since this is a 10-year cohort). Clearly employees receive very large earnings gains during their first decade in this corporation.

In contrast, entry age has minimal impact. Its coefficient is small and not significant. The range of entry ages in this cohort is rather large, from 17 to 53. However, the distribution is very skewed, with only 5% entering after age 35. The entry-age coefficient suggests that the entry-age variation in the 18-year span from 17 to 35 would produce a 1.8% difference in earnings.

---

[4]The reference category in this and in all following regressions (the omitted dummy variable) is actually employees who graduated from middle-Astin colleges (Astin 4), so that significant coefficients for college categories indicate that that category has a significantly different effect than Astin 4 colleges.

Table 5.1

Regression Coefficients for Ln(Earnings) for 1962–1975[a]

Variable	1962	1965	1969	1972	1975
Tenure[b]	.062*	.027*	.013*	.008*	.006*
	(.001)	(.001)	(.002)	(.002)	(.002)
Entry age	.001	−.005*	−.009*	−.011*	−.012*
	(.001)	(.001)	(.001)	(.001)	(.001)
Non-B.A.[b]	−.416*	−.382*	−.393*	−.363*	−.252*
	(.021)	(.021)	(.026)	(.027)	(.021)
M.B.A.[b]	.062*	.048	.013	.026	.034
	(.029)	(.037)	(.041)	(.041)	(.033)
Prestige U	.038	.106*	.116*	.171*	.197*
	(.035)	(.036)	(.046)	(.049)	(.043)
Astin 7	.032	.079*	.110*	.147*	.163*
	(.026)	(.026)	(.034)	(.035)	(.029)
Astin 6	.045	.046	.085	.135*	.144*
	(.034)	(.035)	(.045)	(.049)	(.042)
Astin 5	.029	.043	.066	.094*	.108*
	(.029)	(.029)	(.037)	(.039)	(.033)
State U	−.007	.044	.092*	.128*	.140*
	(.022)	(.028)	(.036)	(.037)	(.031)
Low Astin[b]	.010	.054	.093	.123	.141*
	(.032)	(.046)	(.059)	(.063)	(.056)
Constant[c]	8.854	9.219	9.559	9.766	9.699*
R^2 (%)	72.9	60.2	50.4	47.5	42.3

[a]Asterisk indicates coefficients that are significant at the .05 level. Standard errors for coefficients are indicated in parentheses.

[b]These variables change from year to year, and these regressions use independent variables for the same year as each dependent variable. The remaining independent variables did not change from year to year.

[c]Constant represents middle-Astin colleges (Astin 4).

Although research commonly finds that the lack of a college degree hurts earnings, these results are surprising in finding that the quality of college and entry age do not affect earnings.

Determinants of Earnings in Later Years

The same regression was repeated for this cohort's earnings attainments in 1965, 1969, 1972, and 1975 (Table 5.1).[5] The results indicate

[5]The only variables that required updating were earnings, tenure, M.B.A., non-B.A., State U, and low Astin. Between 1962 and 1975, 16 employees obtained a B.A., all at low-Astin colleges or State U. Although this is a small proportion of the sample (1%) and would not affect the findings greatly, these variables were updated for each period.

that the model becomes increasingly less effective in explaining earnings variance with each successive year studied. The explanatory power of these variables declines in each successive interval from the 73% explained in 1962 to 42% in 1975. It might be inferred that this decline reflects the emergence of other factors in the work situation which influence earnings, an inference supported by the fact that the largest decline (absolutely and proportionately) occurs in the first interval, and the next largest occurs in the second interval. It may be speculated that these background and superficial indicators of an employee's value (or human capital) may diminish in importance because the firm is becoming aware of better indicators of the employees' value (Spence 1974).

Consistent with this, the specific regression coefficients for tenure and M.B.A.'s show important declines. The coefficient for tenure declines in each interval from indicating a 6.2% increase per year of seniority in 1962 to a .6% increase per year in 1975. The finding is consistent with the findings of cross-sectional analyses which have indicated declining returns to experience after the first decade (see also Chapter 7).

The coefficient for M.B.A.'s also shows an important decline. This coefficient indicates a 6.2% increase in earnings for having an M.B.A. in 1962, but it drops to only 4.8% in the next period (1965), and it declines further thereafter. These small values in 1965 and thereafter are all insignificant, even in this large sample. Although an M.B.A. has immediate returns to these employees in terms of early salaries, this return seems to be short-lived, and it becomes insignificant in a very short time. This is precisely the kind of decline that would be predicted by signaling theory. An M.B.A. may be used to screen employee ability at the outset, but over time the organization places less reliance on it as employees become better known.

On the other hand, in the context of these declines, it is all the more striking that several variables show increasing impact on earnings over time. Almost all of the college variables increase in influence over this interval. There are some substantial increases among the higher-Astin colleges, including Prestige U; and the increases seem to be smaller among the lower-ranking colleges (the low-Astin category is the sole exception, for reasons discussed subsequently). Consequently, although the differences among the college coefficients are small and not significant in 1962, Prestige U and Astin 7 have become significant by

---

Between 1962 and 1975, 7 employees obtained an M.B.A., and the M.B.A. variable was updated to reflect employees' degree for each period.

1965, and Astin 6, Astin 5, and State U have also become significant by 1972 and 1975.

The prediction that colleges will affect earnings only according to their Astin score, which is suggested by economic theories, is not confirmed here. Prestige U has greater influence than its corresponding Astin 7 category (a nonsignificant difference), and State U has greater influence than its corresponding Astin 4 category (a significant difference after 1965).[6] Indeed, State U has larger coefficients than the colleges in the next higher Astin category (Astin 5). Apparently the colleges which are socially closer to the employing organization confer greater earnings benefits than their Astin rating alone would suggest. These findings seem to suggest that closer colleges have a specially valued status in this organization.[7]

The other variable which shows increasing influence over time is entry age. Although entry age had an insignificant .1% per year influence on earnings in 1962, it had a significant −.5% per year influence on earnings by 1965; and its negative influence increased further in the following intervals. By 1975, employees lost 1.2% earnings for each additional year of age. This is not merely the effect of the "outlying" ages; for when the 5% of employees who entered over age 35 is excluded, the regression coefficients are minimally reduced. A one-standard-deviation (4.9 years) increase in entry age leads to more than a 5% decrease in earnings. Even after controlling for education and tenure, entry age has a significant influence on earnings.

The continuing influence of these factors is best seen by analyzing their effects after controlling for individuals' previous earnings. In such an analysis, a reversal of influence might be expected as the imperfections of initial indicators are discovered and corrected. The most striking feature of this analysis is the high stability of individuals' relative earnings over time; so that previous earnings have an enormous influence on later earnings, and the influence of all other factors is diminished considerably (Table 5.2). However, despite the enormous change

---

[6]Since Astin 4 is the reference category for this regression, the significant coefficient for State U indicates that it is significantly different than its Astin category. When the regression is repeated with Astin 7 as the reference category, Prestige U does not have a significant coefficient.

[7]Interestingly, the one aberration in these findings may also support this interpretation. The low-Astin colleges tend to have a greater effect on earnings than do the middle-Astin colleges. This may indicate a nonlinear effect of the Astin score; however, this seems unlikely. A more plausible interpretation arises from the fact that most of the low-Astin colleges are local so that the low-Astin coefficient may reflect a positive "local effect" along with a negative "low-Astin effect." Unfortunately, there are too few individuals from nonlocal, low-Astin colleges to analyze these effects separately here.

Table 5.2

Regression Coefficients for Ln(Earnings) for 1962–1975, Controlling for Earnings in
Previous Period[a]

Variable	1962[b]	1965	1969	1972	1975
Tenure[c]	.062*	−.027*	−.015*	−.004*	−.002*
	(.001)	(.001)	(.001)	(.001)	(.001)
Entry age	.001	−.006*	−.005*	−.002*	−.002*
	(.001)	(.000)	(.001)	(.000)	(.000)
Non-B.A.[c]	−.416*	−.046*	−.020	.015	.056*
	(.021)	(.014)	(.017)	(.012)	(.007)
M.B.A.[c]	.062*	−.008	.006	.011	.008
	(.029)	(.018)	(.019)	(.017)	(.010)
Prestige U	.038	.045*	−.020	.047*	.031*
	(.035)	(.021)	(.028)	(.021)	(.013)
Astin 7	.032	.023	.001	.030*	.020*
	(.026)	(.015)	(.041)	(.015)	(.009)
Astin 6	.045	−.023	.010	.041*	.013
	(.034)	(.020)	(.032)	(.020)	(.013)
Astin 5	.029	−.009	−.006	.019	.012
	(.029)	(.016)	(.019)	(.017)	(.010)
State U	−.007	.022	.020	.029	.013
	(.022)	(.016)	(.021)	(.016)	(.009)
Low Astin[c]	.010	.018	.010	.021	.019
	(.032)	(.025)	(.032)	(.027)	(.017)
Ln(earnings)[c] pre-vious period		.873*	1.039*	.983*	.882*
		(.015)	(.019)	(.012)	(.007)
Constant[d]	8.854	1.794	.081	.418	1.131
R^2 (%)	72.9	87.0	82.8	90.4	94.8

[a]Asterisk coefficients that are significant at the .05 level. Standard errors for coefficients are indicated in parentheses.

[b]1962 regression is without previous earnings. It is repeated from Table 5.1 for comparison purposes.

[c]These variables change from year to year, and these regressions use independent
variables for the same year as each dependent variable. The remaining independent
variables did not change from year to year.

[d]Constant represents middle-Astin colleges (Astin 4).

in these coefficients, there is very little indication of the reversal in
coefficients predicted by signaling theory. Only one variable, tenure,
reverses its influence on 1965 earnings from the influence it had on
1962 earnings.[8] Indeed, on the contrary, many variables maintain and
strengthen their 1962 influence in 1965. Not having a college degree,

[8]Actually, the coefficients for several variables change signs, but this is the only case
for which coefficients in both directions are insignificant.

which was highly negative in 1962, has a still larger negative influence on 1965 earnings, net of 1962 earnings. Prestige U and Astin 7 had modest (though insignificant) positive influences on 1962 earnings, and they increase that positive influence on later earnings (except in one interval). Entry age, which had no initial influence, takes on a negative influence in the next interval which continues in the following intervals.

In sum, earnings in this cohort's early years is influenced by only some of the factors which ultimately affect later earnings. Tenure and M.B.A.'s have their greatest influence at the outset and then have progressively less influence over time. However, entry age and the various colleges begin with negligible influence at the outset and then acquire increasingly great influence over time. In terms of these factors, the selection process is a gradually incremental one.

Determinants of Level Allocations

Although the most commonly studied status differences in contemporary sociological literature are between occupational groups, the hierarchy of levels to which jobs are assigned is the most salient manifestation of status differences in organizations. Observers of organizations commonly note that individuals are conferred status according to the job they hold, and the most salient component of their job status is the job's position in the oganizational hierarchy (Martin and Strauss 1959; Goldner 1965).

An employee's job level indicates the way that the employee's job is ranked in the organizational hierarchy. Like occupational status, it is a value ranking conditioned by job attributes. Unlike occupational status, it is an official and visible ranking, which is reflected in very concrete ways in the organization (amount of work, space, authority, autonomy, etc.). The organizational hierarchy has eight main levels: nonmanagement, foreman, lower management, middle management, upper middle management, lower top management, vice president, and president. The present sample includes employees in the first five of these levels.

Repeating the simple regressions from Table 5.1 and taking level as the dependent variable instead of earnings, the results obtained are somewhat different (Table 5.3). Some coefficients in the 1962 level regression are quite similar to those in the earnings regression: Tenure has a strong positive influence, and the absence of a college degree has a strong negative influence.

Table 5.3

Regression Coefficients for Levels for 1962–1975[a]

Variable	1962	1965	1969	1972	1975
Tenure[b]	.054*	.046*	.032*	.022*	.018*
	(.004)	(.005)	(.006)	(.007)	(.007)
Entry age	.009*	.009*	−.003	−.010*	−.012*
	(.002)	(.003)	(.004)	(.004)	(.004)
Non-B.A.[b]	−.613*	−1.014*	−1.397*	−1.258*	−1.213*
	(.073)	(.078)	(.097)	(.100)	(.085)
M.B.A.[b]	.309*	.379*	−.016	.064	.154
	(.114)	(.137)	(.800)	(.143)	(.136)
Prestige U	.616*	.818*	.681*	.737*	.828*
	(.120)	(.134)	(.171)	(.182)	(.178)
Astin 7	.347*	.612*	.630*	.674*	.759*
	(.089)	(.098)	(.124)	(.129)	(.120)
Astin 6	.052	.109	.403*	.609*	.696*
	(.116)	(.130)	(.169)	(.180)	(.174)
Astin 5	.213*	.386*	.377*	.424*	.469*
	(.098)	(.109)	(.138)	(.144)	(.137)
State U	.189*	.483*	.434*	.542*	.622*
	(.093)	(.103)	(.131)	(.137)	(.128)
Low Astin[b]	−.028	−.086	.410	.399	.428
	(.617)	(.157)	(.219)	(.234)	(.233)
Constant[c]	1.445	1.498	2.412	2.670	2.673
R^2 (%)	37.0	53.4	51.5	45.9	46.0

[a]Asterisk indicates coefficients that are significant at the .05 level. Standard errors for coefficients are indicated in parentheses.

[b]These variables change from year to year, and these regressions use independent variables for the same year as each dependent variable. The remaining independent variables did not change from year to year.

[c]Constant represents middle-Astin colleges (Astin 4).

However, while an M.B.A., entry age, and college have modest or negligible influences on 1962 earnings, they have large and significant influences on *levels* in that year. Indeed, among the various college variables, Prestige U graduates surpass the level attainments of graduates of middle-Astin colleges by about the same amount as middle-Astin college graduates surpass the attainments of nongraduates.

The differential college effect on levels helps to clarify one of the more perplexing difficulties raised by the preceding earnings analysis: the lack of initial college effects on earnings. Economic and sociological theories predict an initial effect, yet no earnings differences among colleges were discerned. Particularly perplexing was the subsequent emergence of college effects. Although human capital theory can predict this emergence by assuming that the abilities and skills of individuals become manifest only after experience, social structural theories like internal labor market theory (Doeringer and Piore 1977) and credentials theory (Collins 1979) posit social selection processes which operate from the outset, and selection distinctions which are not made initially but which emerge subsequently are difficult to explain by these theories.

The present findings support the predictions of these theories in showing that colleges have differential effects on levels from the outset. Although this organization does not differentiate initial earnings as a function of colleges, it does allocate graduates of different colleges to different levels from the outset, which in turn could contribute to the subsequent earnings differences observed here.

Furthermore, not only do college effects occur at the outset, but further analyses also indicate that *most* of the college effects on levels come at this time. When the preceding regressions are repeated to control for previous level, the analyses suggest that the college effects have their strongest influence in the initial periods (Table 5.4). Although tenure, entry age, and lack of a B.A. have large net influences through most of the later periods (the non-B.A. coefficient becomes insignificant in the last period), most of the college variables have their influences on levels in the two initial periods and thereafter have minimal (net) influences. Prestige U, State U, and the highest-Astin colleges have large positive influences on the 1962 level and large additional positive influences on the 1965 level (net of the 1962 level), but these colleges have no further significant influences net of the previous level in subsequent years.

This does not mean that the graduates of these colleges stop receiving advantages; the gross influence of these colleges continues to be great (Table 5.3). What it does indicate is that there is no further evidence of direct influences in the later periods. The direct college influences can only be discerned in the early periods. The advantages they receive in subsequent periods are largely transmitted by the operation of the level system in *preserving* their early level allocations. The level system effectively preserves the advantages of the initially influential colleges, and it does so in a way that does not allow their advantages to be eroded.[9]

[9]The anomalous finding that Prestige U loses some of its advantage between 1965 and 1969 (as reflected by the $-.099$ coefficient in 1969; Table 5.4) may be because the firm was experiencing considerable growth during that period and may have been less restrictive in allocating promotions. However, it must be noted that this coefficient is not significant and it only reflects a decrease in advantages relative to other categories. As Table 5.3 makes plain, Prestige U graduates still fare much better than graduates of other colleges in absolute terms (see Chapter 7 for further analysis of this issue).

Table 5.4

Regression Coefficients for Levels for 1962–1975, Controlling for Levels in Previous Period[a]

Variable	1962[b]	1965	1969	1972	1975
Tenure[c]	.054*	.002	−.007	−.008*	−.004*
	(.004)	(.004)	(.005)	(.004)	(.002)
Entry age	.009*	−.002	−.011*	−.008*	−.002*
	(.002)	(.002)	(.003)	(.002)	(.001)
Non-B.A.[c]	−.613*	−.584*	−.607*	−.004	.008
	(.073)	(.055)	(.076)	(.231)	(.023)
M.B.A.[c]	.309*	.165	−.101	.056	.039
	(.114)	(.094)	(.113)	(.079)	(.034)
Prestige U	.616*	.236*	−.099	.073	.046
	(.120)	(.094)	(.128)	(.094)	(.046)
Astin 7	.347*	.248*	.028	.057	.052
	(.089)	(.069)	(.089)	(.068)	(.030)
Astin 6	.052	−.022	.220	.204*	.059
	(.116)	(.070)	(.127)	(.095)	(.043)
Astin 5	.213*	.136	−.040	.040	.010
	(.098)	(.075)	(.126)	(.073)	(.034)
State U	.189*	.253*	−.061	.106	.041
	(.093)	(.072)	(.096)	(.073)	(.032)
Low Astin[c]	−.028	−.138	.393*	−.016	−.011
	(.617)	(.117)	(.163)	(.924)	(.058)
Previous level[c]	—	.823*	.851*	.922*	.998*
		(.020)	(.024)	(.014)	(.006)
Constant[d]	1.445	.759	1.375	.592	.134
R² (%)	37.0	77.8	72.9	84.9	96.7

[a]Asterisk indicates coefficients that are significant at the .05 level. Standard errors for coefficients are indicated in parentheses.

[b]1962 regression is without previous level. It is repeated from Table 5.4 for comparison purposes.

[c]These variables change from year to year, and these regressions use independent variables for the same year as each dependent variable. The remaining independent variables did not change from year to year.

[d]Constant represents middle-Astin colleges (Astin 4).

Although the second-echelon colleges (Astin 6) come to have large and significant influences, their influences emerge later. This later emergence is likely to be related to their lesser effects, and it would also predict a lower maximum attainment of these colleges since later upward mobility has been found to be associated with lower career ceilings (Chapter 2). Moreover, the present regressions suggest support for this inference as well, for the strong negative coefficients for entry age in the later periods would mean that employees who get late benefits from college are simultaneously getting greater penalties because of their age.

As in the analyses for earnings, the most important influence on level attainment is one's attainment in the preceding period. Level allocations are quite stable, and they become increasingly stable as this entering cohort remains with the firm. As Table 5.4 indicates, a one-level difference between employees in 1962 is reduced on average to a .823 level difference by 1965; and over time the amount that existing level differences are changed becomes progressively less so that by 1972, a one-level difference in 1969 is only reduced to a .922 level difference by 1972.

This stability is a stability of relative position, not absolute position. This cohort is rapidly advancing in the level hierarchy over this period. As the large constant terms indicate, the average level advance net of previous level attainment for the residual category representing middle-Astin college graduates is over three-fourths (.759) of a level between 1962 and 1965, over one and one-third (1.375) levels between 1965 and 1969, and over one-half a level (.592) between 1969 and 1972. Therefore, even as this cohort is experiencing large advances up the level hierarchy, previous level attainments preserve employees' rank order relative to others in their cohort.

The most obvious conclusion to come from these findings is that levels and earnings operate in different ways, and different processes may account for them. In particular, different colleges have immediate effects on levels, while their effects on earnings only gradually emerge. The early selection processes described by social structural theory (Berg 1971; Meyer 1977; Collins 1979) seem to be suggested in these level analyses, while the gradual emergence of the influence of skills and abilities described by human capital theory is suggested by the earnings analyses.

However, the finding that college effects on levels precede their effects on earnings suggests the possibility that part of the earnings differences may be derived from the early level allocations. When graduates of better colleges are given initial status advantages in the form of higher-level jobs, albeit without initial salary advantages, this may be providing the initial salary opportunities and conditions that will foster subsequent salary advantages. The early higher levels may be mediating the influence of colleges on later earnings.

As in the analysis of later earnings, the early college effect on levels is not merely due to college quality. State U has significantly greater influence on 1962 level than the other colleges of comparable quality (the Astin-4 residual category). Similarly, Prestige U has much greater influence on 1962 level than the other high-quality colleges. This is not to say that college quality is unimportant, for Astin 7 has a large and significant initial influence and the other high-Astin categories become significant in later years. However, college selectivity does not fully account for the college effects. Some very large and important effects can be explained only by the the special status of socially proximal colleges.

Of course, early status advantages do not necessarily guarantee subsequent earnings advantages, or even subsequent level advantages: The initial level advantages of the employees who entered at an older age and with an M.B.A. were quickly eliminated in later periods. That these advantages are completely erased for employees with an M.B.A. and even reversed for older entrants suggests that the process is more than merely a correction for early screening mistakes. Presumably, such poor predictors would not be used as screening criteria in the first place. These findings probably indicate that level attainment may sometimes be only a temporary reward to recruit employees with particular kinds of experience or training, but the value of this experience or training soon loses its relatively higher status value and never shows up in terms of subsequently greater earnings or level attainments.

While colleges' initial relationships to levels are similar to their subsequent relationships to earnings, the initial relationship of entry age and M.B.A.'s to levels and the subsequent relationship of each to earnings are not similar. This raises the question of the relationship of the two processes which have been analyzed separately until now. To what extent are levels related to earnings? To what extent could the relationship between individual characteristics and levels also account for the relationship between individual characteristics and earnings? To what extent are individual characteristics related to earnings, independent of levels?

A Two-Stage Earnings Determination Process

If the analysis of the relationship of these two processes is to be more than a statistical description, then it is necessary to devise a way to conceptualize the relationship. Labor economists have provided the rudiments of such a conceptualization in their description of "wage structures" or "wage contours" as determinants of wages. As Thurow notes, "the analysis of the labor economist is closer to the sociologist's analysis of relative deprivation than it is to the analysis of the microeconomist. Interdependent preferences and norms of industrial justice influence wages" (1975, p. 53). The status differences associated with different levels and the normative beliefs about the greater responsibility at higher levels in an organization would seem to be prototypical examples of the kind of normative beliefs and equity considerations which might stratify earnings into wage structures.

Other factors associated with levels could also influence salaries. For instance, a Weberian perspective would suggest that salaries have an authority-maintenance function in organizations, with salaries being adjusted to convey the relative authority of employees. By this explanation, salaries are given, not as compensation, but as concrete and visible symbols of legitimacy to enhance the authority of the position (Collins 1975, Chap. 6; Kluegel 1978; Robinson and Kelley 1979; Wright 1978).[10]

By this view, individuals go through a two-stage process that determines their earnings. First they are allocated to a level (specifically, a particular job which is categorized at a particular level in the organizational hierarchy). Since salary ranges are assigned to these levels, this first stage effectively determines a salary range for individuals.

In the second stage, individuals are assigned a particular salary within the range of salaries specified for the level. At this stage, individuals are no longer being judged relative to all others in the firm, for the range of salaries is already determined for the employees at each level. Rather, individuals are judged relative to their immediate peers in the same level.

This two-stage model is quite close to the actual salary determination practices which are described in the management literature and which are applied in many firms. As noted in Chapter 4, management compensation specialists have developed a practice of "job evaluation" that rates jobs on a number of dimensions, generally including status, authority, responsibility, etc. and that assigns the jobs to levels and to associated salary ranges on the basis of a weighted sum of these ratings (see Sibson 1974; Henderson 1976). In other words, job evaluation systems effectively stratify jobs into distinct levels and provide ways of assigning salary ranges to these levels. According to this literature, individuals' salaries are determined first by the evaluation of their jobs (and the associated salary range) and then by their performance and qualifications relative to those of others in the same job or level. Many governmental civil service systems have implemented two-stage pro-

---

[10]Marginal productivity theory would predict that these status considerations would be eliminated by market competition. However, if productivity cannot be judged, and if all competitors share the belief in these status considerations; then competition may not occur in this sector of the labor market.

cedures similar to this, as have many large and middle-sized corporations.

This two-stage model requires some changes in how the earnings determination process in organizations has been conceptualized thus far in this chapter. Earnings have been portrayed as a function of individual characteristics in a one-stage process; and, in so doing, two separate processes were subsumed into an over-simplified single descriptive analysis. However, this model ignores the job evaluation system and its associated level system, which together stratify some of the variation in salaries according to the nature and qualities of jobs, not according to the characteristics and abilities of the individuals who fill them.

Thus, instead of a one-stage model which explains salaries on the basis of individual characteristics and capacities, a two-stage model is now posited: One component of individuals' salaries is determined by the level to which an individual is allocated, and a second component is determined by salary evaluations of the individual within that job. Both stages may be functions of individual characteristics and capabilities, but the two components are conceptually and empirically separate processes, and they may be influenced by particular individual characteristics in different ways and at different times.

In the present analysis, the structurally determined component of salaries is conceived as being the result of the level hierarchy of the organization. Of course, this is a simplifying assumption: It ignores other selection systems which may also contribute to the salary structure,[11] and it ignores antecedent selection and evaluation processes which may contribute to the nature and operation of the level hierarchy. However, for present purposes, an understanding of the two-stage model is attempted through a description of the operation of the level selection system as a distinct system, the ways that the level selection system contributes to the salary structure, and the ways that individual characteristics influence salaries independent of the level system.

The analyses required for the first stage in examining the influences of personal characteristics on levels have already been conducted. The second stage calls for analysis of the influence of levels and personal characteristics on earnings.

The analysis is conducted by adding the level variable to the previous regression of personal characteristics on earnings (Table 5.5). The level coefficient is quite large, and it brings the explained variation of

[11]Finer levels of analysis are possible (see Chapter 6).

Table 5.5

Regression Coefficients for Ln(Earnings) for 1962–1972, Controlling for Current Level[a]

Variable	1962	1965	1969	1972	1975
Tenure[b]	.056*	.019*	.006*	.003*	.002*
	(.001)	(.001)	(.001)	(.001)	(.001)
Entry age	.000	−.006*	−.009*	−.009*	−.009*
	(.001)	(.001)	(.001)	(.001)	(.000)
Non-B.A.[b]	−.353*	−.221*	−.085*	−.062*	.005
	(.020)	(.018)	(.016)	(.013)	(.010)
M.B.A.[b]	.029	−.012	.016	.011	.001
	(.031)	(.027)	(.023)	(.020)	(.016)
Prestige U	−.026	−.023	−.034	−.005	.021
	(.036)	(.030)	(.028)	(.016)	(.021)
Astin 7	−.004	.018	−.029	−.014	.002
	(.231)	(.022)	(.020)	(.017)	(.014)
Astin 6	.040	.028	−.003	−.011	−.003
	(.032)	(.028)	(.150)	(.025)	(.020)
Astin 5	.007	−.019	−.017	−.007	.009
	(.022)	(.024)	(.022)	(.016)	(.016)
State U	−.027	−.033	−.004	−.002	.008
	(.026)	(.023)	(.447)	(.447)	(.015)
Low Astin[b]	.013	.068	.003	.027	.050
	(.329)	(.037)	(.359)	(.030)	(.027)
Present level	.104*	.158*	.220*	.239*	.212*
	(.007)	(.005)	(.004)	(.003)	(.003)
Constant[c]	8.735	9.016	9.027	9.125	9.132
R^2 (%)	76.4	73.9	83.3	88.5	86.7

[a]Asterisk indicates coefficients that are significant at the .05 level. Standard errors for coefficients are indicated in parentheses.

[b]These variables change from year to year, and these regressions use independent variables for the same year as each dependent variable. The remaining independent variables did not change from year to year.

[c]Constant represents middle-Astin colleges (Astin 4).

the previous earnings regressions up to 74–89%. Indeed, the level coefficient increases over time so that it explains increasing amounts of the variance, while the individual characteristics alone explain increasingly less (Table 5.1). The level to which an employee is allocated has a large influence on earnings, even after controlling for individual characteristics; and this influence increases over time.

The influences of most personal characteristics on earnings are markedly reduced after controlling for level. Although entry age retains much of its influence on earnings when level is controlled, tenure and non-B.A. have much smaller influence, particularly in the later periods. By 1969 and 1972, the greater part of their influence on earnings is eliminated when level is controlled. Specifically, over four-fifths of the influence of having a college degree and over three-fifths of the influence of tenure on 1972 earnings are eliminated when level is controlled. Presumably, the primary influences of these factors would seem to be on level allocations in these later periods, an inference supported by the previous finding that they do have large influences on levels (Table 5.3).

However, even more striking is the complete disappearance of differential college effects when levels are controlled. Unlike tenure and non-B.A., which retain some influence, none of the college categories has an influence that is significantly different from that of the middle-Astin (residual) category in any year. Moreover, the coefficients are so small that no other comparisons suggest noteworthy differences between colleges either. It is intriguing that the coefficients for the formerly important college groups (Prestige U, State U, and the high-Astin colleges) are actually negative, suggesting a slight and nonsignificant tendency for them to be underpaid relative to graduates of middle-Astin colleges at the same level and with the same tenure and entry age. Perhaps this is because these individuals are relatively less productive. However, although the coefficients are persistent, they are not significant, and one cannot make much of them.

The central conclusion to emerge from these findings is that the various colleges, which have very substantial influences on earnings— particularly in the later years—have virtually no influence independent of levels. In other words, the level system embodies precisely that component of earnings variation that colleges explain.

Thus, in a model in which level is allowed to mediate the influence of individual characteristics on earnings, these findings indicate that very little of the influence of entry age on earnings is affected. Entry age has a negative influence on both levels and earnings (in the later periods), but controlling for levels does not reduce its influence on earnings very much. On the other hand, these findings indicate that levels mediate most of the influence of tenure and non-B.A., and they mediate virtually all of the influence of the various colleges.

Conclusions

When combined with the results of the previous analyses, these findings reveal some important characteristics of the level system and its operation. Furthermore, they provide some strong evidence for concluding that the level classifications are indicators of a real system, that this system operates in ways which are distinct from those of earnings, and that this system has an important influence in mediating the effect of individual characteristics on earnings. Several aspects of the present findings support these conclusions:

The progression of individuals from level to level seems to operate by some clear processes. Individuals' level attainments at any period are strongly influenced by their previous level attainments. This is not merely a matter of nonmobility, for the actual attainments in this cohort increase dramatically over these intervals. Despite large amounts of mobility, the employees who had attained the highest levels in one period tend to be at the highest levels in the next period. The individual characteristics that influence early level allocations are built into the level system and preserved into the future. For instance, the favored colleges affect initial levels and give an additional benefit between 1962 and 1965. Thereafter, their effect is carried forward into later periods without any further additional impact. Thus individuals are systematically allocated to these level classifications on the basis of some criteria and not others, these selections systematically operate at some times and not at later times, and individuals are systematically transferred between level classifications from one time to the next. These patterns suggest that the level classifications are indicators of a real system.

This level system seems to operate somewhat differently than the earnings system, and in some cases to make selections which are only subsequently manifest in earnings differences. In particular, the preferred colleges affect levels earlier than they affect earnings. If the level system is conceived as having a mediating effect, it is not a simple simultaneous process, but a lagged process. The level system does not immediately pass along the college effect in 1962. Rather it responds to the favored colleges very early, and it transfers these college effects to earnings at a later time.

The level system seems to be an amplifying system for increasing college effects even after they stop having direct effects on levels or earnings. Perhaps the most striking aspect of these findings is that colleges have increasingly large influences on *earnings* over time (Tables 5.1 and 5.2), yet they have no additional direct effects on *levels* after 1965 (Table 5.4) and no direct effects on earnings independent of levels (Table 5.5). The mechanism seems quite automatic; the level system assures that graduates of preferred colleges continually receive even greater earnings, although colleges have no direct influence on earnings (net of level). The level system does this by making a one-level difference have greater effects on earnings as one moves up the level hierarchy. Although promotions are distributed among the graduates of various colleges fairly evenly after 1965 (Table 5.4), the graduates of favored colleges have already received large level advantages before this, so their advantages are preserved by the same amount. However, for this cohort, a one-level difference in 1972 means an earnings advantage that is over 50% greater than the earnings advantage accompanying the same one-level difference in 1965 (Table 5.5). Consequently, by keeping the same amount of level advantage while moving up the hierarchy, the graduates of the favored colleges receive large earnings advantages because of the salary structure of the level hierarchy, although their colleges are no longer having any direct effects on levels or on earnings independent of levels. By this process, the level system can operate quite separately from the earnings system and can pass on its selections to the earnings system in later periods.

The level system can explain much of the influence of individual characteristics on earnings. When a causal model is posited in which levels mediate the influence of individual characteristics on earnings, analysis indicates that levels mediate most of the influence of tenure and non-B.A. on earnings. Similarly, although the various colleges have large effects on earnings which appear at diverse times and which gradually emerge over time, they have virtually no influence on earnings independent of their influence on levels.

Human capital theory does relatively well at explaining the gradually emerging and gradually increasing influence of many of the individual characteristics on earnings in a one-stage model. However, the analyses also suggest some reasons for doubting the one-stage model, and human capital theory fares much less well in the two-stage model. Human capital theory has only minimal value in explaining the determinants of level attainment. Its prediction of gradually emerging and gradually increasing influences does not hold for levels, which show initially large college effects and a sudden discontinuation of additional college effects. Since levels explain the greatest portion of earnings variance, the human capital theory has minimal explanatory value if one accepts the two-stage model.

Although structural theory does poorly at explaining earnings in a one-stage analysis, it does very well at explaining level selections, the first stage of the two-stage model. The large initial effects of high-Astin colleges on levels and the sudden disappearance of their net effects on levels strongly support the structural view of educational credentials having immediate effects due to status considerations, not delayed effects due to performance considerations. Indeed, nearly all of the high-Astin college effects on levels come at the outset, and subsequent changes in effects on earnings are due to the level system. The fact that these effects are largely captured by the organization's status system may be interpreted as even stronger evidence for considering the high-Astin college effects to be arising from their status properties.

Of course, since this study is limited to a single organization, it is not easy to know how generalizable these findings may be. It would be difficult to perform comparable studies of labor markets in large regions because of the difficulty of obtaining comparable measures of level attainment. It is even difficult to know to what extent these findings are generalizable to other organizations. The fact that the procedures advocated by the employee-compensation literature are very similar to the model used in these analyses provides reason for accepting the model tested here, although these considerations do not specify particular coefficients. The generalizability of the particular coefficients obtained here cannot be ascertained without further replications.

The particular coefficients are consistent with those of the few previous studies which have considered the relationship of levels to earnings (Malkiel and Malkiel 1973; Halaby 1978). However, the present study, in considering a more diverse sample (in terms of education, occupation, and level attainments) and in considering additional independent variables (entry age and colleges), is not exactly comparable to those studies.

Although problems of inferring generalizability are created by focusing on a single organization, this approach has permitted a detailed analysis of the social entity in which earnings are determined and careers defined. It has permitted this study to investigate some of the status characteristics of individuals which influence career attainment and to discern some of the organizational processes which determine earnings and define career attainment. While the details may differ in other settings, the general ways that the organizational level hierarchy structures and defines limits for career attainment are likely to be generalizable beyond this corporation. Although analysts of stratification may have difficulty in studying such mechanisms using the survey methods customarily employed in stratification research, the possibility that comparable mechanisms underlie many stratification phenomena in social institutions cannot be ignored.

This analysis also complements White's (1970a) analysis of vacancy movements in hierarchies, for it shows the net results of vacancy-chain processes and organizational selection processes. Moreover, like White's analysis, this analysis suggests that the operation of the hierarchical structure is fundamental in defining careers in organizations.

The implications for policy reform in organizations are clear. Reforms to improve career opportunities within organizations must consider the operation of the organizational level hierarchy. By themselves, changes in individual characteristics (e.g., improved education) or changes in the compensation returns for individual characteristics are likely to create only small increases in earnings. Only if these changes are accompanied by improvements in position in the level hierarchy—particularly improvements which occur early in individuals' careers—will they lead to significant increases in earnings and career opportunities.

Appendix 5.A: College Status Effects on Promotions

This appendix provides an alternative way to analyzing the influence of special college groups on promotions. This analysis extends two studies of a large corporation (Wise 1975a, 1975b) which found that the educational quality of colleges from which employees graduated was correlated with their job success as measured by salary and promotion chances. While this chapter thus far has considered salary and level changes, explicit analysis of promotion chances are now performed using log-linear procedures. The variables are similar to those used in the preceding analysis, although some Astin categories have been aggregated and the level variable has been broken into separate dummy variables.[12] The dependent variable is a dichotomous variable representing whether or not the individual has received a promotion between 1962 and 1965. As in the preceding, the aim here is to test whether the special colleges have additional effects, independent of other colleges of comparable quality on the Astin scale. This model also permits a test of the hypothesis of Chapter 3, that age and tenure have negative effects on promotions, independent of one another.

These analyses are comparable with those of Wise (1975b) in study-

---

[12]The reason for further grouping the Astin categories is to simplify the model. This simplification is supported by the finding that in a multivariate model (controlling for the same independent variables used in Table 5.A.1) the effect of Astin 7 is very similar to that of Astin 6, and the same is true for Astin 4 and 5. Comparisons of the likelihood ratio indexes (a goodness-of-fit statistic) of the simplified model presented in Table 5.A.1 and with the "ungrouped" model reveal no change: The further categorization of the Astin groups does not weaken the fit of the model at all.

ing only managers. The present sample is the universe of white male managers present in 1962 who remained in the firm through 1965. Omitting nonmanagement level from these analyses removes the problems raised by an absence of college graduates with high tenure. Consequently, unlike the analyses reported earlier in this chapter, which studied a 10-year entry cohort which was predominantly in nonmanagement, these analyses exclude nonmanagement level and study the universe of white male managers present over a 3-year period.

Even in studying this universe, problems of small numbers made it necessary to collapse all levels above middle management into a single variable. Consequently, the level variables are represented as follows: upper management, middle management, lower management, and foreman level (which is represented by the constant).

Model and Methods

The customary multivariate regression analysis assumes that the dependent variable is a linear function of the independent variables in the equation. This assumption seems unlikely in the analysis of promotion probabilities. The distribution of promotion probabilities probably resembles that class of phenomena for which a given change in probability is more difficult to obtain when the probability is nearly 0 or nearly certain. This influence is supported by the finding in Chapter 3 that a 5-year age difference among employees in the 25–35 age range made a far greater difference in promotion percentages than a 5-year age difference among employees below or above that age range. That analysis suggests that a linear model would be a poor representation for the upper and lower portion of the promotion probability curve and that a nonlinear function of a general S shape is more plausible.

Such a function is modeled by using logistic analysis. The statistical estimation procedure is based on maximum likelihood techniques, and it treats each case as a separate observation (see Nerlove and Press 1973; McFadden 1974). The procedure has the advantage of dealing directly with the probability function rather than estimating the log of the odds function from contingency tables, and it is consequently not dependent on the requirement of large cell size. The procedure also allows for the use of continuous independent variables. In essence, the logistic distribution function is described as follows:

$$P = \text{Pr(PROMOTE=1)} = 1/(1 + e^{-xb}) \tag{5.1}$$

and

$$1 - P = \text{Pr(PROMOTE=0)} = e^{-xb}/(1 + e^{-xb}) = 1/(1 + e^{xb}). \tag{5.2}$$

Here, the term xb is a vector of exogenous variables and parameters. In the following analysis, this vector is represented by:

$$xb = b_1 + b_2 \text{ (tenure)} + b_3 \text{ (entry age)} + b_4 \text{ (Prestige U)}$$
$$+ b_5 \text{ (State U)} + b_6 \text{ (Astin 4–5)} + b_7 \text{ (Astin 6–7)}$$
$$+ b_8 \text{ (low-mgt.)} + b_9 \text{ (mid-mgt.)} + b_{10} \text{ (upper-mgt.)}.$$

Rearranging and taking the log of Eqs. (5.1) and (5.2) gives

$$\begin{aligned} L &= \ln[P/(1 - P)] \\ &= \ln(P) - \ln(1 - P) \\ &= \ln(1 + e^{xb}) - [\ln(e^{-xb}) - \ln(1 + e^{-xb})] \\ &= xb. \end{aligned} \tag{5.3}$$

In Eq. (5.3), L is the logit or the log of the odds ratio. It can be seen that as P goes from 0 to 1 (or xb goes from $-\infty$ to $+\infty$), L goes from $-\infty$ to $+\infty$; thus, while the probabilities are bounded, the logits are unbounded with respect to the values of x. This means that while the logits are a linear function of the exogenous variables, the probabilities themselves are not: The exogenous factors have declining effects as the actual probabilities approach 0 or 1. This is particularly appropriate since, as mentioned, the previous descriptive analysis in Chapter 3 showed that there is a threshold pattern in the distribution of promotion percentages with respect to changes in employees' age.

Another property of the logistic model is that this function automatically allows for interactions among the variables: That is, the marginal change in the probability P associated with a given variable depends on the values of the other exogenous variables.[13] This feature is also appropriate for these data, for Chapter 3 additionally found that the effects of education and grade level in the firm's hierarchy were dependent on the effects of age: The former two variables ceased to have much influence on promotion percentages among employees past the age of 35 (i.e., where promotion percentages were very small and approached 0 as age increased to the retirement level).

Although the present analysis incorporates variables that were not investigated in Chapter 3, the imposed conditions of this model—that the exogenous variables (1) are interactive and (2) have declining influence as the probability approaches one of the limits—seem reasonable given the nature of the data. This contrasts with additive regression

---

[13]In a two-variable case, the interaction can be seen directly by finding $\partial^2 P/\partial X_i X_j$. This is a function of b_i, b_j and P; $\partial^2/\partial x_i a_{xj} = b_j b_i P(1 - P)(1 - 2P)$. Here the value of the derivative depends on where it is evaluated (in terms of P), and this level of P will depend on the values of both x_i and x_j.

models where linear effects are assumed to be constant in all segments of the population. For example, the effect of age at different education levels would be portrayed by parallel lines. A logistic analysis would portray such effects by a series of S curves which all tend to converge as probabilities approached 1 or 0.

Findings

The results indicate that this logistic model does quite well at fitting these data (Table 5.A.1). The likelihood ratio index (roughly comparable to R^2) is .544, suggesting that over half the variation in promotion probability is explained in this model. More importantly, the goodness-of-fit statistic for the model (i.e., the likelihood ratio statistic) is very significant: The p-level is much smaller than the traditional stringent critical value of 0.001.

Table 5.A.1 presents the logit estimates of promotion probabilities for white managers between 1962 and 1965. Turning first to the estimates

Table 5.A.1

Logit Estimates of Promotion Probabilities among White Managers for 1962–1965

Variable	Logit estimate	Standard error	t Statistic
Tenure	−0.113	0.017	−6.411
Entry age	−0.073	0.029	−2.475
Astin 1–3	0.178	1.176	0.151
Astin 4–5	0.295	0.399	0.743
Astin 6–7	0.582	0.352	1.651
State U	1.630	0.532	3.064
Prestige U	1.051	0.477	2.199
Lower management	−0.524	0.279	−1.873
Middle management	−0.821	0.486	−1.690
Upper management	−0.690	0.575	1.201
Constant	1.649	0.867	1.901

Log likelihood at zero, 630.1; at convergence, 287.3
Percentage correctly predicted at convergence, 88
Likelihood ratio index, .544
Likelihood ratio statistic, 685.5; p level at 10 df, 0.000[a]
n = 908

[a]The likelihood ratio statistic is equal to 2/(L − *L1), where L is the log likelihood at the mean of the dependent variable and *L the log likelihood at convergence. The likelihood ratio statistic is distributed as chi-squared with degrees of freedom (df) equal to the number of parameters, less the constant, estimated in the equation.

for tenure, starting age, and level in the hierarchy, this analysis replicates the findings presented by Rosenbaum and Romo (1979) for a similar group of managers during a different time period. Table 5.A.1 indicates that tenure has a strong negative influence on promotion, and entry age has an additional significant influence. Economists commonly find that earnings increase at a declining rate as careers unfold. The present findings show the same empirical phenomenon for promotions; and, in so doing, they suggest that organizational promotion practices may be partially responsible for these earnings curves. These findings also indicate that entry age has an influence on promotions, and these findings go beyond previous studies (Chinoy 1955; Martin and Strauss 1959) in showing that these effects occur even after controlling for years of experience.

The level coefficients reveal a surprisingly curvilinear pattern. Sociologists studying organizations commonly assume that promotion probabilities systematically decline for those at increasingly higher levels in the hierarchy for the simple reason that organizational hierarchies have a pyramidal shape. The pyramid image is quite appropriate for the organization studied here; however, the inference is not totally correct. Although these coefficients indicate that promotion probabilities do systematically decline as one goes from foreman (constant) to lower-management to middle-management levels,[14] they do not decline further for upper-management level. Indeed, the upper-management coefficient indicates that their promotion probabilities are slightly higher than those of foremen (though not significantly so). The level influence is U shaped, with employees at foreman and upper-management levels having the best promotion probabilities and those in the two intermediate levels having much lower promotion probabilities. Detailed analyses of mobility among levels suggests that company growth and employee retirements in the upper-management levels are sufficient to create additional vacancies despite the narrowing of the corporate pyramid.

Turning to the influence of the college variables, these analyses offer some mild support for the customary importance attributed to the Astin scale. However, the difference between the high- and low-Astin categories is not large enough to be statistically significant; indeed, the graduates of each of the Astin categories of colleges do not have significantly greater promotion probabilities than employees who did not graduate from college.

---

[14]Although both t statistics approach significance, neither is significant at the 5% level. Of course, the usefulness of significance tests when using data on a universe is debatable; however, it is taken here as meaningful.

However, these analyses also reveal that the social proximity of colleges have much greater effects than their Astin ratings. The graduates of both proximal colleges have significantly greater promotion probabilities than employees who do not have a college degree. The coefficient for Prestige U is much larger than the coefficient for the corresponding high-Astin category (Astin 6–7), although the difference is not statistically significant. The coefficient for State U is also much larger than the coefficient for the corresponding middle-Astin category (Astin 4–5), and this difference is statistically significant.[15] The results tend to support the hypothesis that socially proximal colleges have greater influence on promotion probabilities than colleges of corresponding educational quality but less social proximity.

The meaning of the college coefficients can best be understood by plotting the curves described by this logistic model. Figure 5.A.1 portrays promotion probabilities resulting from the interaction between tenure and the different education categories, holding starting age constant at its mean (22.7 years) and level in the hierarchy constant at foreman. The curves do not take the full sigmoid (S) shapes possible with logistic estimation techniques. Instead, the tenure curves for each of the education categories show the tendency to directly decline over the early years of employment (except State U). They slow their decline during the later years of employment, finally leveling out and converging. This indicates that most of the education effects are realized at the beginning of the employee's career. This is depicted in Figure 5.A.1 by the large difference between the education categories at the left-hand margin. Here, State U has the greatest advantage with its graduates maintaining a promotion probability of .83 over their first 3 years of service. The next highest category is Prestige U, with its graduates having a promotion probability of .74 over their first 3 years of service. This is followed by Astin 6–7 with graduates from the schools in this category having a promotion probability of .63. Finally Astin 4–5 and Astin 1–3 graduates and non-college-educated employees have promotion probabilities of .57, .53, and .50, respectively, over the same period of time. Somewhat less pronounced in Figure 5.A.1 is the slight tendency towards increasing difference between promotion probabilities over the first decade of tenure in the firm. For example, during the first 10 years of service, the advantage that the State U graduate has over the Prestige U graduate tends to increase from 9 to 13% before it

[15]The difference between the effect of State U and Astin 4–5 is tested by repeating the analysis with Astin 4–5 as the residual category. The t statistic for State U is significant. Comparable analyses for Prestige U, taking Astin 6–7 as the residual category, find an insignificant t statistic.

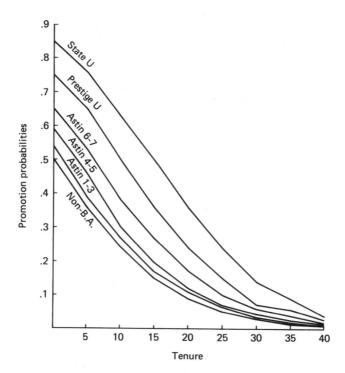

FIGURE 5.A.1.   Promotion probabilities by tenure and college.

converges in the later years. This is also true for Prestige U graduates' advantage over graduates of Astin 6–7 schools, but far less discernible. After this, the tenure curves start to decline more rapidly until they finally converge with the non-B.A. curve, which shows the steepest and most immediate drop. The State U–tenure curve retains its early advantages somewhat longer than the other curves. Its early advantages extend at least through the first decade of service by slowing the declining rate of promotion chances over time.[16] Figure 5.A.1 also dramatically shows that the tenure curves for different college categories converge with the non-B.A. curve during the later stages of employees'

[16]The tendency for the State U–tenure interaction curve to take an S-shape is even more obvious from applying the analysis to B.A.'s only (not shown here). The slower decline in promotion chances over the first decade is observable with both the State U–tenure and Prestige U–tenure curves. Once more, the low-Astin–tenure curves show an immediate and sharp decline.

careers. Although many of these college effects never quite disappear, they are severely reduced over time.

Conclusions

By examining promotions in a single organization, this analysis focuses on the microlevel social selections which lie at the core of economic and structural theories. The present test of these theories considers one particular kind of departure from economic efficiency: promotions of graduates of socially proximal colleges as compared with the promotions of graduates of comparable quality colleges.

The analyses do indicate some support for economic theory. The educational quality of colleges, as measured by the Astin scale, does have the positive influence predicted, although this influence is not large or significant.

However, these analyses also indicate important departures from the predictions of economic theory. The socially important colleges have a greater impact on promotions than the other college categories. The impact of social proximity is particularly great for the middle-status college, State U. These departures from economic theory reflect just the kinds of status considerations which social structural theory predicts.

It is possible to argue that this favoring of socially proximal colleges may occur for efficiency reasons, but these post-hoc arguments seem less than compelling. Of course, socially proximal colleges may offer more information about their graduates; but greater information can be helpful or harmful, and there is no indication that this corporation used any additional information from these colleges. The socially proximal colleges could have produced better graduates than their comparison groups; but, if so, then the Astin index, on which economists rely, is seriously defective. State U, which has the strongest effects in these findings, is rated as Astin 4 and should have had slightly lower effects than the Astin 4–5 variable, and much lower effects than the Astin 6–7 variable. Although it is possible to conceive of efficiency reasons for these findings, such post-hoc speculations are not very satisfying.

Of course, the social proximity of colleges is not the only kind of status that influences promotion decisions. Studies from the 1940s and 1950s reported that promotions were based on ethnic group membership and particularistic family connections. There has been some speculation that these particularistic considerations have declined in importance since 1960, especially in large corporations as these corporations have become less controlled by particular families and as increasing technology has required greater concern for competence and education. Although this analysis cannot examine the influence of family connections, this study does indicate that the reliance on education is not free from the possibility of particularistic selections. Even if particularistic family influences were declining, this analysis indicates that other kinds of particularistic factors accompany the increased reliance on college education.

CHAPTER 6

The Enduring Effects of Early Jobs and Earnings

Introduction

How do employees' early jobs and earnings affect their later careers? The question is important practically, for individuals' entire work lives are at stake. The question is also a central one theoretically; the dominant theoretical viewpoints have contrasting perspectives on the question. Neoclassical economic theories (like human capital theory) posit that ability, skills, and motivation are the main influences on employees' career attainment, that job structures have no impact on earnings, and that early earnings are inversely related to later attainment. In contrast, social structural theory contends that early jobs have a strong positive effect on later careers by channeling employees into discrete job ladders (Althauser and Kalleberg 1981, p. 130).

Numerous studies have sought to test which theory provides a better description of the attainment process, but the results have been inconclusive. In this chapter, the contentions of the two theories are reviewed, and an alternative theory—a signaling theory of promotions—is developed which combines elements of each. Hypotheses about the effects of early jobs and earnings, on which the theories suggest different predictions, are then proposed. The hypotheses are tested using data on a 3-year entry cohort whose attainments are followed longitudinally over a 13-year period. The analyses are able to examine the effects of early earnings, early job status, and even specific job titles on later earnings and status attainment. The results suggest patterns of career mobility which conflict with the "trade-off hypothesis" suggested by human capital theory and the "ahistorical-effects hypothesis" suggested by structural theory. The results most closely support the signaling theory.

Human Capital versus Social Structural Theories

The issue of whether careers are structured by early social forces and barriers is seen theoretically in the conflict between human capital theory in economics (and, more generally, neoclassic economic theory) and social structural theory in sociology. Human capital theory posits that labor markets offer open opportunity and that individuals' attainments are largely a function of their effort, ability, education, and training. It also posits that individuals' ability and effort create productivity, which is the basis for their compensation. In addition, it asserts that individuals create their own productive capacity by making investments in themselves.

In contrast, social structural theory contends that individuals' attainments are determined less by their personal attributes than by structural aspects of labor markets. It posits that the structure of existing jobs controls the "wage contour" for various kinds of employees (Doeringer and Piore 1971; Thurow 1975). As a result, individuals' earnings will not be directly determined by their personal attributes, efforts, or investments in themselves, but by the jobs to which they are allocated. Jobs are assigned wage rates according to normative considerations, and individuals are paid according to the jobs into which they are allocated (Thurow 1975; Granovetter 1981). As a result, the structural model contends that attainments are highly structured, and the effects of personal qualities on earnings is mediated by this structure.

When social structural theory is applied to organizational careers, it is commonly conceived as an internal labor market (Doeringer and Piore 1971). An internal labor market is characterized by a series of discrete job ladders which allow entry only at the bottom and which determine upward movement in response to the development of knowledge or skill (Doeringer and Piore 1971, p. 21; Spilerman 1977; Althauser and Kalleberg 1981, p. 130). Internal labor markets presume that early selections determine the kind of training the organization provides to employees and the ultimate career paths employees will follow.

A Signaling Theory of Promotions

Although human capital and social structural theories are the two main theories to be applied to describing individuals' careers in organizations,[1] a third theory, signaling theory, is also applicable, and this chapter presents qualitative and quantitative evidence which supports this theory. According to signaling theory as it was originally proposed (Arrow 1973; Spence 1973; Stiglitz 1975), employers seek to make their employee selections conform to human capital theory; but, contrary to the assumptions of human capital theory, employers have difficulty knowing which individuals have the most ability. The expense and difficulty of getting information about employees' ability induces employers to use certain social attributes and accomplishments of individuals as signals of their abilities.

Signaling theory is usually applied to explaining hiring decisions, since that is the prototypical case in which employers have little information about individuals. However, the problem continues to exist after employees are hired. Particularly in large organizations, large numbers of employees must be evaluated and compared; and these individuals often occupy very different jobs with incomparable products, and they are evaluated by different supervisors. In addition, most employees considered for promotions are in white-collar jobs for which job performance is difficult to evaluate. While extensive efforts have been made to develop assessment tests and procedures, these have generally been found to have limited validity (Campbell, Dunnette, Lawler, and Weick 1970) and are regarded with mistrust by managers (Shaeffer 1972). A few large corporations have devised elaborate assessment programs (notably UniRoyal and AT&T) (see Bray, Campbell, and Grant 1974); but only the largest companies can afford such programs, and even they cannot afford to implement them for more than one stage

[1]Vacancy theory may be considered a variant of social structural theory, although it generally follows chains of vacancies rather than the sequence of career moves of individuals (see White 1970a; Stewman 1975).

of the promotion process. Clearly, promotion committees face the problem of information scarcity, which suggests the relevance of signaling theory.

According to most accounts, supervisors' ratings are the main determinant of promotions. But complications prevent ratings from being the only criterion. Promotion committees must have some way of comparing high ratings by different supervisors and of comparing good job performance in jobs of different difficulty. Promotion committees need an objective, comparable indicator of job difficulty and of the value of the individual's contribution.

The organization considered in this study, like many large organizations, determines job compensation by a detailed job evaluation system which assesses the difficulty, challenge, and skill requirements of jobs (see Chapter 4; see also Treiman 1979; Grandjean 1981). The job evaluation system in this corporation devotes considerable effort and expense to assure that the job evaluation process is rigorous and that these rankings will be socially accepted as legitimate and fair. Within job statuses, salaries are set by a "merit pay" system which seeks to set pay-in-grade according to individuals' contributions. Given the extensive effort devoted to these compensation systems and to buttressing their legitimacy, job statuses and earnings would seem to be ideal signals of the ability requirements of jobs and of the ability that individuals demonstrate in their jobs. While not formally a part of the promotion process, these two compensation systems permit comparative evaluations of the abilities of individuals occupying different jobs. Are they indeed used as such?

Managers report that they are. In interviews with this researcher, managers report that because of the difficulties promotion committees have in evaluating candidates' abilities, they sometimes infer individuals' abilities from their attainments as indicated by their job status and earnings. Since job status and earnings are objective indicators, and since they have strong salience and importance in the ways individuals are evaluated in this organization on a daily basis, they tend to have particularly strong weighting in these deliberations. What is noteworthy in these accounts is not just that these attainments affect promotion decisions, but also that they do so because they are inferred to be "signals" of individuals' abilities. This inference seems to be based on the assumption that the organization's selection system is meritocratic; consequently, those who have risen the furthest have done so because they are the most able. This rationale is most crisply stated in the frequently cited maxim, "the cream rises to the top." In effect, this maxim seems to be a shared informal "theory" about how to detect ability.

Signaling theory represents a middle course between human capital and structural theories. If promotion committees really do use job status and earnings as ability signals, then signaling theory predicts many of the consequences suggested by social structural theory even though it posits that managers are trying to pursue the aims of human capital theory. It contends that employers pursuing the goals of human capital theory will take structural factors as signals of individuals' ability, but it contends that job attainments affect later career attainments, not by imposing structural constraints, but by conferring information about employees' ability.

Hypotheses

Three hypotheses are proposed about the effects of early jobs on later attainments. The first hypothesis raises the question of simple effects on individuals' career trajectories.

Hypothesis 6.1. The career-trajectory hypothesis: Early attainments have strong effects in setting the career trajectories of entering employees, net of their personal attributes. Two theories clearly support this hypothesis. Structural theory contends that, by putting individuals on different job ladders, entry jobs determine career trajectories. Signaling theory contends that entry jobs influence career trajectories by affecting managers' inferences about individuals' ability. By generally ignoring job effects, human capital theory implies that early jobs would have little influence on later attainment, after controlling for individuals' human capital. However, since any set of information that researchers may have about individuals is unlikely to measure human capital fully, human capital theory can explain a finding of job effects as arising because jobs may reflect unmeasured components of human capital (especially better training). Thus, while human capital theory does not predict early job effects net of individual attributes, such an outcome can be explained by the theory. While early job effects are substantively important, this does not make an interesting hypothesis because it cannot discriminate among the theories. However, the theories do conflict when early job effects are considered net of other attainment effects, as is the case in the other two hypotheses.

Hypothesis 6.2. The historical-effects hypothesis: Early job status attainments have continuing effects on later career attainments independent of intervening attainments. This hypothesis conflicts with structural theories, which generally contend that attainments only have effects in the present; past attainments have no further effects, independent of present attainments. This feature of structural theories has been previously noted in the ahistorical model proposed by Kelley (1973a) and in the path-independence principle in Markov models (Mayer 1972). As Ginsburg (1971) states this position, after an individual enters an organization through an entry port, "the key decisions about his career follow. The occupational decisions that he made earlier will be of relatively little significance" (p. 17).

In the internal labor market literature, conceptions of job structures are fundamentally based on the model of a skill-based job ladder (Doeringer and Piore 1971; Althauser and Kalleberg 1981, p. 130). Like a physical ladder, a job ladder poses barriers to entry except at the bottom and constrains individuals on any particular ladder to remain on that same ladder. Jumping from ladder to ladder is as risky on job ladders as it is on physical ladders. The ladder image implies that the individuals on any rung of a particular ladder have the same career history (i.e., all came from the same lower rungs of that ladder), so historical effects are irrelevant. Of course, the one-dimensional ladder image may be too simple. A career tree is an alternative model which may or may not permit historical effects, but, even here, the customary structural interpretation makes these branches ahistorical (Bartholomew 1968; Kelley 1973a).

In contrast, signaling theory provides a model in which entry jobs could have effects that are carried forward into the future because early jobs provide additional information that could influence later promotions. Signaling theory's assumption that useful inexpensive information about employee ability is scarce and desperately needed makes it likely that promotion committees would consider historical information as well as present information about employees' early attainments.

One may object that these theories do not necessarily have to be interpreted in these ways. In particular, one could imagine a structural theory proposing historical effects. While this is a possibility, it is not the way that structural theory has ordinarily been interpreted.

However, regardless of how the hypothesis relates to larger theories, it raises an important issue on its own. If early jobs are interpreted to have structural force, the hypothesis raises the issue of whether these social forces continue to have a distinctive impact after an individual takes a subsequent job or whether their impact is totally supplanted by, or incorporated in, the effects of the later job. Alternatively, stated in terms of signaling theory, the issue is whether an early job conveys information which is distinctive from what a later job conveys. Regardless of which interpretation is given to the nature of job effects, the question of their historical effects is problematic.

Like the tournament model described in Chapter 2, this hypothesis predicts that early "wins" (higher job statuses) put individuals into competition for better positions than early "losses" (lower job statuses). In terms of the career tree presented in Chapter 2, the tournament model holds that at any particular position in the career tree (i.e., a particular level attainment at a particular time for this cohort), an individual's future attainment is positively related to previous attainment. Of course, the present analysis is more complex than that shown on the career tree diagram in Chapter 2; for it considers a more highly differentiated indicator of attainments (job status), and it controls for individual attributes.

The issue of whether historical effects exist raises a very practical issue for American society and its social institutions. This organization, like American society in general, infers that individuals who overcome great obstacles to attain unexpectedly high positions are more enterprising and more deserving of further advancements than individuals starting at higher positions. "Horatio Alger" stories of mail clerks rising to high positions in the company are important parts of the company culture, so much so that one might expect that individuals replicating the "Horatio Alger" experience might be imputed to have more ability and might be given greater subsequent advancements. Consequently, two different versions of the historical-effects hypothesis can be envisioned. One, a *Horatio Alger version*, would maintain that employees who overcome the obstacles of low-status early jobs to rise quickly in their first 3 years would be imputed to have more ability and be given greater subsequent advancement than others at the same level of attainment in their third year in the firm. The other, a *cumulative-privilege version*, would maintain that employees who began in higher-status early jobs would be given greater subsequent advancement than others at the same level of attainment after 3 years.

Before concluding this discussion, it is worth noting that all three versions of this hypothesis—no historical effects, negative historical effects (Horatio Alger), and positive historical effects (cumulative privilege)—are plausible. Moreover, the issues they raise pervade stratification in all kinds of settings. Do all college students from Northwestern University have the same chance to get a good job regardless of the secondary school they attended, and, if not, do employers prefer the graduates of Andover Academy or those of Hicksville High? Or, do all M.B.A.'s from Northwestern have the same employment chances irrespective of the undergraduate college they attended, and, if not, do employers prefer the ones with B.A.'s from Yale or Illinois State? It isn't clear that the answer to these two sets of questions is the same, and it is quite likely that a different answer might apply to job sequences in a corporation. What is intriguing is that all three different processes are plausible in each example, and there is not an unambiguous answer in any of these cases.

Hypothesis 6.3. The stratified rewards (no-trade-off) hypothesis: Within comparable jobs, employees will face no trade-off between early earnings and later attainments; these rewards will go together. There is considerable variation in early earnings among individuals with similar human capital characteristics. If immediate earnings were the only form of compensation, this finding would contradict human capital theory. According to Mincer's (1974) explanation of the human capital position, employees receive other kinds of compensation besides earnings; they also receive training, which leads to increased future earnings. However, employers will only pay employees for the economic value they contribute to productivity. Providing training to employees is assumed to be costly for employers; and when employers offer training to employees, its cost is subtracted from the employees' current earnings.

Human capital theory also contends that employees choose how they take their compensation. While all individuals with a particular economic value are paid the same total compensation, they can choose whether to accept it in current or future earnings. Accordingly, employees who choose jobs with more on-the-job training are willing to receive lower current earnings, since their additional training will increase their chances of greater career advancement in subsequent years. Indeed, after a certain number of years (the *overtake* period which Mincer estimates at roughly 7–9 years), the earnings of the employees who chose training at the outset will overtake the earnings of those who chose higher earnings. In effect, there is a trade-off between current earnings and later attainment. Newly entering employees may cash in their human capital for either higher current earnings or for training and higher future earnings. However, employees with equal human capital face a trade-off between current and future earnings, and the two will be inversely related.

In contrast, the signaling theory presented here suggests that since employers cannot evaluate human capital directly, they must infer it from consensually accepted social signals. Foremost among these are the rewards and attainments individuals have received, as reflected in their early job status and earnings. Like early jobs, early earnings convey economically significant information about the ability of individuals. For promotion committees, eager for inexpensive indicators for comparing employees' abilities, early earnings and job status provide readily available ability signals on which to base promotion decisions. Thus, in contrast with the trade-off proposed by human capital theory, signaling theory suggests that early earnings are positively, not negatively, associated with later attainment. In other words, there is no trade-off; rewards are stratified: Employees getting more early earnings also get more career advancement.[2]

The present longitudinal data permit examination of Mincer's contention much more closely than he was able to do. Mincer suggests that although on-the-job training is difficult to observe, it can be inferred to have occurred whenever individuals receive subsequent career advancements (if their education does not change). Thus, Mincer would contend that among individuals with the same human capital attributes at the outset, those who receive lower current earnings may be assumed to be receiving more training and consequently greater future career advancement. Mincer's formulation leads to a clear empirical test of the human capital trade-off hypothesis and its converse, the no-trade-off hypothesis proposed by signaling theory.

Analysis

Sample and Dependent Variable

The sample studied in this chapter is composed of the employees who entered the corporation between 1960 and 1962 and who re-

---

[2]Note that the signaling theory need not disregard economic considerations. It proposes that the cost of information is a consideration and that inexpensive information itself has economic value. Moreover, this view need not disregard the economic constraints on employers; it need only maintain that the cost of providing training may not be so expensive as Mincer suggests, it may lead to payback sooner than Mincer suggests, or high-potential employees may receive additional compensation because of their putative future value which an employer is willing to pay for in advance to retain them. In addition, if offered to only a few employees, the cost-effectiveness of early earnings and training compensation can be allowed to overvalue a few employees without upsetting the employers' balance sheet. This is particularly true because most low-seniority employees are willing to be undercompensated in present earnings relative to their marginal product since they anticipate overcompensation in their later years (Lazear, 1981).

mained with it through at least 1975. This permits a longitudinal analysis of 13 years of career mobility for the cohort of 671 employees who
entered the company at roughly the same time. Since this is the same
sample studied in Chapter 2, Chapter 2 provides a graphic description
of these individuals' careers, and this chapter provides a multivariate
extension of Chapter 2.

As noted in Chapter 4, ABCO has two kinds of hierarchical classifications for distinguishing hierarchical attainment: level and status. The
main distinction is the level system, with each successive level indicating a greater amount of authority. Previous chapters have already described level attainments in great detail. However, level attainments do
not distinguish attainments at career entry very well, for nearly all
employees enter this corporation at the same level, nonmanagement.

The other indicator of attainment, job status, is a better indicator of
early attainments. Within each level, jobs are classified by status. Job
statuses are determined according to the task demands and requirements of jobs; and, as noted in Chapter 1, a job's status ranking has a
wide range of implications—defining the job's salary range, benefit
package, and office size and defining an employee's frequency of supervision, discretion in work tasks, and autonomy of work schedule. Since
employees enter the corporation in jobs of different statuses in the same
(nonmanagement) level; status categories distinguish starting positions
better than levels do, and they also indicate more fine-grained distinctions in higher levels as well. For instance, in middle-management
level, higher-status jobs entail supervision of more subordinates or require decisions about larger sums of money than lower-status jobs in
the same level; and they confer greater salary, benefits, etc. To make a
single status variable over all levels in the organization, a single ordinal
scale of strata was constructed by ranking job statuses within successive authority levels.[3]

The other variables studied here are similar to those described in
Chapter 5, with only minor differences. Unfortunately, the factor hypothesized to have the most sharply different effect on earnings and
status—college selectivity—cannot be measured in as much detail in
this small cohort because of the limited number of individuals from

---

[3]The gaps between successive statuses within a level are assigned as one unit, and gaps
between levels (between the top status in one level and the bottom status in the next
higher level) are assigned as three units. This was done because the job classification
administrators in this organization stated that promotions across levels were considered
to convey about three times greater status than promotions across statuses. Moreover,
analyses indicated that the salary increases associated with level promotions were ap-
proximately three times greater than those associated with status promotions.

each college selectivity category, so the 7-point Astin scale is used as a single variable to represent college selectivity effects. Since the non-B.A. variable was used in Chapter 5 to make middle-Astin college graduates the point of comparison (in the constant), and this is not possible here, the more straightforward B.A. variable is used in the present analyses. Of course, it is the exact reverse of the non-B.A. variable in Chapter 5.

Women ($n = 287$) and minorities ($n = 47$) are also included in these analyses, and corresponding variables have been added (e.g., 1 = minorities, 0 = white). In addition, corresponding interaction variables are included to study the extent that B.A., tenure, entry age, and race have different effects for women than for men. The limited number of college-educated women in this cohort ($n = 12$) does not permit interaction terms for college selectivity or M.B.A., and the small number of minorities does not permit further interactions except by gender.

Timing of Earnings and Structural Differentiation

Before turning to the hypotheses, the differentiation of this cohort over the first 13 years of its career can be simply described by two simple analysis. These analyses address the question posed by Chapter 5 about the relative timing of earnings and structural differentiation, and they do so using a more detailed indicator of attainment than that used in Chapter 5 (job status instead of authority level). The present analyses also permit comparison of the careers of women and minorities to those of white males. The regression models of the effects of individual attributes on earnings and job status for this 3-year cohort are shown in Tables 6.1 and 6.2.

Since the white males in this cohort are a subset of the individuals in the 1953–1962 cohort analyzed in Chapter 5 (362 of the 1612 males analyzed in Chapter 5, i.e., 22.5%), it is not surprising to find that the results presented in this chapter are highly similar to those found with the Chapter 5 sample. In both analyses, B.A. and M.B.A. degrees affect earnings and structural attainments from the outset; and, while college selectivity affects job status from the outset, it doesn't begin to affect earnings until later periods. The entry age effect is more complex. While its initial effect on earnings and status is positive (corresponding to the small positive effect commonly found for "previous experience"), it soon becomes negative and increasingly more negative over time. Apparently, the 1953–1962 cohort in Chapter 5 conceals a curvilinear entry age effect during the first decade. With only this excep-

Table 6.1

Regression Coefficients for Ln(Earnings) on Individual Attributes 1962–1975[a]

Independent variable	1962	1965	1969	1972	1975
Tenure[b]	.0751** (.0101)	.0436** (.0103)	.0202** (.0077)	.0082 (.0091)	.0095 (.0096)
Entry age	.0053** (.0010)	−.0040** (.0010)	−.0109** (.0013)	−.0124** (.0015)	−.0130** (.0014)
B.A.[b]	.4145** (.0462)	.3783** (.0487)	.4107** (.0617)	.4081** (.0590)	.2442** (.0480)
M.B.A.[b]	.1409* (.0597)	.0981 (.0629)	.0526 (.0613)	.0764 (.0666)	.0595 (.0559)
College selectivity[b]	.0073 (.0085)	.0075 (.0090)	.0089 (.0115)	.0085 (.0109)	.0190* (.0090)
Race	−.1377** (.0529)	−.2389** (.0557)	−.2912** (.0701)	−.3175** (.0775)	−.3038** (.0769)
Female	−.1770** (.0391)	−.4000** (.0518)	−.4797** (.0740)	−.5381** (.1092)	−.3794** (.1409)
Female–B.A.[b]	−.2387** (.0663)	−.1396* (.0698)	−.1512 (.0880)	−.1588 (.0885)	−.0779 (.0814)
Female–Race	.0751 (.0572)	.1619** (.0602)	.2375** (.0760)	.2707** (.0839)	.2483** (.0833)
Female–Tenure[b]	−.0475** (.0137)	−.0332** (.0107)	−.0144 (.0082)	−.0008 (.0097)	−.0070 (.0102)
Female–Entry age	−.0023 (.0013)	.0048** (.0013)	.0077** (.0017)	.0067** (.0019)	.0065** (.0019)
Constant	8.2984** (.0275)	8.8037** (.0431)	9.1654** (.0636)	9.4440 (.0985)	9.4513** (.1299)
R^2 (%)	79.8	82.4	76.7	72.9	66.3
Adjusted R^2 (%)	79.4	82.1	76.3	72.4	65.7
SEE[c]	.1271	.1339	.1689	.1865	.1852

[a]Asterisk indicates coefficients that are significant at the .05 level. Double asterisk indicates coefficients that are significant at the .01 level. Standard errors for coefficients are indicated in parentheses.

[b]These variables change from year to year, and these regressions use independent variables for the same year as each dependent variable. The remaining independent variables did not change from year to year.

[c]Standard error of estimate.

tion, the findings for white males in this cohort are quite analogous to those found for the larger cohort.

The analyses also permits study of the attainments of women and minorities. A detailed discussion of the effects of discrimination and affirmative action are the focus of Chapter 7. Suffice it to note here that these findings reveal that all groups (non-college-educated and college-educated females, and minority males and females) show large, and generally increasing, disadvantages relative to their white male counterparts. That this occurs in the context of an organization which has implemented a strong, and, by many measures, "successful" affirma-

Table 6.2

Regression Coefficients for Job Status on Individual Attributes: 1962–1975[a]

Independent variable	1962	1965	1969	1972	1975
Tenure[b]	.7388**	.5952**	.3159*	.0643	.1129
	(.0881)	(.1589)	(.1474)	(.1910)	(.2205)
Entry age	.0182*	−.0085	−.0597*	−.1288**	−.1601**
	(.0086)	(.0160)	(.0251)	(.0304)	(.0332)
B.A.[b]	2.8491**	5.1095**	11.1717**	10.7564**	8.6868**
	(.4020)	(.7513)	(1.1785)	(1.2362)	(1.1048)
M.B.A.[b]	2.2921**	2.6323**	3.1241**	3.4209*	1.9794
	(.5198)	(.9711)	(1.1700)	(1.3944)	(1.2854)
College selectivity[b]	.1878*	.3465**	.3361	.2694	.7063**
	(.0741)	(.1384)	(.2198)	(.2292)	(.2072)
Race	−.7261	−1.3257	−1.7653	−2.7056	−2.8517
	(.4602)	(.8599)	(1.3398)	(1.6227)	(1.7692)
Female	.6742*	1.4461	.0633	−3.9450	−3.1672
	(.3401)	(.8004)	(1.4140)	(2.2872)	(3.2408)
Female–B.A.[b]	−2.7707**	−3.7101**	−7.8059**	−6.3702**	−6.1693**
	(.5776)	(1.0769)	(1.6804)	(1.8548)	(1.8709)
Female–Race	.4299	.5434	1.2133	2.3292	2.4390
	(.4981)	(.9298)	(1.4510)	(1.7575)	(1.9160)
Female–Tenure[b]	−.7786**	−.5573**	−.2458	.0385	−.0314
	(.1196)	(.1654)	(.1571)	(.2022)	(.2334)
Female–Entry age	−.0238*	−.0170	.0058	.0438	.0571
	(.0109)	(.0206)	(.0330)	(.0400)	(.0437)
Constant	.8481**	.9885	3.7522**	8.7977**	9.0460**
	(.2393)	(.6659)	(1.2151)	(2.0643)	(2.9858)
R^2 (%)	68.9	65.9	71.9	63.9	60.6
Adjusted R^2 (%)	68.4	65.3	71.5	63.3	60.0
SEE[c]	1.1065	2.0678	3.2256	3.9065	4.2584

[a]Asterisk indicates coefficients that are significant at the .05 level. Double asterisk indicates coefficients that are significant at the .01 level. Standard errors for coefficients are indicated in parentheses.

[b]These variables change from year to year, and these regressions use independent variables for the same year as each dependent variable. The remaining independent variables did not change from year to year.

[c]Standard error of estimate.

tive action program makes these findings puzzling and worthy of more extensive analysis in Chapter 7.

Historical-Effects Hypothesis

Two separate hypotheses are suggested about the effects of early jobs: first, the career-trajectory hypothesis that early jobs (in 1962) have significant effects on later attainment (in 1975), even after controlling for individual attributes; and second, the historical-effects hypothesis that early jobs affect later attainment, even after controlling for intervening attainment.

The first column of Table 6.3 reports the effects of individual attributes on 1975 job status. Adding 1962 job status to this model reduces the unique influence of most individual attributes. Of the 65.2% of variance in 1975 job status explained, individual attributes uniquely explain 12.3% (independent of job status), and 47.7% is explained by attributes and 1962 status jointly. Apparently, most of the influence of individual attributes on 1975 job status is mediated by their effect on early job status.

Early job status does have a large influence on later attainment. A one-unit increase in 1962 job status leads to a 1.36 unit increase in 1975 job status. In effect, early status differences become magnified as individuals proceed through this system. Clearly, the career-trajectory hypothesis is confirmed: The earliest job status attainments have a strong and significant impact on attainments 13 years 'later, independent of individual attributes.

The historical-effects hypothesis can be tested by adding 1965 job status to this regression (Table 6.3, column 3). Controlling for 1965 job status and individual attributes, do 1962 job statuses still affect 1975 attainments?

When 1965 job status is introduced into the regression, it becomes the largest influence in the model. It has increased the explanatory power of the regression by 5%. Evidently, in the 3 years since 1962, some selections have occurred which are not predictable from the earlier period. Turner's (1960) sponsored model is not a totally adequate description of what is happening here.

Nonetheless, although it mediates the greatest part of the effects of earlier factors on later attainment, 1965 job status does not mediate it all. Some individual attributes continue to have an effect independent of this intervening attainment. More pertinent to the hypothesis, early job status attainment continues to have an effect on later attainment,

Table 6.3

Historical-Effects Hypothesis: Effects of 1962 Job Status on 1975 Job Status,
Controlling for Attributes and 1965 Job Status[a]

Independent variable	Attribute alone	Adding 1962 job status	Adding 1965 job status
Tenure[b]	.1129	−.4815*	−.4169*
	(.2205)	(.2136)	(.1977)
Entry age	−.1601**	−.1843**	−.1683**
	(.0332)	(.0310)	(.0287)
B.A.[b]	8.6868**	6.2437**	4.0015**
	(1.1048)	(1.0565)	(1.0012)
M.B.A.[b]	1.9794	1.4803	1.5868
	(1.2854)	(1.1970)	(1.1077)
College selectivity	.7063**	.1456	−.0227
	(.2072)	(.2007)	(.1865)
Race	−2.8517	−2.0668	−1.5412
	(1.7692)	(1.6478)	(1.5257)
Female	−3.1672	−11.4016**	−10.0623**
	(3.2408)	(3.1255)	(2.8951)
Female–B.A.[b]	−6.1693**	−3.1823	−1.4521
	(1.8709)	(1.7660)	(1.6427)
Female–Race[b]	2.4390	2.0024	1.9293
	(1.9160)	(1.7830)	(1.6500)
Female–Tenure[b]	−.0314	.5470*	.4803*
	(.2334)	(.2247)	(.2080)
Female–Entry age	.0571	.0914*	.0909*
	(.0437)	(.0408)	(.0377)
Job status 1962	—	1.3580**	.6285**
		(.1358)	(.1440)
Job status 1965	—	—	.8348**
			(.0804)
Constant[c]	9.0460**	15.4670**	13.1040**
	(2.9858)	(2.8511)	(2.6482)
R^2 (%)	60.6	66.0	70.9
Adjusted R^2 (%)	60.0	65.3	70.3
SEE[d]	4.2584	3.9618	3.6661

[a]Asterisk indicates coefficients significant at the .05 level. Double asterisk indicates coefficients significant at the .01 level. Standard errors for coefficients are indicated in parentheses.

[b]Variables change to be same year as dependent variable.

[c]Constant represents non-college-educated white males.

[d]Standard error of estimate.

independent of intervening attainment, and this effect is not small. A one-status-unit advantage in 1962 has almost as much effect on 1975 attainment as a one-unit advantage in 1965. While the 1962 effect is smaller in terms of standardized coefficients, it is still over 42% of the 1965 effect (a standard deviation advantage in 1962 gives a .184 standard deviation advantage in 1975, and a comparable 1965 advantage gives a .435 advantage in 1975). The findings clearly confirm the historical model.

While the regression findings are sufficient to establish the historical-effects hypothesis, a tabular analysis offers a simple description of the historical effects of particular combinations of early career moves. A tabular analysis cannot easily control for the effects of individual attributes, and since that was done in the regression, no effort is made to do so in the tabular analysis. This type of analysis makes it difficult to evaluate effects for cells which contain few individuals; consequently, the present analysis is restricted to the lowest five job statuses which contain 93% of this cohort.

The results, presented in Table 6.4, indicate the average 1975 job status attained by individuals who move through particular combinations of job statuses in 1962 and 1965, for the 1960–1962 cohort. Inspection of this table clearly indicates that potential "Horatio Alger" types do exist. Many individuals manage to overcome initial disadvantages between 1962 and 1965. For example, the table shows that of the

Table 6.4

Average 1975 Job Status Attained by Employees as a Function of Their 1962 and 1965 Job Statuses For Lowest Five Job Statuses in 1962 and 1965[a]

Job status 1962	Job status 1965				
	1	2	3	4	5
1	3.11	3.52	5.71	10.55	13.00
	(276)	(21)	(142)	(11)	(1)
2	5.00	6.11	5.14	11.00	—
	(4)	(55)	(7)	(1)	—
3	6.00	—	7.14	11.00	—
	(2)	—	(63)	(1)	—
4	—	—	—	11.00	12.59
	—	—	—	(1)	(27)
5	—	—	—	—	12.77
	—	—	—	—	(13)

[a]Number of employees in each cell is shown in parentheses.

employees in status 1 in 1962, 21 moved to status 2, 142 moved to status 3, and 11 moved to status 4 by 1965. Clearly there was much upward mobility for members of this cohort in these first few years.

However, despite overcoming their low origins, the Horatio Alger types still end up in 1975 far behind the cohort peers with whom they shared the same status in 1965. In the above example of the employees in status 1 in 1962, those who attained status 2 in 1965 ultimately attained a much lower 1975 status (3.52 status units) than employees who had been in job status 2 in both 1962 and 1965 (6.11 status units). The same is true for each of the other early Horatio Alger types in this table (except for cells containing a single individual).

This table illustrates the same point that the regression analysis showed. The accomplishment of overcoming low origins does not give Horatio Alger types parity with others in their new status: They remain at a disadvantage compared to those from higher job status origins. Historical effects are positive—not negative—supporting the cumulative-privilege hypothesis and refuting the Horatio Alger hypothesis.

Stratified Rewards (No-Trade-off) Hypothesis

The null hypothesis for this analysis is that employees face a trade-off between their early earnings and their later career attainment; that is, among employees with the same human capital in the same status jobs, those with the highest early earnings will have the lowest career advancement over their next 13 years. The trade-off hypothesis predicts that when early earnings are introduced into the previous analysis, they will have a negative impact (Table 6.3, Column 2 is repeated here in Table 6.5, column 1). Of course, given the very strong correlation between 1962 job status and 1962 earnings for this cohort ($r = .82$), it is not even certain that these two will have independent influences.

The results show that they do have significant independent influences, but not in the direction predicted by the trade-off hypothesis (Table 6.5, column 2). Contrary to the trade-off hypothesis, initial earnings have a significant *positive* influence on employees' career advancement, independent of job status. Indeed, this influence is quite large; among employees in the same job status category, those with 10% higher earnings are a full status unit higher in 1975. Put another way, a one-standard-deviation earnings advantage in job status in 1962 leads to a .439 standard deviation advantage in 1975 job status.

Finally, when this analysis is repeated for 1975 earnings attainment (in logs), the results are virtually the same: Initial earnings have a

Table 6.5

Stratified Rewards (No-Trade-off) Hypothesis: Effects of 1962 Ln(Earnings) on 1975 Job
Status and Ln(Earnings), Controlling for Attributes and 1962 Job Status[a]

Independent variable	Dependent: 1975 job status		Dependent: 1975 ln(earnings)
	Independent		Independent
	1962 job status	1962 job status and ln(earnings)	1962 job status and ln(earnings)
Tenure	−.4815*	−.7436**	−.0331**
	(.2136)	(.2103)	(.0088)
Entry age	−.1843**	−.2277**	−.0163**
	(.0310)	(.0307)	(.0013)
M.B.A.	1.4803	1.4256	.0317
	(1.1970)	(1.1580)	(.0485)
B.A.	6.2437**	4.1450**	.0203
	(1.0565)	(1.0694)	(.0448)
College selectivity	.1456	.0720	−.0128
	(.2007)	(.1945)	(.0081)
Race	−2.0668	−1.1677	−.2211**
	(1.6478)	(1.5999)	(.0670)
Female	−11.4016**	−10.3054**	−.7434**
	(3.1255)	(3.0283)	(.1267)
Female–B.A.	−3.1823	−2.2869	.1159
	(1.7660)	(1.7138)	(.0717)
Female–Race	2.0024	1.3110	.1932**
	(1.7830)	(.7281)	(.0723)
Female–Tenure	.5470*	.5946**	.0245**
	(.2247)	(.2175)	(.0091)
Female–Entry age	.0914*	.1289**	.0100**
	(.0408)	(.0399)	(.0017)
Job status 1962	1.3580**	.7187**	.0381**
	(.1358)	(.1626)	(.0068)
Ln(earnings) 1962		10.5368**	.5038**
		(1.5796)	(.0661)
Constant[b]	15.4670**	−68.0003**	5.7851**
R^2 (%)	66.0	68.2	74.8
Adjusted R^2 (%)	65.3	67.6	74.3
SEE[c]	3.962	3.833	0.160

[a]Asterisk indicates coefficients significant at the .05 level. Double asterisk indicates
coefficients significant at the .01 level. Standard errors for coefficients are indicated in
parentheses.

[b]Constant represents non-college-educated white males.

[c]Standard error of estimates.

strong positive influence on 1975 earnings, even after controlling for initial job status (column 3). Indeed, the influence of initial earnings is almost identical in terms of standardized coefficients (.447), and 1962 job status has a slightly larger influence on 1975 earnings than it did on 1975 job status (a standardized coefficient of .237 versus .210).

It must be concluded that entering employees do not face a trade-off. The alternatives they face are stratified into higher pay with better career advancement and lower pay with lower advancement, regardless of whether advancement is measured in terms of earnings or job status. The organization structures the alternatives it offers to beginning employees so that some employees get more of both pay and advancement and other employees get less of both. Rather than facing a trade-off, employees face a stratified reward structure.

Effects of Individual Jobs

In the preceding analyses, job status was used to represent the structural effects of jobs. Previous analyses provide strong evidence for assuming that job status does indeed represent the most important structural effects of jobs, for they showed that job status alone could explain most of the variance in average job salaries (Chapter 4). Nonetheless, while job status reflects the formal status that is conferred on jobs, jobs may also have informal statuses which also influence their occupants' careers. As a result, it is possible that the job status scale may miss some important features of job effects, particularly distinctions within formal job statuses. If so, then the preceding analyses have *underestimated* structural effects.

A more sensitive indication of job effects would come from allowing each job to be represented by a separate (dummy) variable. This procedure has the advantage of revealing the full effects of each individual job. Of course, since most jobs contain few individuals, such a procedure may also be unduly subject to errors. Any jobs in which a few individuals happen to have had unusually high or unusually low promotion rates will appear to indicate structural effects, which in fact are not properties of the jobs. As a result, this analysis provides an upper limit estimate for structural effects, which is likely to overestimate the actual structural effect.

Historical Effects Net of 1965 Jobs

In the previous analyses, historical effects were inferred from the effects of initial job status independent of intervening job status. However, an alternative explanation would be that 1962 job status only picks up explanatory power because of the imprecision of the 1965 job status scale. If the 1965 job status scale perfectly measured status (for instance, if it took into account both formal and informal job status distinctions), then 1965 job status might totally explain later attainment, and 1962 job status would have no additional effect.

A more severe test of the historical effects hypothesis may be performed by creating a separate (dummy) variable for each 1965 job. In effect, this analysis permits 1965 jobs to have as much effect as they possibly can, freeing 1965 job effects from the possible limitations of the job status scale (such as its linearity or its failure to measure informal status). Of course, this is a particularly severe test of the historical-effects hypothesis, for it allows random variation to be attributed to 1965 jobs.

Does 1962 job status affect later attainment independent of 1965 jobs? As in the previous analysis, 1975 job status attainment is taken as the dependent variable, and the model controls for the same individual attributes. So that jobs containing only 1 person in this cohort will not be interpreted as part of the "job effect," the job variables are limited only to jobs containing 2 or more individuals in this cohort. Fifty-eight individuals in 1965 were in jobs which contained only 1 person in this cohort. These individuals are not represented by job variables in the analyses, and so are represented in the constant term in the regression. Obviously, further limiting the analysis to jobs that contained more individuals would be a more reliable test of job effects, but that would limit the analysis to even fewer jobs. The present analyses study the effects of the 44 jobs in 1965 which contain 2 or more individuals from the 3-year cohort.

For comparative purposes, the third column of Table 6.3 is reproduced here in the first column in Table 6.6. In the second column, 1965 dummy variables are substituted instead of the 1965 job status scale. While these 44 job variables explain more variance than the single 1965 job status scale, the adjusted R^2 is virtually the same. The coefficients for individual attributes do not change very much, and, most importantly, the influence of 1962 job status remains significant. Indeed, somewhat surprisingly, its impact is somewhat greater than it was when 1965 job status was in the equation. Although the 44 job variables explain more variance than 1965 job status, 1962 job status retains an even greater influence. This may be because 1962 job status is explaining some of the effect of the 1965 single-person jobs which are relegated to the constant.

Repeating this analysis after eliminating the 58 individuals in single-

Table 6.6

Historical Effects with 1965 Job Dummy Variables: Effects of 1962 Job Status on 1975 Job Status, Controlling for Attributes and 1965 Job Status or 1965 Job Dummy Variables (Including and Excluding Single-Person Jobs)[a]

Independent variable	1965 job status	1965 jobs[b]	1965 jobs[c]
Tenure	−.4169*	— −.3857	−.4386*
	(.1977)	(.2090)	(.2113)
Entry age	−.1683**	−.1696**	−.1596**
	(.0287)	(.0427)	(.0484)
B.A.	4.0015**	3.9650**	1.7725
	(1.0012)	(1.2150)	(1.3605)
M.B.A.	1.5868	2.2192	2.5080
	(1.1077)	(1.1913)	(1.3070)
College selectivity	−.0227	.0148	.0285
	(.1865)	(.2366)	(.2562)
Race	−1.5412	−1.6711	−.4263
	(1.5257)	(1.5881)	(1.6799)
Female	−10.0623**	−10.5970**	−14.6691**
	(2.8951)	(3.3062)	(3.6728)
Female–B.A.	−1.4521	−1.9421	.3712
	(1.6427)	(1.9504)	(2.1166)
Female–Race	1.9293	1.9664	.7219
	(1.6500)	(1.7198)	(1.7990)
Female–Tenure	.4803*	.4373*	.5064*
	(.2080)	(.2200)	(.2214)
Female–Entry age	.0909*	.0895	.0759
	(.0377)	(.0497)	(.0545)
Job status 1962	.6285**	1.1422**	.9321**
	(.0804)	(.1522)	(.2069)
Job status 1965	.8348**	No	No
	(.0804)		
Jobs 1965	No	Yes	Yes
Constant[d]	13.1040**	16.1004**	18.4761**
	(2.6481)	(2.9862)	(3.4527)
R^2 (%)	70.9	72.5	73.3
Adjusted R^2 (%)	70.3	69.9	70.5
SEE[e]	3.6661	3.6898	3.5335

[a]Asterisk indicates coefficients significant at the .05 level. Double asterisk indicates coefficients significant at the .01 level. Standard errors for coefficients are indicated in parentheses.

[b]Constant includes individuals in single-person jobs in 1965.

[c]Individuals in single-person jobs in 1965 were omitted from this regression.

[d]Constant represents non-college-educated white males.

[e]Standard error of estimate.

person jobs in 1965 (making the largest job in 1965 the constant) does reduce the 1962 job status coefficient. Nonetheless, it still remains quite large and significant (Table 6.6, column 3). Apparently, some distinctions in 1962 job status continue to have effects independent of 1965 jobs.

Of course, the cautions about the interpretation of the job dummy variables still needs to be born in mind. Nonetheless, since the additional sources error introduced by 1965 job dummy variables leads to a bias *against* the historical-effects hypothesis, the net effect of these analyses is to provide even greater support to that hypothesis.

Trade-off within Jobs?

Although it has been shown here that individuals within job statuses face no trade-off, this could be because job statuses are too broadly defined. If different jobs in the same status were very different in the ability they required or status they conferred, the lack of a trade-off could be because individuals are not comparable despite controls for job status and individual attributes. The variation in individuals may be further limited by controlling for jobs.

Analyzing the 1975 status attainments of this cohort—controlling for individual attributes, 1962 earnings, and 1962 job dummy variables (jobs with two or more individuals) as independent variables and single-person jobs as the constant—the effects of most individual attributes are negligible. The 35 job dummy variables in 1962 lead to an adjusted explained variance slightly greater than that of the regression with the 1962 job status variable (comparing the 68.6% adjusted explained variance in Table 6.7, column 1 with the 67.6% adjusted explained variance in Table 6.5, column 2). Nonetheless, 1962 earnings still do not have the negative effect predicted by the trade-off hypothesis; indeed, earnings have a significant positive influence.

Of course as before, the influence of the various single-person jobs which are relegated to the constant may be coming out in the 1962 earnings coefficient. Therefore when the analysis is repeated, omitting the single-person jobs (making the largest 1962 job the constant; Table 6.7, column 2), the effect of 1962 earnings is smaller and not quite significant. But the important point is that earnings still do not have the negative influence predicted by the trade-off hypothesis.

Repeating these analyses taking 1975 earnings (in logs) as the dependent variable reveals comparable findings. In all four analyses, the trade-off hypothesis must be rejected; and early earnings are found to

Table 6.7

Stratified Rewards (No-Trade-off) Hypothesis with 1962 Job Dummy Variables: Effects of 1962 Ln(Earnings) on 1975 Job Status and Ln(Earnings), Controlling for Attributes and 1962 Job Dummy Variables (Including and Excluding Single-Person Jobs)[a]

Independent variable	Dependent: 1975 job status		Dependent: 1975 ln(earnings)	
	Independent		Independent	
	1962 jobs and ln(earnings)[b]	1962 jobs and ln(earnings)[c]	1962 jobs and ln(earnings)[b]	1962 jobs and ln(earnings)[c]
Tenure	−.4826* (.2337)	−.4546 (.2848)	−.0137 (.0091)	−.0185 (.0111)
Entry age	−.1492** (.0426)	−.1238** (.0437)	−.0091** (.0017)	−.0081** (.0017)
B.A.	3.1768* (1.2786)	2.8663* (1.3856)	.0564 (.0498)	.0289 (.0541)
M.B.A.	2.0571 (1.2074)	1.7877 (1.2923)	.0656 (.0470)	.0535 (.0504)
College selectivity	.3922 (.2289)	.1122 (.2509)	.0083 (.0089)	.0016 (.0098)
Race	−1.4561 (1.6078)	−.6728 (1.7385)	−.1865** (.0626)	−.1193 (.0678)
Female	−5.2495 (4.0640)	−11.2324* (4.8505)	−.2163 (.1582)	−.5776** (.1893)
Female–B.A.	−2.2760 (2.0002)	−1.0704 (2.0790)	−.0278 (.0779)	.0395 (.0811)
Female–Race	1.8504 (1.7364)	.9668 (1.8564)	.1873** (.0676)	.1168 (.0724)
Female–Tenure	.3626 (.2335)	.4330 (.2828)	.0086 (.0091)	.0167 (.0110)
Female–Entry age	.0549 (.0493)	−.0287 (.0502)	.0034 (.0019)	.0024 (.0020)
Jobs 1962	Yes	Yes	Yes	Yes
Ln(money) 1962	8.8480** (1.9025)	4.1718 (2.1716)	.3358** (.0741)	.1823* (.0847)
Constant[d]	−55.6240** (15.5291)	−16.4724 (18.0992)	6.8907** (.6045)	8.1427** (.7062)
R^2 (%)	70.9	70.3	80.0	79.9
Adjusted R^2 (%)	68.6	67.9	78.4	78.3
SEE[e]	3.7721	3.7290	.1468	.1455

[a]Asterisk indicates coefficients significant at the .05 level. Double asterisk indicates coefficients significant at the .01 level. Standard errors for coefficients are indicated in parentheses.

[b]Constant includes individuals in single-person jobs in 1965.

[c]Individuals in single-person jobs in 1965 were omitted from this regression.

[d]Constant represents non-college-educated white males.

[e]Standard error of estimate.

be positively associated with attainment 13 years later (a significant effect in all but one analysis).

These results provide no indication that individuals help their careers by making earnings sacrifices in their early years. The contrary seems more likely to be the case; those who get relatively more earnings in their early jobs will also advance further in their later careers.

Another fact of interest in these analyses is that the effects of most individual attributes decline to insignificance in these analyses. Apparently most individual attributes have their effects on ultimate attainments via their effects on early earnings or early jobs. Only a few individual attribute variables retain significant effects in these analyses, and only one—entry age—has a significant effect in all four analyses in Table 6.6. These findings confirm the previous conclusion that entry age is different than most other individual attributes in having an increasingly strong influence as individuals' careers progress. It is the one factor which strongly affects later attainments, net of initial earnings and job attainments.

Conclusions

The findings here reveal an even stronger patterning of careers than anything shown in previous chapters. By studying job status attainment and limiting the analysis to a cohort entering in a limited time period, the analysis reveals the fine-grained selection process which occurs in the very earliest period and traces its subsequent outcomes.

It must be stressed that this continuity is not due to a lack of changes in job status. Job status radically changes over the period studied; for instance, the average attainment of white males increased enormously (comparing the 1962 and 1975 constants in Table 6.2), and the advantage of college-educated over non-college-educated white males also increased a great deal. Despite the great changes in attainment, the general patterns of effects remain largely similar over this period, with many (but not all) of the initially advantaged groups retaining their advantage 13 years later.

The underlying reason for the enduring patterns of influence is the stability of individuals' relative rankings in the job status structure. Job status attainments in employees' first years in the firm are moderately good predictors of their attainment 13 years later. First selections have an impact on later career attainments independent of the most salient individual attributes.

Moreover, the findings of historical effects are particularly important because they contradict American norms about opportunity. According to American societal norms, individuals who overcome low-status origins can advance to high status, and such Horatio Alger stories are often cited in this organization. Indeed, the findings of this study indicate that some Horatio Alger types do manage to overcome initial disadvantages and reach the same attainments as many of their cohort peers who began at higher-status positions. These Horatio Alger types also end up doing better, on average, than their peers who began at the same low-status jobs and rose less quickly from the outset. However, the central contention of the Horatio Alger stories, that fast starters from low-status origins can overcome their initial disadvantages and achieve parity with those beginning higher, is clearly contradicted. Kelley's (1973a, p. 492) ahistorical conclusion that "past failures are forgiven and past successes forgotten" is, generally speaking, not true.

Similarly, early earnings advantages are also carried forward in future attainments, and the human capital theory's prediction of a trade-off is unambiguously contradicted. Instead of earnings sacrifices being associated with greater subsequent career attainments, lower initial earnings are associated with lower subsequent career attainments in virtually all analyses, even with individual attributes and job status (or jobs) controlled. Rewards are stratified; either one gets more of both rewards or one gets less of both.

This chapter began with the conflict between human capital theory, which posits open advancement opportunity, and structural theory, which posits no opportunity for advancement. The results find both theories to be inadequate.

Human capital theory is difficult to challenge, and the findings of these analyses strike serious—but not necessarily lethal—blows to that theory. The findings indicate that early jobs strongly affect individuals' ultimate attainments independent of individuals' attributes, a finding which implies that the organization's job assignments cause a greater structuring of career attainments than human capital theory suggests. However, the limitations of our measures of individuals' attributes—which are unavoidable limitations—provide a ready-made escape clause for human capital theory to interpret job effects as indicating unmeasured human capital.

It is also clear from these analyses that employees do not seem to face a trade-off between early earnings and later career advancement; early earnings are not negatively related to later attainments, even after controlling for individual attributes and initial jobs. This finding does seem to be a clearer contradiction of the trade-off prediction of human capital theory, but even here the escape clause can be invoked that this study has not adequately measured human capital, particularly the ability component. College selectivity, which may be considered a measure of ability (as it has been interpreted in previous economic research [Weisbrod and Karpoff 1968; Wise, 1975a]), has been controlled, but it is difficult to maintain that college selectivity is a perfect measure for the kinds of ability that employers compensate. If this ability measure is imperfect, then advocates of human capital theory may contend that the apparent influences of early jobs or early earnings may actually be due to the effects of unmeasured components of ability. Since this research, like all research, lacks a perfect measure of ability, this possibility must be conceded.

Of course, this difficulty of fully measuring ability cuts both ways. Since ability is a central component of human capital, the fact that ability is not fully measurable makes it impossible for this or any other analysis to refute human capital theory. However, an irrefutable theory has limited usefulness as a scientific theory. Although these findings cannot refute human capital theory, the fault may lie not in the analyses but in a deficiency of the theory.

Moreover, refutability issues aside, these analyses do demonstrate career patterns and social influences which are not directly suggested by that theory and which conflict with the predictions that the theory seems to suggest. At the very least, human capital theory does not seem very useful in predicting the features of career patterns found in this study.

These findings have a clearer impact on social structural theory. Contrary to that theory, these analyses find that the structural influence is not an all-encompassing ahistorical effect that subsumes the influence of all previous attainments. The findings force an expansion of the notion of structural effects. While the effects of early jobs are a prototypical example of structural effects, the effects of early earnings and the historical effects of early jobs (net of intervening jobs) are not easily interpreted by this theory. Initial earnings also operate as a social status variable, but their effect cannot be interpreted as structural in the traditional sense; nor are historical effects of early jobs generally seen as compatible with structural theory. Either structural theory must be seriously modified or the signaling theory must be chosen instead.

CHAPTER 7

Continuity and Change in the Career Attainment Process in a Corporation during Growth and Contraction

Introduction

"Structural" theories have generally described the stable characteristics of social institutions. They are often contrasted with "economic" theories that posit highly responsive institutions. The social structure of organizations is sometimes portrayed as a skeletal diagram of a hierarchy of fixed positions which must be filled (White 1970a; Stewman and Konda 1983). Other times, it is portrayed as an internal labor market in which administrative rules and institutional customs define hiring, firing, pay, and promotion practices in fixed and enduring ways (Doeringer and Piore 1971). What these diverse views share is their assumption that inequalities are not very responsive to short-term changes, particularly economic changes.

The polarity between social structural theory and economic theory—particularly the distinct positions each takes regarding persistence and change in economic institutions—has been useful theoretically, but it is obvious that an explanation of the real dynamic of economic institutional change lies somewhere between the views proposed by each of these theories. As Granovetter (1981) and Jencks (1981) have noted, advocates of social structural theory concede that social structures must eventually change in response to economic forces just as economists concede the existence of temporary disequilibria and imperfect markets which sometimes make earnings temporarily unresponsive to change. The more important issues here, however, which neither theory adequately addresses, are, according to Granovetter and Jencks, more complex. Rather than investigating whether or not change occurs, the real issues to deal with here are what kinds of forces, over what periods of time, create what kinds of changes in economic and social inequalities.

While sociological models portray organization structures as rigid and unchanging as the buildings in which they are housed, the corporation analyzed in this volume did in fact grow and subsequently contract during the period studied; and this growth and contraction affected the demand for various kinds of employees. Like the Weberian model of bureaucracy, the model of the career selection process presented here presumes distinctive preferences among employee attributes. This model also portrays the selection system as a series of selections operating over time, and this sequential nature of the process may make selections susceptible to change from external influences. However, until now, the ways that career structure may be changeable have not been specified.

The present chapter shifts the focus from specifying how individual careers unfold over time to describing how career trajectories are affected by historical forces. It describes careers by comparing cross-sectional analyses of random samples of employees in four different periods. Although this procedure does not yield quite the same parameters as longitudinal analysis, it does make it possible to investigate how these parameters change over periods of increasing and decreasing growth, contraction, and affirmative action.

Neither economic nor structural theories are entirely satisfactory for predicting outcomes here. While economic theory provides a dynamic mechanism to explain a system's responsiveness to such changing influences, it assumes that the structure is "rational" in the economists' radically individualistic sense of the term. On the other hand, while most structural theories pose explanations for lack of changes, they generally do not pose explanations for changes.

This chapter presents a dynamic structural model which posits that career selections are the result of tournament processes, and the tournament's selectivity is affected by a dynamic supply–demand mechanism. This dynamic structural model is in many ways similar to economic theory: Increased demand raises attainments and decreased demand lowers attainments. But, unlike economic theory, the dynamic structural model posits that changes in the supply–demand relationship affect the selectivity of the promotion system; and, as a result, some structural limitations are imposed which are not imposed by economic theory. The dynamic structural model proposes two sets of hypotheses to explain these structural limitations.

One set of hypotheses—the *developmental hypotheses*—describes differential responsiveness as careers progress. They contend that individuals' job status attainments become increasingly enmeshed in the career structure over time, so that careers become increasingly less responsive to external forces as they unfold. The other set of hypotheses—the *selectivity hypotheses*—describe the differential responsiveness of different employee groups. These hypotheses contend that the balance of supply and demand, rather than affecting all groups equally, has least influence on the highest and lowest status groups. While economic theory provides a parsimonious model of the outcomes in many cases, these hypotheses suggest that the actual selection process is more complex, and the changeability of career trajectories is dependent on employees' career stages and status attributes.

This chapter analyzes job status attainments in ABCO over a 10-year period, using official personnel records. Because several important changes occurred in the organization over the period studied, this organization provides an unusually good opportunity to study the effects of diverse economic and social changes on the organization selection system and the structural attainments of various kinds of employees. The study begins by analyzing attainments in 1965, following a period of modest growth. This makes a good baseline period, for it is fairly representative of most of the postwar period for this corporation. The subsequent period (1965–1969) was a period of much faster organization growth; the next (1969–1972), a period of sharp decline in organization growth; and the last (1972–1975), a period of organization contraction.

These three periods were also times of dramatic changes in the treatment of women and minorities. Increasingly strong efforts at affirmative action were introduced over the various periods considered here.

Even before the first period, a modest program for helping minority males had begun, but little attention was given to women. Only in 1970, at the beginning of the second interval, did the advancement of women become the primary emphasis, and this affirmative action program was considerably strengthened in the final interval (1972–1975). These diverse influences provide a severe test of the persistence of the career model proposed in this volume. In addition, these strong influences also provide a good opportunity to test the developmental and selectivity hypotheses about the nature of responsiveness of career structures.

Changes in Career Trajectories: Developmental Hypotheses

The tournament model of careers in many ways resembles the developmental model in biology. Both models posit that development is patterned by an underlying structure, and both characterize the structure of development quite similarly. Like the developmental model, the tournament model posits that careers advance through stages, and these stages are irreversible (see Chapter 2). The stages suggested by the tournament model are similar to those described by the developmental model: Early careers are characterized by rapid advancement and differentiation of a cohort, middle stages are characterized by increasingly slower advancement and differentiation, and later stages by a plateau and perhaps a decline (see Bloom 1964; Kagan 1969; Kohlberg 1969). Like the developmental model, the tournament model suggests that individuals may advance at different rates and to different final attainments and that rate and final attainment are related: Those who fail to advance in early career are less likely to continue advancing thereafter. The loss of developmental "momentum" is likely to lead to a plateau.

The previous chapters describe some features of career trajectories which fit this developmental model. The career-tree analysis shows that individuals become increasingly "locked into" a particular career trajectory (Chapter 2). The cohort analyses show that different employee groups (distinguished in terms of education, race, sex, and entry age) have different career trajectories, with different initial starting attainments, different initial rates of advancement, and different later advancement rates, and that these are all related (Chapters 5 and 6). Since much of the effect of individual attributes on later attainments is mediated by early attainments, these analyses suggest that structural mechanisms may have a large influence in determining career trajectories, particularly in influencing their responsiveness to change.

Most important for the present chapter, both models also contend that development is structured in another sense: It is resistant to change. The developmental theory in biology posits that organisms become increasingly resistant to change over time. According to developmental theory, organisms are responsive to external environmental forces in the early stages of their development when their most rapid changes are taking place; thereafter, as development slows over time, responsiveness also declines. For instance, studies of the relationship of drug consumption during pregnancy and infant malformation conclude that "developing structures are most vulnerable during the period of their most rapid development" (Fein et al., 1983). Similarly, developmental theory also suggests that there are differences among organisms in how responsive they are. It posits that organisms which exhibit more changes in their normal development are also more responsive to external forces than are organisms which change less.

The tournament model suggests analogous predictions for careers. It suggests that careers are most responsive to external forces in their early stages, for that is the period when the tournament system allows many selections to occur and when individuals' career trajectories are still unfrozen. Thereafter, as careers become increasingly well defined and limited and as individuals increasingly receive specialized training, socialization, and an accumulation of signals defining their career futures; the tournament model predicts that careers become less responsive. Similarly, the tournament model specifies that employee groups differ in how much career change they may anticipate in the normal development of their careers; and, following the prediction of developmental theory, it is predicted here that employee groups that normally receive more advancement will be more responsive to external influence than those who normally receive little advancement. These parallels may be stated as two developmental hypotheses:

Hypothesis 7.1. Career trajectories can be changed most during their early stages when their most rapid changes ordinarily take place; thereafter, as development slows over time, responsiveness also declines.

Hypotheses 7.2. The career trajectories of employee groups which ordinarily advance more quickly will be more responsive to social and economic forces than those which advance less quickly.

Changes in Career Trajectories:
Selectivity Hypotheses

The preceding discussion considered the changeability of career patterns as a function of developmental considerations. However, this is
not the only factor to affect the changeability of career patterns. The
nature of selection systems also imposes another kind of constraint.

According to the model proposed here, the organizational career system takes certain individual attributes as selection criteria. Assuming
that the organization has a strong commitment to these criteria, what
happens, then, when organization growth or contraction changes the
numbers of individuals the organization needs (i.e., demand changes)?

According to conventional economic theory, large increases in vacancies increase the demand for qualified personnel. This, in turn,
increases the pay offered for these positions in order to draw additional
candidates to compete for the vacancies. However, this cannot happen
in an internal labor market which has fixed entry portals only at the
bottom and which requires prior company experience for higher-level
positions; higher-level vacancies can only be filled by the employees
already in the organization. Since internal labor markets recruit new
employees only into low-level jobs, the organization cannot quickly
alter the supply of employees available for higher levels. If the demand
for high-level employees increases, the only way the organization can
increase the supply of employees is to reduce its minimum requirements for selections into each level.

Whereas in the economic model, earnings are a direct function of
supply and demand, in the dynamic structural model, structural positions become the important outcomes; and it is the matching processes,
particularly the selection criteria, which change individuals' status attainments and their earnings (see Granovetter 1981). But selection criteria can also be conceived as a function of the balance between demand (the number of vacancies) and supply (the number of qualified
candidates). Unlike economic theory in which prices are elastic, what
is elastic in this model is how selective the firm can be in choosing
individuals to fill job vacancies (which confer predetermined wages).
In effect, this dynamic structural model contends that when demand
(vacancies) increases faster than the supply of qualified employees, the
organization must become less selective in filling its vacancies; and,
conversely, when demand declines relative to supply, selectivity
increases.

The dynamic structural model is similar to Thurow's job competition
theory (Thurow 1975). In Thurow's model, wages are fairly fixed prop-

erties of jobs: "In the job competition model, instead of competing against one another based on the wages that they are willing to accept, individuals compete against one another for job opportunities based on their relative costs of being trained to fill whatever job is being considered" (p. 75). Jobs offer different amounts and kinds of on-the-job training so that "marginal product resides in the job and not in the man" (p. 77), and, consequently, jobs offer fairly fixed wages. Instead of supply and demand changing the wages of a job, "markets clear by altering hiring requirements and the amount of on-the-job training they provide" (p. 77). Since Thurow's discussion focuses on hiring (the aspect of labor markets most affected by market mechanisms), he does not consider advancements within firms in as great detail as the dynamic structural model presented here, and so he does not develop hypotheses about career trajectories.

One implication of the dynamic structural model is that some groups will benefit less than others from increased demand. Specifically, it predicts that the most valued employees will experience little benefit from increased demand. It implies that an organization first selects its most valued employees for any vacancies that arise. Accordingly, any small, highly preferred group will be fully utilized under all circumstances, even during periods of limited growth. Consequently, if they are already fully utilized, then organizational growth cannot increase their utilization, and they will experience no gains during periods of growth.

These processes can be stated more formally. Assume for the sake of simplicity that organizations consider employees as falling into three ranked categories. The categories could be ranked in terms of qualifications or status. Here they shall be called elite, semi-elite, and nonelite; however, what they are called is of no importance in the model. Furthermore, assume that during periods of modest growth, the organization fully utilizes all elite individuals in the highest-status jobs they can hold and puts some, but not all, of the semi-elite in the same jobs.[1]

---

[1]This assumption is quite reasonable. Indeed, the notion of an elite (or high selectivity) presupposes that this group is ordinarily fully utilized and in short supply. If elite individuals were not in short supply, they would not be regarded as so precious. Of course, at the very top of organizational pyramids this assumption may not apply, for the number of vacancies at the very top may be smaller than the number of qualified elite individuals. However, this condition is unlikely to apply at middle-management levels and below, which is the focus of this study and where 99% of all employees are located. The model also assumes that, under ordinary circumstances, the organization does not fully utilize all employees to their highest potential. Put another way, if strapped, the organization could put most people into more demanding jobs. Although they might not perform as well as in their previous positions, they would perform adequately.

From these assumptions, it may be inferred that during periods of enormous growth, when there is increased demand for manpower, the elite group receives no further advancement because it is already fully utilized (or nearly so). Since the organization cannot increase the number of elite candidates for high-level jobs, the organization can fill these vacancies only by lowering eligibility requirements, making the selection criteria less stringent, and promoting a greater proportion of the semi-elite to higher positions. Consequently the increased demand will "spill over" to the next most desired group, the semi-elite. As a result of this spillover, the semi-elite group gains during periods of organization growth, and the difference between the elite and the semi-elite declines. In effect, the organization becomes less selective.

Declining growth or labor oversupply reverse these changes. These circumstances reduce the demand for manpower relative to its supply, and the organization selection system can increase its selectivity. Except in the case of extremely severe contraction, the elite will not experience declines; for, even with reduced demand, elites will still be in short supply; however the attainments of the semi-elite will be reduced. The nonelite will continue to be unaffected by both growth and contraction.[2]

Thus, dynamic structural constraints create two kinds of processes: one which creates flexibility of minimum requirements and another which creates stability for elites and non-elites. The following selectivity hypotheses are suggested:

Hypothesis 7.3. When demand (growth of advancement opportunities) increases faster than the supply of qualified employees, the organization must become less selective in filling its vacancies; and conversely, when demand declines relative to supply, selectivity increases.

Hypothesis 7.4. The career trajectories of the most-preferred employees ("elites") are relatively unaffected by social and economic forces and, as a result, their advantage over the semi-elite varies as the

---

[2]Although this trichotomy is an oversimplification, the essential point is likely to hold for greater numbers of subgroups. Any hierarchical distinction among employee groups may lead to one group having some or all of the properties I have attributed to the elite (i.e., being the most preferred group, which the selection system will fully utilize before dipping down to the next group). Of course, under what circumstances this procedure holds is an open question. It must be noted that a greater number of subgroups could make the spillover process more complicated and more difficult to analyze. It might also be noted that the problem of exits does not affect this model. Periods of growth are likely to increase the numbers of elite individuals leaving the organization, but, while this might increase the numbers of semi-elites promoted, it is unlikely to increase the promotions of the elite individuals who remain or to affect non-elites.

fortunes of the latter are affected by external economic events. The career trajectories of the least preferred employees ("nonelites") are also relatively unaffected by social and economic forces since they are not considered for advancements.

Effects of Affirmative Action

Another radical change occurred in this organization over the period considered here: a decline in sex and race discrimination and the implementation of an increasingly strong affirmative action program. Some sociologists have been skeptical about the effectiveness of such reforms. This skepticism is based in large part on the notion of an unchanging organizational structure. Moreover, the traditional structural model provides a good description of the specific practices which militate against affirmative action's effectiveness. The gender allocation practices in organizations are so ingrained in job definitions and job evaluations that these practices seem to be part of the fixed structure of organizations. Furthermore, these structural barriers seem to define role relations among employees so that affirmative action would also require behavioral changes in interpersonal relations among employees. The organization behavior literature is full of examples of women's difficulties in gaining acceptance even in low-level managerial positions, and such acceptance is likely to be a prerequisite to further advancements. Moreover, the structural model suggests that if changes occur, they are likely to be structurally trivial; and observations and studies provide many examples of ostensibly serious efforts which advance only a small number of "token" individuals or which advance individuals into jobs that become stigmatized by the process (Kanter 1977).

Sex differences in attainment would seem to be rooted in the very structure of organizations and to be extraordinarily difficult to alter. While the structural model does not necessarily predict barriers to improved earnings parity between men and women, it posits that status parity would face barriers that are inordinately resistant to change.

However, again it would seem that the traditional structural model, while fundamentally correct, may be excessively rigid. While the social processes suggested by the structural model may be durable and raise appropriate skepticism about social change, the customary concept of structure also seems to be unduly static.

A more dynamic model of social structure would portray the diverse mechanisms that go into creating the structure and would suggest which mechanisms would endure when changes were made in any others. For instance, while affirmative action policies are vague and do not specify which groups of women will benefit, a dynamic model of social structure would predict which women would benefit most and which least. It might also suggest which men would be hurt by the process and which men would be less affected.

The simple prediction one would make for an affirmative action program is that, if successful, it would lead to parity for women compared to men with the same qualifications. Discrimination not only reduces women's attainment, it also reduces the variation in their attainments so that women with a certain degree of education or experience do not receive the same benefits as comparable males (Malkiel and Malkiel 1973; Kanter 1977; Halaby 1979; Rosenbaum 1980). Consequently, affirmative action would not only increase the status attainments of women generally, but it would also make them increasingly differentiated on the same selection criteria applied to men. An important corollary of this prediction is that elite female groups are likely to receive even greater gains than female semi-elites (see Jencks 1983).

Superficially, this would seem to contradict the selectivity hypothesis; however, the past condition of discrimination creates an important difference. Discrimination creates a situation where supply has been underutilized and thus is highly available. Consequently, after a period of discrimination, the increased demand from affirmative action does not exceed the supply and, as a result, it does not require the organization to become less selective. Rather, affirmative action increases differentiation of women's attainments (benefitting the women with the most valued attributes more than it benefits other women), and, consequently, it increases the system's selectivity with respect to women.

Indeed, this prediction, if confirmed, provides an additional confirmation of the particular selection criteria studied thus far in these analyses. Until now, the variables in the regression model used here have described actual empirical outcomes. However, it may be predicted that this regression model is also the ideal pattern toward which affirmative action strives; that is, it may be predicted that the coefficients for the various groups of women increasingly resemble those of men's. Since the organization did not state its affirmative action goals in terms of targeting particular groups of women based on degree of education or tenure, and since it did not even acknowledge some variables in the model proposed here (age or high-status colleges); a movement toward this model implies that it is an implicit ideal of the career structure.

However, since the first developmental hypothesis (7.1) posits that career trajectories change most during their early stages, it predicts an important departure from parity. It predicts that affirmative action helps women in early career more than it helps senior women.[3]

In sum, these considerations lead to the following hypotheses:

Hypothesis 7.5. Affirmative action increases parity between men and women, and thus it increases selectivity among women (subject to the exception noted in Hypothesis 7.6).

Hypothesis 7.5a. Consequently, educated women at preferred colleges will benefit from affirmative action even more than other groups of women.

Hypothesis 7.6. Women in early career will receive more attainment benefits than senior women; that is, the tenure coefficients for women will become increasingly less positive.

Affirmative action is likely to change men's career trajectories, in the same ways already predicted by declining economic growth in these periods. To the extent that affirmative action reduces the attainments of men (since it occurs during periods of declining growth and contraction), the first developmental hypothesis (7.1) predicts that it will affect more-senior men less than it affects less-senior men, and the second selectivity hypothesis (7.4) predicts that it will affect M.B.A.'s and graduates of high-status colleges less than it affects other male B.A.'s. Non-college-educated males will also be less hurt by affirmative action because they received few promotions before affirmative action, and those few promotions may have been necessary to preserve morale in this group, as noted in Chapter 3. Although the coincidence of affirmative action and declining growth makes it difficult to infer the extent to which each affects men's careers, both influences predict the same changes in men's career trajectories.

The two sets of forces have contradictory influence only for women. In the history of this organization (as in the United States generally), affirmative action began helping women as the organization began to experience declining growth, and the program got stronger as the organization contracted. Since parity is being analyzed here in terms of total attainments, the reduced number of advancement possibilities makes total parity more difficult to achieve in a given amount of time.[4] Consequently, any improvements that the affirmative action program introduces in these circumstances are all the more impressive.

[3]This will be the case at least in its immediate impact. Long-run outcomes, extending beyond the period of this study, may be different.

[4]If promotion rates were the dependent variable considered here, declining growth and contraction would make parity easier; fewer individuals would be needed for the limited promotion opportunities.

Comparable contradictory influences also occur for women in the 1965–1969 period of growth and discrimination. Since women had limited opportunities because of discrimination in this period, they represented underutilized abilities and skills, which raised an important conflict for the organization as its need for experienced employees increased: How committed was the organization to sex discrimination? In a period in which it needed to promote large numbers of individuals, did the organization sacrifice its tradition of discrimination to draw on the pool of promotable women? If so, which groups of women did it choose to promote?

The present analysis makes an initial effort at analyzing changes in status attainments in these terms. The analyses provide a dynamic picture of the effects of an affirmative action program on various groups of women and men over successive periods as the affirmative action program is increased in strength. While these analyses cannot produce definitive conclusions about the intrinsic properties of career systems, the findings suggest that a career system can change in important respects, but that it does so in predictable ways and enduring aspects can be discerned.

Even a cursory inspection clearly indicates that the affirmative action program accomplished some sizable gains over the periods studied here. Over the decade 1965–1975, minority earnings increased 38.5% and white females' earnings increased 32.9%, while white males' earnings only increased 18.2% (in constant dollars). Clearly the earnings of women and minorities greatly improved; however, what remains problematic is the extent to which their earnings improved within job status classifications and the extent to which their earnings improved because they improved their job status attainments. Moreover, if there were job status gains, did the affirmative action program accomplish these gains by helping all women equally or did some groups benefit more than others?

The Empirical Model

As previously noted, the tournament model suggests the same stages as the developmental model in biology: early rapid advancement, subsequent slower advancements, and thereafter advancement plateaus and perhaps declines. Moreover, the analyses of cohorts' careers in Chapters 5 and 6 have shown that although different employee groups have different career patterns, all of these patterns are variants of these same stages. This pattern is quite consistent with the parabolic curves which are commonly found by the cross-sectional studies of economic attainment in external labor markets (e.g., Hanushek and Quigley 1978). Of course, the previous analyses, which longitudinally studied status attainment in an internal labor market, differ from those studies in many respects, so it is noteworthy that the same pattern is found in both.

Since the tournament model predicts and the analyses performed in this study thus far have shown parabolic patterns of advancement with increasing tenure, the regression model used for these cross-sectional analyses must permit such patterns to emerge. Following the procedure in economic research, both tenure and tenure-squared terms are included. This permits the model to describe parabolic patterns, with the tenure coefficient indicating the initial rate of rise and the tenure-squared coefficient indicating the rate of deceleration (or acceleration). Of course, if a particular group has a linear advance, then the tenure-squared term will be negligible. (Note that this was not necessary in the previous analyses of the cohorts because of the limited range of the tenure variable.)

In principle, a model in which all variables would interact with both tenure and tenure-squared terms could be constructed, and the results would demonstrate whether each interaction term was important. However, since this would make the model extremely complex, it is desirable to simplify the model somewhat. Preliminary analyses indicate that men and women who attended high-status colleges and those with M.B.A.'s, have similar career trajectories to those of their B.A. counterparts (nonsignificant tenure interactions). For the sake of simplicity, interaction terms are included here only for the four largest groups in the model, non-college-educated males and females and college-educated males and females.

Analyses are conducted on 25% random samples of the complete files from the personnel records, using the above-described model. The same analyses are run for the four separate periods, 1965, 1969, 1972, and 1975. Because race data are missing for 1962, the analyses could not be conducted for that year.

Cross-sectional Analysis for 1965

Table 7.1 reports the analysis of the 25% random samples for each of the 4 years. This section focuses on the first year, 1965 (Table 7.1, column 1). In 1965, the model explains 53.5% of the variance in job

Table 7.1

Regression Coefficients for Job Status for Random Samples of All Employees in the
Corporation in Each Year: 1965–1975[a]

Variable	1965	1969	1972	1975
Tenure	.2973**	.3043	.3983**	.3259**
	(.0291)	(.0255)	(.0299)	(.0443)
Tenure^2	−.0028**	−.0029**	−.0059**	−.0031**
	(.0007)	(.0007)	(.0009)	(.0012)
B.A.	4.5198**	6.6516**	6.0366**	4.1263**
	(.7330)	(.6294)	(.6954)	(.7683)
B.A.–Tenure	.9880**	.6610**	.5225**	.7386**
	(.1018)	(.0858)	(.0991)	(.1138)
B.A.–Tenure^2	−.0227**	−.0144**	−.0137**	−.0193**
	(.0027)	(.0025)	(.0031)	(.0036)
M.B.A.	3.3979**	2.1419*	2.1819*	2.3078**
	(1.0572)	(1.0299)	(1.0161)	(.8618)
High-status colleges	1.5770**	1.0648	2.1407**	2.3002**
	(.5870)	(.6405)	(.6997)	(.7062)
Entry age	−.0925**	−.0639**	−.0667**	−.0490*
	(.0194)	(.0176)	(.0172)	(.0197)
Race	.0192	.0132	−.0818	−.0116
	(.9402)	(.5011)	(.4006)	(.4340)
Female	−1.5016*	−1.0899*	−.5586	.4286
	(.6297)	(.5480)	(.5661)	(.6951)
Female–Tenure	−.1676**	−.1282**	−.1943**	−.1308*
	(.0401)	(.0364)	(.0415)	(.0588)
Female–Tenure^2	.0017	.0003	.0034**	.0008
	(.0011)	(.0011)	(.0012)	(.0016)
Female–B.A.	−1.9934	−1.3704	.0398	3.6538**
	(1.8853)	(1.3193)	(1.2211)	(1.1158)
Female–B.A.–Tenure	−.3683	−.3126	−.3415	−.7591**
	(.5694)	(.4137)	(.3317)	(.2552)
Female–B.A.–Tenure^2	−.0015	−.0013	.0035	.0171*
	(.0262)	(.0163)	(.0119)	(.0080)
Female–M.B.A.	−3.2340	−1.0965	.0865	1.9048
	(2.6652)	(4.4870)	(2.1316)	(1.8404)
Female–High-status colleges	.2930	−.7189	.3592	1.8491
	(1.9509)	(2.1090)	(1.7838)	(2.0281)
Female–Entry age	.0453*	.0171	.0060	−.0214
	(.0228)	(.0202)	(.0200)	(.0229)
Female–Race	−.5274	−.4018	−.1975	−.2634
	(1.0476)	(.5760)	(.4981)	(.5318)
Constant[b]	4.0290**	3.8304**	3.8179**	2.9942**
	(.5391)	(.4652)	(.4652)	(.5628)
R^2 (%)	53.87	52.57	44.97	43.50
Adjusted R^2 (%)	53.55	52.29	44.66	43.16
SEE	3.6549	3.6874	3.8452	4.0623

[a]Asterisk indicates coefficients significant at the .05 level. Double asterisk indicates coefficients significant at the .01 level. Standard errors for coefficients are indicated in parentheses.

[b]Constant represents non-college-educated white males.

status. While this is less than the 68% explained in the first period of the 3-year cohort's career (Chapter 6), it is still much greater than the 20–40% of earnings variance which most analyses of society-wide earnings can explain (Thurow 1975, p. 67). Indeed, analyses of earnings do even better. This model regressed for the log of earnings explains 79% of the variance, and a simpler model without tenure interactions explains over 70% of the variance. The strength of these relationships may be taken as evidence that we are modeling important underlying relationships in this corporation. By extension, this finding suggests that society-wide analyses' failure to explain more than 20–40% of earnings variance is possibly due to insufficient controls for type of institution, not basic defects in the empirical model (although this is conjecture). In this micro-analysis of a single case, where institutional factors are highly controlled, the empirical model explains well over 50% of the variance of job status and earnings (as have comparable studies in other organizations; Malkiel and Malkiel 1973; Wise 1975a; Halaby 1978).

These findings offer many familiar patterns from previous analyses. College degrees offer great benefits to men, and high-status colleges and M.B.A. degrees further increase these benefits. An older entry age significantly reduces male employees' attainment. (An increase in entry age of 7.1 years [one standard deviation] reduces attainment by 0.67 status units). Male minorities have roughly the same attainments as their white peers (i.e., the race coefficient is not significant).

In contrast, women have much lower attainments. College-educated women have even greater disadvantage relative to their male peers; indeed, after summing the female disadvantage (−1.5016) with the college advantage (+4.5198) and the college-educated-female disadvantage (−1.9934), college-educated women start out only slightly above non-college-educated males (+1.0248).

Moreover, female M.B.A.'s receive no benefit from their additional degree (3.3979 − 3.2340). Although female high-status-college alumni receive all of the advantage over other college-educated females that their male counterparts receive (and slightly more [0.2930] besides), they still suffer the enormous penalties of other college-educated females. In sum, most college-educated women have attainments little better than those of males without college degrees, and non-college-educated women have even lower attainments.

However, those findings consider only initial attainments, not career trajectories; and the tenure coefficients indicate that the disparities between college-educated and non-college-educated employees and between men and women increase with tenure. Non-college-educated males show an initial average increase of less than 0.30 status units each year, while college-educated males show an additional 1-status-unit advantage over non-college-educated males each year.

Non-college-educated females not only start lower than their male counterparts, but they also receive less than half the initial tenure increases of their male counterparts. (The initial female tenure advance is calculated as the sum of the tenure coefficient and the sex–tenure coefficient: .2973 − .1676 = .1297). College-educated females begin even lower than their male counterparts, and they suffer an increasingly strong disadvantage over time. While college-educated males receive initial increases of 1.2853 status units per year (.2973 + .9880), their female counterparts receive only a 0.75 status-unit increase per year (1.2853 − .1676 − .3683 = .7494). Consequently, college-educated females begin 3.5 units lower than their male counterparts and their disadvantage increases by over 0.5 status units each year.

The tenure-squared interactions indicate the rate of deceleration of these curves. Deceleration is quite small for the non-college-educated male and female curves; their careers can be described as having almost linear advancement. Deceleration is quite sizable for college-educated males and females, producing parabolic curves. For college-educated males this leads to a plateauing at 25 years of tenure; for college-educated females, the plateau occurs at 15 years of tenure, and more-senior college-educated females actually have lower attainments. (A check of average data points indicates that this decline actually occurs, as noted later.)

Like the previous longitudinal findings, these cross-sectional analyses support the developmental model, showing rapid early advancement which declines over time. The career trajectories of employees in 1965 tend to fit the parabolic patterns posited here (particularly for B.A.'s). Each employee group has a different parabolic trajectory. Compared with non-college-educated males (who increase 0.3 status unit per year), non-college-educated females begin about 1.5 units lower and increase about half as fast, college-educated females begin about 1.0 unit higher and initially increase at about one and one-half times the rate, and college males begin 4.5 units higher and initially increase at more than four times the rate (1.2853 / .2973 = 4.3) These analyses provide a baseline for comparison with later years.[5]

---

[5]Of course, deceleration gradually diminishes the divergence of these curves. For instance, by 10 years of tenure, college-educated females are increasing in status at about the same rate as non-college-educated males, and college-educated males are increasing at less than three and one-half times the rate of non-college-educated males.

Historical Effects on Career Trajectories

Having described career trajectories at one period of time, it is now possible to test the proposed hypotheses. Judging from the previous results, high-status-college alumni and M.B.A.'s are the most preferred groups and may be interpreted as the "elites" in the hypotheses. College-educated males would then be the semi-elites, and non-college-educated males would be the nonelites. The same will be true for females, but only after the affirmative action program begins.

Before proceeding to the analyses, the predictions of the hypotheses should be specified more clearly in terms of this regression model. The second selectivity hypothesis (7.4) predicts that organizational growth (in the 1965–1969 period) will lead to increases for semi-elites (college-educated males) and to little change for elites (male M.B.A.'s and high-status-college alumni) and nonelites (non-college-educated males). The effects of entry age as a selection criterion will also decline. The first developmental hypothesis (7.1) predicts that college graduates with high tenure will benefit relatively less than their peers with less tenure (i.e., the B.A.–tenure coefficient will decline).

Since affirmative action had not yet begun for women in the 1965–1969 period, it is impossible to state with any certainty how much women might have benefited from organization growth. However, if women had benefited, those who had been most underutilized should have benefited most: college-educated females (particularly M.B.A.'s) and, according to Hypothesis 7.1, those with low tenure.

Declining growth, contraction, and increasingly strong affirmative action are predicted to lead to declines for most groups of males, with elites (high-status-college alumni and M.B.A.'s) and nonelites (non-college-educated males) and senior men less affected than less-senior semi-elites (male B.A.'s). Increased selectivity will increase the effects of entry age.

Increasingly strong affirmative action over these periods is predicted to lead to increased parity for women, and thus increased selectivity among them, so that high-status-college alumnae and female M.B.A.'s will gain most, and other college-educated females will gain more than their non-college-educated counterparts. Women will also be increasingly subject to the same influence of entry age as men experience. The first developmental Hypothesis (7.1) suggests that females with higher tenure will not fully share in these gains.

The effects of organization growth are seen by comparing the 1969 results with those from 1965 (Table 7.1; the career trajectories for the

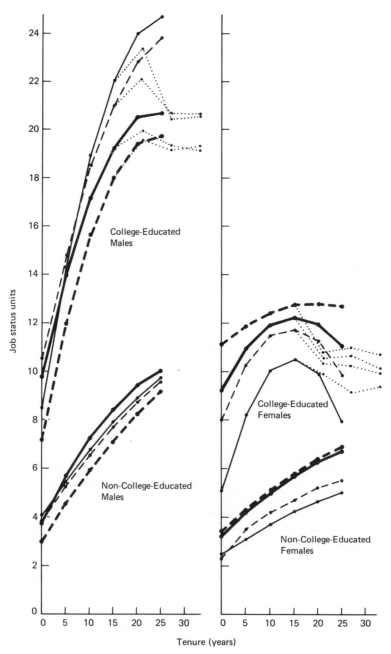

FIGURE 7.1. Job status by tenure for cross-sectional random samples of college-educated and non-college-educated males and females for 1965 (thin solid line), 1969 (thin dashed line), 1972 (thick solid line), and 1975 (thick dashed line). Dotted lines, which begin in the second decade of tenure, are averages of actual data.

four main groups are plotted in Figure 7.1).[6] As predicted, a large increase for male B.A.'s is found while the advantages of high-status-college alumni and M.B.A.'s decline. The attainments of these elite groups seem to be limited as if they were already fully utilized.

As predicted, non-college-educated males do not benefit from organizational growth; indeed, they experience a small decline in attainment (in the constant), and their tenure trajectory is minimally affected. As the developmental hypothesis predicts, more-senior college-educated males gain much less than their less-senior counterparts (as indicated by the marked decline in the B.A.–tenure slope), and the same is true for college-educated females. Also as predicted, the reduced selectivity resulted in a considerable reduction in the influence of entry age.

The results indicate that women benefit from organization growth, and they do so in a way that differentiates the educational groups of women. Non-college-educated females benefit a little (0.2 status unit), college-educated females gain a great deal (3.0 status units), and female M.B.A.'s gain even more (3.9 status units) (numbers represent changes in total attainment at zero tenure, adding all components). The gain for high-status-college alumnae is not as large, but it is still considerable (1.5 status units). Evidently, even before the affirmative action program was implemented, women benefited from organization growth, generally in ways that made them increasingly subject to the same selection criteria as men. The results also suggest that white women are treated more like white men with respect to entry age, and minority females are treated somewhat more like their male counterparts too.

The results of declining growth, contraction, and affirmative action are shown in the 1972 and 1975 columns of Table 7.1 and in Figure 7.1. As predicted, college-educated males decline in attainment over both periods, and, also as predicted, the decline is larger over the 1972–1975 period when the contraction and the affirmative action program are both more pronounced than over the preceding period. Hypothesis 7.4 is confirmed by these findings: The career trajectories of male M.B.A.'s and high-status-college alumni suffer less loss than those of other male college graduates. That is again true in 1975, but both groups nonetheless suffer from the strong B.A. decline. Hypothesis 7.3 is less clearly supported in terms of the entry age coefficient, which slightly increases

---

[6]The present discussion concerns the graphs of the regression analyses, plotted as solid and dashed lines in Figure 7.1. To make this figure more readable, curves for many groups are not plotted, so the reader must refer to Table 7.1 for the data on the effects of college selectivity, M.B.A. degree, minorities, and entry age. Data averages, plotted as dotted lines, are explained subsequently in the text.

as predicted over the 1969–1972 period and declines sharply in the following period.

Affirmative action did bring increased parity for and increased selectivity among females. College-educated females gain more than non-college-educated females and high-status-college alumnae and M.B.A.'s, gain much more than other female college graduates. Women also become increasingly subject to the influence of entry age, so much so that they are more strongly affected by entry age than their male counterparts by 1975.

Hypothesis 7.2 predicts that career trajectories of non-college-educated individuals will be fairly unresponsive to external influences since the careers of these individuals normally show little advancement with increasing tenure. The non-college-educated male curves in 1972 and 1975 are highly similar to the 1969 curve, never amounting to a full status unit in difference (in contrast with much larger changes for B.A.'s). Similarly, the non-college-educated-female curves show small gains in entry status and minimal changes in overall slope (tenure and female tenure).

The first developmental hypothesis (7.1) receives mixed support from the college-educated male-curves. The total slope for college-educated males declines slightly over the 1969–1972 period (.9653 versus .9208), contrary to the predicted increase. This may be because the decline in growth is relatively small and has a relatively small impact. In contrast, when the organization actually contracts over the 1972–1975 period, the first developmental hypothesis is strongly supported: The B.A. slope increases sharply. More-senior college males are relatively less affected by declining growth.

The first developmental hypothesis (7.1) receives strong support from the college-educated-female curves. While college-educated females receive increasingly strong advantages over the two periods after 1969, their tenure slopes become increasingly less steep, indicating that more-senior college-educated females do not fully share in the gains of their less-senior counterparts.

Moreover, the support provided by the regressions for college-educated males and females for the first developmental hypothesis (7.1) is actually understated. Due to attrition, random samples overrepresent low-tenure employees relative to those with high tenure; consequently, employees in their third and fourth decades in the corporation are underrepresented in the regression curves. If average job statuses for college males are plotted, the data points are quite close to the regression curves through the first two decades, but not in the third and fourth decades.

The dotted lines in Figure 7.1 show actual data points for white, college-educated males and females, who neither attended high-status colleges nor have M.B.A. degrees (without controlling for entry age). The first 18 years of tenure are ignored, because those data fit the curves quite closely. Data points are calculated for three 6-year tenure spans in order to have sufficient numbers of cases in all spans (18–23 years, 24–29 years, and 30–36 years, arbitrarily represented as 21, 27, and 33 in the figure).[7]

The college-educated male data curves indicate a stronger deceleration than the regression curves at the end of the second decade, declines early in the third decade, and leveling off thereafter. Demotions, though rare generally, are much more common among senior employees. The data curves imply that college-educated males may experience real declines in status at higher tenures, and these declines occur earlier and to a greater extent than the regression curves suggest.[8] The declines are particularly great in 1965 and 1969, reducing much of the advantage of this group over the 1972 and 1975 curves. Moreover, although 1975 attainments are much lower than 1972 attainments in early career, the disadvantage declines in late career and vanishes in the third decade. This convergence in the third decade suggests that declining growth and affirmative action take less of a toll on college-educated men's attainments in their later careers than in the second decade of their careers.

The same is true for the college-educated female curves. The data curves for college-educated females in their third and fourth decades also tend to be much lower and closer together than the regression models indicate. The third-decade data curve for 1965 is higher than the regression model indicates, and those for other years are generally lower. As a result, these curves tend to be within two status units of each other by the end of the third decade, and they converge into the fourth decade. Cross-sectionally, the data curves in 1969, 1972, and 1975 show that in the third and fourth decades college-educated wom-

[7]Since the data after 1969 represent historical periods separated by 3-year intervals, the 6-year tenure ranges have the additional advantage that each 1969 tenure span represents a sample from the same universe of individuals as the next tenure span in the 1975 curve. Consequently, these data points represent the advancement of comparable individuals from the same cohort. Note that since these data are based on independently drawn 25% random samples, they include very few of the same individuals.

[8]An alternative interpretation would be that senior employees may have started out in lower-status jobs than young employees. These cross-sectional data cannot address this possibility, but longitudinal analyses do show real decreases in status for higher tenure individuals.

en have much lower attainments than their less-senior peers, suggesting that they were left behind when less-senior college-educated women benefited from organizational growth and affirmative action. Similarly, comparing data points longitudinally in the way suggested in footnote 7, the gains from 1969 to 1975 also indicate that more-senior college women do not fully share in the gains of their less-senior peers. The data curves indicate that organization growth, contraction, and affirmative action had much less influence on the attainments of college-educated males and females in their third and fourth decades than in earlier periods. Consequently, both cross-sectional and longitudinal evidence support the first developmental hypothesis (7.1).

The results generally confirm most hypotheses in most periods. The changes in college-educated males' attainments conform quite well to the predictions; and, in the context of this marked changeability, the stability of attainments exhibited by M.B.A.'s, high-status college alumni, and more-senior college-educated employees are particularly striking in their consistency with the hypotheses. Indeed, the findings that more-senior college-educated females failed to benefit from affirmative action and that their male counterparts failed to be hurt by contraction have important implications which are considered later in this chapter.

Components of Earnings within and across Statuses

Economic theory conveys an image of earnings being determined by judgments about the value of individuals. For instance, human capital theory posits that individuals' earnings are determined by the value of their personal attributes, while marginal productivity theory posits that individuals' earnings are determined by their contribution to the organization's productivity. Both descriptions convey an image of the earnings-determination process as being quite individualistic, that is, as judging employees individually in terms of their value or contributions.

A job evaluation compensation system such as the one implemented in this organization clearly differs from this model; job evaluation does not reward individuals per se, but only pays them according to the jobs they occupy. As has been shown, job evaluation policy stipulates that jobs are evaluated based on social judgments about what the job demands from its occupants (rather than what the jobholders have to offer), and the pay levels of jobs are set in a way that will reinforce the authority and status differences in the organization hierarchy. Little mention is made of market rates; internal equity comparisons are the dominant considerations in setting wage levels.[9]

As noted in Chapter 4, job statuses are based on three main factors: requirements, working conditions, and responsibility, none of which is adequately described by human capital theory. The first, job requirements, is likely to be related to individuals' human capital, but individuals' capabilities may sometimes fall short of job requirements (e.g., during tight labor markets) and sometimes exceed job requirements (e.g., during loose labor markets), and, in both circumstances, job evaluation dictates that individuals be paid according to job demands, not their individual human capital: Engineers forced to do janitorial work are paid as janitors. The second, harsh working conditions, is likely to be negatively related to human capital. The third, responsibility, which is primarily indicated by a job's position in the authority hierarchy, may be positively related to human capital, but the incremental human capital needed for a promotion is likely to be much smaller than the pay gains conferred by the promotion. Indeed, managers report that promotion selections are generally difficult decisions made about highly similar competitors, but the promotion decision leads to these marginally superior individuals receiving much greater earnings on the day that they move into their new jobs. The human capital they bring with them is clearly not what determines their increased earnings.[10] Moreover, Thurow (1975) contends that human capital theory reverses the causal direction: Jobs determine the value of individuals' human capital, rather than human capital determining jobs and salaries. Clearly, earnings differences across statuses are difficult to attribute solely to human capital.

---

[9]Of course, individuals are assigned to job statuses in part based on their personal resources (human capital), but, given the difficulties of assessing human capital per se, even these assignments are likely to be based on social signals of ability and features of their job histories, such as original and subsequent job statuses, and recency of job moves. Although one may interpret earnings conferred by job statuses as vaguely indicative of individual human capital, this relationship is at best a very indirect one, mediated by diverse social processes.

[10]Of course, after individuals have occupied a higher-level job for some time; they will have acquired the skills necessary to perform its functions, and they will have the human capital commensurate with the value attributed to the job. But that acquired human capital is less a property of the individual than it is the property of the job which conferred the skills. As Thurow (1975) states in his job competition theory, fairly equivalent individuals compete for jobs, and the winners win both the better jobs and the on-the-job training required to permit them to do the job.

Table 7.2

Regression Coefficients for Ln(Earnings), Controlling for Job Status for Random
Samples of All Employees in the Corporation in Each Year: 1965–1975[a]

Variable	1965	1969	1972	1975
Tenure	.0297** (.0010)	.0214** (.0008)	.0187** (.0010)	.0214** (.0014)
Tenure^2	−.0006** (.0000)	−.0004** (.0000)	−.0004** (.0000)	−.0005** (.0000)
B.A.	.1058** (.0239)	.0888** (.0206)	.0215 (.0221)	.0156 (.0240)
B.A.–Tenure	−.0162** (.0033)	−.0166** (.0028)	−.0060* (.0030)	−.0126** (.0036)
B.A.–Tenure^2	.0003** (.0001)	.0003** (.0001)	.0001 (.0001)	.0003** (.0001)
M.B.A.	−.0047 (.0343)	−.0037 (.0331)	.0007 (.0319)	.0131 (.0268)
High-status colleges	−.0038 (.0190)	.0000 (.0206)	−.0235 (.0220)	−.0368 (.0220)
Entry age	−.0032** (.0006)	−.0024** (.0006)	−.0026** (.0005)	−.0026** (.0006)
Race	−.0679* (.0304)	−.1076** (.0161)	−.1253** (.0126)	−.0357** (.0135)
Female	−.4361** (.0204)	−.4184** (.0176)	−.3639** (.0178)	−.2482** (.2159)
Female–Tenure	−.0021 (.0013)	.0048** (.0012)	.0009 (.0013)	−.0050** (.0018)
Female–Tenure^2	.0001** (.0000)	−.0001 (.0000)	.0000 (.0000)	.0002** (.0001)
Female–B.A.	−.0469 (.0610)	.1600** (.0424)	.1024** (.0383)	.0688* (.0347)
Female–B.A.–Tenure	.0371* (.0184)	.0073 (.0133)	.0142 (.0104)	.0258** (.0079)
Female–B.A.–Tenure^2	−.0011 (.0009)	−.0000 (.0005)	−.0003 (.0004)	−.0006* (.0002)
Female–M.B.A.	.1987* (.0862)	.0832 (.1442)	−.0553 (.0669)	.0039 (.0572)
Female–High-status colleges	.1156 (.0631)	.1076 (.0678)	.0735 (.0560)	.1033 (.0630)
Female–Entry age	.0040** (.0007)	.0028** (.0007)	.0025** (.0006)	.0006 (.0007)
Female–Race	.0707* (.0339)	.0842** (.0185)	.0846** (.0156)	.0195 (.0165)
Job status	.0391** (.0006)	.0412** (.0006)	.0413** (.0005)	.0362** (.0006)
Constant[b]	8.6316** (.0176)	8.6883** (.0151)	8.8566** (.0148)	8.9126** (.0176)
R^2 (%)	91.47	91.19	88.08	82.44

Table 7.2 (Continued)

Adjusted R^2 (%)	91.41	91.13	88.01	82.33
SEE	.1182	.1185	.1207	.1261

[a]Asterisk indicates coefficients significant at the .05 level. Double asterisk indicates coefficients significant at the .01 level. Standard errors for coefficients are indicated in parentheses.

[b]Constant represents non-college-educated white males.

But there is another aspect of compensation which does resemble the economic theories in being individually based. According to company policy, part of compensation is based on *merit* considerations; individuals are paid within jobs according to their personal productivity as judged by their supervisors. Since job statuses often contain many different jobs, and since jobs often contain many individuals; it is quite possible that considerable earnings variance could occur within structurally equivalent jobs, and this unstructured earnings variance could resemble the pure, individually based process described by human capital theory. To what extent is the variation in individuals' earnings mediated by structural positions and to what extent does it occur within structurally equivalent positions?

This question, originally raised in Chapter 5, can be tested here for random samples of the corporation's employees over several periods, and the job status scale provides a better estimate of the full extent of structural effects. More important, by comparing analyses over different periods, the extent to which social and economic forces affect earnings through the status structure and the extent to which their influence is independent of the status structure can be discerned. Structural theory generally posits that the component of earnings mediated by status is less responsive to external forces than the component of earnings which is independent of status. The dynamic structural theory proposed here, while contending that structurally mediated earnings may be somewhat responsive to external forces, still posits that their responsiveness is subject to constraints, such as those described by the selectivity and developmental hypotheses and by structural discrimination. In contrast, earnings differences within statuses, being determined at the discretion of supervisors, would be unfettered by these structural constraints and may be fully responsive to market influences and individual contributions.

Elaborating the regression model discussed previously permits an investigation of this issue. The empirical analysis is modified by making earnings (in logs) the dependent variable, and by introducing job status as an additional independent variable. The job status coefficient indicates how much an additional unit of job status advancement contributes to earnings, and the coefficients for individual attributes then indicate their contributions to earnings independent of job status (Table 7.2).

Although the table is complex, it is immediately obvious that job status is strongly related to earnings. The magnitude and nature of this relationship can be seen most clearly by analyzing the contribution of job status to earnings variance. As Table 7.3 makes clear, job status mediates about two-thirds of the relationship between individual attributes and earnings. In addition, job status is related to earnings over and above the component that is mediated by individual attributes. This additional "unique influence" of job status on earnings increases over these historical periods. Consequently, if the relationship between job status and earnings is subject to structural constraints as posited, then structural constraints will also have a great influence on individuals' earnings, since so much of individuals' earnings is determined by job status.

This partitioning of effects can also be done for each individual attribute. The extent to which each individual attribute has its influence across or within job statuses can also be compared by combining Tables 7.1 and 7.2. For instance, a college degree adds 4.52 units of job status in 1965 (Table 7.1) for newly entering males, and a 1-unit increase in 1965 job status contributes 3.91% to earnings (Table 7.2); consequently, the structurally mediated effect of a college degree on earnings is 17.67% (i.e., 4.52 × 3.91). In contrast, within job statuses, a college degree contributes 10.58% to earnings (Table 7.2). These two sources of contributions to earnings are portrayed in Table 7.4. Despite the com-

Table 7.3

Earnings Variance Explained by Individual Attributes and Job Status[a]

| | 1965 | | 1969 | | 1972 | | 1975 | |
Variable	Unique	Total	Unique	Total	Unique	Total	Unique	Total
Individual attributes	27.0	79.2	23.1	75.3	20.0	67.4	19.3	58.6
Job status	12.3	64.5	15.9	68.1	20.7	68.1	23.8	63.1
Shared	52.2		52.2		47.4		39.3	
	91.5		91.2		88.1		82.4	

[a] The explained variance of components is derived from the model in Table 7.2. Variance is expressed as a percentage.

Table 7.4

Contributions to Ln(Earnings) across and within Job Statuses[a]

Variable	1965	1969	1972	1975
Tenure	.0116	.0125	.0164	.0118
	.0297	.0214	.0187	.0214
Tenure^2	.0001	.0001	.0002	.0001
	−.0006	−.0004	−.0004	−.0005
B.A.	.1767	.2740	.2493	.1492
	.1058	.0888	.0215	.0156
B.A.–Tenure	.0386	.0272	.0216	.0267
	−.0162	−.0166	−.0060	−.0126
B.A.–Tenure^2	.0009	.0006	−.0005	−.0007
	.0003	.0003	.0001	.0003
M.B.A.	.1329	.0882	.0901	.0835
	−.0047	−.0037	.0007	.0131
High-status colleges	.0617	.0439	.0884	.0833
	−.0038	.0000	−.0235	−.0368
Entry age	.0036	.0026	−.0028	.0018
	−.0032	−.0024	−.0026	−.0026
Race	.0008	.0005	−.0034	.0004
	−.0679	−.1076	−.1253	−.0357
Female	.0587	−.0449	−.0231	.0155
	−.4361	−.4184	−.3639	−.2482
Female–Tenure	−.0066	−.0053	−.0080	−.0047
	−.0021	.0048	.0009	−.0050
Female–Tenure^2	.0000	.0000	.0001	.0000
	.0001	−.0001	.0000	.0002
Female–B.A.	−.0779	−.0565	.0016	.1323
	−.0469	.1600	.1024	.0688
Female–B.A.–Tenure	−.0144	−.0129	−.0141	−.0275
	.0371	.0073	.0142	.0258
Female–B.A.–Tenure^2	.0001	−.0001	.0001	.0006
	−.0011	−.0000	−.0003	−.0006
Female–M.B.A.	.1264	.0452	.0036	.0690
	.1987	.0832	−.0553	.0039
Female–High-status colleges	.0115	.0296	.0148	.0669
	.1156	.1076	.0735	.1033
Female–Entry age	.0018	.0007	.0002	−.0008
	.0040	.0028	.0025	.0006
Female–Race	.0206	.0166	−.0082	−.0095
	.0707	.0842	.0846	.0195

[a]For each variable, upper values are across-status coefficients calculated from Tables 7.1 and 7.2; lower values are within-status coefficients copied from Table 7.2.

plexity of the table, some findings are easily noted. For example, in all years, the college variables (college degrees, M.B.A. degrees, high-status colleges, and the B.A.-tenure interaction) affect men's earnings predominantly through their influence on job status. The earnings of the various groups of college-educated men are strongly differentiated across statuses and minimally differentiated within job statuses. Consequently, most of their earnings advantage is likely to be subject to the structural constraints described by the selectivity and developmental hypotheses which affect job status attainments, and relatively little of their earnings advantage is independent of job statuses.

As has already been seen, changes in job status attainments support the predictions of the dynamic structural model; however, since economic theory is meant to explain earnings, the earnings changes provide a better test. Indeed, within job statuses, the results provide some support for economic theory. Within statuses, the earnings advantages of M.B.A.'s and high-status colleges mostly change in the directions predicted by economic theory. (Both have slightly increasing earnings advantages within statuses over 1965–1969 and high-status alumni have declining advantages over the next two periods, as shown in Table 7.4). However, while the earnings advantages of M.B.A.'s and high-status colleges within statuses are small and insignificant, their earnings advantages across statuses are much larger; and these advantages change—not according to the predictions of economic theory, but according to the predictions of the selectivity and developmental hypotheses. The advantages of the elite college-educated groups (M.B.A.'s and high-status college alumni) decline with organization growth and increase with declining growth; and college-educated men's gains in 1965–1969 are largest for those with low seniority, while their declines in the final period are also greatest for those with low seniority.[11] The greatest part of earnings variance for college-educated men is across statuses, and the changes in the effects of these factors are subject to the constraints described by the dynamic structural model.

Economic theory and the dynamic structural model make the same predictions about the changing effects of college degrees for men's earnings: Both predict increased influence with growth and declining influence with declining growth, contraction, and affirmative action. The results indicate that the across-status effects conform to these predictions, but the within-status effects do not always do so (Table 7.4). The within-status effects of college are contrary to prediction over the

[11]The results in the middle period conflict with the developmental hypothesis, but the modest changes make this a minor conflict, as noted in the discussion of status changes.

period of organizational growth (when they decline for most values of tenure) and over the 1969–1972 period (when they increase for those with more than 7.37 years of tenure). These differences are small and perhaps not important. However, if earnings within statuses are the best indication of the value of human capital (unmediated by structure), these changes clearly offer no support to human capital theory.

These analyses also help in understanding the source of women's earnings disadvantages and the way they change. In 1965, non-college-educated women suffer their largest earnings disadvantages within statuses rather than across statuses. Apparently, within jobs of equivalent status, non-college-educated women do not receive "equal pay for equal work" in this period. College-educated women in this period suffer from the same problem. Although their status disadvantage relative to college-educated men reduces their earnings by almost 8%, the 44% "women's penalty" within job statuses is the major source of their earnings disadvantage.

Although structural factors continue to have little influence on non-college-educated women's earnings in later years, structural factors do begin to have a large influence on college-educated women's earnings, but only after the advent of the affirmative action program. True to the prediction of economic theory, organizational growth does improve the earnings of college-educated women, but this is only true for the unstructured component of earnings—their earnings within statuses. While their earnings within statuses increase by nearly 20% between 1965 and 1969, their earnings across statuses change very little. Evidently, economic forces alone are not sufficient to overcome the structural barriers to their status advancement.

It is only with the increasingly strong affirmative action program between 1969 and 1975 that college-educated women received earnings increases across statuses. Over this period, college-educated women's earnings began to resemble the college-educated male pattern of being predominantly determined across job statuses. Apparently, while organization growth led to large earnings gains within statuses, strong affirmative action efforts were required to overcome the status obstacles and create major earnings gains across statuses.

The developmental hypotheses have a large impact on the economic gains of college-educated women. While newly entering college-educated women have achieved parity with their male counterparts in terms of across-status earnings by 1975, they receive virtually none of the gain for tenure that their male counterparts receive (so that those with 10 years of tenure have 45% lower earnings than their male counterparts due to their status disadvantage). These developmental barriers do not apply within statuses; the affirmative action program gives high-tenure college-educated women bigger earnings gains within statuses than their lower-tenure female peers. But since the developmental character of status gains prevents high-tenure college-educated females from fully sharing in the status gains of their lower-tenure peers, their earnings gains within statuses are effectively cancelled.

Conclusions

This chapter supports, clarifies, and extends the conclusions of previous chapters. The empirical findings are consistent with those of the age-promotion curves in Chapter 3.[12] These findings also support the conclusions of the longitudinal analyses by showing that the diverging career trajectories for different employee groups are also evident in cross-sectional analyses in each of the periods considered. These career trajectories are not merely products of a particular cohort or particular historical sequence; they are enduring properties of the organization career system.

The dynamic structural model also extends the conception of career systems presented in this volume by proposing specific hypotheses about the ways that careers respond to change. The first developmental hypothesis (7.1) suggests that career trajectories will be most susceptible to change in their early periods. This inference, already supported by the age–promotion curves, is further supported in the present analyses, which extend the conclusion to the career trajectories of various employee groups, including various subgroups of women.

The dynamic structural model, and particularly its selectivity hypotheses, lead to predictions that cannot easily be explained by economic theory. The constraints that prevent elite college groups from gaining during organization growth and limit their losses during contraction do not follow from any principles in economic theory, but they do follow directly from the dynamic structural model. This is not to say that human capital theory could not be modified to incorporate these

---

[12]The main differences are that the present chapter's parabolic model formulates career trajectories as a function of tenure (not age) and portrays age as an additive influence. For explaining empirical outcomes, the use of age or tenure does not make much difference (since the two are so highly correlated, particularly for B.A.'s). However, for the model discussed in this chapter, which conceptualizes career trajectories as components of organization structure, tenure is preferred.

results, for instance, by positing some special properties of elite college-educated groups, but such complications seriously detract from the primary virtue of the theory: its parsimony. Moreover, the most plausible modification of human capital theory would require superimposing a structural mechanism on economic theory (e.g., contending that these groups are already fully utilized).

The tournament mechnism underlying the dynamic structural model also provides a serious competing explanation for the "fanning-out" patterns in lifetime earnings. While Mincer (1974) develops an elaborate model which posits hypothetical differences in individuals' investments in their human capital in order to explain the fanning out of earnings, the tournament provides a simpler explanation. Positing that jobs are distributed in structural hierarchies conferring commensurate pay (on a logarithmic scale), the tournament model makes job statuses and, consequently, earnings "fan out" over time as sequential selections occur in the career tournament.[13]

Admittedly, the findings predicted by the developmental hypotheses could also be explained by human capital theory. Human capital theory posits that investments in human capital decline with seniority because of the shorter time remaining to receive benefits from these investments (to amortize the investments). This could explain why the earnings of senior employees are less responsive to social and economic forces than the earnings of their less senior counterparts. For example, the relative lack of losses by senior men and the relative lack of gains by senior women over the 1972–1975 period may be explained by the organization's protection of its former investments in the men and its reluctance to invest in women with too few years remaining for amortizing the investments. The main problem with this human capital explanation arises if the amortization contention does not apply, and Chapter 10 suggests that it may not apply under certain common circumstances, including rapid turnover and rapid changes in job requirements. Nonetheless, in the abstract, human capital theory cannot be ruled out as a possible explanation for the findings pertinent to the developmental hypotheses.

The analyses suggested by the dynamic structural model permit human capital mechanisms to be separated from structural mechanisms. The human capital component can be seen in earnings within

---

[13]Obviously, the tournament model is only meant to describe the career system within large organizations, not in the labor market as a whole. However, given their size, visibility, and influence, large organizations are likely to influence the pay and job structures of smaller organizations if the latter are to be competitive for employees.

statuses, since structural mediation is not involved, employees' productivities are more comparable, and equity norms reinforce paying employees for their performances (not for their status attributes). In contrast, for reasons outlined earlier, earnings differences across statuses, though possibly reflecting some human capital influences, are likely to be reflecting other influences as well, such as the normative considerations incorporated in the job evaluation system.

The findings suggest that human capital theory is right for the wrong reason. The predictions are confirmed, but not because the value of human capital attributes per se changes. Instead of individual attributes explaining earnings, the direct effect of human capital attributes (M.B.A.'s, high-status colleges, senior B.A.'s) on earnings is small and often negative within job statuses (where the value of human capital attributes per se is best gauged). It also changes very little in response to changing demand, and mostly in the wrong direction.

Rather, the predictions of human capital theory are confirmed only because the organization status structure, operating according to the mechanisms of the dynamic structural model, selects individuals for positions in ways that often support human capital theory. In other words, its predictions are confirmed not by individual human capital's economic value per se, but by the value conferred by the status system. This value may bear some resemblance to human capital, but it need not do so; also there will be important sources of lags and discrepancies and, as has been shown in these analyses, structural attainments will even affect earnings independent of individual attributes. Most important, changes in external circumstances will affect earnings largely through the mediating influence of the job status structure, and changes in job status are seriously constrained by the mechanisms described by the dynamic structural model presented here.

The dynamic structural model and its component mechanisms described by the selectivity and developmental hypotheses explain the ways that the organization status system responds to various social and economic influences and to affirmative action; as a result, it explains the largest part of changes in earnings. Insofar as it explains phenomena which are not well explained by human capital theory or rigid structural theories, it identifies important shortcomings of each theory.

Contrary to the prediction of human capital theory, elites will experience smaller gains than semi-elites during increasing growth and smaller losses during declining growth and contraction. Moreover, although organization growth increases college-educated women's earnings within job statuses, as human capital theory suggests, it does not increase their earnings across statuses, and the structural barriers of the job status system—which are the most important determinants of earnings differences—are only overcome by the extraordinary intervention of the affirmative action program.

The dynamic structural model and the present findings also have important implications for structural theory, both supporting the stability it predicts and indicating dynamic mechanisms which structural theory must incorporate. A distinctive feature of this chapter's results is the fundamental stability of structural attainments. Despite the enormous changes occurring in this organization over these periods, the same groups tend to maintain their same relative positions. Although females' gains provide a dramatic exception, the fact that females' career trajectories increasingly resemble the structural model for males suggests that the model describes a latent ideal.

The dynamic structural model also indicates dynamic mechanisms which structural theory must incorporate. In this chapter the selection processes for matching employees with job statuses were found to change over different social and economic conditions, and the dynamic structural model proposed here explains these changes better than other structural models. Vacancy models, though dynamic, do not readily describe career timing and subgroup differences (see Chapter 1). Traditional structural theories do not describe mechanisms for changes in selection processes. In contrast, the dynamic structural model proposes several mechanisms which explain changes in the career timing and trajectories of employee subgroups. Moreover, the empirical analyses confirm that career trajectories often change in the ways predicted by these mechanisms (as stated by the selectivity and developmental hypotheses).

In addition to its theoretical value, the dynamic structural model also has practical implications. The dynamic structural model explains some of the successes and failures of the affirmative action program. The greatest gains of affirmative action went to females in the elite college-educated groups. They suffered the greatest disadvantages relative to their male counterparts of any group of females in 1965 and 1969,[14] they gained the most during the weak affirmative action program (over the 1969–1972 period), and they attained the greatest status advantage relative to their male counterparts by 1975.

Indeed, as Hypothesis 7.5a predicted, females' gains seem to be directly commensurate with credentials. The elite college-educated females gained the most, other college-educated females gained the next most, and non-college-educated females gained much less. Col-

[14]This is the case except for high-status-college alumnae in 1965.

lege-educated females' gains both precede and surpass the gains of non-college-educated females. One cannot help speculating that a strong reliance on credentials made it easier for this organization to overcome its previous strong reluctance to advance women. This is consistent with findings that suggest that educational credentials have been important in fostering Blacks' earnings gains since 1964 (Jencks 1983).

The dynamic structural model also identifies some serious shortcomings of the affirmative action program in this organization, and it explains why they occur. The developmental character of career trajectories tend to make the affirmative action program, though highly successful in the aggregate, a complete failure in rectifying past injustices. The relative lack of gains for senior women and the relative lack of losses for senior men creates serious departures from parity. The processes underlying the developmental hypotheses lead to a form of structural inertia which partially undermines the effects of affirmative action.

These findings are not only theoretically important; they are also important for policy concerns. From the perspective of individual equity, this set of outcomes is particularly unjust for it means that while the "average" woman receives great gains and the "average" man receives losses, the program does not rectify past injustices against the particular individuals concerned. For the particular individual women who were held back the longest because of discrimination, affirmative action provided little gain in status; and for the individual men who benefited the longest from discrimination, affirmative action had relatively little cost. The mild decrease in growth and mild affirmative action program over the 1969–1972 period provides a partial exception, since the costs initially increase with tenure; nonetheless, even over this period, the most-senior college-educated men decline less than college-educated men in the second decade of their careers. Moreover, the strong contraction and strong affirmative action program in the following period provides unqualified support: The amount of males' decline decreases uniformly with tenure between 1972 and 1975. The affirmative action program did not cancel the normal operation of the career structure, and the developmental character of career trajectories meant that the attainments of senior men and women, established during the period of discrimination, were maintained, even after the discriminatory practices stopped.

Meanwhile, the least-senior men and women are strongly affected by the affirmative action program. The least-senior women, who were not members of the organization when discrimination was occurring, gain the most; and they gain relatively more status than parity in order to offset the lesser gains of more-senior women who attain less than parity. The least-senior men, who never benefited from past discrimination, suffer the biggest decline in job status relative to what their more senior counterparts received in an earlier period and relative to that of their female counterparts.

These shortcomings of the affirmative action program are perhaps the most important implications of the dynamic structural model for policy concerns. While the average situations for men and women move toward an aggregate balance, the dynamic structural model suggests mechanisms by which organization structure creates new inequalities which are likely to be fraught with frustration and envy. The psychological implications of these inequalities are considered in Chapter 8, and policy implications are considered in Chapter 10.

CHAPTER 8

*Organization Careers and Life-Cycle Stages: Social Psychological Implications of Career Structure**

Introduction

The previous chapters have shown that age has a major influence on employees' career patterns in this corporation over all periods studied. The present chapter explores some implications of this finding.

Careers and the adult life cycle have received considerable attention from researchers and the public media. The reasons are manifold. The entrance of women, minorities, and the large postwar generation of youth into career-ladder jobs, the effects of declining economic growth, legal issues related to age discrimination, and declining productivity

*This chapter is an expanded version of a paper presented at the annual meeting of the American Sociological Association, New York City, August 30, 1980, at the session on Life Cycle chaired by Frank Furstenberg. I wish to thank Glen Elder, Melvin Kohn, Carmi Schooler, and Richard Suzman for their helpful comments.

236

among employees in their middle and later careers have all created new pressures for change on organization career systems and on commonly held conceptions of careers.

However, most of the attention to this issue has been from a psychological perspective, which tends to view life-cycle changes in isolation and to give the impression that life-cycle changes are inevitable and immutable aspects of people's biological and psychological makeup. Although interesting insights have emerged from this perspective, its orientation on the individual places blinders on inquiry and prevents it from determining where biology and psychology end and social forces begin.

Sociological research has mostly addressed life-cycle questions using survey methods; and, as a result, it has been unable to obtain good indicators of social context factors. For instance, Morse and Weiss (1955) found that work satisfaction steadily declined with increasing age, and Campbell, Converse, and Rodgers (1976) and Kalleberg and Loscocco (1983) obtained similar findings decades later. But this research has difficulty relating psychological outcomes to features of the work context, such as the structure of career opportunities. While individuals' perceptions of context can be measured, people have difficulty seeing important aspects of social contexts, particularly opportunity structures, as the review in Chapter 1 suggested.

Consequently, what remains unexplored in the survey research on the life cycle is whether social institutions have age-graded practices which might be contributing to life-cycle phenomena. If studies of social institutions did reveal age-graded practices, then age-related phenomena which are commonly attributed to an individual's internal life cycle might alternatively be explained by external influences. The present study has performed just such an examination of a social institution, and it has found clear age-graded practices. This chapter explores some implications of these findings for interpreting life-cycle phenomena.

This chapter begins by presenting some alternative conceptions of aging. After describing the view of aging as a biological phenomenon, I propose and develop a conception of aging as a social phenomenon, particularly as a phenomenon creating social inequalities. The previous analysis of employees' careers in the corporation under study in this volume is used to show the ways that this organization creates distinct career stages for different kinds of employees. These findings suggest the possibility that organization career structures may contribute to aging, and particularly to social inequalities among different age groups.

In addition, some further hypotheses are proposed about the ways that organization career structures may affect individuals and the underlying processes involved. In contrast with the traditional psychological model of careers, the model proposed here suggests ways that an organization's career structure may influence the attitudes and behaviors which are commonly attributed to the adult life cycle. This model indicates that the occurrence and timing of these attitudes and behaviors may not be inevitable and immutable aspects of the life cycle per se, and it suggests ways that they may be altered by reforms of organization career systems.

Biological and Sociological Explanations of the Midcareer Life Stage

This chapter focuses on one particular life stage—what has been called the midcareer stage. This life stage has received increased attention since 1970. Sheehy (1974) calls this the midlife-crisis stage, and she defines it in terms of confronting the loss of youth. Sofer (1970) identifies this period as the time when people "come to realize the implications of the commitments they have made during the last 15–20 years" (p. 69), and they realize this is their last chance to make a fundamental change in their lives. Super (1957) labels this period the maintenance period; and, distinguishing it from the previous periods of striving and achievement, he describes it as a plateau, where one tries to maintain what has already been achieved. Kaufman (1974, pp. 46–48) identifies this period as a time of obsolescence of career skills.

One possible explanation for the midcareer life stage is that it is a response to biological declines. Biological aging occurs in this period, and it is commonly thought to have profound effects on people. Without asserting biological determinism, Hall (1976) nonetheless implies it by preceding his discussion of the midcareer life stage by a discussion of the biological changes occurring in this period, leaving the implication that they may be influential on individuals' psychological responses during this stage.

The list of biological changes occurring after age 40 is lengthy and depressing: loss of energy, visual acuity, hearing capacity, muscle tone, skin elasticity, and same-sex hormone. These biological declines might seem to be the fundamental causes of career plateauing and the onset of the midcareer stage of life.

However, although this list of biological declines represents important changes for individuals, these biological declines are not necessarily pertinent to work careers, particularly for white-collar jobs. Surely muscle tone and skin elasticity have little relevance to most kinds of work. And, although loss of visual acuity and hearing could be quite important in some jobs, studies suggest that the declines at age 40 are trivial and serious declines only tend to occur after age 60—well after the midcareer stage (Weiss 1959; see Figures 8.1 and 8.2). The studies of biological aging suggest that gradual changes take place, and these studies give little support to discrete stages of aging. Biological changes alone are not likely to be sufficient causes for partitioning career stages of individuals.

An alternative explanation for the midcareer life stage is that it is socially determined. As Riley (1976) has stressed, "age is a continuum." Consequently, the problem to be explained is why aging is commonly viewed in discontinuous stages. Riley infers that "partitions of the population by age *acquire* meaning as age strata only as they index *socially* significant aspects of people and roles" (p. 192). Riley's survey of the literature documents the ways that "the numbers of [age] strata and their age-related boundaries differ from one time and place to another" (p. 192). Her analysis suggests that life stages are actually the product of social conceptions which society and its institutions *impose* on the age continuum. If an understanding of where these social conceptions originate is to be reached, the ways that society and social

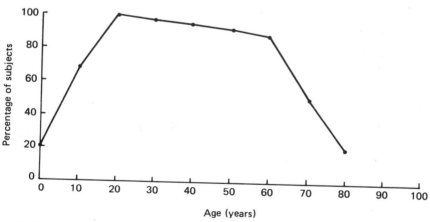

FIGURE 8.1. Changes in visual acuity with age: percentage of subjects having normal 5/5 acuity at different ages. (Adapted from Weiss. 1959." Sensory Functions." In *Handbook of Aging and the Individual: Psychological and Biological Aspects*, edited by J. E. Birren, p. 510. Courtesy of the University of Chicago Press. © 1959 by the University of Chicago.)

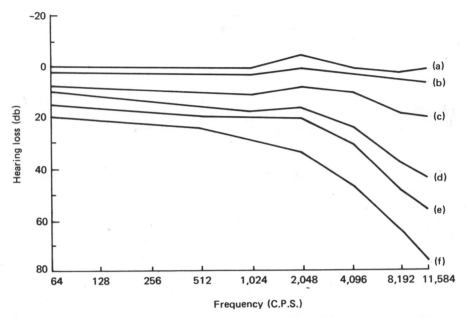

FIGURE 8.2.   Hearing loss at various frequencies with age: (a) 11–15 years, (b) 21–25 years, (c) 41–45 years, (d) 51–55 years, (e) 61–65 years, and (f) 70–82 years (Adapted from Weiss. 1959. "Sensory Functions." In *Handbook of Aging and the Individual: Psychological and Biological Aspects*, edited by J. E. Birren, p. 521. Courtesy of the University of Chicago Press. © 1959 by the University of Chicago.)

institutions respond to age must be examined (Foner 1974, 1980; Dannefer 1982).

The importance of social conceptions in defining adult life stages can be seen in the descriptions of these stages. Unlike Piaget's (1952) stages of child development, which are defined in terms of *competencies* at specific physical tasks and which may be considered to be properties of individuals, the adult life stages are defined in terms of attitudes and behaviors which seem to depend on socially conditioned expectations. Sheehy's "sense of loss of youth" and Sofer's "one last chance" refer to a sense of deprivation relative to what one's social experience has led one to expect. Although most definitions of the midcareer life stage have stressed the psychological changes in this stage, changes in the social environment have been implicit in most descriptions of this period.

Reversing the emphasis of such descriptions may provide a new understanding of these life-cycle stages. Rather than focusing on the subjective experiences of individuals, the sources of these changes may be better understood by focusing on changes that occur in the social environments that individuals confront as they become older. Bringing the social deprivations implicit in the psychological literature into the foreground, a sociological definition of the *midcareer life stage* would be the life stage when the social environment stops offering individuals new opportunities because of their age. The events described by Sheehy, Sofer, and Super identify a multitude of ways that the social environment begins cutting off options, reducing challenges, and reducing expectations for what individuals can do and become as they approach the midcareer stage. Note that this definition clearly portrays aging as a matter of social inequality, with the onset of the midcareer being a form of status loss.

Homogenization or Differentiation

Much of the analysis in social science is based on central tendencies. Whether measured by means, medians, or modes, phenomena are described by what is taken to be "typical." However, this is only one way of representing reality, and, as social scientists are aware, descriptions of "typicality" are all too conducive to stereotypes which ignore important sources of variation. Indeed, the degree of variation is another feature of social phenomena, which, though often neglected, may be highly revealing about social processes.

The notion of *stage* is based on the assumption that members of an age cohort are highly similar to each other with regard to certain attributes and differ from other age cohorts with regard to these same attributes; that is, that stages are discrete and coherent. However, many researchers have suggested that, rather than leading to discrete stages, aging leads to increasing variability among the individuals in an age cohort on many social, psychological, and physiological characteristics (see Botwinick and Thompson 1968; Neugarten 1973; Butler 1975). Obviously, if a cohort is becoming increasingly more heterogeneous, it will be increasingly less well typified by a distinct stage description.

Other researchers have suggested the contrasting view that aging makes a cohort more homogeneous over time (Palmore 1981; Bornstein and Smircina 1982). This view is derived from the notion that biological declines impose increasingly lower limits on performance, and that they will have greater impact on high performers than on low performers. By this view, performance is increasingly homogenized at a low level.

Dannefer (1982) reviews the literature on this question, and he suggests that the answer probably depends upon the outcome being measured and the structure of environmental contexts.[1] For instance, he notes the observation of Riley and Bond (1982) that the way health services are distributed to aging people could "increase heterogeneity if made available selectively . . . or could decrease heterogeneity if made universally available" (Dannefer 1982, p. 25).

Thus, the homogenization–differentiation issue brings up the same question about causation as the stage theory: To what extent do biological forces predominate and cause aging to be manifested by reduced variability and to what extent do environmental forces predominate and cause aging to be manifested by increased variability? Of course, to address this question, a better understanding of the environmental forces and structures which individuals experience is needed.

The Tournament Model of Career Structure

Sociologists have studied the career stages of a wide variety of occupations, including dance musicians, hockey players, doctors, lawyers, and business executives (e.g., Glaser 1968; Slocum 1974; Van Maanan 1977). By drawing on individuals' perceptions, this literature has been able to describe the ways that individuals conceive of the career stages in their occupations and to relate these stages to individuals' perceptions of the institutional and social constraints in the occupation. However, if many employees misperceive the nature of the career system, as the findings in Chapter 1 suggest, then the reliance on individuals' perceptions, without having access to objective data for checking these perceptions, presents a serious risk of distortion. Moreover, the study of perceptions makes it difficult to discover systematic patterns of career paths, particularly the kinds of complex patterns shown in the analyses presented in this study (however, see Lawrence 1983, 1984). The analyses presented in previous chapters provide an objective description of the career structure of the organization under study, which suggests a general model of career options and con-

---

[1]One problem with both sets of issues is the disparate types of changes being discussed. Dannefer (1982) notes the common finding of increasing income inequality with aging (U.S. Bureau of the Census 1967) as an example of increasing variance and the finding of increasing homogeneity of blood pressure with aging (Maddox and Douglass 1974) as an example of decreasing variance. These findings, notes Dannefer, do not really conflict. If a conflict is to be identified, more precision is needed about the phenomena being considered.

straints. From these findings and this model, the present chapter offers some speculations about the kinds of incentives and social conceptions this career structure provides to employees and how this structure is likely to affect the socialization of employees through the middle portion of their careers.

The previous chapters describe the way that an organization allocates career trajectories to individuals at various times in their careers. However, by itself, the empirical description is not sufficient. To understand *why* an organization treats various age groups differently and *how* these promotion practices influence individuals' attitudes and behaviors, it is necessary to have a theory of organization career selections.

Briefly stated, the organization career system is conceptualized in this volume by the tournament model. As opposed to systems which defer selections as late as possible (Turner's contest model) or those which make selections as early as possible (Turner's sponsored model), the tournament model makes selections sequentially. The rule for tournament selection can be simply specified: When you win, you win only the right to go on to the next round; when you lose, you lose forever. This leads to a system in which selections are continually occurring among members of the current winner's group in order to decide which ones will receive the next available promotions and which ones will be eliminated from the tournament and moved into the category of loser, from which there is limited opportunity to advance.

As a selection system that stratifies individuals' future options, the tournament model defines the structure of incentives to which individuals must respond. Moreover, it also conveys information about individuals' probable career futures, and this information, being a social evaluation, is likely to have important social implications for how individuals will be treated by supervisors and peers.

The tournament model is more than a description of a structure; it also posits that the mobility patterns described by the tournament model result from a pattern of investments in individuals, which represents a compromise between the contest and sponsored norms. The continual winnowing down of the winner's group has been inferred in previous chapters to represent an effort to achieve the economic efficiency of early selection and training; but, if this is a dominant goal of the system, then the tournament structure is also likely to encourage supervisors to begin rationing their investments in their subordinates in anticipation of these selections and in ways that would facilitate these selections. Consequently, in addition to describing a selection structure, the tournament model also suggests several underlying social processes which may have effects in socializing employees. These are discussed in the following section.

Opportunity Effects on Socialization: Four Propositions

Selection systems define the range of options that individuals' future careers may take and the probability of each option occurring, defined here as their *set of future advancement opportunities* or, more simply, their opportunities. Opportunities are likely to affect individuals by four kinds of socialization processes. In this section, each of these is described in detail, the rationale of each is presented, and, where possible, pertinent research regarding each is reported. Subsequent sections then develop two hypotheses about how these socialization processes would affect various kinds of employees in this career structure. These socialization processes could be mediating mechanisms which explain how career structure could affect psychological changes in the mid-career stage, and they could provide a resolution of the differentiation–homogenization question.

Opportunities may affect individuals by four kinds of socialization processes. The set of future advancement opportunities offered to an individual defines the structure of incentives to which he or she must respond; it defines the ways an individual prepares for the future (*anticipatory socialization*); it defines the *labels* which affect how an individual is treated by others; and it defines the investments that supervisors will make in an individual. For lack of a better name, these are here called socialization processes, although in many cases they refer to changes which are not as deep-seated as socialization usually connotes. A discussion of each of these processes follows.

Proposition 1. Advancement opportunities define the incentive structure: Individuals who have advancement opportunities will be more highly motivated than those who do not. In my previous study of a high school (Rosenbaum 1976, 1978), students who retained the opportunity to attend college remained involved in school activities. Students in the business track, which offered job training and the opportunity for getting a skilled job, were less involved but still showed some effort in school. Students in the general track, which offered opportunity neither for college nor for a skilled job, were highly withdrawn and apathetic to all aspects of the school (Rosenbaum 1976). Although the direction of causality cannot be determined with certainty, students who were moved to a lower track reported that course difficulty, not low motivation, was the cause of their downward mobility and that their motivation declined after the move because they felt there was no longer any reason to work (a rationale that was given some support by teachers, as shall be noted later). Of course, as with any retrospective account, this explanation must be accepted cautiously.[2] Nevertheless, studies in high schools also have found a similar association between opportunities and motivation (Stinchcombe 1964; Schafer and Olexa 1971).

A great deal of research has found that advancement opportunity is related to employees' motivation in work organizations. Many studies have found that individuals at upper echelons of a hierarchy, "more than those at lower levels, are likely to experience greater motivation, involvement, and interest in their jobs; [and] stronger identification with and loyalty to the organization" (Tannenbaum et al. 1974, p. 1). They conclude, "Thus, hierarchy, which is a basic *organizational* characteristic, has profound *psychological implications for members*" (p. 8). Moreover, even for individuals in comparable jobs, advancement opportunity has been shown to be related to job satisfaction and motivation (Morse 1953; Sirota 1959; Bonjean, Grady, and Williams 1967; Pennings 1970; Pruden 1973) and inversely related to absenteeism and turnover (Friedlander and Walton 1964; Ronan 1967; Hulin 1966; Porter and Steers 1973; Anderson and Milkovich 1980). Even managers in high-level jobs who felt that their careers were at a dead end showed signs of lower motivation than their counterparts who retained advancement opportunity (Kanter 1977, p. 144).

An experimental study of task performance in a hierarchy created in a laboratory setting found that low-status groups who had the possibility of advancement showed greater task motivation than those with no advancement opportunity (Cohen 1958). The finding of this correlation in an experimental study clarifies the causal inference. Since subjects were randomly assigned to conditions, the motivational differences found in the study cannot be attributed to selection effects (i.e., assignments based on initial motivation), so it must be attributed to the experimentally imposed difference in advancement opportunity.

The motivating effects of holding out the possibility of a promotion is well known to managers. In the words of one salary administrator, "Money is not a motivator, anyway. It's just a way for the company to cut its losses by ensuring that people do their job at all. The reward we really

---

[2]Attributing their move to course failures rather than to declining motivation would not seem to be a self-flattering distortion.

control is the ability to promote" (Kanter 1977, p. 129). Promotions are particularly powerful motivators because they have implications for earnings, status, power, and, as the tournament model suggests, the possibility for continued promotions. Moreover, as economists have noted, the prospect of a promotion is a particularly inexpensive reward for an organization since the possibility of a single future promotion can be used to motivate many individuals (Williamson 1975).

Proposition 2. Advancement opportunities affect the ways an individual prepares for the future (anticipatory socialization). The notion of the future affecting the present seems strange. It is surely foreign to the traditional stimulus–response version of psychology. However, it has become an established part of cognitive social psychology and sociology.

Individuals act differently on their own as they receive clues about their likely career futures; they begin to prepare themselves for their future statuses. This anticipatory socialization can be a powerful influence, and it can lead to surprising outcomes. Thus, upwardly mobile working-class men show sexual practices typical of middle-class men (Kinsey et al. 1946). Clearly, career futures can have a very strong impact on present behavior.

Proposition 3. Advancement opportunities define the labels which affect how an individual is treated by others. Individuals' future social roles and statuses are very real phenomena in social institutions. An individual who is "on the way up" is likely to be treated with greater deference, both because of the esteem that upward mobility potential confers and because of the future power the individual will hold. In contrast, there is a common assumption that "if you're not going up, you must be going down" (Ference 1979). Indeed as a vice-president of a major New York firm reported to Ference, "If I remain in this job for three, or five, or seven years, many will come to see me as a failure because I have 'leveled off' " (p. 176). This special treatment is likely to have effects on socialization.

The effects of labeling on socialization were demonstrated in the classic "Pygmalion" experiment. Randomly chosen students who were arbitrarily labeled "late-bloomers who would soon show increased ability" did indeed show subsequent test score improvements, ostensibly because teachers had begun treating them differently (Rosenthal and Jacobson 1968).

Proposition 4. Supervisors will invest attention, help, and resources in an individual who has advancement opportunities. Supervisors will *invest much less attention, help, and resources in an individual with little advancement opportunity.* This proposition is similar to the former one, in this case applied to the treatment of an individual by supervisors rather than by peers. But supervisors' behaviors do not just confer informal status and esteem; supervisors' attention is often an *investment* in subordinates, and it may lead to increased training, increased job challenge, and increased official status in the organization. This proposition combines sociologists' observation of the preferential treatment by supervisors (sponsorship; see Becker and Strauss 1956) with economists' concept of "investments in individuals' human capital." It suggests that the tournament model leads to a distinctive pattern of investments in employees.

The tournament model can be seen as having economic implications for how employees will be treated. In defining which individuals will be subject to further selections and which will not, the tournament model also defines where the organization should invest its finite resources. According to economic theory, investments are made in those productive units which have the potential to produce the greatest returns to investment, and the potential returns to investment are defined by the potential capability of the productive unit and the potential demand for its products. Human capital theory applies this principle to investments in individuals, asserting that investments in employees will be made if there is sufficient potential economic return from the investment.

But human capital theory focuses only on the supply side of the equation (the human capital attributes of individuals), not on the way the organization structures the demand for individuals. While human capital theory considers the potential returns to investments only in terms of individuals' attributes (their education, experience, and ability), the potential returns to investments are also determined by the advancement opportunities that the organization career system permits. Individuals who have been removed from the tournament for top positions can only produce very limited returns to investments, since they cannot advance to more demanding positions that permit much greater productivity. In contrast, individuals who remain in the tournament for top positions still have the chance to produce great returns to the investment.

The effect of opportunity structure on supervisor investments was seen in the high school study mentioned previously (Rosenbaum 1976, 1978). That study found that the track system resembled the tournament model: College-track students had to compete to remain in that track, and upward mobility into the college track was not possible.[3] That study also found that teachers devoted very little attention and resources to lower-track students, while they devoted a great deal of attention and resources to upper-track students. Indeed, teachers who taught students in both kinds of tracks reported how demanding the college-track classes were, while they described the non-college-track classes as periods when they could relax because so little was required of them.[4] The tournament system placed serious demands on teachers of the college-track classes to prepare these students for college, to test their mastery of the material, and continually to make selections of those most suited for the best colleges and those who were unsuited to continue receiving the college curriculum.

Of course, the mandate to look out for students to eliminate from the college track along with the high demands that are made on teachers' limited time in these classes encouraged teachers to make "economic" decisions about how to allocate their time investments among students in the college track. In contrast with a remedial model, which would have encouraged teachers to devote more time to slower students in the college track, a tournament model encourages teachers to devote less time to these students, for they will be candidates for downward track mobility in the future.

In effect, by channeling students' future opportunities, the tournament system provides a way of channeling investments to a limited number of individuals. It defines which students have the opportunity to fulfill the organization's goal, in this case the goal of getting students into college, and it implicitly dictates that investments in students who are likely to attend college will be worthwhile but that investments in other students will produce little visible return.

Having observed such differential investments in an ostensibly non-economic organization like a school, it would seem all the more likely that tournament selection in the career system of the organization under study would encourage similar socialization processes. Supervisors have several kinds of incentives for treating upwardly mobile subordinates better. First, a supervisor is often evaluated on subordinates' performance. A supervisor who turns out good subordinates is more valuable to the company. Second, a supervisor's advancement is often

[3]In other communities or in other times in which college access might be easier it might be expected that college track would have less complete control over college attendance, yet it still might control access to the best colleges (Rosenbaum 1983).

[4]The non-college-track students demanded little of teachers; these students only wanted to get through school and get the diploma, and the school placed few demands on the teachers of these classes.

contingent on having a good replacement to move up into his or her job, so the supervisor who grooms one or more candidates for his or her own position is making him or herself more available for further advancement.

Moreover, supervisors have limited time and resources. They cannot give maximum attention and resources to everyone. As economic actors, they will restrict their attention and the resources at their disposal to those employees whom they believe can most benefit from them.[5] To the extent that career development of subordinates is a supervisor's goal, the tournament model suggests that supervisors would be wasting their time and resources to devote much attention to employees who have little opportunity to advance.

Kanter describes the manifestation of such a process. She notes that "continuing to do the same thing well over time seemed hardly to deserve anyone's notice" (1977, p. 130). In contrast, fast-track employees received a great deal of attention from higher-level supervisors. In the words of one fast-track employee, "[Suddenly higher-level supervisors, including some I did not know] were friends, knew my name, had personal details [about me]. . . . [They were] pulling me aside, not through channels [and] trying to pirate me to their department . . . [Y]ou could see the brown-nosing" (Kanter, 1977, pp. 133–34). This informal attention was also accompanied by very practical benefits. Kanter reports that "fast-track employees were given career reviews much more often than usual . . . and placed in positions that would maximize their exposure . . . for close attention and special observation" (p. 133). Like the teachers in the Pygmalion study, supervisors also tend to invest their attention and resources in individuals labeled to have greater potential.

These socialization processes provide a link between findings reported in this volume about this organization's career structure and the attitudes and behaviors associated with the life-cycle stages. The previous chapters and the underlying tournament model which has been proposed to explain this organization's selection system provide a description of the ways opportunity is allocated to individuals in this organization. Taking these propositions about "opportunity effects on socialization" as axioms permits some specific hypotheses about the effects of organization selection systems in contributing to the psychological life-cycle changes described in the literature. Indeed, these hy-

[5]This might not happen if the organization allowed subordinates to move into positions that would put them in competition with their former supervisors, but, for this reason, organizations seek to avoid constructing such situations (Williamson 1975).

potheses suggest distinctive patterns of attitudes and behaviors at each juncture on the career-tree diagram (in Chapter 2) and the likely changes in attitudes and behaviors in individuals as they proceed out from a juncture along one branch or another.

Age–Promotion Curves and Their Implications for Motivation

Since the concern here is with the work career, the definition of the midcareer stage adopted for this discussion is Super's (1957): a maintenance period in which challenges stop increasing. As Super notes, this leveling off of challenges is also likely to be accompanied by a lack of further job advancement, since organizations often use status advancements as a form of compensation for individuals who take more difficult jobs. Of course, in the organization under study in this volume, as in many others, the relationship between challenge and job advancement is formalized by the job evaluation system. As a result, the analyses of promotions may be a singularly appropriate indicator of organization challenge, and the previous analyses of promotions over time may give a precise description of the onset of the midcareer stage.

Instead of identifying Super's maintenance period in terms of its psychological manifestations, it is identified here in terms of individuals' positions in the career structure and the advancement opportunities associated with these positions, which are posited to have implications for individuals' psychological adaptations. According to this approach, psychological manifestations are dependent variables, which can be explained by the social structural conditions associated with the midcareer stage. The organization selection system determines when an individual reaches the "plateau" of work challenge, which in turn leads to the psychological changes customarily associated with the "midlife" stage.

For this analysis, age–promotion curves (Chapter 3) can be taken as a simple description of organization selection systems. From Proposition 1 (advancement opportunity is a motivator) and from this description of the incentive structure of organization selection systems, a structural explanation of the psychological changes in midcareer may be inferred. This is stated in the following hypothesis:

Hypothesis 8.1. Because increasing age leads to declining promotion chances, individuals' motivation will decline with increasing age.

College-educated employees will experience sharp declines in motivation with increasing age. Non-college-educated employees, though having lower motivation, will experience more gradual declines over time. This hypothesis provides a structural explanation of the psychological changes in midcareer. If it is assumed that promotion chances are an important determinant of motivation, the analyses of promotion chances presented in earlier chapters can explain changes in motivation over employees' careers.

The implications of this hypothesis can be seen most simply and precisely by inspection of the age–promotion curves from Chapter 3. These curves suggest that the career system is quite different for non-college-educated individuals than it is for college-educated individuals. For non-college-educated individuals, changes in career stages are gradual: Promotion chances increase gradually until age 35–40, and they decline gradually thereafter; but there are no abrupt changes. It is not clear that distinct stages are suggested for these employees. In contrast, for college-educated employees, there is an abrupt decline in promotion chances from a peak of over 60% at about age 35 down to less than 20% only 5–10 years later. These findings suggest that the selection system tends to withdraw active consideration from these employees after age 40. Although some are promoted after age 40, the proportion is so much smaller than it was even 5 years previously that the decline suggests a discrete and qualitative change in these individuals' career stage. A college-educated employee under age 35 can expect to continue advancing, while the same employee who holds this expectation 5 years later is bucking the odds and is very likely to be disappointed. This change is so abrupt that it is quite likely to be experienced as stressful, and, as a result, it might precipitate what has been called the "midcareer crisis."

Of course, these simple graphs ignore many factors; however, even after suitable multivariate controls are added, the findings seem to be supported. As Chapter 3 showed, even after years of experience in the company are controlled, the age–promotion curves tend to be replicated for non-college-educated employees. (Comparable analyses for college-educated employees could not be done because of multicollinearity.) Further multivariate controls continue to show strong negative effects of entry age on level changes (Table 5.4), status changes (Table 6.3), and promotion chances (Table 5.A.1), and this influence becomes more strongly negative as careers unfold.

It is instructive to compare these curves with the biological age declines considered previously in this chapter. The biological age declines were rather trivial in the years during which the midcareer life stage occurs, and the declines seem too gradual to explain the onset of a discrete life stage (Figures 8.1 and 8.2). Such is not the case for the age declines in promotions, particularly for college-educated employees. The precipitous declines in the promotions of B.A.'s after age 35 are likely to be traumatic and to be conducive to the psychological "crisis" reactions which are attributed to this life stage.

Of course, the possibility that these promotion declines are a response to these biological declines cannot be rejected; however, if this were so, then these pronounced promotion declines would seem to be an overreaction to rather trivial biological declines. It is as if the first slight signs of biological decline are taken as social signals that are interpreted to have vast social significance. The promotion decline may indeed be a response to other kinds of biological or psychological declines; however, the aging literature does not suggest any biological or psychological attribute which shows that kind of sharp decline.

Stratification of Socialization Processes: Differentiation and Homogenization

While the preceding discussion considered changes in individuals in isolation, this section considers the issue of differentiation or homogenization, which pertains to individuals in relation to their peers in their cohort. Although still referring to psychological consequences, the concern here is with their distribution in a cohort, so the phenomenon is even more clearly sociological.

Wheeler provides a conceptual basis for this analysis. He describes two different socializing environments: "homogenizing settings that tend to reduce the relevance of prior experience for present adjustment . . . [and] differentiating settings [in which] authorities may urge recruits to give expression to the different backgrounds and interests they bring into the organization" (1966, p. 76). Furthermore, Wheeler's examples suggest that upper-status settings (e.g., liberal colleges) differentiate their members, but lower-status settings (e.g., prisons, army training units) homogenize their members. Other examples of homogenizing socialization can be seen in studies of deprived people: the deviant (Sudnow 1965), the sick (Scheff 1966), and the poor (Piven and Cloward 1971). In contrast, differentiating settings generally exist to serve those at the other end of the stratification hierarchy: Human potential centers, psychoanalysis, and open-education schools largely serve the upper-middle class.

While the just-mentioned examples are of two socialization processes operating in different institutions, the two can coexist within the same institution. Indeed, the preceding analyses provide a basis for inferring the structural sources of these two socialization processes, which are proposed in the following hypothesis:

Hypothesis 8.2. Within an organization which has a career system that operates by the tournament model, socialization processes will be stratified: Promotable employees will be differentiated and non-promotable employees will be homogenized. These two different kinds of socialization may be structurally determined. Supervisors will need to discern differentiations among employees so that promotion committees can decide which ones to promote, and, after the fact, these employees will be differentiated further by the consequences of the promotions. In contrast, employees who are no longer in the tournament will be homogenized because whatever differences exist among them will not be socially important for any selection decisions; nor will any subsequent selections be made that will cause them to be differentiated.

The pyramid structure creates an imperative to make differentiations among eligible candidates, and the tournament model focuses this differentiation on employees who have won all their past competitions. After several selections, the competitors at a given level of attainment will probably be very similar (at least with respect to the selection criteria used for past promotions), but the mandate to differentiate employees is inescapable. Even if competitors were identical, as long as there are more competitors than positions at any time period, the system requires differentiations to be created in order to make the required selections. This demand of the selection system encourages supervisors to make more fine-grained differentiations among employees than had been made previously. For instance, previously unnoticed differences could be identified as newly important attributes. Or, if individuals were totally identical, competitions could be arranged to guarantee that some would win and others lose.

These tests, competitions, and labeling processes are likely to identify individual differences which previously did not exist or were not socially important, and they will attribute social importance to these differences. By focusing the pyramidal imperative on a highly pre-selected group of employees, the tournament assures that these individuals will become increasingly differentiated. What may have looked like a "close call" before the selection decision will not appear so after these socialization processes have had time to operate.

The previous propositions about socialization processes suggest more detailed explanations of how these changes may occur. Once the selection system has identified certain individuals as being in contention for advancement, supervisors will invest greater attention, help, and resources in them. These investments, in turn, will lead to increases and differentiation of motivation and skills, and lack of investments will lead to declines and homogenization of performance near the minimum standards. Economic theory posits that investments in productive units (such as factories, machines, or individual workers) tend to increase their productivity and increase the variance in their productivities (because of different returns of investments). Similarly some psychologists suggest that educational programs' investments increase children's skills and increase the variation among them (Cook et al. 1975).

In contrast, a lack of investments leads to declines and homogenization to a low level of performance. Developmental psychology suggests that a lack of environmental stimulation leads children to regress to more infantile behavior (Bowlby 1951). Economic theory also posits that a lack of investment leads to stagnation of factories and, as a result, productivity declines to a very low level.

Similarly, the tournament model suggests that those eliminated from the tournament will only be judged relative to the minimum standards for their jobs, and, as a result, some tendency for performance to become homogenized near that low standard might be expected. Only for these employees is the traditional phenomenon of bureaucracies failing to recognize and respond to individual differences found (Weber 1946). Of course, employees as individuals may resist this homogenization and performance decline because of their own personal standards, but organization career structures provide few incentives for this.

Although presently there is a lack of data for testing this hypothesis for corporation employees, the results of my study of high school students support this hypothesis. Analyses of students' IQ test scores found that the variance of students' IQ scores increased over time for the two college tracks and the variance declined for the three non-college tracks (Rosenbaum 1975). Modeling the change processes revealed that the differentiation in the college tracks was a random process (i.e., it was not a matter of high scorers improving more, or less, than the low scorers; Rosenbaum 1976, pp. 145–148). However, the homogenization in the noncollege tracks was not at all random; students above a low "target" score tended to decline, and that target was lower for the lower general track (IQ = 83) than for the upper general track (IQ = 98). While teachers' behaviors were not observed, these results suggest that something in the experience of these students was serving to homogenize them to successively lower "targets" depending on their track position.

This homogenization and decline are the very same outcomes that have been attributed to biological aging, but of course that explanation would not apply to high school students; and, moreover, it would not explain why college-track students were differentiated and tended to increase in IQ. The stratification of socialization hypothesis provides an alternative explanation which is far more compelling in this situation. Of course, without appropriate data on changes in employees in their work contexts, the issues between the biological aging explanation and the stratification-of-socialization explanation cannot be resolved at this time.

However, the point of this analysis is that these theoretical issues can only be resolved by analyses which take account of organization career structures. Other studies have analyzed changes in employees, but, by ignoring the structural context and the relationship of individual changes to their career trajectories, these analyses could not examine the possibility that employee changes were related to their position in the career system. And, almost by default, these studies have tended to suggest that the causes of the observed changes were in the individuals themselves.

An alternative explanation in terms of the structural demands of the selection system and the socialization processes which are likely to accompany it has been provided here. Unlike the biological aging explanation, which predicts the same aging changes for all individuals at the same age; the structural explanation predicts that some individuals will face these age declines in performance later than others. Of course, even these individuals who delay the age declines must eventually be eliminated from the tournament—everyone stops rising eventually— but they will not start showing these psychological manifestations of aging until the social structure eliminates these individuals from the tournament.

Rather than aging being accompanied by either differentiation or homogenization; according to Hypothesis 8.2, both occur, albeit to different groups of individuals. Individuals are segmented into groups, some are differentiated and others are homogenized, and the result is the stratification of socialization processes. Employees who are in the competition for career advancement are increasingly differentiated, and those who are no longer in competition for career advancement are homogenized to a low level of performance near the minimum standards required to hold the position. The selection systems' imperative to winnow down the winner's cohort and the labeling, anticipatory socialization, and supervisor investments which occur in the process mean that fewer and fewer individuals can put off the manifestations of aging.

Conclusions

In this chapter it has been argued that many aging phenomena which are often attributed to biological changes can be better explained by social processes that are likely to occur in workplaces. In a similar argument, Riley (1977) compares reactions to unemployment with reactions to old age. She notes that studies have found that unemployment sometimes leads people to experience resignation, low self-esteem, apathy, indolence, and physical or mental illness. These attitudes and behaviors are precisely the reactions that have often been attributed to the phenomenon of old age; however, their prevalence among younger people who are unemployed raises the question of whether the social condition of unemployment, which usually accompanies old age, may be responsible for these reactions. Similarly, my research raises the question of whether work conditions also contribute to middle age.

Four socialization processes have been proposed as mediating the impact of work organizations on employees: incentives, anticipatory socialization, labeling, and supervisors' investments. All four are likely to affect employees' motivation, skills, and other outcomes which are commonly attributed to biological aging. These various processes provide a social psychological explanation of aging phenomena.

But while these socialization processes are the proximal causes of individual changes, these processes are set in motion by what has been called here employees' future opportunities. It is customarily assumed that future events are consequences, not causes; but this assumption is oversimple. In the context of an organization where the future is patterned and predictable, expectations for the future are generated, and these expectations can have very real effects on the present. As long as employees are in the organization tournament and can anticipate future selections, the organization must continue recognizing, responding to, and even fostering individual differences among these employees in order to continue the selection process. Once employees are excluded from the tournament and can anticipate no further selections, the organization can stop recognizing and responding to individual differences among such employees and may consider them as interchangeable and homogeneous.

Although socialization processes occur at the level of individual interactions, they are not divorced from larger organization purposes. They are very much a part of the operation of the larger organization. This is true in large part because the organization structure defines career futures. Career futures can only be inferred if careers are patterned and well defined, so organization career structures provide the basis for career futures to become social facts, and thus to set in motion the various socialization processes. These career futures, in turn, create the incentives, expectations, labels, and investments which generate the socialization processes.

The analyses presented here suggest the existence of an organization career structure that defines which individuals have advancement opportunity and which have none. The career tree, the age–promotion curves, and their multivariate extensions even suggest precise inferences about the probability of promotion for particular employee groups, based on individual attributes and previous career history. Indeed, if the actual structure of advancement opportunity were to be represented by the career tree or some multivariate extension of this, then at each selection point, one could infer not only individuals' promotion chances, but also their motivation, the investments they may be receiving from supervisors, and whether they can anticipate being differentiated or homogenized in the future. No doubt this model is too simple, but this skeletal model of careers and the associated socialization processes provides a crisp overview of the influence of structure on socialization, which is difficult to convey in other career models.

The perspective presented here has been one-sided to stress the influence of structure on life cycle. Surely, biological aging is also likely to affect careers. However, structural influence has been stressed here because that view has been so ignored in most of the discussions of this issue. In fact, both kinds of influence must be considered.

It should be noted that unlike the biological view, which encourages fatalistic acceptance, the structural determinant view does suggest that some things can be done to change the life-cycle declines. The changes that would be required are not simple ones, but there are actions that can be taken. Chapters 9 and 10 propose some such changes.

CHAPTER 9

Conceptualizing Organization
Career Systems

Introduction

Organizations are complex phenomena: they are difficult to see and difficult to conceptualize. Even at the simplest descriptive level, the pattern of careers within an organization is difficult to discern because of the large numbers of individuals involved and the many factors which any analysis must include. The task of describing career patterns is beyond the capacity of simple individual perception.

Accurate perception of career patterns is made additionally difficult by the fact that personnel policies are confusing on the issue, reflecting the fundamental conflict in social norms. Society provides strong conflicting mandates on issues involved in organization career systems, and organizations which seek to convince their employees that they operate in socially appropriate ways are caught in a dilemma as they attempt to reconcile these conflicting norms with their particular operational demands. Organizations must do the best that they can to resolve this dilemma, and their policies and practices reflect these efforts.

The analysis of the conflict between human capital and structural theories presented in this volume is really an effort to understand how much and what kind of structuring an organization imposes to constrain individuals' career options. To the extent that the human capital theory holds, early selections will be minimally constraining, and individuals' efforts, abilities, and investments will have great impact on their subsequent careers. To the extent that structural theory holds, early selections will be highly limiting, and they will define many constraints on what directions individuals' careers can take.

Of course, the persistence of the conflict between these two theories and the inability of previous research to make much progress in settling these questions did not bode well for the present enterprise. Ultimately, the conflict is not likely to be definitively settled by any empirical inquiry; the concepts are too difficult to operationalize, and some of the most important factors cannot be measured at all.

However, the present inquiry begins with some distinct advantages since it is able to look at career attainments more closely than much of the previous research efforts have and is able to consider individuals' attainments over long periods of time, controlling for many kinds of individual attributes. Moreover, at times, these analyses have drawn on knowledge and observations of individuals who were involved in making key decisions that determine careers.

How can a system with unequal attainments preserve equality of opportunities? What are the effects of early selections on subsequent careers? These are the focal questions of these analyses. The human capital and structural theories are brought to bear on these data because they are conceptually clear ways of representing the polar opposite conclusions one could reach on these questions. However, given the fundamental difficulties of ever reaching conclusive inferences on this theoretical conflict, the success of this enterprise needs to be judged in terms of how far these empirical analyses and conceptual explorations can go in seeing the merits and limitations of each theory and in assessing which theory is the better explanation of the basic elements of the findings.

In the following sections, this chapter reviews what the findings presented in this volume thus far have suggested about the merits and limitations of each theory. Several findings are not well explained by either theory, and instead they suggest the need for another kind of model. The tournament model is proposed as an alternative way of explaining these findings, and it has implications for understanding the concept of "ability" implicit in organization career systems. A conclusions section considers the tournament model's implications for reconciling some of the main features of the human capital and structural theories. Finally, Appendix 9.A addresses two complexities of the tournament model—job statuses and minor tournaments.

Evidence for and against Human Capital Theory

The strongest support for human capital theory comes from the finding that the structure of careers is less rigid than structural theory generally implies. Rather than the organization being a rigid hierarchy composed of an invariant set of jobs, in fact jobs are continually being created and disbanded. Rather than the age–promotion curves being stable over time, the promotion chances of young employees are quite flexible. In particular, the career trajectories for most college graduates (except those from high-status colleges and those with M.B.A.'s) show considerable flexibility.

Human capital theory can explain some aspects of these findings. The flexibility in career trajectories and promotion chances can be explained as the result of changing economic demand for human capital attributes, and some aspects of the findings are consistent with this economic explanation. Human capital theory can also explain the phenomenon described by the developmental hypotheses (the declining changeability of career trajectories as careers unfold) either by assuming that aging reduces individuals' ability to cope with advancement or by assuming that investments in individuals' human capital decline over time due to the diminished time to amortize these investments. Either of these is a plausible assumption, though (as is noted subsequently) each is subject to serious criticisms.

However, the findings reveal six kinds of evidence that challenge human capital theory. First, the strong structural regularities in career advancement challenge human capital theory because this theory ignores structural phenomena. Since this theory contends that structural regularities in attainments are a by-product of processes occurring at the individual level, it predicts that structural relationships are weaker than the underlying individual influences on earnings. In fact, the opposite has been found in this study.

Second, historical effects pose a fundamental challenge to human capital theory, just as they do to structural theory. Human capital theory contends that individuals are paid and promoted according to the value of the human capital they bring to a job, which, if very little decay over time is assumed, includes most of the human capital the individual previously possessed. Consequently, time-2 compensation (either in job status or earnings) always includes paying for an individual's human capital at time 1, and the theory suggests no way for time-3 status (or earnings) to compensate for time-1 human capital that was not compensated in the intervening period. To explain historical effects requires a mechanism by which value can differentially emerge in different jobs, and human capital provides no such mechanism. Of course, the job evaluation policy provides just such a process, and the empirical findings reported in this volume confirm that most human capital effects on earnings are mediated by job status. Although the possibility that these historical effects might be interpreted as measurement error cannot be ruled out, the most plausible substantive interpretation of the findings entails structural processes which challenge human capital theory.

Third, the absence of a trade-off between initial job status and initial earnings challenges human capital theory. Human capital theory suggests that individuals face trade-offs between earnings and job training, yet the findings reported in this volume provide no indication of such a trade-off. The generalizability of these findings is suggested by reports of the widespread overcompensation of young, preferred employee groups (Shaeffer 1972). The findings are more consistent with the structural theory's prediction that rewards are stratified.

Fourth, the selectivity hypotheses also pose a challenge to human capital theory. They indicate a lack of responsiveness for certain employee groups, which suggests that the advantages of these groups are not merely determined by economic considerations. Structural constraints seem to be involved in creating this lack of responsiveness. Human capital theory suggests no simple explanation for these phenomena (although no doubt the theory is sufficiently resilient to offer a post hoc explanation).

Fifth, although college-educated women's earnings increase with organization growth, as predicted by economic theory, their status attainments do not increase very much. Only after the affirmative action program is implemented do their status attainments increase appreciably, and then they become a major source of earnings gains. Economic theories cannot explain this differential responsiveness, while structural theories can.

Sixth, individuals' structural attainments are differentiated before their earnings are differentiated in ways that can explain their later earnings differences, and this temporal priority poses a serious challenge to human capital theory. If structural differentiation occurs before earnings differentiation, then the most plausible causal interpretation would make structure, not earnings, the prior cause. Indeed, by looking at structural attainments in terms of the organization's own labels, the findings of this study indicate that college status affects employees' attainments much earlier than analyses of earnings or occupational attainment have shown (cf. Karabel and McClelland 1983).

The findings of this study have very practical implications for employees' decisions about investing in education. The diminished benefits from delayed education have been noted in analyses of national survey data (Hogan 1980). The present study suggests some of the mechanisms which may account for this finding. The analyses of these mechanisms as they operated in the organization under study indicate that the benefits employees receive from their investments in education depend on their investments being made at a young age, being accomplished quickly, and being completed before they enter the organization. If employees invest in additional education after they enter the organization, their additional education is likely to have little impact. Early jobs have such large influences on career trajectories that B.A. and M.B.A. degrees have negligible additional effects on later earnings and job statuses after early jobs have been assigned.

If individuals invest in additional education before they enter the organization, these investments could have a large impact since individuals' education before entry strongly affects initial job assignments. However, these benefits may be diminished if they take a long time to get the additional degree. If individuals invest in part-time continuing education while working in another firm, they avoid the structuring of their career trajectories by first-job effects. However, since part-time schooling before entry increases entry age, it confers lesser benefits than full-time schooling. Therefore, as previously stated, individuals who want to invest in their human capital through formal education must do so at a young age, in a full-time program, and before entering the organization to get the full benefits from the investment.

The other investments suggested by human capital theory are salary sacrifices that employees could make to get more job training. However, the findings are quite clear in refuting this process. Employees who take lower earnings in their first years in the firm attain lower—not higher—job statuses in the future, even after controlling for individual attributes (including the proxy for ability, college selectivity).

In summary, the individual processes customarily emphasized by human capital theory are likely to have a relatively minor influence on employees' careers within organizations like this one. The results here suggest that individuals might well benefit if they can get the organization to make investments in their human capital through rapid job advancements, but it is not clear that individuals have much control over these selections—they are primarily controlled by the organization. Fundamentally, structure dominates the career process.

The point here is not to refute human capital theory. Indeed, the contention of this study is that human capital theory is not refutable; nor does this study contend that human capital theory is not useful, for it is a useful statement of an economic ideal which would obtain in ideal hypothetical circumstances. Rather, the point here is that it is not a very useful explanation for the empirical reality described by the findings of this study. It stresses individual factors, which, according to the analyses presented in this volume, have relatively small unique impact. It ignores structural factors which have been found here to be central in mediating the effects of most individual factors on earnings and career attainments and which determine the responsiveness of career trajectories.

Human capital theory is a versatile and resilient theory, and it can explain most of the findings of this study if additional untestable assumptions about unmeasureable components of human capital, particularly the elusive concept of ability, are adopted. However, saving the theory by increasing its baggage of untestable assumptions raises questions about whether it is worth carrying. Some testable hypotheses derived from the theory are not supported, and strong empirical effects are explained by vague untestable assumptions or not explained at all. While human capital theory may not be refuted, these findings indicate ample room for a structural theory to provide an alternative explanation of the phenomena. At a minimum, structural phenomena cannot be adequately explained by human capital theory, and a separate structural theory is required.

Evidence for and against Structural Theory

Many aspects of the findings of this study support a structural model of careers and conflict with the human capital model. The description of career moves show such clear patterns of mobility that implicit, if not explicit, rules are suggested. The precipitous declines in the age–promotion curves of college graduates are more steep than one would expect from a model based on human capital declines. Indeed, age seems to have almost categorical impact on the promotion of college graduates after a certain age, with the age boundary being a function of organization factors, such as organization growth or contraction (Chapter 3). In addition, the dramatically different promotion curves for college-educated and non-college-educated employees suggests another dimension on which the labor market is stratified. While these two groups represent different amounts of human capital in economic theory, their mobility patterns across authority levels suggest qualitatively different promotion mechanisms, better described by structural theory than by human capital theory. Although human capital theory describes variations in a continuous quantity such as earnings quite well, a structural theory explains the clear-cut discontinuities in the age–promotion curves much better than can human capital theory.

Even in explaining earnings, a structural theory is required; for human capital theory does not adequately take into account the extent to which job structure factors precede and mediate economic outcomes. Human capital composition of jobs (measured by the two most important human capital factors) explains very little of the variance in the average salaries of jobs, probably because job demands and responsibility are not strongly related to the human capital individuals bring to these jobs. Rather than paying for human capital, organizations pay only for the human capital that the job structure permits individuals to utilize. Comparable conclusions emerge from the analyses of individuals' earnings within statuses.

The longitudinal analyses of individuals' careers give the clearest indication of the relative importance of structure. Structural selections precede some of the important earnings differentiations.

Finally, and most importantly, the strong enduring features of career trajectories found in this corporation over the 1965–1975 decade indicate that careers are patterned by a fairly durable structure. Many aspects of this structure appear to be relatively unresponsive to dramatic changes in organization growth and contraction.

Nonetheless, although these findings clearly call for a structural theory to explain these findings, a rigid structural theory is not adequate for the task. Structural theories sometimes contend that selections are rigid in constraining individuals to fixed career paths (e.g., the sponsored model), or they contend that the selection structure is rigid in being unresponsive to historical changes. Neither contention is supported by the findings of this study.

Structural theories, including segmented labor market theories, sometimes suggest that careers are rigidly patterned in ways that resemble the sponsored mobility norm. While the analyses of this study find a great deal of structuring of mobility, they do not indicate a sponsorship system. Early selections have lasting impact, but they are not totally determinative. Subsequent selections also have a large additional independent impact in ways that sometimes cancel the "sponsoring" effect of first selections.

Structural theories also tend to posit unresponsiveness to social and economic changes. The findings of this study suggest that this is only partially true. The career trajectories of elite individuals and those in the later part of their careers are unresponsive to the changes in economic growth and contraction and the changes brought on by the affirmative action program. On the other hand, the career trajectories of young, semi-elite employees are highly responsive to these historical forces. The notion of a rigid, unresponsive structure must be modified by the kinds of mechanisms suggested by the developmental and selectivity hypotheses.

The Tournament as a Structural Theory of Ability

As noted in Chapter 6, signaling theory reconciles much of the conflict between human capital and structural theories by allowing structural attainments to be viewed as signals of ability. Performance in most kinds of jobs is difficult to assess, and ability is even more difficult to assess since it is based on an inference from performance. Signaling theory contends that in such circumstances, employers use certain social attributes and accomplishments of individuals as signals of their abilities. Specifically, it is proposed in Chapter 6 that managers take employees' job status attainments as signals of their ability. If ability, which is a key component of human capital theory, is signaled by structural attainments, then the conflict between the human capital and structural theories largely disappears.

Moreover, the tournament model proposes a structural mechanism which creates these ability signals and justifies the signaling inference. Indeed, this is the purpose of tournaments. In sports events, tournaments identify and communicate individuals' ability relative to the individuals against whom they have been pitted, and, by extension, the tournament implicitly identifies their ability relative to everyone else in the tournament. Tournaments imply that the losers at any stage are less able than the winners at that stage. The statement that an individual "survived the semi-finals" implies that the individual is more able than those who did not. By pitting winners at each stage against each other, tournaments can differentiate ever more finely among degrees of ability. This procedure is prevalent in sports tournaments, and it is implicit in the "social Darwinism" of the business ethos.

The tournament model functions the same way in an organization as it does in a sports event. Individuals who are promoted first are the winners of the initial competitions, while members of the same cohort who are promoted later (even from the same jobs) were the losers of earlier competitions and consequently are inferred to be less able. In positing that competitions for promotions occur continually, early promotions become signals of greater ability.

Since ability is detected by an individual's history of attainments, ability is not solely a property of individuals. In the tournament, ability is a socially assigned status, determined at least as much by the needs and properties of the career system as by the attributes of the individuals involved. If an organization needs to promote many individuals, then many ability statuses will be assigned, regardless of the actual distribution of ability. If none are to be promoted, then no ability statuses need to be assigned. An organization's career system influences the number of ability statuses assigned.

The career system defines how many winners there will be at any particular time, how quickly they will be tested for further advancements, when (if ever) tournament losers will be offered subsequent competitions, and the positions for which they will be able to compete. The career system's rules define the ways that ability labels will be assigned and even what ability labels individuals may subsequently compete for in the future.

This is in marked contrast to ordinary ideas about ability. Commonsense notions and psychological and economic theories conceive of ability as a property of individuals. By this notion, individuals possess high or low ability as personal qualities. Ability is an individual attribute just as eye color is, and the social world of teachers and employers seek to assess this property of individuals and to respond to individuals accordingly. In contrast, the tournament model asserts that the career system has a major role in defining how the status of ability will be identified and assigned to individuals.

The conception of ability as a status resembles the conception of social labeling in symbolic interactionist analyses, although that literature mostly discusses deviant labels. "High ability" or "high potential" is the socially recognized status that organizations confer to their most-valued members, and the career system regulates how many and which individuals are assigned this status.

This conception is most similar to what Meyer (1977) describes as "legitimation theory which treats education [or other institutions] as both constructing or altering roles in society and [as] authoritatively allocating personnel to these roles" (p. 56). According to Meyer, while the evidence regarding education's effects on competence is mixed, education still constitutes a system of "institutionalized rites" which define "new roles and statuses for elites and members" (p. 56). Moreover, different schools receive distinct social "charters to define people as graduates and therefore as possessing distinctive rights and capacities in society" (Meyer 1977, p. 59; see also Kamens 1971, 1974, 1977). However, Meyer's notion can apply to other institutional contexts besides education (Meyer and Rowan 1977), and the differentiation of roles and statuses not only occurs between institutions, but also within institutions, with high school tracking being a noteworthy example (Meyer 1977, p. 61; see also Rosenbaum 1976).

The tournament is a particularly effective way of legitimizing selections in work institutions and in schools (Rosenbaum 1976, ch. 9). As in Meyer's conception of an allocation system, the tournament makes selections and assigns new roles and statuses, but the tournament is a mechanism which provides an additional source of legitimation—the presumed open competition at the outset and the gradual winnowing down of the winner's cohort by successive competitions. While Meyer's conception explains how the outcomes of selections at any point in time are legitimized, the tournament also explains how career patterns over time are legitimized. The tournament is particularly effective within institutions where career-history information about individuals can be preserved and easily communicated and where the status value of an individuals' attainments is easily interpreted.[1]

What is noteworthy here is that relationships between macrolevel career systems and microlevel social interactions are posited, with each reinforcing the other (see also Collins 1981). The career system defines how many individuals and which individuals receive ability status, and these ability assignments, in turn, tend to legitimate the career system.

[1]These conditions sometimes hold in assessing careers across institutions, particularly for educational careers. The status value of various colleges and graduate schools is easily interpreted, and individuals' career histories across these institutions tend to be well known and easily communicated. So it may be expected that if career patterns are traced through college and graduate school and on into work environments, they might be found to follow tournament principles. Similarly, academic jobs may also meet these conditions. The same is not true for most jobs in the labor market, however, for the status value of these jobs are not easily interpreted and individuals' job histories are not always well known or easily communicated.

Career systems specify that a certain number of individuals must be promoted quickly, and, consequently, they create a need for conferring the high-potential labels that justify these rapid promotions. Even if talented employees did not exist, organizations would have to invent them to fill the fast track of the career system. And while talent cannot be created, the label of talent can be; and the tournament model contends that this is done by conferring rapid career advancement.

Human capital theory may have the facts right for the wrong reason. High pay is associated with high ability not only because talent advances, but also because most people tend to see the world in that way; and thus high ability is imputed to those with high pay, high status, and fast-rising career trajectories.

Of course, managers are not the only people to use these tournament signals to infer ability. The practice is common in other areas of society as well. For instance, university faculty are impressed by an individual who has attained the rank of full professor at a major university at an unusually young age. Moreover, if the situation is comparable to the situation that managers face in which the individual's performance is difficult to assess (if, for instance, the young professor's work is esoteric and few scholars can judge it), then this ability label inferred from past mobility might continue to be the main way that this young professor would be judged for a long time. Career histories are commonly used to signal ability, and the human capital predictions become true by a process of reverse causality.

This is all the more true if career advancement routes are predefined. The organization under study here persistently promotes high percentages of young college graduates, particularly from elite colleges, in all periods, regardless of whether it is a period of growth or contraction; and the career system maintains fast advancement channels for this small elite group at all levels. By maintaining these mobility paths, the career system guarantees that the organization will have a pool of individuals designated with the status of "high potential" from which to recruit its future top executives.

Structurally Determined Properties
of Ability Signals

Career systems define the properties and signals of ability. For instance, in a contest system, ability is conceived as transitory and subject to change; high-ability individuals may subsequently falter, while initial losers may be "late bloomers." That is one reason why the contest system delays making final selections as long as possible.

A tournament system is more complex. It sets a "ceiling" on ability for individuals after they lose a competition and a higher "floor" on ability for individuals after they win a competition. A decision not to promote an employee at a particular stage communicates the message that the individual lacks the requisite ability, and this social fact has irreversible consequences in limiting the individual's chances of subsequent advancement and in reducing the individual's maximum career attainment. Those who lose an early selection are assigned a "low-ability" status which sharply limits their future opportunities. The tournament implies that there are no "late bloomers."

Although the tournament sets a higher floor on ability when individuals win a competition, it does not define how much ability the individual has or how far the individual is going to advance. A tournament is far more pragmatic than a sponsorship in this respect. While a sponsorship makes far-reaching decisions about which individuals are destined for top executive positions (because it considers ability permanent and easy to detect), the tournament makes incremental decisions at each stage in the process (see Lindblom 1959). The tournament continually asks "What have you accomplished recently?" Each win connotes more ability, but a win never guarantees more than one advancement. For instance, in the 3-year cohort discussed in Chapter 2, employees in high-status jobs in 1962 who were promoted to foreman level by 1965 have the best chance of attaining middle management, but even they are not guaranteed such attainment. Thus, while low ability is conceived as permanent, irreversibly eliminating the individual from competitions for top positions; high ability is conceived as unspecified and subject to change, requiring continual reaffirmation by continued winning.

Besides defining properties of ability, career systems also create signals of ability. While the tournament does not give any guarantees about future mobility, it implies that individuals who advance relatively more quickly are more able and that previous advancement rate could be used as a signal of ability.

The career patterns described in this study are consistent with this interpretation. It seems reasonable to expect that any manager who noticed these patterns might very well have made this signaling inference. The parabolic career trajectories show this by their smooth curves of advancement rates for each employee group (Chapter 7). The career tree also shows this; individuals who do not advance in one period are less likely to do so subsequently, while those who did advance in the previous period are more likely to continue doing so in the next. The impact of rate of advancement is seen most directly in the multivariate analyses of the cohort. Future career attainments (net of present attainments) are negatively related to tenure and entry age. Among individuals at the same job status, those who achieved it sooner (with lower tenure or at a younger age) had greater chances of subsequent advancement (Chapters 5 and 6). These results are consistent with the interpretation that rate of past advancement is a signal of ability.

Consequently, when managers have difficulty in inferring individuals' abilities, these patterns suggest that they could use individuals' job histories to assist in inferring their potential for future advancement, and managers report that they do indeed use these as signals. The tournament definition of the ability signal might be expressed as the quotient of job status divided by tenure and entry age. This quotient is similar to the signals that informants said they used in promotion committees. Based on observations of another corporation, Kanter (1977) has also suggested such a relationship. It is also consistent with descriptions of still other corporations. For example, based on observations of many firms, Kellogg (1972) notes that most employees expect that high-potential managers will advance every 2 or 3 years, a belief which implies that those who do not are not good candidates for advancement; and Ference (1979) notes that employees who "level off" are seen as failures with no ability to advance further.

The simple quotient expresses the net result of the tournament norm: Ability is indicated by how high one has risen in a particular span of time. Other historical features of careers may also be taken into account—entry job status, subsequent job status, and timing of selections—and these may be similarly used as signals of ability.

Critical Periods: Properties of Individuals or of Career Systems?

Perhaps the best example of the tournament defining properties of ability signals is illustrated by the critical-period conception of ability proposed by Berlew and Hall (1966). In a study which has become a cornerstone of the psychological study of organization careers, Berlew and Hall (1966) found that the company's early expectations for a manager, and the concomitant challenge posed by his first job, were strongly related to his success 5 years later. The researchers conclude that the first year is

> a critical period for learning, a time when the trainee is uniquely ready to develop or change in the direction of the company's expectations. This year would be analogous to the critical period, probably between six and eighteen months, when human infants must either experience a close emotional relationship with another human being or suffer ill effects ranging from psychosis to an inability ever to establish such a relationship. (p. 221)

While noting that work orientation is unlikely to be "fixed" in the first year, and "corrective experiences are certainly possible," Berlew and Hall conclude that "probably never again will [a manager] be so 'unfrozen' and ready to learn as he is in his first year" (p. 222).

However, the tournament model raises the question of whether it is the person or the career system which becomes increasingly "frozen" over time. Just as Chapter 7 proposed that the tournament career system—not individual development—is responsible for the greater responsiveness of career trajectories in early career (the developmental hypotheses), the tournament career system may also explain this critical-period aspect of careers. Berlew and Hall's findings are certainly open to alternative interpretations, for they only study individuals and do not look at properties of the career system. Since Berlew and Hall do not analyze what stimulation or challenge employees are offered, their data do not define what it is that vanishes at the end of the critical period: Does an individual's ability to benefit from challenge vanish or does the challenge from the environment vanish? If it is the former, as Berlew and Hall imply, then the critical period is a property of individual development; but if it is the latter, as the tournament model suggests, then the critical period is a property of the career system.

The tournament model advances a structural counterpart of the critical-period notion. It suggests that there is a critical period during which organization career systems will notice ability in individuals and will offer them challenge. After this critical period, the career system will no longer notice employees' ability and will no longer offer them challenge. Instead of the critical period being an attribute of individuals, the tournament makes it a property of the career system and what the career system allows individuals to do. Once the career system has determined that some employees have no potential for advancement, either it assigns them to jobs which do not permit them to manifest the skills needed for advancement or it does not notice those skills if exhibited. As a result, the abilities which individuals are allowed to manifest (or which are recognized by the career system) are limited by the jobs to which the tournament has assigned them.

If a career system has critical periods for allowing individuals to demonstrate ability, then the career system can prevent individuals from manifesting ability after they have passed its critical period (i.e., after the organization stops paying attention and stops offering challenge). One's performance after being eliminated from the tournament is irrelevant, and consequently it goes largely unnoticed.

The concept of a career system which has differential responsiveness to individuals' performance makes it impossible to know whether the patterns of individuals' attainments are due to individuals' abilities or to the abilities which the career system permits the individual to manifest. This problem is not ideosyncratic to organization careers, it is true whenever ability is assessed. Ability is an inference from performances, and in all such inferences, doubts arise about whether the "testing" situation has allowed the individual the opportunity to show the appropriate ability.

Besides raising this question, career systems also raise the question of how long "tests" continue to occur. The contention here that career systems operate essentially like tournaments, with implicit competitions which determine subsequent job assignments, implies that the critical period for ability is determined by the career system, that an individual's critical period for showing ability remains open as long as he or she continues winning in the career tournament, and that a history which includes a loss will be taken as a clear signal of the limits of the individual's ability, justifying elimination from the tournament for top positions.

It is ironic that human capital theory views the assessment of ability as a trivial problem. It makes ability central to its explanation, but it does not attempt to define or operationalize it, conveniently assuming that managers can easily assess it. The personnel literature on the assessment of managerial and professional ability makes it plain that managers do not know how to measure it, and the statements of managers in this study confirm their confusion on the matter.

The answer proposed here to the human capital problem of ability is that the social structure determines it. The tournament career system determines the way ability is conceived and the way it is used to affect careers. It stipulates how ability can be recognized, where it is likely to be found, how long it takes to appear, and when to stop looking for it.

This book is a study of organization career systems, not a study of ability. Nonetheless, from these analyses, it is clear that the career system describes a map of where organizations allocate employees who are presumed to have ability, and the patterning of careers describes some properties which organizations attribute to ability. In effect, the sociology of organization careers leads to a sociology of ability.

With the exception of a few reports by managers of how they use signals for determining promotions, this study has not analyzed the signaling process empirically. The preceding speculations can only be studied by fine-grained observations of the assessment activities that occur in organizations. However, just in describing the organization career system and showing that it is patterned as it is, this analysis has gone a step further than the psychological approach by showing that an entirely different kind of mechanism could possibly explain the phenomena psychologists usually attribute to individuals. While further research is needed to decide the issue, this study indicates the plausibility of an alternative conception.

Conclusions

The fundamental issue between human capital and structural theories is whether individuals' worth (human capital) is continually reassessed in determining their careers or whether their careers are prestructured from the outset by their first job assignments. The difficulty in testing this issue comes down to the difficulty of measuring human capital; and, of the components of human capital, ability has proven particularly intractable to measurement. This unmeasurability of ability has become the standard "escape clause" for discrediting any empirical test of human capital theory. If a structural factor is shown to affect earnings independent of measurable components of human capital, it can always be said that the model does not fully measure human capital because a measure of ability is inadequate. In fact, given the impossibility of fully measuring ability, this escape clause is always applicable.

Surely, employers do consider ability to be an important factor, and, admittedly, social research can do no better than to measure surface indicators of ability. However, supervisors also have great difficulty identifying ability, and they experience normative constraints on what ability indicators they can use for selections. It seems likely that supervisors, like researchers, have great difficulty in assessing productivity in most jobs, and their inferences about ability are likely to be highly speculative and based on scanty information.

Sociologists may have conceded too much in allowing economists to use ability as an escape clause to protect human capital theory. Although economists are surely correct that "true ability" is the ideal causal factor, managers generally do not have very good information about ability. Moreover, the information they use must be interpreted and, in actual practice, ability assessments are likely to be affected by all kinds of contextual factors, not the least of which is the structure of the selection system.

The tournament model suggests that "ability status" is assigned to individuals based on their job histories, effectively providing an operational definition of ability. In stressing ability, the tournament model resembles human capital theory, but unlike that theory, it views ability as a status attribute which is derived from individuals' histories of structural attainments. In viewing past structural attainments as determining present and future careers, the tournament model is like other structural models; but unlike ahistorical structural models, the tournament is a dynamic process and consequently it predicts the patterns of successive competitions indicated in the career-tree diagram (Chapter 2). Moreover, as a dynamic process, the tournament model is less rigid in the outcomes it predicts. It suggests that contextual factors (i.e., changes in social factors) can affect career trajectories of different employee groups in the ways described by the selectivity and developmental hypotheses.

By positing a mechanism in which ability status is determined by individuals' histories of structural attainments, the tournament combines the central mechanisms of human capital and structural theories in a distinctive model. In many ways, this model makes human capital theory a by-product of structural forces, yet the model also incorporates dynamic elements from economic theory.

The net result is a model which is neither as focused on the individual as human capital theory is portrayed nor as static and rigid as structural theory is sometimes portrayed. Neither individuals' attributes and performances nor rigid barriers and narrow career paths are the basis of career patterns in the model. Rather the tournament portrays dynamic structural processes by which early selections are related to later ones, regardless of the individual attributes or performances involved. Although the particular selection criteria will change according to the social and economic circumstances of the period, the same tournament mobility processes will occur—regardless of what kinds of individuals are selected or what particular job paths are available—and these processes will confer ability status to whatever individuals are involved.

Organization careers have been ignored by human capital and status attainment theories. They represent a complication which detracts from the simplicity and elegance of these theories. However, even in arguing in favor of economic theory's neglect of the firm, Machlup (1967) concedes that economic theory is most appropriate for analyses of marginal changes in large aggregates and that more-complicated, institutional studies are required for analyses of attainments in specific institutional contexts. Similarly, Baron and Bielby criticize status attainment theory for ignoring institutional factors, and they suggest that research must focus on "the units which comprise the structure of the work and the dimensions underlying economic segmentation" (1980, p. 737).

The present inquiry has focused on the agenda recommended by Baron and Bielby, and it has described career patterns within these units. It has described structural properties and mechanisms which determine these career patterns, and it has suggested an underlying model which connects these structural features to conceptions of ability. In so doing, this model creates linkages between economic and structural theories. It also creates linkages between social normative models and concrete institutional properties of organizations, and between institutional properties and career patterns experienced by individuals. These relationships permit a view of organization careers from a more general perspective. Individuals' sequences of jobs can be seen as being part of general career patterns, and these career patterns may be seen as part of an organization career system which is subject to external social and economic constraints and which is patterned by the mechanisms of the tournament model.

The most important contribution of the tournament model is to provide an institutional model of careers. It describes career patterns, suggests social processes, and provides a link at the institutional level between macrosocietal theories and individual interactions and experiences. In effect, it provides linkages between economic theories, social structural theories, organization theories, and psychological theories. Quite apart from the specific new knowledge this study has provided, this model suggests new interpretations of and connections among previously well-established phenomena.

For example, the tournament model provides a new interpretation of the Berlew–Hall (1966) psychological model of job effects on careers, it challenges the relevance of Kelley's (1973a) ahistorical status-attainment theory and the corresponding path independence assumption in Markov models (Bartholomew 1968), and it suggests an alternative explanation for the fanning out of earnings attainments which Mincer (1974) attributes to human capital theory. The tournament model suggests a simple alternative interpretation for each of these diverse phenomena, and it suggests connections among them that the various separate disciplines have not explored.

Note that all of these approaches are studying the same phenomena whether they be called individuals' careers, organization personnel systems, earnings trajectories, or status attainments. The approaches differ mostly in the viewpoints from which they consider these phenomena and in the processes and mechanisms to which they attribute them. The empirical findings of this study and the tournament model provide a description of the phenomena at an intervening institutional level of analysis which may provide a new understanding of the ways that the macro- and microlevels interact.

Appendix 9.A: Complexities in the Career Tournament—Job Statuses and Minor Tournaments

Although tennis tournaments are a good analogy for career tournaments, they are less complex. Two complexities involved in analyzing careers via the tournament model—job statuses and minor tournaments—are addressed in this appendix.

While all competitions at a particular stage in a tennis tournament (e.g., semi-finals) are implicitly assumed to present equal challenge, jobs represent different amounts of challenge. While the effects of hundreds of entry jobs can be explained by the effects of only a few job statuses, job statuses still make the model more complex than it is portrayed in Chapter 2.

Nonetheless, the fundamental processes still resemble the tournament even when job status attainments are considered. For instance, as discussed in Chapter 6, although new employees in the top job status of nonmanagement level in 1962 have much higher career trajectories than others in the 3-year cohort, they still must win the competition in the next 3 years to retain their advantage. Of those in the top job status who do receive promotions by 1965, almost half (45.8%) attain middle-management positions or higher and virtually all (96.0%) attain lower-management positions or higher in the next decade. In contrast, of the top job status employees who do not receive promotions by 1965, none reached middle management in the next decade and 35.7% do not even attain lower-management positions. Entry job status helps, but it is not sufficient to guarantee success. This implicit career timetable is also indicated by the significant negative effects of tenure and entry age, even after controlling for 1962 and 1965 job statuses and other individual attributes (Table 6.3). As the tournament implies, one has to keep winning to stay in the competition for top management, even if one begins in the top job status.

Even after controlling for many indicators of ability (education, college quality, earnings, job status), the tournament timetables are supported by the continuing significant negative effects of tenure and entry age (Chapter 6). This may indicate the workings of unmeasured components of ability (e.g., that "late bloomers" do not exist); but the most plausible interpretation is that the tournament imposes structural timetables on when ability must emerge to affect trajectories. Of course, regardless of interpretation, the tournament remains a good description of career patterns even when the complexities of job statuses are considered.

The career tournament is also more complex than tennis tournaments in that it involves minor tournaments. In tennis tournaments, losers are eliminated from further competitions, so that individuals at a given stage of the tournament do not really have different career histories. They have all won the same number of previous competitions. The only kind of heterogeneity one's career could show would be a loss, and a loss is the last event in one's history in an elimination tournament.

However, that is not the form of the tournament indicated by the career-tree analysis. Although losers are indeed eliminated from competing for top positions, the career tree indicates that losers of early competitions can still compete for middle-range positions. In effect, "minor tournaments" occur for these lesser positions, and these are not elimination tournaments. For instance, although the 604 individuals who did not advance in their first period may be out of the competition for middle management, many receive subsequent promotions (Figure 2.2). Most of the individuals receiving a promotion do so in the second period (1965–1969; 128 individuals), but even this is not necessary. A sizable number (62 individuals) who lost the first and second competitions were still able to win the next round.

These individuals may be conceived of as being in a minor tournament in which the odds of advancement are less than those for individuals who won the major tournament. They retain the option to advance to foreman level, and even to lower management. Within this minor tournament, timing does not present rigid barriers. Although these individuals may not be in contention for middle management or higher positions, lower management remains a possibility, even for relatively late winners. The probability of advancement does decline gradually over time, but advancement still remains an option.

The major and minor tournaments do seem to operate differently. While individuals in the minor tournament continue receiving advancements from nonmanagement and foreman levels even after two losses, only a negligible number of those in the major tournament continue advancing after experiencing one loss. Of the 37 individuals in lower management in 1972 who failed to advance in one period, only two individuals were promoted in the final period (Figure 2.2). In the major tournament for high-level positions, a single loss has clear-cut implications.

This dual structure is interesting because it suggests that like the different career patterns noted in Chapters 3 and 7, the major and minor tournaments operate to serve different goals. The major tournament selects the elite to run the organization, while the minor tournament is more in conformity with the contest norm and seems designed to preserve motivation.

However, the complexities just discussed do not diminish the importance of the tournament model for describing the major tournament in this system. This may be properly termed the *major tournament* not only because the most important positions are involved, but also because these are the selections which are most salient in the system and these are the selections to which the most resources and attention are given.

This dual structure of career patterns (major and minor tournaments) helps to elaborate the distinction between subordinate and independent segments of the primary labor market (Gordon 1972; Carnoy and Rumberger 1975; Osterman 1975; and Edwards 1979). The two sets of distinctions address the same distinction among jobs. The minor tournament applies to low-status (subordinate) entry jobs, and the major tournament applies to high-status (independent) entry jobs. The same predictions may also be made about the career ladders for each. The major–minor tournament distinction may help elaborate the subordinate–independent segment distinction by indicating the nature and timing of selections in the two segments. The findings of this study reinforce the notion that career ladders are used in the subordinate segment to control and motivate, for the minor tournament preserves opportunity as an incentive over a longer portion of employees' careers. The findings caution against exaggerating the openness of opportunity in the independent segment, since status distinctions are found to have large effects and the major tournament is continually making selections which reduce career options for increasing portions of this segment.

While the analyses of average earnings do indicate "a substantial return to experience through the first nineteen or so years" for this segment (Edwards 1979, p. 176), the findings presented in this volume suggest that this average conceals the fact that the large earnings increase is only for those who continue advancing in job status and that advancement is restricted to an ever smaller portion of those who began in the most-advantaged jobs. Indeed, the timetables are found to be particularly abrupt; those who fail to advance in their first 3 to 5 years (in the 1962 cohort, by 1965) have dramatically curtailed advancements in the next decade (Figure 2.2). The major–minor tournament distinction reinforces the analyses of the labor market economists, and it also suggests that the internal stratification of these labor markets may be even more highly structured than previously indicated.

Despite these complexities, the fundamental principles underlying the tournament remain fundamentally intact. Job statuses and minor tournaments add complexity to the tournament, making the ability inference more complex and the ability conception more differentiated. Nonetheless, the tournament principles continue to operate, and the tournament continues to create ability signals.

CHAPTER 10

Policy Implications:
Reconceptualizing and Redesigning
Career Systems

Introduction

As Kurt Lewin once said, "Nothing is more practical than a good theory." While the previous chapters have stressed the theoretical implications of the tournament model, theoretical models also have practical implications. In drawing connections between the phenomena and their contexts, theoretical models explain why things happen as they do and what preconditions are assumed.

The tournament model has several implications for personnel policies. The tournament model may be used both to reconceptualize and to redesign the career systems in organizations. It can help employees understand their career options, and it can help organization planners redesign career systems to achieve a better resolution of the conflicting ideals. By suggesting the preconditions that career systems must satisfy to offer opportunity and efficiency, the tournament identifies whether specific features of career systems are appropriate for their particular organization context, and, if not, what aspects of the career system could be redesigned to match its context. The final sections of this chapter propose policy implications of this analysis for procedural and structural reforms of career systems. However, before turning to these issues, this chapter begins by summarizing the rationale for the career system conception in terms of this study's findings.

The Effects of Career Systems: Beyond the Pyramid Imperative

Much has been made of the limits imposed by the pyramid shape of organization hierarchies. The shape of organization hierarchies surely does limit the number of positions at each level, and it does curtail the maximum attainment that the average employee can expect to achieve. Since the pyramid shape of an organization's hierarchy cannot be easily altered, this approach quickly leads to a fatalistic attitude about the possibilities for structural solutions to career development problems. Limited growth during the late 1970s and early 1980s has thrown additional gloom over this approach.

Although the pyramid shape of hierarchies imposes limits on careers, the present analysis contends that it is not the only factor imposing limits, and it is not necessarily the most important constraint. Since jobs are continually being created and disbanded (Chapter 4), vacancies are neither necessary nor sufficient for career advancements. Moreover, the finding that certain employee groups are so strongly and consistently preferred in good times and bad (Chapter 7) suggests that the career system might guarantee their advancement even if the required vacancies did not exist. Managers in this firm report that positions are sometimes created to advance the career of a valued employee. Granovetter (1974, p. 14) also reports that new positions are often created for new recruits. The interdependence of jobs and individuals is further suggested by Baron's (1982) finding that 47% of the jobs in a sample of 415 organizations had only one incumbent.

The central contention of the present inquiry is that careers are two-dimensional: Individuals' careers must be measured by their status attainments and by their timing. While the pyramid imperative may impose unavoidable constraints on maximum available status attainments, it says very little about which employees will be considered for those attainments, when individuals will be considered for advancements, or what their rate of advancement will be. To explain these features of careers in organizations, it has been posited here that organizations have "career systems" which result from explicit policies and implicit norms about how careers should unfold. Many of the problems which are often attributed to the pyramid imperative are also affected by aspects of the organization career system.

For instance, the strong effects of early jobs in limiting career advancement are not dictated by the hierarchy (Chapter 6). Indeed, these early job effects actually contradict hierarchical models which predict ahistorical effects. Moreover, these effects are so strong that they undermine the possibilities for Horatio Alger successes, in spite of strong norms to the contrary. Given the great latitude this career system allows for special treatment of elites, it is curious that Horatio Alger types are not also treated as elites. Whatever the reasons, this is not dictated by the pyramid shape of the hierarchy.

The "sudden-death" quality of the tournament and the sharp promotion declines with age lead to radical discontinuities in the opportunities for college-educated employees (Chapter 2). The hierarchy does not impose this age distribution on promotions. Indeed, noncollege graduates have a different age distribution of promotions than college graduates at the same levels, and college graduates have similar age distributions of promotions over different hierarchical levels. These patterns seem to be determined more by the way the career system treats employee groups than by hierarchical shape.

Young employees often say that they must sacrifice their family commitments to achieve career advancement. This is often based on the fears that the top positions in the hierarchy will become filled up. The analyses presented in this volume suggest that the hierarchy per se is less to blame than the rigid timetables imposed by the tournament system.

The strong preferences for certain elite educational groups are certainly not dictated by the shape of the hierarchy. When organization growth is curtailed and the hierarchy provides fewer vacancies, the elite are minimally affected.

While the pyramid imperative imposes some limits on ultimate attainments, it says very little about features of the career system. The career system imposes additional constraints on attainments beyond the constraints imposed by hierarchical shape. Even if the organizational hierarchy were broadened to increase advancement opportunity at certain levels, the career system would still define which employees received the increased opportunity. On the other hand, changing the career system, even without changing the hierarchy, could increase the availability of advancement opportunity. A reform of career systems which increased the number of groups considered for advancement and which delayed selections would prolong advancement opportunity for many employees, even if the pyramid shape remained unchanged.

The key to doing this is an understanding of the organization's career system. Although organization policies describe some aspects of career systems, the analyses presented in this study provide examples of how the operation of organization career systems could be better understood. Describing the career trajectories of various groups and the ways they change over time can reveal the underlying career system which governs employees' careers.

The tournament model provides a way of conceptualizing the issues raised by career systems, a way of inferring their preconditions and outcomes, and a way of inferring policy alternatives for better achieving the system's goals. These considerations are reviewed in the following sections.

The Tournament As a Model of Entire Career Systems

Organization planners and other employees desperately need a model of career systems, for career systems are not easy to see or understand. Selections in organizations occur through the operation of many diverse career programs and practices: programs for recruitment, career planning, succession planning, out-placement, and so on. Each is somewhat vague about the ways it makes its selections, its implications for later careers, and its relationships to other programs. In addition, these programs tend to exaggerate the amount of opportunity they allow, and they give widespread attention to Horatio Alger stories far out of proportion to their frequency of occurrence. These stories not only serve the interests of supervisors seeking to motivate employees, they also "ring true" with what employees (and supervisors) have been told in school and in the media, and they provide strong distractors preventing individuals from seeing the career system in perspective. Consequently, it is not surprising that employees' perceptions of career systems are piecemeal and often incorrect.

However, even if career systems cannot be seen directly, they can be described in terms of their outcomes. In much the way that physicists describe magnetic fields by the patterns they make on iron filings, career systems can be described by the patterns they make on the job mobility of an entering cohort. Morever, just as physicists use models to conceptualize magnetic fields, the tournament model can be used to conceptualize career systems.

The tournament model describes a selection mechanism that pervades the many different career programs in organizations. It describes how they are interrelated, how they create a coherent system, and how this system accomplishes some of the organization's goals. As such, this model can help individual employees to understand career realities and to make plans and choices about their careers. It may be a particularly good way of portraying this information because the model not only shows present choices, but also shows the probable long-term consequences of these choices.

This model could also be useful to organizations. While personnel managers surely have more information about career systems than do other employees, some kinds of crucial information can only be revealed by systematic research on career patterns. More important than information is the question of how it is conceptualized; the conflicting social norms operating in this corporation and in many others (Chapter 1) make it difficult for corporate employees to have a coherent picture of what is happening.

It seems quite conceivable that organization members, even those at high levels, are ignorant or confused about these issues. Perception is difficult on these matters and social norms are likely to distort perception. Of course, there is no way of knowing what top executives actually believe since there is no way to force them to be candid. But Vroom's example of the high-level personnel officer who took steps to eliminate structural barriers after learning the results of Vroom and MacCrimmon's (1968) research tends to suggest that this was new information and it was considered cause for concern.

The findings of this study and the tournament model provide a way of conceiving of careers and career-related issues at a structural level. They also permit identification of the sources of career problems at a structural level, rather than attributing them only to individuals' deficiencies.

Although the tournament is a good reconciliation between the opportunity and efficiency norms, its success in reconciling this conflict is based on a particular set of assumptions about preconditions. If these preconditions do not exist, then the tournament will fail to satisfy one or the other aspect of this conflict. In the following sections, the preconditions for opportunity and efficiency in career systems are identified and are assessed in terms of the findings of this and other studies.

Preconditions for Opportunity in
Tournament Career Systems

Tournaments offer opportunity by allowing all employees a chance to compete for advancement at the outset. However, to offer opportunity, tournament career systems must meet certain preconditions which are suggested by the tournament model: Employees must know the rules of the game, they must start at similar positions, and they must be allowed to begin the tournament when they are ready to compete. The findings of this study raise doubts about each of these points.

Do employees know the rules of the game? My interviews with 163 foremen and lower-management ABCO employees suggest that they do not (Chapter 1). Similarly, in a study of an electric utility, Lawrence (1983) reports that managers seem to perceive that promotion opportunity continues forever and that no one gets stuck in the lower levels of the hierarchy. These results are given further support by the misperceptions found by Vroom (personal communication) and Goldner (1970) described in Chapter 1. Evidently, many managers in various firms do not know important rules of the career tournament. This is even more true for workers, at least in their early years (Chinoy 1955; Sennett and Cobb 1972).

Do employees start at similar positions? Employees begin at different positions in this firm's career tournament, and, unlike auto races where the "pole position" gives only minimal advantages over a 500-mile race, early jobs give decisive advantages to some employees. The tournament is not equal from the outset.

Are individuals allowed to begin competing at the time of their own choosing? Tennis tournaments implicitly assume that individuals enter the tournament when they are ready to do so. Tennis tournaments are held every year, and individuals who are not ready can wait another year before entering. This is not the case with the career tournament. As soon as one begins working in an organization, one must enter the career tournament. Individuals do not have the option to say that they are not ready to compete for advancement. Indeed, the management literature warns that when a boss asks a subordinate to take a more demanding job (a new test in the tournament), the subordinate does not have the option of delaying the test (Shaeffer 1972). Individuals who refuse this request usually do not get a second chance.

Consequently, women and men who are not ready to compete for advancement in their early years because they want to devote time to starting their families, caring for an ill parent, or developing an avocational interest are effectively ruled out of the tournament. If they subsequently develop ambition and a willingness to devote time to the organization, the tournament structure provides no opportunity for them to do so.

The logic of the tournament specifies certain conditions to make the competition fair, open, and efficient. The findings of this and other studies provide evidence suggesting that these conditions are not met. Clearly, for a career system to satisfy its aim of opportunity and efficiency, some modifications are required along these dimensions.

The policy implications of these findings are straightforward. For a tournament to conform to its assumptions, it must make its rules public, it must reduce the effects of starting positions, and it must allow employees more choice about when they wish to begin competing. Organizations which fail to meet these preconditions for a tournament will tend to be unfair to employees and may deprive the organization of the full use of employees' talents.

Of course, as a practical matter, some of these preconditions may be difficult to satisfy. Starting all employees in equal positions may not be possible, since different entry jobs are likely to be differently valued. Efforts to make entry jobs more equal may be desirable in such circumstances, but it's not clear that equality can be accomplished (Dahrendorf 1968). On the other hand, equal knowledge and choice about when one competes should be relatively easy to accomplish, and these factors may reduce the importance of initial status inequalities.

These preconditions are not just important for the fairness of the selection system, they also affect its efficiency. At a time when men are increasingly more involved with child-care and household responsibilities and women are increasingly more career oriented, the timetable imposed by the tournament forces the career system to neglect important segments of the work force. The tournament's timetable may have been relatively more appropriate in previous decades (when men may have been less family oriented and women less career oriented), but in the present era, this system is likely to eliminate some top candidates (Bailyn 1980).

Preconditions for Efficiency in Tournament Career Systems

Tournaments offer efficiency by making early selections which limit the number of employees requiring investments and by permitting the organization's investments to be amortized over longer periods of time.

However, to be efficient, tournament career systems must meet certain preconditions: (1) they must use appropriate selection criteria, (2) they must increase amortization time, and (3) they must not reduce productivity by their selections. The findings of this study raise doubts about each of these points.

Tournaments Must Use Appropriate Selection Criteria

Besides being determined by explicit decisions, selection criteria are also determined implicitly by the structure of the selection process. An early selection system like the tournament limits the type of ability and performance that it evaluates, and it permits certain kinds of errors which raise doubts about its appropriateness for contributing to efficiency. It defines ability in terms of "fast starters," it limits assessments to short-term performance outcomes, it specifies how much selection error will be permitted, and it even suggests what kinds of selection errors will or will not be corrected by the system. The following review of these considerations indicates that an early selection system requires the use of selection criteria and procedures which may be inappropriate for selecting the most able employees.

A central feature of this selection system is that it makes its decisions very early. Early job statuses have lasting effects on career attainments; and, according to the career-tree diagram (Figure 2.2), subsequent selections are made soon after individuals arrive in each successive job. Individuals who get to the top rarely spend more than 3 years in any level and less than 2 years in each job (since employees are expected to hold more than 1 job at a level before being promoted).

One implication of an early selection system is that it selects only "fast starters." Ability must emerge very quickly if it is to be recognized and selected. According to popular idiom, *fast starters* are individuals who show their ability from the outset, although the term may carry connotations of superficiality. *Late bloomers* are individuals who take longer to show their abilities. Although this selection system does not state an explicit preference between these types of ability, its early selections make it inevitable that fast starters have great advantages in this system, and late bloomers are likely to be left behind and never recognized.

The earliness of selections causes the assessment of ability to be based only on short-term performances. Outcomes which stretch out past the 2-year timetable will be ignored by this selection system. Employees who can exhibit short-term performance, perhaps even to the detriment of long-term outcomes, will be promoted in this system.

A career structure which makes early and rapid selections tends to allow more selection errors than one that makes late and slow selections, for the former's selections will be based on fewer performances. Indeed, March and March (1977) suggest that performance sampling error could be a major factor determining which employees are selected as fast-starting top executives. Moreover, individuals may also use this to their advantage; they may scheme to present misleading impressions and to take advantage of these "errors," knowing that their opportunism cannot be discovered in the short run. Opportunism is even more likely when individuals cannot be blamed for the long-term costs of their short-term decisions (see Williamson [1975] for a discussion of the economics of opportunistic behavior). Rapid, early selections increase the risk of errors due to both the limited performance samples and the short-term nature of the outcome.

Selection systems can also determine what kinds of selection errors can be remedied and what kinds of selection errors cannot. A tournament selection system is particularly well suited to catching mistakes of inclusion. Low-ability individuals mistakenly retained in the tournament will be repeatedly tested; and if they lack ability, this will be discovered in subsequent competitions.

A tournament is particularly weak at discovering errors of exclusion. It does not have any way to bring former losers back into the competition for top positions. The lack of second chances means that high-ability individuals who begin in low-status jobs or those who are mistakenly eliminated in an early competition (due to selection error or a temporary performance lapse) will not have much chance to show their abilities subsequently. This is even more of a problem because entry jobs have such a great impact on career trajectories, and entry jobs are assigned before much is known about employees' work performance.

The risks of selection errors are even greater in a sponsored system. For instance, a small sponsored program for high-potential people may rapidly advance a few young employees to be contenders for top management, but in so doing may exempt them from some of the scrutiny of a tournament, thereby creating a risk that low-ability individuals in these programs will not be discovered. Moreover, sponsored programs tend to operate regardless of the abilities of the individuals who happen to be in any particular cohort, and such a system carries the risk that the term "high-potential people" does not so much describe a type of person as it describes a predefined role to which some individuals will be assigned regardless of their personal qualities. By the training, socialization, and social labels it confers, the career system may be creating many of the individual differences which it presumes to be using for its selections. Although organizations go through intermittent periods of concern about whether they are finding the most talented managers, they less often attend to the question of whether the talent they are identifying is really as good as their high-potential programs assume. If the ability differences are not great, then later selections would less seriously prejudice the issue and might give more extensive performance samples from which to infer ability.

From a policy perspective, the short-term orientation in tournament and sponsored career systems could be a particularly serious problem for organizations. It gives the message that ambitious employees do not need to consider long-term consequences of their behavior. These consequences will be someone else's concern if they are successful in continuing in their fast-rising trajectory, and their career histories teach them to expect that they will be. No doubt some do get caught. If they get stuck in their job more than 2 years, they may have to face up to the consequences of their having ignored long-term outcomes. This may even be a factor in explaining why those who stay in a level more than 3 years are unlikely to advance further (Chapter 2). But the individuals who were successful do not have to face these consequences, and they are the ones who end up filling the top levels of the organization hierarchy.

This speculation is supported by several managers whom I interviewed in this firm. They noted that young, high-potential people tend to make decisions that help their careers but do not necessarily help their department's long-term operation.[1] The present analysis suggests that this problem is endemic to the structure of the career system. It is not just that high-potential people happen to be opportunistic and shortsighted, or even that the career system permits such behavior; but rather the career system actually creates an incentive structure which encourages this behavior.

Observers of American corporations have often noted that corporate managers are so concerned with improving quarterly profits that they ignore long-term investments and long-term planning. The blame is usually directed at stockholders' attitudes and managerial decision-making models. However, this analysis suggests another possible source of the problem which has largely been neglected: that manageri-

---

[1]Of course, this perception may be somewhat due to a "sour-grapes" reaction on the part of the respondents since the high-potential people have clearly passed them by, and these respondents may be jealous. However, even after discounting the distortions implicit in these reports, the fast-rising career trajectories created by the tournament inevitably pose the risk of this problem arising. This is a potential problem which is worthy of future study.

al career systems provide direct incentives for managers to make short-term decisions and sacrifice longer-term outcomes.

Tournaments Must Increase Amortization Time

Economists justify early selections on the grounds that they allow employers more time to amortize their investments. If the training costs for a foreman job are the same, regardless of how long an employee has been at the nonmanagement level (within some span of years), then economists argue that the selection should be made as early as possible to give the organization more years to benefit from its investment. This might explain why the age–promotion curve shows such pronounced drop-offs at age 35. Given a universal retirement age of 65 at that time, the organization may need 30 years for amortizing its investments, and it would not have enough time to recover the costs of training individuals for new jobs if it promoted older employees.

However, it is not clear why 30 years is required to amortize investments. Why not 25 or 20? Even 10 years is a long time to amortize investments during periods when the organization of work is changing rapidly (as suggested by the extensive changes in job titles in Chapter 4). Obviously, how long an organization has to amortize its investments in employees depends on how much change occurs in job tasks.

In addition, while the amortization argument considers the *potential* amount of time that an individual might stay with a firm, assuming that no one leaves the firm, employees do leave firms; and young employees leave more often than older ones. Since older employees tend to be more likely to stay with the same employer, older employees might actually provide the company more time to amortize its promotion investment than younger employees provide.[2]

Moreover, it is quite possible that the early selection system actually contributes to the rapid turnover of young, high-potential people. Because organizations create this great demand for young, high-potential people; employees who are so labeled raise their expectations, and their career decisions are effected by the external labor market which bids highly for them. Indeed, some reports have warned that major corporations may be overcompensating high-potential people beyond

[2]One reason the human capital analysis is wrong here is that human capital is different from physical capital. Unlike physical capital, human capital (i.e., people) is highly portable and highly susceptible to voluntary turnover.

what the organization can expect to get as returns (Shaeffer 1972; Hayes and Abernathy 1980).[3]

This extensive analysis of economic principles like amortization is not meant to belittle the previous discussions of legitimizing processes (Chapters 8 and 9). Legitimizing processes provide an alternative explanation of early selections, overcompensation, and persistent elite preferences. When organizations make early investments in a select group of young employees, they may *confer* additional value to those employees, over the amount needed to compensate them. These selections and investments give these employees the image of being very able and very valuable. A fast-track program is an ideal way of legitimating the authority of top executives, for it gives a very high reputation to the employees who are destined to fill these positions. By such a process, *overcompensation* (the awarding of salaries beyond the individuals' apparent economic value) is a signal that the individual is more valuable than he or she appears.

As previously noted, career systems leave ample room for legitimizing processes to operate. Early selections signal ability and justify differential training and socialization of early winners. The legitimizing interpretation could explain early selections at least as well as the amortization interpretation, and the conflict between the two cannot easily be settled empirically. Moreover, the legitimizing interpretation provides a serious critique of the assumption by economic theory that early selections are economically rational and efficient. However, this section has focused on the economic interpretation in order to show that even if one takes the "best case" economic argument for early selections (i.e., amortization), its applicability is limited to only certain circumstances.

The amortization argument is a particularly compelling justification for early selections. It has been used to justify sponsored selections in a diversity of circumstances from utopias like Plato's "Republic" and Young's (1958) "meritocracy" to fast-track programs in modern corporations. The arguments presented here do not refute the general conten-

---

[3]Of course, if employees made all the investments in themselves, then organizations would not need to be concerned about amortization, and they could grant promotions in later career periods since individuals would pay for the training conferred by promotions by accepting lower wages. Organizations' concern about amortizing these investments, as reflected in justifications of early selections, is further evidence that individuals do not face trade-offs between training and wages. The two are stratified, and organizations pay for both.

tion that having more time to amortize investments contributes to economic efficiency.

However, the point is that, while the general principle might hold, specific organization conditions might limit its applicability. If work tasks change greatly over time, then the value of initial investments cannot be amortized over long periods. If young employees leave the firm more often than older ones, then they may not offer the firm longer periods of time for amortization. Obviously, the applicability of the amortization principle depends on the organization meeting specific preconditions, and its merits must be assessed in terms of the specific conditions. While this analysis does not provide conclusive arguments against early selections, it does raise questions that need to be considered in judging the appropriateness of early selection systems for attaining amortization goals.

Tournaments Must Not Reduce Productivity

The efficiency of early selections is also premised on the assumption that early selections per se do not reduce the productivity of employees. In personnel practice, as in economic theory, employee productivity is assumed to be a product of an individual's personal attributes (ability and skills), which are assumed not to decline as a function of the selection system.

Although the personnel literature has shown great concern about how organizations can preserve the motivation and skills of midcareer employees (Kaufman 1974), particularly as they have become a greater proportion of the work force (Pfeffer 1983), these problems have been treated as individuals' problems, and so solutions have been sought through individual counseling and training. In response to the midcareer crisis, organizations have implemented psychological counseling sessions. In response to the problem of obsolescence, organizations have variously implemented retraining programs and early retirement programs. But they have not considered whether their career systems contribute to these problems.

The tournament model suggests that career systems may have an important impact. The career system determines employees' first jobs, their future career options, and their timetables. It defines some employees as having no possibility for further advancement, and in so doing, it defines a structural situation in which it makes no sense to invest further resources or training in these employees. In effect, the career system makes these individuals obsolescent, and, as Chapter 8 noted, it sets in motion many social psychological processes which are conducive to creating the midcareer crisis. Without denying the possibility that midcareer emotional changes and skill obsolescence would occur independently of the selection system, the career system is nonetheless likely to contribute further to these kinds of changes.

The career system may be instrumental in building up the skills, status, and expectations of high-potential people, and it may be powerful in its destructive force in lowering the skills, status, and expectations of employees who have been eliminated from further competitions. It withholds further investments from them, it attributes low-ability status to them, and it creates the expectation that these individuals are not going any further in their careers.

The transition to "loser" status is likely to be particularly difficult. The tournament encourages the belief in open opportunity, and, in the early stages of their careers, young managers are encouraged to hold high expectations. Indeed, some corporations devote considerable effort to increasing young employees' ambitions in order to increase their motivation. These programs may work quite well in the short term in increasing ambition and the motivation to compete in the tournament, but they may make the inevitable loss all the harder to take. The personnel literature voices a concern about the problem of getting new employees to raise their expectations for themselves (Hall 1976), while it simultaneously voices the reverse concern about the problem of getting midcareer employees to lower their ambitions to their plateaued position (Ference 1979). The tournament selection system forces organizations to "heat up" the ambitions of young employees very rapidly while it also forces them to "cool down" the ambitions of the middle-aged. If, instead of an early selection system, organizations were slower to make decisive selections or if they reduced the consequences of all selections, the problems of quick "heating up" or "cooling down" of ambitions would presumably be less pressing.

Of course, this study is not in a position to evaluate how much the tournament selection system contributes to these problems. The problems are manifest at the "microlevel" of personal feelings, performances, and interpersonal interactions, and there is no way of knowing from the data gathered to what extent these problems originate at the macrolevel of organization structure. Surely, the microlevel processes to which psychologists attribute causal forces also contribute, and there is no way to sort out the relative effects of these causal factors within the design of this study.

Yet it is striking how much these microlevel problems are consistent with the structural model observed in these analyses. The structural model is able to explain many of these individual problems quite well. It is particularly impressive that this structural model has been able to describe careers to a very strong degree with only surface indicators of individual status attributes and job status and without knowledge of the data which have been the basis of most psychological analyses. Moreover, the clarity of career patterns found in this study have been remarkable, providing further support for analyzing careers as the product of career systems. Clearly, career systems cannot be ignored if social scientists are to reach an understanding of how motivation changes over employees' careers.

This analysis of preconditions, though nominally theoretical, has policy implications. If the preconditions required for a tournament's early selections do not hold, then concerns about legitimacy and efficiency may require procedural and structural reforms of career systems, as outlined in the following sections.

Policy Implications for Procedural Reforms

The findings and conceptualization offered by this study provides a new resource for employees and organization planners. The model that it provides of the entire career system of organizations suggests new information that individuals need to know for their career choices and that planners need to know for their policy decisions. It also suggests additional standards that policy analysts must apply in assessing and designing career systems.

Obviously, we must bear in mind the limitations of this research in proving the validity of approaching organization policy reform through career system redesign. The study of a single organization can do no better than show the possible usefulness of this approach and provide examples of the issues suggested by it. However, a great deal of policy is currently based on an individual-focused approach, which has never been tested against structural approaches; and so, at the least, policy analysts would be wise to consider the policy implications of an alternative approach which presents important practical issues in entirely different ways and suggests quite different remedies. While it may be premature to implement these policies, the same might also be said of the psychological policies aimed at the individual, which are so widely implemented today. Moreover, if this study has had an impact, I would hope that it has shown the possibility of an alternative interpretation of career phenomena. If I have succeeded in showing that the choice of approaches is indeed an open and unresolved question, then personnel policy analysts must consider the implications of conceptualizing organization careers in terms of career systems. This approach has several kinds of policy implications which are quite different than the policies and practices suggested by individual-focused approaches. The following are specific policy changes suggested by this approach.

1. *Intrapsychic counseling will not be an adequate response to aging.* The use of psychological counseling as a means of encouraging people to accept aging as a biological reality may help people adjust to their situations, but this kind of adjustment may be particularly harmful to individuals' self-esteem and sense of control—and needlessly so. If aging is largely a socially caused phenomenon, then assertions about biological causality misplace the blame. They are blaming the victim rather than blaming the system. Moreover, such assertions will tend to discourage individuals from being aware of their real strengths and abilities and from trying to find social systems that are less age-graded and more responsive to their abilities. By ignoring social context influences, psychologists may have inadvertently fallen into a trap in which only internal factors can have causal force. The need to remove these blinders should be apparent from this work.

2. *Career education and counseling must inform individuals about the structural factors which influence careers.* Career education and counseling are usually limited to describing work tasks and skill requirements. They sometimes discuss "organizational politics" and "impression management," but they rarely convey information about career timetables or about the kinds of organization factors and personal attributes which influence advancement opportunities. This kind of information is at least as important as the kinds of information about work environments and job demands which are usually conveyed. Just as counselors help individuals choose how much day-to-day pressure they face at work, they could also help individuals choose how much career pressure will be imposed by the timetables of their chosen career. This kind of information can be disseminated to students and others who are choosing careers.

Of course, this kind of information is not presently available for many careers. It is difficult to obtain much specific information about career systems in various occupations and organizations. Some work with census data has begun to illuminate the career timetable of selected occupations (Spilerman 1977; Spenner, Otto, and Call 1982). More of this work needs to be done and the results communicated to career counselors.

This kind of information is even more difficult to obtain for specific organizations, but it would help individuals in choosing employers. Career counselors have an important role to play in making the need for this kind of information apparent, and in persuading organizations to make such information available. Career counselors are supposed to act as agents of their counselees, and they have a responsibility to obtain this information for their clients. Moreover, just by asking organizations for this information, they will make personnel officers aware of the importance of these aspects of careers.

3. *Organizations must inform their employees about the structural factors which affect careers.* While there are serious limits to what career counselors can learn about the career systems in the many organizations in their locale, personnel staff in a single organization can convey information about that organization's career system to its employees. But unlike career counselors, who are agents of their counselees, personnel staff who do career counseling are agents of the organization. Personnel staff may believe that the interests of employers and employees conflict, and they may believe that the organization's interest in obtaining the best efforts of employees may dictate that they withhold information about career realities.

Indeed, this may be a conscious policy choice. Some managers with whom I have discussed these findings have confessed that, although they do not communicate deceptive information, they try to hide unpleasant realities from employees. The statement of one personnel manager in a large manufacturing firm exemplifies the underlying rationale: "There isn't much employees could do about it, so why tell them? They will figure it out sooner or later. In the meantime, I'll have a more motivated employee." Hall and Lawler (1969) note an aspect of this in a study which found that managers do not report negative performance ratings to subordinates. Ference (1979) also notes that managers feel they can not tell employees that they have plateaued, because this information tends to demoralize employees and hurt organization productivity.

From my discussions with managers, I suspect that conscious deception or withholding of information are less common than the practice of communicating vague generalities which are open to misinterpretation. Since opportunity myths are so much a part of the culture of U.S. society and its organizations, managers may even do this in good faith without realizing that the opportunity myths are untrue. Of course, like conscious deceptions, these vague generalizations confer the benefits of making managers feel more comfortable than they would if they had to confront the truth. Consequently, it is hard to know to what extent the use of vague generalizations is a conscious expedient strategy and to what extent it is an inadvertent mistake.

Despite the benefits of misleading information, it may also have considerable costs. If individuals do not know about these barriers, they will keep butting up against them and not understanding why they are failing to advance. They will retain unrealistically high expectations, which will be even more disappointing when they finally realize that their expectations have been unrealistic. Moreover, if employees do not realize that their failures are structurally determined, they will internalize the blame, and this will make them unhappy and make them blame themselves more than is warranted (Sennett and Cobb 1972). This can undermine the morale and effectiveness of an employee far more than an initial statement about that employee's prospects.

Employees may also come to realize that they have been strung along and deceived, and they are likely to be angry. They may direct their anger at the organization, and they may try to get back at the organization for its cruel manipulation. Although self-blame and system-blame are contradictory, both may happen in the same individual over time. Individuals may realize their failure before they realize its cause, and only with more experience will they come to understand how it came about. Since deception is particularly prolonged in management levels where the fiction of open opportunity is proclaimed most strongly, trusted managers in positions of considerable responsibility will be feeling the most anger. Hostile managers in such positions could be quite costly for an organization.

Instead of manipulating information, organizations could be candid about career systems and their operation. Information could be disseminated early in employees' careers so that they can clearly understand what they are up against and what they must do in order to attain their aspirations. Moreover, such information would reduce the likelihood that individuals would be caught by surprise after they have hit an age barrier, so it might tend to reduce disappointment. As noted previously, my preliminary comparisons of employees' perceptions with the organization reality in the personnel records have suggested that many employees do not correctly perceive the age basis of promotions or their own promotion chances. Other studies also support this conclusion (Goldner 1970; Lawrence 1983). I expect that individuals would face less severe disappointment if they perceived their career chances more accurately from the outset.

4. *Career policies must be assessed by additional standards, including behavioral outcomes.* This analysis has suggested that the career problems commonly observed in organizations must be seen as

interconnected and as possibly caused by the structure of the organizational career system. Instead of dismissing career problems as individual problems of psychological origin, the model presented here suggests that career problems spring from the career system; and any assessment of a career system must also take employees' career problems into account.

For instance, early career stress has been identified as a serious problem among young managers (Kotter 1973; Webber 1976). The two most common remedies proposed in the literature are individual "stress management" techniques and reduction of stress inducers in work tasks. This literature, though acknowledging that this problem is particularly acute in early career, fails to relate it to the career system. However, this study suggests that the tournament system makes stress endemic to the career system.

This prediction is supported by the observations of a health care consultant who was studying the feasibility of a stress management program for young managers in a large corporation in the health services industry (E. Blake, personal communication, December, 1983). She reported that job tasks per se were not the cause of stress, and stress would probably not have been reduced by job redesign. Rather, she concluded that young managers' stress was due to the rigid promotion timetable to which they were subjected. As in the corporation studied here, promotions declined sharply after age 35 (though managers seem to have been more aware of this timetable in the firm she observed). Managers in their early 30s were highly aware of the impending "sudden-death" implications of this timetable. The stressors in the environment could not be traced to particular job tasks; they were a property of the career system. Only by broadening the timetable for advancement would this corporation be able to reduce this career-related stress.

Ironically, the opposite is also identified as a problem: How can the work involvement of talented new employees be increased? Managers report that some new employees seem "too" involved with family responsibilities, and managers are concerned that some of the most talented young employees are not sufficiently engaged in their work. Of course, this problem arises in large part because the career system makes its most important selections—and consequently its greatest demands—at precisely the period when individuals customarily have had the greatest demands from their family responsibilities (Rapaport and Rapaport 1978). Therefore, these selection systems are making fateful decisions about employees at precisely the time when employees are relatively less free to immerse themselves fully in their work.

This is unfair to young employees and their families, and it may also hurt work organizations. Rather than selecting the most able employees, early selection systems may be selecting those employees who have the least demands from, or least concern about, their families. By making its demands coincide with the period of greatest family responsibilities, the organization wins only if the family loses, and the organization does not win employees who are strongly committed to their families. This analysis suggests a remedy to the problem of "greedy institutions" (Handy 1978): A shift in career timetables would reduce this conflict.

Institutional sources of sex discrimination are another pressing concern. It is the great work demands during the 25–35 age period which have been used to justify discrimination against married women who have, or might have, children. One common response to avoid that form of discrimination has been for families to purchase child-care assistance so that child rearing will not detract from work. However, the present analysis suggests that the great demands during the 25–35 age period could be changed, and another response might be for work environments to allow men and women to reduce their involvement in work during these years without penalty to their later careers. If work environments extended the period during which the most important career selections were made so that selections did not end at age 35 or 40, then men and women could diminish their work commitment during their early child-rearing years and increase it later without penalty to their careers.

The midcareer crisis is another acute problem in corporations. It leads to lower motivation and indifferent performance among individuals who are in key positions of considerable responsibility and in whom the organization has invested considerable training. The personnel literature has devoted increasing concern to this problem, and considerable resources have been devoted to initiating psychological programs to ameliorate the psychological distress and to making these valued employees more productive.

However, the present analysis suggests a structural explanation for the midcareer crisis. According to the structural explanation proposed here, the midcareer crisis arises because the selection structure withdraws important inducements from employees in their midcareer periods.

If early selections increase early career stress, midcareer crises, work–family conflict, and sex discrimination, then the economic justifications of early selections require rethinking. Although early career selections may increase amortization time (under some conditions), they also create important costs that are generally ignored in assessments of early selection systems.

Ironically, the personnel literature identifies these problems and associates them with particular career stages, but it fails to relate these problems to each other or to career systems. As long as careers are attributed only to individuals' actions, the systematic factors that constrain career outcomes will not be seen, and their potential impact on employees' motivation and performance will not be considered.

The tournament model of career systems provides a structural map of the career incentives that employees are likely to experience in different parts of the career system. Just as a highway map tells drivers their travel options, the tournament model tells employees their career options, depending on their position, direction, velocity, and acceleration. Since different career options provide incentives of various strengths, this "career map" may tend to stimulate varying amounts of motivation commensurate with the strength of the career incentive. Career incentives will be important determinants of employees' motivation, and, other things being equal, the intensity of motivation will tend to be higher at those positions in the tournament where the career incentives are strongest.

In particular, the tournament model of career systems relates career structure to some common motivation and performance problems, in effect suggesting additional costs which are generally ignored in the cost–benefit analysis of career systems. Indeed, changes in motivation and performance may undermine the amortization argument, for the midcareer crisis reduces the dependability of managers' later performance and thus reduces the time available to amortize investments in employees' human capital. The tournament also identifies some prerequisite conditions which must obtain if early selections are to confer their presumed benefits. Consequently, this model suggests additional standards which must be considered in assessing selection systems.

Redesigning Career Systems: Destratification for Structural Reform

I propose a program of reform which seeks to reduce the structural factors observed in this research and to increase the options and opportunities available to employees. This program for structural reform may be characterized as destratification. I propose that career systems be redesigned to open employees' advancement opportunities later in their careers, both by delaying selections and by diminishing their impact on later career attainments. In addition, I propose that job challenge be freed from the constraints of job status.

In many respects these reforms lead to the ideal described by economic theory. It might seem ironic that the economic model criticized throughout this work is held up as the ideal in the final chapter, but this is quite consistent with the contention throughout. While the economic model is not an accurate statement of career realities in organizations, it is a good statement of the normative ideals in this society. It posits circumstances which would foster opportunity, choice, and individual initiative, conditions which career systems generally do not encourage but which could be increased by organization reforms suggested by this analysis.

This analysis has repeatedly shown the influence of career structure on individuals' careers. Social structures are like highways in the ways they delineate specific paths and options for movement. While individuals may wish to take a certain route with a certain timetable, the direction and condition of the roads define where the car can go and at what speed.

But unlike highways, which are set in concrete, career systems are not so immutable, and there are various ways to modify them. This does not require dismantling the whole system, for, as noted, the system does serve a useful purpose. Instead, the goal must be to reorganize the career system, make it less stratified, and allow individuals to have more options over a longer period of time.

The findings of this study and the tournament model suggest that a program of destratification would tend to increase individuals' options and opportunities and consequently to increase motivation and commitment. Moreover, this analysis suggests that this may not reduce efficiency nearly as much as is commonly presumed. It may even introduce some new efficiencies by providing better ability signals and reducing counterproductive stresses. Two kinds of reforms are proposed that might aid in destratifying career systems.

Freeing Job Challenge from the Constraints of Job Status

One way of destratifying career systems would be to decouple job challenge from the constraints of job status. This analysis has described careers only in terms of job statuses. This is not because all individuals are status seekers, but because organizations make status a prerequisite for attaining the other goals that individuals seek. Organizational psychologists have noted that employees seek many kinds of personal fulfillment from their work: qualities such as variety, autonomy, challenge, and interpersonal influence (Argyris 1964; Hall 1976). However, the organizational structure tends to make them all contingent upon status advancement. Job evaluation systems formalize this relationship by using these features of jobs as factors in the determination of job pay and job status.[4] As a result, while an individual may be indifferent to job status and may desire any of these personally fulfilling qualities of work (which for simplicity may be represented here by job challenge), job evaluation makes job challenge a "compensable factor" which increases job status. In such a system, if one wants job challenge, one must seek job status. Indeed, organizational psychologists sometimes inadvertently fall into this one-dimensional perspective when they speak of "personal development" and "hierarchical advancement" interchangeably, as if they were the same thing. They are not necessarily interchangeable; they only happen to be interchangeable because organizations' job evaluation practices constrain rewards onto a single status dimension.

The best critique of job evaluation comes from economic theory. Economic theory indicates the irrationality of stratified rewards. If individuals believed the job evaluation assumption that job challenge deserves to be compensated, then they would refuse to accept a promotion to a more challenging job if it didn't also offer greater pay. However, as economic theory rightly indicates, refusing one reward just because it is not accompanied by another reward is an irrational self-sacrifice.

Economic theory also contends that stratifying rewards reduces individuals' choices. By making all rewards correlated, job evaluation prevents individuals from having the option to choose among trade-offs. Individuals cannot choose to sacrifice immediate earnings and take a more challenging job, for job evaluation makes job challenge a "compensable factor" which increases job salaries. Since there are no trade-offs, individuals' latitude for making choices is markedly reduced.

By stratifying rewards, organizations are firmly in control of individuals' careers, since the organization is paying the bill. Job evaluation makes job challenge doubly costly to organizations; organizations must pay to make the job more challenging, and they must also offer greater status and pay for the challenging jobs. This puts organizations firmly

---

[4]Job demands and responsibility, which are used as factors in many job evaluation systems, are likely to include ratings of the variety, autonomy, challenge, and influence which jobs allow.

in control of the process, for they are paying a big cost for these over-compensated jobs.

Indeed, stratified rewards may increase the tendency to create elites. When an organization assigns employees to a higher status job, it is making a large investment in them which has great cost and which confers many kinds of benefits, including the benefit of higher career trajectories. Given the many kinds of investments at stake, organizations will limit these highly desirable jobs to those employees who are considered to be suitable for overcompensation, that is, elites.[5]

Although job evaluation's practice of paying individuals for "sacrifices" would seem to be equitable and economically efficient, it ignores the nonmonetary rewards conferred by jobs. If "sacrifices" are also rewarding—if, for instance, individuals enjoy job challenge—then job evaluation leads to overcompensation.

Organizations could distribute rewards and incentives over a greater number of employees by uncoupling job evaluations from job challenge and other rewarding features of jobs. Decoupling these rewards would permit organizations to offer pay rewards for unpleasant difficult jobs, while pleasant difficult tasks would require lesser monetary compensation after their nonmonetary rewards were factored into the pay equation. In addition, if job evaluation did not force organizations to pay greater salaries for challenging jobs, then organizations would find it less costly to allow jobs to become more challenging, and organizations could afford to increase challenge in a greater number of jobs. Moreover, although managers could still infer ability signals from more challenging jobs within job statuses, the signal would be less visible and less stigmatizing if the various kinds of job enrichment (i.e., challenge, autonomy, etc.) were decoupled from job status.

Job evaluation ignores nonmonetary rewards and ignores the motivational costs of stratified rewards. As a result, job evaluation risks wasting organizational rewards on some jobs, while leaving the organization with too few incentives for motivating employees in other jobs. While this analysis cannot say in the abstract what combination of monetary and nonmonetary rewards are "overcompensation" without

[5]One implication of this analysis is that job evaluation makes the allocation of statuses more important since job statuses also constrain job enrichment. Consequently, although job status was the dependent variable in the analyses throughout this volume, status was not the only outcome at stake. Given the way that job evaluation stratifies rewards, many qualities of jobs were also at stake—including variety, autonomy, challenge, and interpersonal influence. The analyses in this volume not only describe the allocation of job status attainments in this corporation, they also describe the ways that many rewarding qualities of work are assigned to employees over their careers.

having specific information about particular contexts, this analysis can make managers aware of problems which are rarely considered, and it suggests options they have to make better use of available resources.

However, this reform alone probably would not induce organizations to distribute rewards into later career periods. If the tournament's contention of the presumed efficiencies of early selections remains widely accepted, then it is likely to be applied to selections into challenging jobs, even if challenge were decoupled from job status. The same logic which dictates early status selections would suggest that it is also more efficient to make early selections into challenging jobs: Job challenge is an investment, and organizations would seek to amortize it. While decoupling job challenge from job status would permit rewards and incentives to be dispersed over more employees, the rewards and incentives would not necessarily be dispersed into middle or later career periods unless assumptions about the efficiencies of early selections are questioned. The issues of timing in the career system still remain to be addressed by separate reforms, which are described in the next section.

Opening Opportunities Into Later Career: Delaying Selections and Diminishing Their Impact

The tournament model is in many ways an ideal reconciliation of the conflict between opportunity and efficiency. It offers the efficiencies of early selections, and it also holds out opportunity to many employees. Some variant of the tournament is likely to be the best reconciliation one can hope for. However, while the tournament is rational to make selections as early as possible and to make selection probability decline over time, many questions still remain.

1. Are organizations making their selections before they have adequate information about employees and before they can assess long-term implications of individuals' performance? Given the limited information organizations have when they assign employees to their early jobs, the strong effects of early jobs on later careers is particularly troubling.
2. Are organizations assuming that amortization occurs over a period of time which is inconsistent with employee turnover or with changes in jobs tasks in the organization?
3. Can organizations offer second chances to employees? The lower career ceilings of early losers in the career tournament and the inability of Horatio Alger types to overcome initial disadvantages

suggest that this career system allows no room for second chances.[6] Besides violating the contest norm, irreversible selections create inefficiencies by preventing the organization from discovering its early mistakes.

4. Are the precipitous declines in promotion chances after age 35 due to arbitrary assumptions about aging? Biological aging is unlikely to create such precipitous declines in ability or performance as occur in these promotion curves (Chapter 8), although the precipitous promotion declines may make aging assumptions a self-confirming prophesy.

5. Are organizations creating their own problems by these early selections? This chapter has speculated that early irreversible selections might contribute to many common problems in organizations: early career stress, the midcareer crisis, sex discrimination, and work–family conflicts. If these are counted as costs of early selections, and if the benefits of early selections are considered more skeptically, then delaying selections may reduce these costs without seriously reducing the benefits of the tournament.

Organizations persist in making early selections because certain assumptions (like the amortization assumption) are accepted uncritically and because early selections are not perceived as affecting employees' motivation. Organizations seem to be getting benefits and to be getting them costlessly. However, if the above analysis is correct, then the apparent benefits may be less than assumed and the motivational costs, though delayed, may nonetheless emerge belatedly, in other forms and at other times that prevent personnel analysts from realizing their origin. If this is indeed true, then the designers of these career systems may not only be deceiving employees, they may also be fooling themselves.

Diminishing the impact of early selections on later careers would further extend the availability of opportunity into later career periods.

---

[6]The tournament model is vague about what constitutes a "competition." Unlike tennis tournaments in which each competition is a single game, I suspect that a competition in a career tournament entails a number of events, actions, or decisions over a one- or two-year period. However, the tournament may not always be so generous. A manager in a bank told me of a middle manager who had already been offered a promotion when the offer was rescinded because he failed on a single project in his current job. He was never considered for another promotion, and it was well known by all his subordinates that he was "stuck." In this case, one event cancelled his previous record of successes and eliminated him from the tournament. The present research was not able to investigate what events constitute a competition, but it would be a fruitful area for more detailed study.

It would allow individuals to make salary sacrifices to obtain better training and better chances of advancement. It would also allow employees who overcome their initial disadvantages in Horatio Alger fashion to shift to new career trajectories.

But, one may object, if organizations stop relying on signals and proxies for ability, then they will need better assessment techniques. This is not necessarily so. Surely organizations would have to rely more on assessments of individuals' performances and capabilities, but these assessments might also be easier to make if selections were delayed, for organizations would have more information about individuals' performances. Indeed, the need for easy signals of ability is partially due to the tournament's mandate to make early selections before an adequate performance sample is available. If the career system were to allow selections to be made later, then better information would be available and selection decisions would be based on a longer track record in a greater number of jobs.

Delaying selections would also offer important motivational gains. It would reduce the excessive incentives which create stress in the early career period, and it would prolong incentives into the middle career period, delaying the midcareer decline in motivation. Retaining promotion chances in the later career period would increase employees' motivation and would allow organizations to utilize their most experienced employees in the ways assumed by the amortization argument. Since the gains of amortization can only be achieved if employees' motivation is preserved, amortization may even be increased by not making all selections in the early career period.

Interestingly, the current period of declining growth provides an unusually good opportunity to implement this kind of reform. Although Chapter 7 suggests that ABCO has used periods of declining growth to increase its selectivity and give increased advantages to youth, the opposite strategy might be more reasonable. While job vacancies do not control selection criteria, the reduced numbers of job vacancies certainly reduce the pressure to advance employees quickly for expected future vacancies. Declining growth permits organizations to make their selections more deliberatively, with firmer knowledge of employees' abilities.

Moreover, the aging of the organization caused by declining growth makes fast-track advancement policies and youth preference increasingly inappropriate. Youth preference excludes an increasing proportion of the work force from advancement, while it leads to the promotion of employees who are increasingly younger than their peers and subordinates, a fact which may reduce their authority and effectiveness. The proposed reforms would seem to be particularly appropriate in the current period.

Conclusion: Toward a New Conception of Careers in Organizations

The American penchant for focusing on individuals creates a tendency to see all attainments as the result of individual performance and to decide selections on a case-by-case basis. Consequently, promotions are decided individually and personal problems are counselled individually, and these are not related to one another. However, the contention here is that there are systematic features of promotion decisions which may be described as a career system, and this career system is likely to have an impact on problems like early career stress and the midcareer crisis.

This book has described the patterns that individuals' careers follow over time in ABCO, and it has shown some of the ways that structural factors affect these patterns. The case is presented for considering these patterns as the result of systematic features of the organizational career selection system. This career system also defines an incentive structure which may affect employees' motivation and behavior and contribute to commonly identified personnel problems. The central conclusion to be drawn from these findings and conceptions is that career attainments, career motivation, and career problems must be seen as interrelated and as parts of systems, not as isolated pieces, if selections are to be truly efficient and career problems are to be addressed effectively.

This conception is more important than the particular reforms proposed. The relevance of the proposed reforms and the actual form they should take will depend on the particular circumstances in particular organizations, and this must be determined in each organization. The present conception provides a way of approaching the problem, and it shows the kinds of relationships that must be investigated. This is the main message of this work.

Of course, managers may think that they are better off not dealing with these issues, leaving them hidden and unconsidered. However, the world is changing, and even if these career systems served their purpose at one time, they are not well suited to the enormous changes which are now occurring. Informal adaptations cannot be counted upon to be adequate to meet the challenges of the current era.

Organizations are concerned about how they are making use of their human resources. They are investing in costly piecemeal psychological programs to deal with the many problems identified here. Moreover, an era of declining growth has reduced the hiring of new employees, and the reduced numbers of young employees makes selections among them increasingly important. Middle-aged and older employees have become an increasing proportion of the work force in organizations, and this has raised particularly great concern about the loss of energy and commitment shown by employees in middle and later career stages. Organizational leaders are aware that they must attend to these problems, but they lack the conceptual apparatus to see the structural underpinnings of these problems. Consequently, their piecemeal psychological programs do not deal with the fundamental causes.

While the generalizability of the specific findings cannot be accurately assessed at present, given the meagerness of existing research, the tournament model of career systems describes a dynamic mechanism which may be generalizable. Although it is not a sufficient basis for making specific policies, it raises the conceptual issues that need to be considered. These issues are not now being raised by traditional individual-focused explanations. This study has succeeded if it has raised sufficient doubts to make the individual-focused model problematic, for it will have opened new ways of understanding careers, of understanding the causal factors which make them operate as they do, and of designing new alternatives for career systems. This is the great practical value of a good theory.

References

Akalin, Mustafa T. 1970. *Office Job Evaluation*. Illinois: Industrial Management Society.

Althauser, Robert P., and A. L. Kalleberg. 1981. "Firms, Occupations, and the Structure of Labor Markets: A Conceptual Analysis." Pp. 119–152 in *Sociological Perspectives on Labor Markets*, edited by Ivar Berg. New York: Academic Press.

Argyris, Chris. 1964. *Integrating the Individual and the Organization*. New York: Wiley.

Arrow, Kenneth J. 1973. "Higher Education as a Filter." *Journal of Public Economics* 2:193–216.

Astin, Alexander W. 1965. *Predicting Academic Performance in College*. New York: Free Press.

Bailyn, Lotte. 1980. "The Slow-Burn Way to the Top." Pp. 94–105 in *Work, Family and the Career: New Frontiers in Theory and Research*, edited by C. B. Derr. New York: Praeger.

Baltes, Paul B., and O. G. Brim, Jr. (eds.). 1980. *Life-span Development and Behavior*. Vol. 3. New York: Academic Press.

Baron, James N. 1984. "Organizational Perspectives on Stratification." In *Annual Review of Sociology*, Vol. 10, edited by Ralph Turner. Palo Alto, Cal.: Annual Reviews Inc.

Baron, James N., and W. T. Bielby. 1980. "Bringing the Firms Back in: Stratification, Segmentation, and the Organization of Work." *American Sociological Review* 45:737–765.

Bartholomew, David J. 1968. *Stochastic Models for Social Processes*. London: Wiley.

Bartlett, Susan, and C. Jencks. 1978. "Returns to Schooling, Experience, and Age in 1959 and 1969." Unpublished manuscript, Northwestern University.

Beck, E. M., Patrick M. Horan, and Charles M. Tolbert. 1978. "Stratification in a Dual

Economy: A Sectoral Model of Earnings Determination." *American Sociological Review* 43:704–720.

Becker, G. 1964. *Human Capital.* New York: Columbia University Press.

Becker, Howard, and A. Strauss. 1956. "Careers, Personality, and Adult Socialization." *American Journal of Sociology* 62:253–263.

Berg, Ivar. 1971. *Education and Jobs: The Great Training Robbery.* Boston: Beacon Press.

Berk, Richard. 1977. "Proof? No. Evidence? No. A Skeptic's Comment on Inverarity's Use of Statistical Inference." *American Sociological Review* 42:652–656.

Berlew, D. E., and D. T. Hall. 1966. "The Socialization of Managers: Effects of Expectations on Performance." *Administrative Science Quarterly* 11:207–223.

Bibb, Robert, and William H. Form. 1977. "The Effects of Industrial, Occupational, and Sex Stratification on Wages in Blue-Collar Markets." *Social Forces* 55:974–996.

Birren, James E. (Ed.). 1959. *Handbook of Aging and The Individual: Psychological and Biological Aspects.* Chicago: University of Chicago Press.

Blau, Francine D. 1977. *Equal Pay in the Office.* Lexington, Mass.: Lexington Books.

Blau, P., and O. D. Duncan. 1967. *The American Occupational Structure.* New York: Wiley.

Blaug, Mark. 1976. "The Empirical Status of Human Capital Theory." *Journal of Economic Literature* 14:827–855.

Bloom, Benjamin. 1964. *Stability and Change in Human Characteristics.* New York: Wiley.

Blumen, I., M. Kogan, and P. J. McCarthy. 1955. *The Industrial Mobility of Labor as a Probability Process. Cornell Studies in Industrial and Labor Relations.* Vol. 6. Ithaca: New York State School of Industrial and Labor Relations, Cornell University.

Bonjean, Charles M., Bruce D. Grady, and J. Allen Williams, Jr. 1967. "Social Mobility and Job Satisfaction: A Replication and Extension." *Social Forces* 46:492–501.

Bornstein, R., and Mark T. Smircina. 1982. "The Status of the Empirical Support for the Hypothesis of Increased Variability in Aging Populations." *The Gerontologist* 22(3):258–260.

Botwinick, J., and L. W. Thompson. 1968. "A Research Note on Individual Differences in Reaction Time in Relation to Age." *The Journal of Genetic Psychology* 112:73–75.

Bowlby, John. 1951. *Maternal Care and Child Health.* London: Penguin.

Bowles, Samuel, and H. Gintis. 1976. *Schooling in Capitalist America.* New York: Basic Books.

Bray, Douglas W., Richard J. Campbell, and Donald L. Grant, 1974. *Formative Years in Business.* New York: Wiley.

Bridges, William P., and Richard A. Berk. 1974. "Determinants of White-Collar Income: An Evaluation of Equal Pay for Equal Work." *Social Science Research* 3:211–234.

Breiger, Ronald L. 1981. "The Social Class Structure of Occupational Mobility." *American Journal of Sociology* 87:578–611.

Breiger, Ronald L. 1982. "A Structural Analysis of Occupational Mobility." Pp. 17–31 in *Social Structure and Network Analysis,* edited by Peter V. Marsden and Nan Lin. Beverly Hills, Calif.: Sage.

Brim, Orville G. 1976. "Theories of the Male Mid-life Crisis." *The Counseling Psychologist* 6:2–9.

Butler, Robert N. 1975. *Why Survive: Being Old in America.* New York: Harper & Row.

Cain, Glen G. 1976. "The Challenge of Segmented Labor Market Theories to Orthodox Theory." *Journal of Economic Literature* 14:1215–1257.

Campbell, Angus, P. Converse, and W. Rodgers. 1976. *The Quality of American Life.* New York: Russell Sage Foundation.

Campbell, Richard J. 1968. "Career Development: The Young Business Manager." Paper presented at the Annual Meeting of the American Psychological Association, San Francisco.

Campbell, John P., M. D. Dunnette, E. E. Lawler, III, and Karl E. Weick, Jr. 1970. *Managerial Behavior, Performance, and Effectiveness*. New York: McGraw-Hill.

Caplow, Theodore. 1954. *The Sociology of Work*. New York: McGraw-Hill.

Carnoy, Martin, and R. Rumberger, 1975. *Segmented Labor Markets: Some Empirical Forays*. Palo Alto, Calif.: Center for Economic Studies.

Cassell, Frank H., S. M. Director, and S. I. Doctors. 1975. "Discrimination within Internal Labor Markets." *Industrial Relations* 14:337–344.

Chinoy, Ely. 1955. *Automobile Workers and the American Dream*. New York: Random House.

Clark, B. 1960. "The 'Cooling-Out' Function in Higher Education." Pp. 513–526 in *Education, Economy, and Society*, edited by A. H. Halsey, J. Floud, and C. A. Anderson. New York: Free Press.

Cohen, Arthur R. 1958. "Upward Communication in Experimentally Created Hierarchies." *Human Relations* 11:41–53.

Cohen, Y. and J. Pfeffer. 1983. "Employment Practices in a Dual Economy." *Industrial Relations*. 22:41–53.

Coleman, James S., E. Campbell, C. J. Hobson, J. McPartland, A. Mood, F. Weinfeld, and R. York. 1966. *Equality of Educational Opportunity*. Washington, D.C.: Government Printing Office.

Collins, Randall. 1974. "Where are Educational Requirements for Employment Highest?" *Sociology of Education* 47:419–442.

Collins, Randall. 1975. *Conflict Sociology*. New York: Academic Press.

Collins, Randall. 1979. *The Credential Society*. New York: Academic Press.

Collins, Randall. 1981. "On the Microfoundations of Macrosociology." *American Journal of Sociology* 86:984–1014.

Cook, Thomas D., H. Appleton, R. Conner, A. Shaffer, G. Tamkin, and S. Weber. 1975. *"Sesame Street" Revisited*. New York: Russell Sage Foundation.

Dahrendorf, R. 1968. "On the Origin of Inequality among Men." Pp. 151–178 in *Essays in the Theory of Society*. Palo Alto, Calif.: Stanford University Press.

Dalton, Melville. 1951. "Informal Factors in Career Achievement." *American Journal of Sociology* 56:407–445.

Dannefer, Dale. 1982. "Adult Development, Social Structure and Ideology: Toward a Sociogenic Paradigm of Change in Adulthood." Unpublished manuscript, University of Rochester.

Davis, Kingsley, and W. E. Moore. 1945. "Some Principles of Stratification." *American Sociological Review* 10:242–249.

Doeringer, Peter, and Michael Piore. 1971. *Internal Labor Markets and Manpower Analysis*. Lexington, Mass.: Heath Lexington Books.

Dreyfuss, Carl. 1968. "Prestige Grading: A Mechanism of Control." Pp. 145–149 in *Organizational Careers*, edited by B. Glaser. Chicago: Aldine. (Originally published, 1938.)

Duncan, Otis, D., David L. Featherman, and Beverly Duncan. 1972. *Socioeconomic Background and Achievement*. New York: Seminar Press.

Edwards, Richard C. 1979. *Contested Terrain: The Transformation of the Workplace in America*. New York: Basic Books.

Esterlin, Richard. 1973. "Does Money Buy Happiness?" *The Public Interest* 30:3–10.

Etzioni, Amitai. 1964. *Modern Organizations*. Englewood Cliffs, N.J.: Prentice-Hall.

Evans, Peter B. 1975. "Multiple Hierarchies and Organizational Control." *Administrative Science Quarterly* 20:250–259.

Farkas, George, 1977. "Cohort, Age, and Period Effects upon the Employment of White Females: Evidence for 1957–1968." *Demography* 14:33–42.

Faulkner, Robert R. 1974. "Coming of Age in Organizations." *Sociology of Work and Occupations* 1:131–173.

Featherman, David L. 1971. "A Research Note: A Social Structural Model for the Socioeconomic Career." *American Journal of Sociology* 77:293–304.

Featherman, David L. 1973. "Comments on Models for the Socioeconomic Career." *American Sociological Review* 3:785–796.

Featherman, David L., and Robert M. Hauser. 1976. "Sexual Inequalities and Socioeconomic Achievement in the U.S., 1962–1973. *American Sociological Review* 40(June):462–483.

Featherman, David L., and Robert M. Hauser. 1978. *Opportunity and Change.* New York: Academic Press.

Fein, Greta G., P. M. Schwartz, S. W. Jacobson, and J. L. Jacobson. 1983. "Environmental Toxins and Behavioral Development: A New Role for Psychological Research." *American Psychologist* 38:1188–1197.

Ference, Thomas P. 1979. "The Career Plateau: Facing Up to Life at the Middle." Pp. 175–179 in *Career Management,* edited by Mariann Jelinek. Chicago: St. Clair Press.

Findlay, W., and M. Bryan. 1971. *Ability Grouping: 1970.* Athens, Ga: Center for Educational Improvement.

Fitzpatrick, Bernard H. 1949. "An Objective Test of Job Evaluation Validity." *Personnel Journal* 28:128–132.

Foner, Anne. 1974. "Age Stratification and Age Conflict in Political Life." *American Sociological Review* 39:187–196.

Foner, Anne. 1980. "The Sociology of Age Stratification: A Review of Some Recent Publications." *Contemporary Sociology* 9:771–779.

Fox, William. 1962. "Purpose and Validity in Job Evaluation." *Personnel Journal* 41:432–437.

Freeman, Richard B. T. 1976. *The Overeducated American.* New York: Academic Press.

Fuchs, Victor. 1971. "Differences in Hourly Earnings between Men and Women." *Monthly Labor Review.* 94:9–15.

Ginsberg, R. B. 1971. "Semi-Markov Processes and Mobility." *Journal of Mathematical Sociology* 1:233–262.

Glaser, Barney. 1964. *Organizational Scientists: Their Professional Careers.* New York: Bobbs-Merrill.

Glaser, Barney. 1968. *Organizational Careers: A Sourcebook for Theory.* Chicago: Aldine.

Goffman, Erving. 1952. "Cooling the Mark Out: Some Aspects of Adaptation to Failure." *Psychiatry* 15:451–463.

Goldner, Fred. 1965. "Demotion in Industrial Management." *American Sociological Review* 30:714–724.

Goldner, Fred. 1970. "Success vs. Failure: Prior Managerial Perspectives." *Industrial Relations* 9:453–474.

Goldner, Fred H., and R. R. Ritti. 1967. "Professionalization as Career Immobility." *American Journal of Sociology* 73:489–502.

Goodman, Leo A. 1961. "Statistical Methods for the Mover–Stayer Model." *Journal of the American Statistical Association* 56:841–868.

Goodman, Leo A. 1962. "Statistical Methods for Analyzing Processes of Change." *American Journal of Sociology* 68:57–58.

Gordon, David. 1972. *Theories of Poverty and Underemployment*. Lexington, Mass.: Lexington Books.

Grandjean, Burke D. 1981. "History and Career in a Bureaucratic Labor Market." *American Journal of Sociology* 86:1057–1092.

Granovetter, Mark. 1974. *Getting a Job: A Study of Contacts and Careers*. Cambridge, Mass.: Harvard University Press.

Granovetter, Mark. 1981. "Toward a Sociological Theory of Income Differences." Pp. 11–48 in *Sociological Perspectives on Labor Markets*, edited by Ivar Berg. New York: Academic Press.

Grusky, Oscar. 1966. "Career Mobility and Organizational Commitment." *Administrative Science Quarterly* 10:489–502.

Halaby, Charles N. 1978. "Job-Specific Sex Differences in Organizational Reward Attainment: Wage Discrimination vs. Rank Segregation." Madison, Wis.: Institute for Research on Poverty.

Halaby, Charles N. 1979. "Sexual Inequality in the Workplace: An Employer-Specific Analysis of Pay Differences." *Social Science Research* 8:79–104.

Hall, Douglas T. 1976. *Careers in Organizations*. Pacific Palisades, Calif.: Goodyear.

Hall, Douglas T., and E. E. Lawler. 1969. "Unused Potential in Research and Development Organizations." *Research Management* 12:339–354.

Hall, Douglas T., and Khalil Nougaim. 1968. "An Examination of Maslow's Need Hierarchy in an Organizational Setting." *Organizational Behavior and Human Performance* 3:12–35.

Hall, Richard H. 1982. *Organizations*. 3rd ed. Englewood Cliffs, N.J.: Prentice-Hall.

Hall, Robert E. 1982. "The Importance of Lifetime Jobs in the U.S. Economy." *American Economic Review* 72:716–724.

Handy, Charles. 1978. "Going Against the Grain: Working Couples and Greedy Occupations." Pp. 36–46 in *Working Couples*, edited by Robert and Rhona Rapoport. New York: Harper Colophon.

Hanushek, Eric A., and John Jackson. 1977. *Statistical Methods for Social Scientists*. New York: Academic Press.

Hanushek, Eric A., and John M. Quigley. 1978. "Implicit Investment Profiles and Intertemporal Adjustments of Relative Wages." *The American Economic Review* 68:67–79.

Hayes, Robert, and W. Abernathy. 1980. "Managing Our Way to Economic Decline." *Harvard Business Review* 58:66–77.

Hartmann, Heidi I., Patricia A. Roos, and Donald J. Treiman. 1980. "Strategies for Assessing and Correcting Pay Discrimination: An Empirical Exercise." Staff paper prepared for the Committee on Occupational Classification and Analysis, National Research Council, National Academy of Sciences, June. Washington, D.C.

Hetzler, Stanley. 1955. "Variations in Role Playing Patterns among Different Echelons of Bureaucratic Leaders." *American Sociological Review* 20:700–706.

Hodge, Robert W. 1966. "Occupational Mobility as a Probability Process." *Demography* 3:19–34.

Hogan, Dennis P. 1978. "Order of Events in the Life Course." *American Sociological Review* 43:573–586.

Hughes, Everett. 1958. *Men and Their Work*. Glencoe, Ill.: Free Press.

Hulin, Charles L. 1966. "Job Satisfaction and Turnover in a Female Clerical Population." *Journal of Applied Psychology* 50:280–285.

Jacobs, D. 1983. "Industrial Sector and Career Mobility Reconsidered." *American Sociological Review* 48:415–421.

Jencks, Christopher. 1980. "Structural Versus Individual Explanations of Inequality: Where Do We Go From Here?" *Contemporary Sociology* 9:762–767.

Jencks, Christopher. 1983. "Discrimination and Thomas Sewell." *New York Review of Books* 30: March 3 and March 17.

Jencks, Christopher, M. Smith, H. Ackland, M. Bane, D. Cohen, H. Gintis, B. Heyns, and S. Michelson. *Inequality: A Reassessment of the Effect of Family and Schooling in America.* New York: Basic Books.

Jencks, Christopher, S. Bartlett, M. Corcoran, J. Crouse, D. Eaglesfield, G. Jackson, K. McClelland, P. Mueser, M. Olneck, J. Schwartz, S. Ward, and J. Williams. 1979. *Who Gets Ahead?* New York: Basic Books.

Jennings, Eugene E. 1971. *Routes to the Executive Suite.* New York: McGraw-Hill.

Kagan, Jerome. 1969. "The Three Faces of Continuity in Human Development." Pp. 983–1004 in *Handbook of Socialization Theory and Research,* edited by D. A. Goslin. Chicago: Rand McNally.

Kalleberg, Arne L., and K. A. Loscocco. 1983. "Age Differences in Job Satisfaction." *American Sociological Review* 48:78–90.

Kamens, David. 1971. "The College 'Charter' and College Size: Effects on Occupational Choice and College Attrition." *Sociology of Education* 44:270–296.

Kamens, David. 1974. "Colleges and Elite Formation: The Case of Prestigious American Colleges." *Sociology of Education* 47: 354–378.

Kamens, David. 1977. "Legitimating Myths and Educational Organization: The Relationship between Organizational Ideology and Formal Structure." *American Sociological Review* 42:208–219.

Kanter, Rosabeth Moss. 1977. *Men and Women of the Corporation.* New York: Basic Books.

Kanter, Rosabeth Moss. 1983. *The Change Masters: Innovations for Productivity in the American Corporation.* New York: Simon & Shuster.

Karabel, Jerome, and Katherine McClelland. 1983. "The Effects of College Rank on Labor Market Outcomes." Paper presented at the Annual Meeting of the American Sociological Association, Detroit, September.

Kaufman, H. G. 1974. *Obsolescence and Professional Career Development.* New York: Amacom.

Kaufman, Robert L., and S. Spilerman. 1982. "The Age Structure of Occupations and Jobs." *American Journal of Sociology* 87:827-851.

Kelley, Jonathan. 1973a. "Causal Chain Models for the Socioeconomic Career." *American Sociological Review* 38:481–493.

Kelley, Jonathan. 1973b. "History, Causal Chains, and Careers: A Reply." *American Sociological Review* 38:785–796.

Kellogg, Marion. 1972. *Career Management.* New York: Amacom.

Kimberly, J. R. 1976. "Organizational Size and the Structuralist Perspective: A Review, Critique, and Proposal." *Administrative Science Quarterly.* 21:571–597.

Kinsey, A. C., W. B. Pomeroy, and C. E. Martin. 1948. *Sexual Behavior in the Human Male.* Philadelphia: Saunders.

Klevmarken, Anders, and J. Quigley. 1976. "Age, Experience, Earnings and Investments in Human Capital." *Journal of Political Economy* 84:47–72.

Kluegel, James R. 1978. "Causes and Costs of Racial Exclusion." *American Sociological Review* 43:185–301.

Kohlberg, Lawrence. 1969. "Stage and Sequence: The Cognitive–Developmental Approach to Socialization." Pp. 347–480 in *Handbook of Socialization Theory and Research,* edited by David Goslin. Chicago: Rand McNally.

Kohn, Melvin. 1977. *Class and Conformity: A Study in Values.* 2nd ed. Chicago: University of Chicago Press. Homewood, Ill.: Dorsey Press, (Originally published, 1969).

Kohn, Melvin, and Carmi Schooler. 1978. "Reciprocal Effects of the Substantive Complexity of Work and Intellectual Flexibility." *American Journal of Sociology* 84:24–52.

Kohn, Melvin, and Carmi Schooler. 1983. *Work and Personality: An Inquiry into the Impact of Social Stratification.* Norwood, N.J.: Ablex.

Kornhauser, William. 1952. "The Negro Union Official: A Study of Sponsorship and Control." *American Journal of Sociology* 57:443–453.

Kotter, John Paul. 1973. "The Psychological Contract: Managing the Joining-Up Process." *California Management Review* 15:91–99.

Ladinsky, Jack. 1975. "Notes on the Sociological Study of Careers." Paper presented at an SSRC Conference on Occupational Careers Analysis, Greensboro, N.C.

Landau, Hyman G. 1965. "Development of Structure in a Society with a Dominance Relation When New Members Are Added Successively." *Bulletin of Mathematical Biophysics* 27:151–168.

Lawrence, Barbara S. 1983. "The Age Grading of Managerial Careers in Work Organizations." Unpublished dissertation, Sloan School of Management, MIT, Cambridge, Mass.

Lawrence Barbara S. 1984. "Age Grading: The Implicit Organizational Timetable." *Journal of Occupational Behavior* (forthcoming).

Lazear, Edward P. 1981. "Agency, Earnings Profiles, Productivity and Hours Restrictions." *American Economic Review* 71:606–620.

Lazear, Edward P., and S. Rosen. 1981. "Rank-Order Tournaments as Optimum Labor Contracts." *Journal of Political Economy* 89:841–864.

Lester, R. A. 1946. "Shortcomings of Marginal Analysis for Wage–Employment Problems." *American Economic Review* 37:135–148.

Lester, R. 1967. "Pay Differentials by Size of Establishment." *Industrial Relations* 7:57–67.

Levenson, Bernard. 1961. "Bureaucratic Succession." Pp. 362–375 in *Complex Organizations: A Sociological Reader,* edited by Amitai Etzioni. New York: Holt.

Levinson, Daniel J. 1978. *The Seasons of a Man's Life.* New York: Knopf.

Lillard, L. E., and R. Weiss. 1976. *Dynamic Aspects of Earnings Mobility.* Research Working Paper No. 150. New York: National Bureau of Economics.

Lindblom, Charles E. 1959. "The Science of Muddling Through." *Public Administration Review* 19:79–88.

Lipset, Seymour M., and R. Bendix. 1952. "Social Mobility and Occupational Career Patterns, Part 2: Social Mobility." *American Journal of Sociology* 57:494–504.

McArthur, Leslie Z. 1983. "Social Judgement Biases in Comparable Worth Analysis." Paper presented at the Seminar on Comparable Worth, sponsored by the National Academy of Sciences and the Ford Foundation, Hilton Head, S.C., October.

Maccoby, Michael. 1977. *The Gamesman.* New York: Simon & Schuster.

Machlup, Fritz. 1967. "Theories of the Firm: Marginalist, Behavioral, Managerial." *American Economic Review.* 57 (1):2–33.

Maddox, George L., and Elizabeth R. Douglass. 1974. "Aging and Individual Differences: A Longitudinal Analysis of Social, Psychological and Physiological Indicators." *Journal of Gerontology* 29 (5):555–563.

Malkiel, Burton B., and Judith A. Malkiel. 1973. "Male–Female Differentials in Professional Employment." *American Economic Review* 63:693–705.

March, James C., and James G. March. 1977. "Almost Random Careers: The Wisconsin

School Superintendency, 1940–1972." *Administrative Science Quarterly* 22:377–409.

March, James C. and James G. March. 1978. "Performance Sampling in Social Matches." *Administrative Science Quarterly* 23:434-453.

March, James, and Herbert Simon. 1958. *Organizations*. New York: Wiley.

Martin, Norman H., and Anselm L. Strauss. 1959. "Patterns of Mobility within Industrial Organizations." Pp. 85–101 in *Industrial Man*, edited by W. Lloyd Warner and Norman H. Martin. New York: Harper & Row.

Matras, Judah. 1975. *Social Inequality, Stratification, and Mobility*. Englewood Cliffs, N.J.: Prentice-Hall.

Mayer, Thomas. 1972. "Models of Intragenerational Mobility." Pp. 308–357 in *Sociological Theories in Progress*, Vol. 2, edited by Joseph Berger, Boston: Houghton Mifflin.

McFarland, David D. 1970. "Intragenerational Social Mobility as a Markov Process." *American Sociological Review* 35:463–476.

McGinnis, Robert. 1968. "A Stochastic Model of Social Mobility." *American Sociological Review* 33:712–722.

McLaughlin, David I. 1975. *The Executive Money Map*. New York: McGraw-Hill.

Medoff, James L., and K. G. Abraham. 1980. "Experience, Performance and Earnings." *Quarterly Journal of Economics* 95:703–736.

Medoff, James L., and K. G. Abraham. 1981. "Are Those Paid More Really More Productive? The Case of Experience." *Journal of Human Resources* 16:186–216.

Meyer, John. 1977. "The Effects of Education as an Institution." *American Journal of Sociology* 83:55–77.

Meyer, John, and B. Rowan. 1977. "Institutional Organizations: Formal Structure as Myth and Ceremony." *American Journal of Sociology* 83:341–363.

Mincer, Jacob. 1974. *Schooling, Experience, and Earnings*. New York: National Bureau of Economic Research.

Montagna, Paul D. 1977. *Occupations and Society: Toward a Sociology of the Labor Market*. New York: Wiley.

More, Douglas, 1962. "Demotion." *Social Problems* 9 (3):213–221.

Morse, Nancy. 1953. *Satisfaction in the White Collar Job*. Michigan: Survey Research Center.

Morse, Nancy C., and R. S. Weiss. 1955. "The Function and Meaning of Work." *American Sociological Review* 20:191–198.

Nerlove, Marc, and S. J. Press. 1973. *Univariate Log-Linear and Logistic Models*. Santa Monica, Calif.: Rand Corporation.

Neugarten, Bernice L. 1973. "Personality Change in Late Life: A Developmental Perspective." In *The Psychology of Adult Development and Aging*, edited by E. Eisdorfer and M. P. Lawton. Washington, D.C.: American Psychological Association.

Neugarten, Bernice, and Nancy Datan. 1974. "The Middle Years." Pp. 592–608 in *American Handbook of Psychiatry*, edited by Silvano Arieti. New York: Basic Books.

Oaxaca, Ronald. 1973. "Sex Discrimination in Wages." Pp. 124–151 in *Discrimination in Labor Markets*, edited by Orley Ashenfelter and Albert Rees. Princeton, N.J.: Princeton University Press.

Ornstein, Michael D. 1976. *Entry into the American Labor Force*, New York: Academic.

Osterman, Paul. 1975. "An Empirical Study of Labor Market Segmentation." *Journal of Industrial and Labor Relations* 19:79–88.

Palmore, Erdman. 1981. *Social Patterns in Normal Aging: Findings from the Duke Longitudinal Study*. Durham, N.C.: Duke University Press.

Patten, Thomas H. 1977. "Job Evaluation and Job Enlargement: A Collision Course?" *Human Resource Management* Winter:2–8.

Pennings, J. M. 1970. "Work-Value Systems of White-Collar Workers. *Administrative Science Quarterly* 15:397–405.

Peres, Sherwood H. 1966. *Factors Which Influence Careers in General Electric.* Crotonville, New York: Management Development and Employee Relations Service, General Electric Company.

Pettigrew, T. F. 1967. "Social Evaluation Theory: Convergence and Applications." *Nebraska Symposium on Motivation* 15:241-311.

Pfeffer, Jeffrey. 1977. "Toward an Examination of Stratification in Organizations." *Administrative Science Quarterly* 22:553–567.

Pfeffer, Jeffrey. 1983. "Organizational Demography." Pp. 299–359 in *Research on Organizational Behavior,* edited by L. L. Cummings and B. Staw. Vol. 5. Greenwich, Conn.:JAI.

Phelps-Brown, H. 1977. *The Inequality of Pay.* Berkeley: Univ. of Calif. Press.

Piaget, Jean. 1952. *The Origins of Intelligence in Children.* New York: International Universities Press.

Piven, F. F., and R. Cloward. 1971. *Regulating the Poor: The Functions of Public Welfare.* New York: Random House.

Porter, L. W., and R. Steers. 1973. "Organizational, Work, and Personal Factors in Employee Turnover and Absenteeism." *Psychological Bulletin* 80:151–176.

Rapaport, Robert, and Rhona Rapaport. 1978. *Working Couples.* New York: Harper Colophon.

Rainwater, Lee. 1974. *What Money Buys: Inequality and the Social Meaning of Income.* New York: Basic Books.

Reynolds, L. G. 1951. *The Structure of Labor Markets.* New York: Harper.

Riley, Matilda W. 1976. "Age Strata in Social Systems." Pp. 189–217 in *Handbook of Aging and the Social Sciences,* edited by Robert H. Binstock and E. Shanas. New York; Van Nostrand Reinhold.

Riley, Matilda W. 1978. "Aging, Social Change and the Power of Ideas." *Daedaeus* 107 (4): 39–52.

Riley, Matilda W., and Kathleen M. Bond. 1982. "Beyond Ageism: Postponing the Onset of Disability." In *Aging in Society,* edited by Beth Hess and Kathleen M. Bond. Hillside, N.J.: Lawrence Erlbaum Associates.

Riley, Matilda W., Anne Foner, and Marilyn Johnson. 1972. *Aging and Society, Vol. 3: A Sociology of Age Stratification.* New York: Russell Sage Foundation.

Robinson, Robert V., and Jonathan Kelley. 1979. "Class as Conceived by Marx and Dahrendorf: Effects on Income Inequality and Politics in the United States and Great Britain." *American Sociological Review* 44:38–58.

Romo, Frank, P., and J. E. Rosenbaum. 1984. "College Old-Boy Connections and Promotions." Unpublished paper, Yale University.

Roos, Patricia A. 1981. "Sex Stratification in the Workplace: Male–Female Differences in Economic Returns to Occupation." *Social Science Research* 10 (3).

Rosenbaum, James E. 1975. "The Stratification of Socialization Processes." *American Sociological Review* 40:48–54.

Rosenbaum, James E. 1976. *Making Equality: The Hidden Curriculum of High School Tracking.* New York: Wiley-Interscience.

Rosenbaum, James E. 1977. "Analysis of Opportunity in Organizations." Paper presented at the Research Symposium on Sociological Indicators of Institutional Discrimination, University of California, Los Angeles, April.

Rosenbaum, James E. 1978. "The Structure of Opportunity in School." *Social Forces* 57:236–256.

Rosenbaum, James E., 1979a. "Tournament Mobility: Career Patterns in a Corporation." *Administrative Science Quarterly* 24:220–241.

Rosenbaum, James E. 1979b. "Organizational Career Mobility: Promotion Chances in a Corporation during Periods of Growth and Contraction." *American Journal of Sociology* 85:21–48.

Rosenbaum, James E. 1980. "Hierarchical and Individual Effects on Employees' Earnings." *Industrial Relations*, 19:1–14.

Rosenbaum, James E. 1983. "Changes in Men's and Women's Promotion Chances after an Affirmative Action Program." Unpublished paper, Northwestern University.

Rosenbaum, James E. 1983. "Why do the Rear Wheels Fall Further Behind? The Impact of Jobs and Job Statuses on Women's Earnings Gains from Affirmative Action." Paper presented at the Seminar on Comparable Worth, sponsored by the National Academy of Sciences and the Ford Foundation, Hilton Head, S.C., October.

Rosenbaum, James E., and Frank P. Romo. 1979. "College Status Effects on Promotions: A Test of Credentialling versus Signalling Theories." Paper presented at the Annual Meeting of the Society for the Study of Social Problems, Boston, August.

Rosenthal, Robert, and L. Jacobson. 1968. *Pygmalion in the Classroom.* New York: Holt.

Roth, Julius. 1963. *Timetables.* Indianapolis: Bobbs-Merrill.

Runciman, W. G. 1966. *Relative Deprivation and Social Justice.* Berkeley:University of California Press.

Sanborn, H. 1964. "Pay Differences between Men and Women." *Industrial and Labor Relations Review* 17:534–550.

Sargent, Henry A. 1972. "Using the Point Method to Measure Jobs." Pp. 231–241 in *Handbook of Wage and Salary Administration*, edited by Milton L. Rock. New York: McGraw-Hill.

Schafer, W. E., and C. Olexa. 1971. *Tracking and Opportunity.* Scranton, Penn.: Chandler.

Scheff, T. J. 1966. "Typification in the Diagnostic Practices of Rehabilitation Agencies." In *Sociology and Rehabilitation*, edited by Marvin B. Sussman. Cleveland: American Sociological Association.

Schein, Edgar. 1978. *Career Dynamics: Matching Individual and Organizational Needs.* Reading, Massachusetts: Addison-Wesley.

Schrank, H. T., and Y. T. Wesley. 1977. "Sex, Rank and Mobility in a Complex Organization." Paper presented at the Symposium on Social Indicators of Discrimination, University of California, Los Angeles, April 29–30.

Schwab, Donald P. 1983. "Job Evaluation and Research Needs." Paper presented at the Seminar on Comparable Worth, sponsored by the National Academy of Sciences and the Ford Foundation, Hilton Head, S.C. October, 1983.

Sennett, Richard, and J. Cobb. 1972. *Hidden Injuries of Class.* New York: Random House.

Shaeffer, Ruth G. 1972. *Staffing Systems: Managerial and Professional Jobs.* New York: The Conference Board.

Sheehey, Gail. 1974. *Passages.* New York: Dutton.

Sibson, Robert E. 1974. *Compensation.* New York: Amacom.

Singer, Burton, and Seymour Spilerman. 1976. "Some Methodological Issues in the Analysis of Longitudinal Surveys." *The Annals of Economic and Social Measurement* 5 (4):447–474.

Sirota, David. 1959. "Some Effects of Promotional Frustration on Employees' Understanding of, and Attitudes toward, Management. *Sociometry* 22:273–278.

Slocum, Walter. 1974. *Occupational Careers*. Chicago: Aldine.

Sofer, C. 1970. *Men in Mid-Career*. Cambridge, England: Cambridge University Press.

Sofer, C. 1972. *Organizations in Theory and Practice*. New York: Basic Books.

Sommers, Dixie. 1974. "Occupational Rankings for Men and Women by Earnings." *Monthly Labor Review* 97:34–51.

Sørensen, Aage B. 1975. "The Structure of Intragenerational Mobility." *American Sociological Review* 40:456–471.

Sørensen, Aage B. 1977. "The Structure of Inequality and the Process of Attainment." *American Sociological Review* 42 (6):965–978.

Spence, A. Michael. 1973. "Job Market Signaling." *Quarterly Journal of Economics* 83:355–374.

Spence, A. Michael. 1974. *Market Signaling: Information Transfer in Hiring and Related Processes*. Cambridge, Mass.: Harvard University Press.

Spenner, Kenneth I. 1981. "Some Elementary Properties of Career Lines." Unpublished manuscript, Boys Town Center for the Study of Youth Development, Boystown, Nebraska.

Spenner, Kenneth I., L. B. Otto, and V. R. A. Call. 1982. *Career Lines and Careers*. Lexington, Mass.: Lexington Books.

Spilerman, Seymour. 1972. "Extensions of the Mover–Stayer Model." *American Journal of Sociology* 78:599–627.

Spilerman, Seymour. 1977. "Careers, Labor Market Structure, and Socioeconomic Achievement." *American Journal of Sociology* 83:551–593.

Stern, David. 1982. *Managing Human Resources: The Art of Full Employment*. Boston: Auburn.

Stewman, Shelby. 1975. "Two Markov Models of Open System Occupational Mobility: Underlying Conceptualizations and Empirical Tests." *American Sociological Review* 40:298–321.

Stewman, Shelby. 1981. "The Aging of Work Organizations: Impact on Organization and Employment Practice." Pp. 243–290 in *Aging: Social Change*, edited by S. B. Kiesler, J. N. Morgan, and V. K. Oppenheimer. New York: Academic Press.

Stewman, Shelby, and S. L. Konda. 1983. "Careers and Organizational Labor Markets: Demographic Models of Organizational Behavior." *American Journal of Sociology* 88 (4):637–685.

Stiglitz, Joseph P. 1975. "The Theory of 'Screening,' Education, and the Distribution of Income." *American Economic Review* 65:283–300.

Stinchcombe, Arthur, 1964. *Rebellion in a High School*. Chicago: Quandrangle.

Stinchcombe, Arthur. 1965. "Social Structure and Organizations." Pp. 142–193 in *Handbook of Organizations*, edited by James G. March. Chicago: Rand McNally.

Stolzenberg, Ross M. 1975. "Occupation, Markets, and Wages." *American Sociological Review* 40:298–321.

Stolzenberg, Ross M. 1978. "Bringing the Boss Back in: Employer Size, Employee Schooling and Socioeconomic Achievement." *American Sociological Review* 43:813–828.

Stolzenberg, Ross M. 1979. "The Measurement and Decomposition of Causal Effects in Nonlinear and Nonadditive Models." Pp. 459–488 in *Sociology Methodology 1980*. San Francisco: Jossey-Bass.

Super, Donald. 1957. *The Psychology of Careers*. New York: Harper & Row.

Talbert, J., and C. Bose 1977. "Wage Attainment Processes: Retail Clerk Case." *American Journal of Sociology* 83:403–424.

Tannenbaum, Arnold S., B. Kavcic, M. Rosner, M. Vianello, and G. Weiser. 1974. *Hierarchy in Organizations: An International Comparison*. San Francisco: Jossey-Bass.

Thompson, James D., Robert W. Avery and Richard O. Carlson. 1968. "Occupations, Personnel, and Careers." *Educational Administration Quarterly*, 4:6–31.

Thurow, Lester. 1967. "The Occupational Distribution of the Returns to Education and Experience for Whites and Negroes." Pp. 233–243 in *Proceedings of the Social Statistics Section of the American Statistical Association*.

Thurow, Lester. 1973. "Proving the Absence of Positive Associations." *Harvard Educational Review* 43:106–112.

Thurow, Lester. 1975. *Generating Inequality*. New York: Basic Books.

Treiman, Donald J. 1979. "Job Evaluation: An Analytic Review." *Interim Report of the Committee on Occupational Classification and Analysis to the Equal Employment Opportunity Commission*. Washington, D.C.: National Research Council, National Academy of Sciences.

Treiman, D. J., and H. I. Hartmann (eds.). 1981. *Women, Work, and Wages: Equal Pay for Jobs of Equal Value*. Washington, D.C.: National Academy Press.

Treiman, D. J., and K. Terrell. 1975a. "Sex and the Process of Status Attainment: A Comparison of Working Women and Men." *American Sociological Review* 40:174–200.

Treiman, D. J., and K. Terrell. 1975b. "Women, Work, and Wages—Trends in the Female Occupational Structure since 1940." Pp. 157–200 in *Social Indicator Models*, edited by Kenneth C. Land and Seymour Spilerman. New York: Russell Sage Foundation.

Tuma, Nancy B. 1976. "Rewards, Resources, and the Rate of Mobility: A Nonstationary Multivariate Stochastic Model." *American Sociological Review* 41:338–360.

Turner, Ralph. 1960. "Modes of Social Ascent through Education: Sponsored and Contest Mobility." *American Sociological Review* 25:855–867.

U.S. Bureau of the Census. 1967. *Trends of Incomes of Families and Persons in the U.S. 1947–1964*. Technical Paper 17. Washington, D.C.: Government Printing Office.

Van Mannen, John (ed.). 1977. *Organizational Careers: Some New Perspectives*. London: Wiley.

Van Maanen, John, and E. H. Schein. 1977. "Improving the Quality of Work Life: Career Development." Pp. 30–95 in *Improving Life at Work*. edited by J. R. Hackman and J. L. Suttle. Santa Monica, Calif.: Goodyear.

Vanneman, Reeve. 1977. "The Occupational Composition of American Classes: Results from Cluster Analysis." *American Journal of Sociology* 82:783–807.

Veiga, John F. 1973. "The Mobile Manager at Mid-Career." *Harvard Business Review* 51:115–119.

Veiga, John F. 1981. "Plateaued versus Nonplateaued Managers: Career Patterns, Attitudes, and Path Potential." *Academy of Management Journal* 24:566–678.

Vroom, Victor H., and K. R. MacCrimmon 1968. "Toward a Stochastic Model of Managerial Careers." *Administrative Science Quarterly* 13:26–46.

Webber, Ross A. 1976. "Career Problems of Young Managers." *California Management Review* 18:19–33.

Weber, Max. 1946. *Wirtschaft und Geselschaft*. Part 3, Chapter 6, pp. 196–266 in *From Max Weber*, translated and edited by H. H. Gerth and C. W. Mills. New York: Oxford University Press.

Weisbrod, B., and P. Karpoff. 1968. "Monetary Returns to College Education, Student Ability, and College Quality." *Review of Economics and Statistics* 50:491–497.

Weiss, Alfred. 1959. "Sensory Functions." Pp. 503–542 in *Handbook of Aging and the Individual: Psychological and Biological Aspects*. edited by James E. Birren. Chicago: University of Chicago Press.

Wellbank, Harry L. 1979. "Planning Job Progression for Effective Career Development and Human Resources." Pp. 361–369 in *Career Management*, edited by Mariann Jelinek. Chicago: St. Clair Press.

Wheeler, Stanton. 1966. "The Structure of Formally Organized Socialization Settings." Pp. 51–113 in *Socialization after Childhood*, edited by Orville Brim and S. Wheeler. New York: Wiley.

White, Harrison C. 1970a. *Chains of Opportunity*. Cambridge: Harvard University Press.

White, Harrison C. 1970b. "Stayers and Movers." *American Journal of Sociology* 76:307–324.

Whyte, William H., Jr. 1956. *The Organizational Man*. New York: Simon & Schuster.

Wilensky, Harold L. 1961. "Orderly Careers and Social Participation: The Impact of Work History on Social Integration in the Middle Mass." *American Sociological Review* 26:521–539.

Williamson, Oliver. 1975. *Markets and Hierarchies*. New York: Free Press.

Wing, Richard. 1972. "Achieving Internal Equity through Job Measurement." Pp. 219–230 in *Handbook of Wage and Salary Administration*, edited by Milton L. Rock. New York: McGraw-Hill.

Wise, David A. 1975a. "Academic Achievement and Job Performance." *American Economic Review* 65:350–366.

Wise, David A. 1975b. "Personal Attributes, Job Performance and Probability of Promotion." *Econometrica* 43:913–931.

Wright, Erik Olin. 1978. *Class Structure and Income Inequality*. New York: Academic Press.

Wright, Erik Olin, and L. Perrone. 1977. "Marxist Class Categories and Income Inequality." *American Sociological Review* 42:32–55.

Young, Michael. 1958. *The Rise of the Meritocracy*. Baltimore: Penguin.

Index